HISTORY OF PHILOSOPHY

History of Philosophy

Y N Thakur

MD Publications Pvt Ltd
New Delhi
www.mdppl.com

Published by :

MD Publications Pvt Ltd
"MD House", 11, Darya Ganj,
New Delhi - 110 002
Phone : +91-11- 45355555
E-mail : contact@mdppl.com
Website: www.mdppl.com

ISBN : 978-81-7533-335-2

Published and Printed by Mr. Pranav Gupta on behalf of **MD Publications Pvt Ltd** at Repro India Limited.

PREFACE

The history of philosophy is the study of philosophical ideas and concepts through time. Issues specifically related to history of philosophy might include but are not limited to how changes in philosophy can be accounted for historically.

All cultures are they prehistoric, medieval, or modern; Eastern, Western, religious or secular have had their own unique schools of philosophy, arrived at through both inheritance and through independent discovery. Such theories have grown from different premises and approaches, examples of which include but are not limited to rationalism theorics arrived at through logic, empiricism and even through leaps of faith, hope and inheritance.

History of philosophy seeks to catalogue and classify such development. The goal is to understand the development of philosophical ideas through time. This book has a dual purpose. Primarily I hope to introduce the subject "History of Philosophy' to those philosophy students, academics and teachers who may to varying degrees be unfamiliar with an extensive branch of writings relating to their discipline. Nowadays such relative unfamiliarity is commonplace amongst philosophies'. There are at least two reasons for this first, a claustrophobic compartmentalisation of disciplines, certainly in the Anglo-American world, where professional pressures tend towards narrow discipline bases and second, specifically in historians, an air of indifference towards "philosophy of history', either as an example of such compartmentalisation, or as a more deliberate stance emanating from some unfortunate encounter with philosophy, best forgotten. Such diffidence may be justified, but only on the basis of some familiarity with "philosophy of history' and a principal purpose of this 'guide' is to furnish precisely that.

A secondary purpose of this 'guide' relates more urgently to the contemporary nature of historical study, for it is under attacks sourced precisely from the two branches of History of Philosophy, namely, 'speculative'and 'analytic'. First, from recent signs of a revival in 'speculative' History of Philosophy which, as we shall see, tries to construct some kind of "universal history' of the world (the rise and decline of great states, empires and cultures, complaints have arisen that modern historians have lost that sense of the grand sweep of time - that their writings are narrowly focused specialist studies, more akin to the mentality of 'antiquarians' or laboratory workers' than efforts to make sense of the unfolding of human history.

It is in the light of all these considerations that this book on History of Philosophy is offered to help familiarise with the principal outlines of an extensive, multi-faceted literature so they can better assess its relevance for them. Each reader will doubtless sort out the dross from the gold within ' the History of Philosophy ' in his or her own way despite any critical edge offered in this exposition.

I am very grateful to Mr. Pranav Gupta, Director of MD Publications Pvt Ltd, New Delhi, for his kind cooperation and support for this book.

Y N Thakur

CONTENTS

	Preface	*v*
1.	History of Philosophy: Pindar	1
2.	Sophocles in Philosophy	19
3.	Plato in the History of Philosophy	29
4.	Aeschylus in the History of Philosophy	53
5.	Gorgias in Philosophy	63
6.	Medieval Discussion of Intentionality in Philosophy	77
7.	Augustinian Argument for Philosophical Dialogues	123
8.	Ockham and Textbooks on Scholastic Philosophy	139
9.	Nicholas of Autrecourt to Bernard of Arezzo for Philosophy	161
10.	Rejection of Authority in Philosophy	171
11.	Emergence of Philosophy and its History	209
12.	Anti-Cartesianism of Philosophy	249
13.	Les Philosophes in Philosophy	281
14.	Idealist Tradition in England for Philosophy	329
15.	Revolution in History of Philosophies	377
	Bibliography	397
	Index	403

Contents

	Preface	*v*
1.	History of Philosophy: Pindar	1
2.	Sophocles in Philosophy	19
3.	Plato in the History of Philosophy	29
4.	Aeschylus in the History of Philosophy	53
5.	Gorgias in Philosophy	63
6.	Medieval Discussion of Intentionality in Philosophy	77
7.	Augustinian Argument for Philosophical Dialogues	123
8.	Ockham and Textbooks on Scholastic Philosophy	139
9.	Nicholas of Autrecourt to Bernard of Arezzo for Philosophy	161
10.	Rejection of Authority in Philosophy	171
11.	Emergence of Philosophy and its History	209
12.	Anti-Cartesianism of Philosophy	249
13.	Les Philosophes in Philosophy	281
14.	Idealist Tradition in England for Philosophy	329
15.	Revolution in History of Philosophies	377
	Bibliography	397
	Index	403

1

History of Philosophy: Pindar

Introduction

The tradition of Greek choral lyric culminated with the odes of Pindar. These are not easy to evaluate and appreciate, but it is still more difficult to comprehend and assess the poet who composed them. Even to his contemporaries, Pindar must have seemed an aloof and somewhat enigmatic figure. As an aristocrat he would more naturally have been a patron of poetry than himself a poet; he came from a part of central Greece that had made a relatively small contribution to literature and the arts. A modern reader needs a sympathetic insight into the nature and traditions of Greek aristocratic society before he can begin to understand how Pindar's subject matter victory in an athletic contest or in a chariot race—could inspire poetry characterized by high seriousness and deep feeling. Pindar cannot, indeed, speak across the centuries with the directness of Homeric epic poetry or Sophoclean tragedy, but he does create, with disciplined mastery of a sophisticated and complex art form, a choral lyric of unsurpassed splendor and sustained nobility.

I hope to begin to supply the "modern reader" the "sympathetic insight" needed to read Pindar properly, a poet who exploited the differences among the Greek cities in order to advance Panhellenic standards and interests.

It has been said of Pindar that "he was not the creator of any new kind [of choral lyric], as Simonides of the *epinikian* [victory odes]; nor again, was he the first who gave a new artistic value to any old form of song, as Simonides gave it to the dirge. What Pindar did was to set the stamp of an original and strongly individual genius on every lyric form in which he composed". And it has also been said that the "all-pervading, selfconscious, Greek individualism is no more evident than in Pindar, who likens himself to the eagle, the divine bird of Zeus".

Perhaps, indeed, Pindar may be the most self-conscious of the Greek poets, very much aware of his great gifts and not shy about asserting his superiority. It has been suggested that his aspiration was to be preeminent among poets as the athletic victors he celebrates were preeminent among their rivals. It seems particularly fitting, then, that a poet who made so much of his own preeminence should have devoted so much of his poetry to celebrating the victories (the momentary superiority?) of others in the great Games of his time. Perhaps it should be considered for him an apt, if not even a divinely ordained, fate that he survives primarily in the poetry that celebrates the athletic feats of others.

The victory odes were dedicated to the winners of the great Games of Greece. Such odes, usually commissioned by the city or family of the winner, were evidently performed with the aid of dance and music. The odes were only a part, but they were a particularly spectacular part, of the rewards showered upon the most spectacular athletes of the day. Among the rewards for these winners might be free meals for life bestowed upon them by their proud and grateful cities.

Such lavish recognition of winners is called into question, as are perhaps the poets and citizens who make much of them, by what Socrates said when the time came for him to discuss an appropriate punishment upon conviction at his trial:

> *What, then, is fitting for a poor man, a benefactor, who needs to have leisure to exhort you? There is nothing more fitting, men of Athens, than for such a man to be given his meals in the Prytaneum, much more so than if any of you has won a victory at Olympia with a horse or a two- or four-horse chariot. For he makes you seem to be happy, while I make you to be so; and he is not in need of sustenance, while I am in need of it. So if I must propose what I am worthy of in accordance with the just, I propose this: to be given my meals in the Prytaneum.*

It is the kind of winner Socrates speaks so slightingly of that Pindar celebrates in his victory odes. We might well wonder what Pindar would think of Socrates' comparison of himself to those winners, a comparison which reflects Socrates' opinions both as to what is worthwhile for its own sake and as to what is helpful to the city:

> *It has been noticed that "no Greek poet says so much as Pindar about his art". This may be related, I have already suggested, to the self-consciousness and self-confidence of athletes who display their powers. But would not Pindar regard his poetry as superior to the athletes and contests that he celebrates, and superior because of attributes that should win the respect of a Socrates? Thus, he might have been inclined to agree with Socrates if he (Pindar) had seen the winners merely as athletes. But he moves beyond the surface of the victories, examining what is really being exhibited (or at least celebrated by him) in such winning.*

In the foreground of Pindar's odes are indeed the Games and their winners and these the typical Greek citizen and Greek city would probably have been immediately most interested in. In the background of Pindar's odes, however, are the doings of gods and demigods and heroes, especially as founders and saviours of cities. The depiction of this background takes up most of the lines of the odes. In the "deep" background of the odes are the opinions Pindar himself may have had about the games, gods, and cities. For example, can the gods (if omniscient and omnipotent) be as most people evidently believed them to be? Are the Games as important as people generally took them to be? These underlying opinions furnish the most critical subject Pindar deals with, even though he rarely makes that subject explicit.

Whatever reservations Pindar may have about the Games, or for that matter about the gods (as the gods were generally regarded), the odes do provide him opportunities to discourse on the greatest and deepest things. Of course, Pindar writes the things he does for money. The question remains, What are the things he is willing to write for money? The simplest answer to this question is that he is hired to write about winners. We should consider, therefore, what this kind of winning requires and means.

It seems, especially when the competition is "world-class," that winning usually requires determination, discipline, various physical (or natural) attributes (which may even be hereditary in some cases), and (for some events, such as chariot racing) considerable resources. Thus, it must have taken a certain kind of city, and training not available everywhere, to produce the very best.

Winning *means* various kinds of excellence. Pindar in one of his odes passes on the "true saying," "Trial is the true test of mortal men". (One may wonder whether Pindar himself is not also being tested by all this.) Thucydides complains in his *Peloponnesian War* (1.21) that poets unduly glorify events, thereby distorting them. But Pindar records in one of his odes a saying, "Do not bury high success in silence". Elsewhere he observes (in one of the fragments) that the minds of men are blind without poetry. "To me," he says, "have [the Muses] handed on this immortal task," the task of enlightening mankind. In still another fragment he says something which can stand as a rationale for his career, "'Tis meet for the good to be hymned with fairest songs. For this is the only tribute that vergeth on the honours due to the immortals; but every noble deed dieth, if suppressed in silence". Thus, an excellence, or image of the good, is displayed when the winner of a Game is celebrated in a poem. It is such celebration that permits Pindar to go on to bigger things, to talk about the parallels to gods and heroes suggested by one winner after another. This is not only because the gods and heroes originally founded the Games and remain their patrons. The winners themselves display something godlike in their issuing forth victorious.

Very little is said in Pindar's victory odes either about the athletes and their families or about the condition of the athletes' cities. Nor is there much said even about the contests themselves. Pindar's odes are quite different, in this respect, from the modern sports page. They are different as well from the victory odes prepared by many of his contemporaries, who did so much more than he did with the athletes and the contests in which the athletes had triumphed. One learns very little from Pindar's odes about just how the various contests were conducted. This may be compared to the plays (a generation later) of Sophocles and of Euripides in which there are detailed and graphic accounts of a chariot race in which Orestes is "killed." Those accounts, which so far as Orestes is himself concerned are simply not true, may be accurate enough about what can happen in such a race. In Pindar's own times, his older and younger contemporaries, Simonides and Bacchylides respectively, provided detailed descriptions of the contests that had led to victory odes.

There can be little doubt about what Pindar regarded as important, as he devotes himself much more to retelling old stories (about gods and heroes) than to developing new ones about the most recent heroics. In Sophocles and Euripides, on the other hand, the accounts of Orestes' supposed chariot race are as detailed as they are in order to show how those who dreaded Orestes' return were persuaded to let down their guard. It usually suffices for Pindar to say that a certain athlete won such and such a contest at this or that place. In a sense, for his purposes, all winning athletes can be taken to have done much the same (the exceptions include such achievements as a son following a parent as a victor or an athlete winning several contests in the same year). To say much about the event itself is, for Pindar, to waste a precious opportunity.

It is likely, however, that those who commissioned victory

odes must often have wanted to hear much more about the particular event. Pindar appeals to this kind of desire by recognizing "that words are necessary if deeds are to be properly rewarded by being long remembered". So it came to be believed that one of the greatest rewards for victors was to have poems, such as Pindar's, prepared for them, poems that would be remembered as having been elicited by the thushonored victors. These would be poems in which something beyond one's victories would be looked to, just as the games themselves could be considered as looking beyond mere physical activity.

Were the people who commissioned the poems aware of what was likely to happen at the hands of a Pindar? Were they reconciled, for instance, to the fact that the poem commissioned would say little about the athlete personally, however much it would draw upon gods and heroes and legendary episodes somehow appropriate to the city of the athlete? It does seem, at times, that patrons were primarily interested in getting the best artistic "caterer" for their event and Pindar had come to be recognized as one of the best, if not the very best. Did this recognition depend upon an informed awareness of his qualities as a poet, aside from the personal portraits he provided (or failed to provide)? To commission Pindar, then, might have been somewhat like persuading Pablo Picasso to do one's portrait: the subject of the portrait may not be recognizable, but one could expect that the resulting picture would be noticed and that having one's name attached to the picture would somehow redound to one's fame. Or, this is like commissioning a museum in which to house works of art—only to find that the architecture of the museum itself is more imposing and of more enduring artistic significance than any of the pictures housed therein.

Pindar did say (or, some might say, advertise), "In payment for praiseworthy deeds, we ought to celebrate the noble man in poetry, extolling him with grace". Still, it is hard to believe that Pindar himself did not recognize that his poetry would outlast the athletic deeds he praised. So little were the contests themselves his concern that few of the losers, or the winner's opponents, are identified by him. If the contests themselves had been critical, the achievements of the winners could have been pointed up by describing the prowess of the challengers they had overcome, which is to be seen in Pindar's accounts of the achievements of gods and heroes.

It can be said, therefore, that we owe these poems in part to the pride if not even the vanity of those who commissioned them. Not only were the odes originally brought into existence because of a desire to see oneself thus celebrated but they may have been preserved, by families and cities, for that reason. "Seventeen volumes of Pindar's poetry, comprising almost every genre of choral lyric, were known in antiquity. Only four books of [victory odes] have survived complete". This is attributed to the fact that they chanced to be selected by a teacher as a school book in the second century A.D. But, we must wonder, what permitted them to be available so long for such selection?

Those who commissioned the poems did get their money's worth from Pindar. His vivid accounts of gods and heroes ennobled the athletic deeds that had inspired those accounts. Few would have wondered, as we might well do, whether those accounts somehow showed up the athletic events as petty by comparison. Nor would many have wondered whether Pindar's art did not display itself as higher in its class than even the winners in the great Games were in their respective classes. It probably sufficed for them, winners and patrons alike, to be told by Pindar that "it is those that are prosperous [victorious?] who are deemed wise, even by their fellow citizens". The winners must have seemed eminently worthy, the honour they received assuring them of their virtue. Pindar could tell them that "poets sing the happy man as one who wins by excellence of hands or feet and who, before he dies, sees his young son [win as well]" (Pythian 10). One cannot do what the gods do—but one should go as far as men can, recognizing all the while one's limitations and thereby avoiding presumptuousness (or *hubris*). (In some ways, Pindar identifies his own poetic achievements as "athletic."

All in all, then, Pindar presents the athletic contest, and

especially victory, in the best light possible. He can speak, as in Olympian 10, of "the joy of winning, the light in life that compensates for all exertion." Or, as put in a different translation, "Few indeed have won, without trial, the joy that is a light of life above all labours." This would seem a salutary teaching, especially since the winners and their cities are repeatedly reminded by the odes of the gods and heroes who throw the best light upon their momentary achievements.

Critical to Pindar's victory odes is the proposition that the winner "shares the marvellous munificence of deity". He can add that "a mortal who achieves the praise of fame and great possessions" has reached the peak. It has been noticed that in the time of Simonides, Pindar's great predecessor and evident originator of the victory ode, "the man to whom a hymn was addressed would feel that he was receiving a distinction which had hitherto been reserved for gods and heroes".

It is not said in the odes that these winners *can* do what the gods had done. Thus, Pindar insists, "I think that nothing done by deity exceeds belief or merits puzzled awe". The gods are presented by him and by others as pervading everything, certainly manifesting themselves in achievements. The gods "lay out all paths to human excellence, on which the wise, the strong, the eloquent will walk". By the gift of a god alone does a man flourish forever. It is evident that it is Pindar's opinion that the gods, or at least stories about the gods, are needed for the founding and perpetuation of cities. The great Games, then, are the visible manifestations of the gods and heroes who established not only those Games but the cities as well. Even so, the gods are *not* presented in the victory odes as involving themselves in the affairs of men in Pindar's day. That is, they do not "intervene," in the ordinary sense of that word, however much victory is seen as reflecting the favour of the tutelary god of this or that Game.

The gods and heroes *are* presented as being themselves reflections of something which continues to be influential among men in Pindar's time, something which may be more fundamental than the gods as ordinarily conceived.

Standards and ends are affirmed thereby, promoting in this way both virtue and the common good.

Pindar considers it the obligation of the poet to praise excellence. The notion of the best is again and again pointed up by him. In this way, the contemporary winner is both exalted and put in his place. One eminently successful man is advised, "Don't try to be a Zeus; if you get a share of these advantages, then you have everything". This may be a useful corrective of what has been called the "selfish individualism" summed up in a famous line of Homer, that one should strive "ever to excel and to surpass other men".

The limits of human achievement are suggested, of course, by the mortality of man. At times, indeed, victory in the games is extolled as somehow a conquest of Hades, of death. It can be said, "You know that the grave is forgotten by him who has won befitting fame". Still, it seems that winning can do no more than make death more endurable. Does this apply also to those who "identify" themselves with winners? It can be said as well that the dead will welcome news of their survivor's victories. Elsewhere, however, it is indicated that the dead should be left to praise the dead, that one cannot reach across the barrier between life and death. On another occasion, Pindar refuses to supply a poem for a ruler to whom he cannot send a remedy for what seems to be his fatal illness. It is on that occasion that he instructs this man (and us) that there are two ills accompanying each good for mankind.

With these observations we can again be reminded of Socrates' suggestion that the Olympic winners merely seem to make the people of Athens happy. Do they do this, in part, by offering the appearance of the conquest of death? We are reminded also of Thucydides' criticism of the pleasantness of hearing Herodotus. Are people easily beguiled from facing up to the way things truly are?

How things truly are, especially in the great contests in which one may be engaged, is suggested by the Churchillian observation that one can, in war, deserve victory, but one cannot guarantee it. One is obliged, that is, to do all that one should do to achieve the best; but one should recognize that providence (or chance?) may have much to say about whether one does indeed achieve what one is entitled to. It is prudent thus to recognize the limits of even prudence.

This means that one should do certain things ultimately for their own sake, that the consequences are beyond one's complete control. How much is Pindar aware of this? That is, what does Pindar really believe about the gods and about what makes things happen as they do? Is there something about art itself which not only places the emphasis upon the concrete or particular but also sees all things as decisively subject to an overall order? The sovereignty of art is thereby asserted, a sovereignty which insists that there is an intimate relation between one's character and one's fate.

Even so, victory (however much it is due to providence) is not enough in itself. Or so Pindar is obliged to say, as when he reports, "But when a man works hard and wins, he needs the melody of praise, in prelude, and a pledge in honour of his excellence". He gives a more poetic account of this sentiment in the same ode: *"My words are wont to herd the sheep of glory, and god makes poems blossom in the meadow of the heart."* The victor, then, is dependent upon the poet. So, perhaps, is the conscientious loser, who can have explained to him that, indeed, one cannot guarantee victory but only deserve it.

In any event, Pindar's victory does routinely exhibit a competitiveness (*vis-à-vis* other poets) that may be more intense than that evident in any other great poet we know. In this way he can be said to have very much gotten into the spirit of the Games he took as his point of departure in telling the world how things truly are.

It may be in what Pindar did *not* say, however, that he most dramatically revealed how things are. His great silence, a virtually complete silence, is about the Persian Wars, which were fought while he was in his prime.

The Persian Wars were, of course, far more glorious for the Greeks than anything performed in any of the Games that Pindar wrote about. Pindar must have recognized this.

His use of ancient wars and heroic feats testifies to his opinion that war provides a better test of virtue (whether of men or of cities) than do games. After all, games are but images of greater contests. Simonides, we know, wrote some of his most famous poems about the Persian Wars; Herodotus wrote about them in his famous history. It is obvious that subsequent ages have been far more interested in the exploits of those Wars than in the exploits of any Games mounted during Pindar's time.

But, alas, circumstances were against Pindar here. The Theban city to which he owed allegiance by birth had considered itself obliged, because of its geographical location, to collaborate with the Persian enemy against its fellow Greeks, thereby depriving itself of the great renown won by cities such as Athens and Sparta.

We observe here the limits even of art. For Pindar could not, as a citizen of Thebes, sing the praises of the Greeks in the Persian Wars. Even to notice the specialness of Athens, in cultural matters, earned him the rebuke of his fellow citizens. We see here, in a particularly difficult situation, the political judgment that the makers of victory odes had to exercise. Thus, it has been noticed, "The choice of the myth for an *epinikian* was a good test of political tact. In some cases, the task was a simple one–namely, when the traditions of the victor's city or family supplied a suitable legend".

In some ways, then, Pindar was in the position of German writers after the Second World War. And, drawing upon an example closer to home, we can usefully think of Pindar as the Greek William Faulkner, an artist who must make the best of a lost cause as he tries to affirm the humanity of his people and restore their self-respect and their confidence, working all the while for a general reconciliation.

It is possible, of course, that something even deeper is responsible for Pindar's virtually complete silence about the Persian Wars, a silence that found him saying so much by saying so little. Perhaps, that is, there were profound differences between Pindar and, say, Simonides, who did deal both with the actual Games in some detail and with the Persian Wars. These would be differences as to how seriously the modernity of their day should be taken. For one reason or another, Pindar does find his most instructive stories in antiquity. He is certainly freer to say what he wishes by staying away from modernity.

Whatever the reputation of Thebes among the Greeks, however, that of Pindar was most elevated. Thus, a century or so after Pindar's death, Alexander the Great could order the Theban house of Pindar's family spared in the general destruction of that city by the Macedonians in 335 B.C. This despite Pindar's acknowledgment, "Verily, as no stranger, nor as ignorant of the Muses, was I reared by famous Thebes". He may allude to the nightmare of the Persian Wars in these lines: *"Now the darkness of the wintry months is past and on the coloured land red roses bloom again"*. But it may not have been tactful, or kind, of him to say much more than this openly.

Pindar is often taken by readers today to avow the belief that all human excellence comes by divine dispensation. (See Olympian 14.) Thus, in Olympian 8, he says, *"Some blessings are wont to come to one man, some to another; and, with the favour of the gods, there are many paths of prosperity."* Elsewhere he observes that men become good and wise by fate divine. And yet Pindar can, in still other odes, make much of fortune. Sure tokens of the future, he can warn, do not exist; reversals can be sudden and unexpected.

What, then, should be understood to be responsible for what happened to Thebes during the Persian Wars? Did its geographical location, which may have been favourable to its development for centuries, happen to become a liability when the Persians appeared as enemies of the Greeks? That is, was it chance that determined what happened to Thebes? If chance is so critical, how important is the fact that one's achievements (whether in war or in games) happen to be recognized? What does all this say, that is, about the claims of art?

Is it possible to conquer chance? And if so, what is the

best way to do so? Does art offer the best hope? Or statesmanship (a special form of art)? Or philosophy (which makes explicit the concern with nature that is implicit in art)? Or religion (which shares, in critical respects, the resources and interests of art)?

The use of victory odes as an important, if not the principal, vehicle of one's poetry means, among other things, that one thereby enlists cities and families in an effort to preserve one's poems despite the ravages of chance. On the other hand, we can see, in our attempts to read Pindar, how much depends upon what we happen to know about the things he refers to. Each ode, it seems, was intended to stand alone (although there do seem to be references in some to others). This induces us to wonder, once again, how much of what Pindar says and wants depends upon the accidental—and what this says about (if not even against) what he seems to say about the role of providence and art in ordering human affairs.

Our own circumstances may happen to be such that we do not appreciate as we should certain influences upon Pindar's poetry. Two influences should be noticed here. The first is the Theban character itself. We have wondered whether it was due to chance that Thebes found itself "obliged" to collaborate with the Persian enemy. Or was it the character of Thebes that was more responsible? Perhaps the greatest Theban stories were devoted to Oedipus and his family, who would be understood by many as born losers (however splendid Oedipus' apotheosis at his death, and however noble Antigone's sacrifice). One does get the impression, at least from the surface of those stories, that it was believed that an inexorable divine will was at work.

What the desperate Oedipus says about Apollo brings us to the second major influence upon Pindar that we should notice, the importance for him of Delphi and its oracle. Pindar says in one of the fragments we have, "Muse! be thou mine oracle, and I shall be thine interpreter". And to a Syracusan ruler he could indicate that the god's favour comes somehow through the poet, who becomes a kind of priest. It does seem, sometimes, that Pindar believes himself to speak, even among the poets, from a superior position—and there are hints, here and there, that it is the influence of Delphi, and all that Delphi stands for, which had put him in a privileged state of mind. And so he can speak "with a voice as of Delphi".

Although Pindar recognizes that poets are often mistaken, he himself proposes to tell the truth. In the process, he reshapes (as Socrates does later) some of the old stories about the gods, denying in effect that they can do the questionable things sometimes imputed to them. His retelling of old stories, which the victory odes license him to do, is from the perspective of one who sounds as if he has access to special revelation himself.

A truly thoughtful winner, whether man or city, would know that a victory ode from a Pindar is more important than the victory itself. The ode is a challenge, somewhat artificial and accidental to be sure, just as the athletic contests celebrated in the odes themselves are. One's mettle as a poet is tested; an opportunity is given to show what one can do, especially if one is working against a deadline; and acclaim can be earned. But it seems obvious that Pindar, in the final analysis, does not really care for the acclaim, except as it contributes to something greater, a Panhellenic reconciliation. In this, too, Pindar can be seen to reflect the Delphic influence. That the securing of peace among the Greeks is to be prized is evident even as Pindar celebrates the victory of one city over all the others in a Game. Thus, Pindar can be recorded as saying, *"To the inexperienced, war is pleasant, but he that has had experience of it sorely fears in his heart its approach"*.

Pindar makes much, whenever he can (it seems), of heroes who can be connected with Thebes (directly, or indirectly through Aegina), people such as Aeacus, Telamon, Ajax, Peleus, Achilles, and even Heracles. No doubt this is partly in order to cater to local interests. But is it not also partly because of Pindar's interest in reintegrating Thebes into the Greek world, something which can be advanced by noticing how much the great Greek heroes are connected with Thebes (or, at least, how much they can be *said* to be connected with

Thebes)? The further Pindar can move from contemporary events whether at the Games or in the Persian Wars—the better he can show the Greeks what they share. In this way, the partisan passions and politics which lead to commissions for Pindar can be employed by him in inducing the Greek cities to rise above their differences in acknowledging their deep, if not even eternal, affinities. (Consider how Thebes and Athens are brought together in Sophocles' *Oedipus at Colonus* and how Argos and Athens are brought together in Aeschylus' *The Eumenides*, Even so, Arrian reports that when Alexander destroyed Thebes a century after Pindar's death, "people felt that Thebes, at long last, had been punished for her treachery she had paid the penalty for her betrayal of Greece in the Persian war [etc.]")

To speak of Pindar as I have is to return to the Socrates of Plato and to the Platonic use of Pindar, whatever Socrates found it prudent to say about the treatment afforded in Athens to Olympic victors. Certainly, Pindar can be taken to caution us not to allow athletic contests to become ends in themselves, so much so that they can be made too much of as particular events, promoting and legitimizing in us the lust for victory, if not even for blood. Here, too, there can be seen something Socratic. Something Socratic may be seen as well, especially when we recall the philosopher-king, in the sovereignty Pindar asserts again and again, as he organizes all the elements that he enlists in his service: *the gods and heroes of antiquity and the winners of the Games in his day. And so Pindar can ask that "war and all battle remain far from the immortals".*

It is consistent with the theme of reconciliation I have attributed to Pindar that I should say more about the differences between philosophy and poetry, differences rooted perhaps in opinions about the relation between bodies and the ideas. It is salutary, in these circumstances, to place an emphasis instead upon affinities between philosophy and poetry, including their ability if not their duty to say different things (about both divine and human affairs) to different kinds of people (depending upon how attentive and thoughtful one is).

In what is regarded as Pindar's last ode that is, the last

ode we have and can date the concluding passage recognizes that human beings are but "things of a day". Pindar thereby acknowledges most emphatically the limitations of human beings and hence of his art. He indicates this elsewhere as well, such as when he says, *"Beyond this neither the wise nor fools must go. I'll go no farther. I'd be a fool".*

We are once again reminded of Socrates, with his lively awareness of his limitations. But it was also Socrates who could, like Pindar, recognize his true worth. If Socrates is correct in the *Apology*, he deserves, better than do the winners of the Olympic Games, the largesse that the city is prepared to lavish upon them. Would this largesse not include victory odes of the kind Pindar provided *his* winners? Should we not say that the dialogues of Plato and the recollections of Xenophon are, in effect, Socrates' victory odes? (These are reinforced by the treatises of Aristotle.)

Socrates, we also remember, was spoken of in the highest (human) terms for his wisdom by the oracle of Delphi, the very oracle with which Pindar allied himself. Thus Pindar could say, *"Me too hath the Muse raised up for Hellas as a chosen herald of wise words."*. A Socratic approach may also be noticed in another saying by Pindar: *"Yet measure due is meet in all things, and the fitting moment [kairos] is the best aim of knowledge."*

Still, we should not forget that there *are* differences between the poet and the philosopher, and, with perhaps profound implications, between Pindar and Socrates. Not the least of these differences is related to the fact that Socrates is remembered (along with Sappho?) for talking in the most down-to-earth fashion, employing everyday speech even for the most exalted things. Pindar, on the other hand, was entitled to say of himself, "My voice is sweeter than the bee-wrought honeycombs".

Would Socrates have been entitled to say about Pindar what he said about poets generally, that "they do not make what they make by wisdom, but by some sort of nature and while inspired, like the diviners and those who deliver oracles"? For, Socrates added, "they too say many noble things, but they know nothing of what they speak." Does the considerable self-consciousness of Pindar, which some can mistake for mere arrogance, suggest a thoughtfulness that anticipates, if it does not even help instruct, both the dramatists and the philosophers who succeeded him?

There is considerable discussion about why Athenian culture democracy. It is known from Plato's writings that many sophists maintained schools of debate, were respected members of society, and were well paid by their students. Orators influenced Athenian history, possibly even causing its failure. Another theory explains the birth of philosophical debate in Athens with the presence of a slave labour workforce which performed the necessary functions that would otherwise have consumed the time of the free male citizenry. Freed from working in the fields or other manual economic activities, they were able to participate in the assemblies of Athens and spend long periods in discussions on popular philosophical questions. Students of Sophists needed to acquire the skills of oration in order to influence the Athenian Assembly and thereby increase respect and wealth. In response, the subjects and methods of debate became highly developed by the Sophists.

The key figure in transforming Greek philosophy into a unified and continuous project the one still being pursued today — is Socrates, who studied under several Sophists. It is said that following a visit to the Oracle of Delphi he spent much of his life questioning anyone in Athens who would engage him, in order to disprove the oracular prophecy that there would be no man wiser than Socrates. Through these live dialogues, he examined common but critical concepts that lacked clear or concrete definitions, such as beauty and truth, and the virtues of piety, wisdom, temperance, courage, and justice. Socrates' awareness of his own ignorance allowed him to discover his errors as well as the errors of those who claimed knowledge based upon falsifiable or unclear precepts and beliefs. He wrote nothing, but inspired many disciples, including many sons of prominent Athenian citizens, which led to his trial and execution in 399 B.C. on the charge that his philosophy and sophistry were undermining the youth, piety, and moral fiber of the city. He was offered a chance to flee from his fate but chose to remain in Athens, abide by his principles, and drink the poison hemlock.

2

Sophocles in Philosophy

Introduction

It is presupposed in the play that the divine exists, with direct references to gods and their doings in one-third of the lines and with the divine and its effects evident throughout the play. It is never questioned that the gods exist, but only whether, and if so how, they manifest themselves to human beings.

It is also presupposed that the gods interest themselves in human affairs. The gods, we are told by the Chorus in *Oedipus Tyrannus*, prescribed "the laws [with respect to piety] that live on high, laws begotten in the clear air of heaven, whose only father is Olympus [Zeus?]." Teachings and moral standards are furnished by the gods. These are backed up, it seems, by prospects of eternal rewards and punishments as well as by the temporal consequences of one's deeds. But, we can wonder, what does the play say about whether the gods intervene in the everyday life of human beings and, if so, how, why, and when?

How do the gods express interest in particular cases? It seems that they speak in response to efforts by human beings to secure divine guidance. For example, men seek out oracles at shrines. They seek help elsewhere as well. In Rome, we recall, much was made of the examination of such things as the entrails of animals.

Sometimes an oracle is sought by someone for his own sake, as Oedipus did when he went to Apollo's shrine at Delphi to learn about his parentage. The disclosure made there was personal to Oedipus, even though it had public consequences. The same can be said about the disclosure decades before to Oedipus' parents, Laius and Jocasta.

Sometimes an oracle is sought on behalf of the city, as when Creon was sent by Oedipus to Delphi to learn what could be done about the blight that had settled upon Thebes. This disclosure was about public affairs, even though it had profound personal consequences.

The gods can also express interest in particular cases without waiting upon human inquiries. The very passivity of men with respect to key matters may lead the gods to approach them. The blight that settled upon Thebes, which is connected with vital unfinished business in the city, prompts the Thebans to make inquiries of the gods, inquiries that they should perhaps have made decades before about who had presumed to kill the ruler who preceded Oedipus.

The signs sent by the gods to men sometimes provide guidance enough on their face, thereby encouraging or deterring action. Sometimes the signs, such as the Theban blight in this play, serve to encourage inquiry and investigation.

The signs that move human beings to wonder can be connected with birds, fire, altars, dreams, earthquakes, lightning and thunder. Some people, it seems, are better equipped than others to read these signs.

Oracles, such as those coming from the priests at Delphi or those that come from Tiresias, the blind Theban seer, offer more precise information than signs usually provide. For example, the career of Oedipus can be given in its awful detail to Oedipus' parents before his birth, to Oedipus himself as a young man, and to Oedipus by Tiresias in the play. Nothing is said in Oedipus Tyrannus about how the priests or seers secure the information they relay.

The play opens with the people of Thebes imploring Oedipus for help with the blight. A priest says to him, *"Perhaps you'll hear a wise word from some God"*. Everyone remembers that Oedipus had been able to "read signs" effectively when he dealt with an earlier Theban calamity, the presence there of the deadly Sphinx. Oedipus has been able to think of only one thing to do so far this time, to send Creon to Delphi for help from Apollo.

Jocasta (Oedipus' wife and Creon's sister), has come to discount oracles, remembering the one she and Laius had had which had been "proved" false, since Laius had died by a stranger's hand, not by the hand of the infant that they had disposed of in their terror. She counsels Oedipus not to allow himself to be intimidated by such prophecies. Questions are thus raised in the play as to who, if anyone, speaks reliably for or about the gods or about what we call the supernatural. (Another way of putting this may be to ask, "Whose general understanding of things, or metaphysics, is sound?")

It should be noticed that the speech of the divine is not usually regarded in this play (or in the Greek plays generally?) as the kind of action that speech is sometimes regarded in the Bible or in the Koran to be, where to speak can be to make or to do. Thus a priest can pray, *"May Phoebus who gave us the oracle come to our rescue and stay the plague"*. It is one thing for a god to speak; it is another thing for him to act.

Indeed one can wonder whether the gods of the Greeks, as described in this play, ever operate independently of men in human affairs. Do most, if not all, of their meaningful activities depend upon human beings? Does meaningfulness depend upon the fact, including the implications and possibilities, of mortality? To what extent, and in what way, do the things that happen to human beings flow from what mortals have done without immediate divine intervention? This bears upon the question of the relation between revelation and philosophy. Before we return to that perennial question, we should consider further what revelation means by considering, now that we have surveyed how the gods speak to men, why the gods speak at all.

The gods speak in order to advise, to condemn, to encourage—and perhaps out of sheer exuberance? The whyness depends in part, that is, on the whatness. What is there that needs to be said?

We have seen that the gods sometimes speak to men without any deliberate inquiry by men. Signs may be provided which are designed either as immediate guidance or as spurs to inquiry. Sometimes signs from god may not be recognized as such. Thus, the young Oedipus was prompted by a drunkard's slur, in Corinth, to go to Delphi to inquire about his parentage, which led to his learning that he was destined for patricide and incest. Was the drunkard in effect an agent of the divine? Was it not critical for what happened to Oedipus that he learn the Delphic prophecy and that he try to avoid it?

Oedipus' parents in Thebes had had to be told his fate also, or they would not have abandoned him as they did and this, in turn, permitted him to fulfil the prophecy, in its most literal sense, without seeming to be a degenerate monster. Nor would it do, it seems, for Oedipus to have fulfilled the prophecy without his ever learning that he had done so.

Would it have been better if Oedipus had not lived at all? No doubt some think so. We venture to hope that the world is better for all this having been exposed, once it had happened. Perhaps it was even fitting and proper that these things happened when and how they did. It sometimes does seem, however, that men are the gods' playthings, and even that the gods are malevolent.

But should we not insist that the gods are, by and large, benevolent, especially as promoters of piety and guarantors of justice? Are they not bound to be so if they are wise, with wisdom intimately related (as we shall see in our Aristotle chapter) to the moral virtues? But if wisdom is critical to the gods' being, might not a wise man be able to figure out what should be done without immediate divine intervention to guide him? Did not Oedipus, who had been celebrated as the reasoner who had liberated Thebes from the Sphinx, long have available to him, without the spur of Delphi, what he needed to make the inquiries he eventually did? (Was he, then, clever but not wise?)

I will say something about this further on. But more should be said now about the intrinsic goodness of life, especially human life—that is, the life of rational beings. Rationality depends upon, and issues in, speech. Is it possible, ultimately, to lie about the divine? No doubt there have been charlatans and impostors, to say nothing of madmen, posing as prophets and diviners. No doubt, also, there have been men who have believed themselves to be lying about the divine. But, we must wonder, is there not likely to be some truth in what "catches on" because of their lies, a truth that they themselves may not be aware of?

When, then, do the gods speak to men? When they speak, we have seen, is determined in part by when men seek guidance, in part by when men need guidance, whether or not they seek it. Thus, it can be said, the divine speaks intermittently to men, especially when there is more than one god.

The signs, miracles, and oracles used may differ from time to time, depending upon the circumstances of human beings. A god, like any other skilled speaker, can be expected to take account of his audience. Thus, if birds or dreams or thunder should become the provinces of scientific inquiry, then it would no longer be persuasive (or dignified?) for the divine to make use of them as signs. Or if an oracular site should happen to lose its reputation, then it might no longer serve as a source for prophetic utterances. Or, perhaps in other circumstances, Oedipus' character and doings would have as their consequences leprosy or paralysis in him personally rather than in a general blight.

These observations remind us that the gods of the Greeks

seem more "civic-minded" than "personal" in their interests. They are the gods of cities. (This may be seen in the ultimate fate of Oedipus, in Oedipus at Colonus, with the partnership forged between Oedipus and King Theseus and hence Athens.) Especially is this so in the more serious plays, where the heroes tend to be men and women of stature whose fates very much affect what happens to their cities. In any event, there may be far less emphasis than we are used to upon personal salvation as the primary concern of religious observances.

If, as we have noticed, the gods speak, however intermittently, then this means that the divine must exist. But if the divine exists, is it not likely to have a continuous effect, whether or not always perceived (or indeed looked for) by human beings?

The variety of gods, as among the Greeks, testifies not only to continuous involvement but to comprehensiveness as well. All facets of life seem to be provided for. The divine seems to pervade everything.

If the divine is seen as significant if not even as comprehensive in its effects, questions must be raised about the status of nature. Nature may not be recognized as such, however much an awareness of it as critical as the background against which divine interventions can be noticed. What we call the natural ordering of things may itself be a vital sign of the divine, if not even a limitation upon the divine.

We may wonder, however, whether the blight on Thebes *came naturally* because of the pollution of an unexamined regicide, or *was sent by the gods* because the Thebans had shirked their pious, as well as their natural, duty with respect to the regicide. In the play itself it is said again and again that the things that come about, and especially the inexorable fate visited upon Oedipus, are due to the gods, with Zeus and Apollo as the leading influences on this occasion.

To ask whether the divine or the natural is ultimately in control may be to ask, still another way, whether revelation or philosophy is the better means to human understanding. Natural religion (as in the Declaration of Independence?) may try to combine revelation and philosophy, with philosophy in control, just as certain kinds of theology make use of philosophy. Also, some may see philosophy as still another way that the divine speaks, so much so that the gods need not speak directly to the truly wise man.

But, in everyday terms, there is an inevitable tension between a reliance upon revelation and a reliance upon philosophy. Not only are these two approaches to the world likely to be quite different, but the world itself seems quite different from the two viewpoints. The world of the philosophers tends to be impersonally organized. Vice is harmful, not because of any particular or divine intervention but rather because of a general or natural system of cause-and-effect.

The prophets, and the poets to whom they are closely allied, insist that everything means something. Jocasta, in attempting to reassure Oedipus, argues that chance is critical in human affairs. Oedipus can come even to revel in himself as the Child of Fortune. These emphases on chance, by Jocasta and then by Oedipus, are designed to minimize reliance upon prophecies, oracles, and the like, leaving human beings free to reason about, and control, their destinies. But we can see in the *Oedipus* how unpredictable things can be. For example, the Messenger from Corinth happens to have deadly information, blithely volunteering it as a remedy. The most fortunate-looking thing can thus become the most devastating. Or, another example: Oedipus' conscientious efforts to escape his fate make matters worse for him.

It is difficult for common sense to do much with such unpredictability. But poets, like the prophets, present stories that display what happens to people over many years because of their character. Poets "read" signs the way that priests and seers do; they, too, work by inspiration. Is there not something godlike, then, in the way that poets organize things? Rulers, too, can be regarded as godlike, as Oedipus is at the beginning of the play—not necessarily in how they comprehend the whole but rather in how they take charge of things.

The better (or true?) poets sense that there must be *will* and *choice* if a story is to be significant. Things may appear meaningless, if not even malignant, to an Oedipus but is there not a significant pattern working its way out in his life? Whatever the diversity of the gods and their doings, is there not a god of gods, or a divine principle, which guides the overall direction of things? The poets seem to think so.

The philosophers may think so also, but in a different way. Would not they suggest, in any event, that it is important to notice the impulse, or ability, in human beings to rely upon, or to turn to, the gods? Is there not something natural about this human openness to the divine?

What does it mean to say that human beings are receptive to divinity? It may reflect a desire to worship, to enter into a proper, or helpful, relation with the greatest power. Or it may reflect the desire to know, to grasp the sense of the whole. Or it may reflect the overall order in things that human beings can and do notice and that they need and want.

Are men better off for what they learn from or about the gods? But for signs from the gods, diligently investigated, Oedipus' unnatural deeds might never have come to light. Would this, we again ask, have been better or worse for Oedipus? Are these the questions of a philosopher, not of the pious man? Both might agree that it is generally better to know than not to know. But the pious man might recognize certain things as properly concealed, things not to be said or even known. And the philosopher would agree that there are things not to be said in some circumstances.

The philosopher advances knowledge because to understand is fully human, the pious man because knowledge may be necessary in order to avoid impiety. The pious man recognizes his dependence upon what the gods say from time to time as well as always. But what about philosophy? *Can* the wise man, who is listened to by fewer people than either the poet or the pious man is likely to be, figure out the divine will? That is, can he discern on his own the ultimate good by which God also is guided? Is there a correspondence between what follows naturally and what the gods ordain?

Creon reported, upon returning to Thebes from Delphi, that Apollo had said that "the clue is in this land". This and other clues, relating to the cause of the oppressive blight, had evidently been there all along for the discerning (not-yet-blinded!) eye to notice. Oedipus, we remember from his encounter with the Sphinx, is good at solving mysteries. He might have been somewhat better than he was if he had not believed himself to be much better than he was. That is, he is rather presumptuous, as well as at times unduly fearful, and that clouds his talents.

One vital clue, of which Oedipus should be more aware than he is, is his own temper (like the temper of Laius before him?). Is his temper related to his desire to master things as well as to his deep fears? That temper, along with his failure to investigate properly the fate of his predecessor (which, like his temper, is perhaps an undue emphasis upon himself), contributes to his fate. What the gods say and do may be a poetic way, then, of explaining what human beings should do and say.

In this chapter I have considered, first, *how* the gods speak to human beings by request or on their own, through signs and in the very organization of the world; second, *why* the gods speak to men to instruct, chastise, and otherwise guide them; and third, *when* the gods speak to men continuously or intermittently, as needed. Perhaps another way of putting all this is to say that the divine speaks to human beings in part, if not primarily, through inspired poets who present the world in a certain way, reinforced as this is by the interest generated in us by an account (called prophecy) which dramatizes the remarkable events we encounter. These events may not truly depend upon any prophecy for their significance. In a sense, that is, the events come first; the prophecy (whether curse or blessing) or poem comes afterwards for the benefit of those who cannot or will not or perhaps even should not confront events in themselves.

All this, it can be said, Aeschylus anticipates, Sophocles teaches, and Euripides questions and perhaps thereby teaches even more.

3

Plato in the History of Philosophy

Introduction

Once one is *told*, presumably by someone who has read the proper scholars what "the Greeks" thought about the burial of a corpse, one is then well on the way to understanding what Antigone did and why. Without this vital information about Greek opinion, one would have to determine what to make of what she did; one would have to *think* about the meaning and significance of what is said and done. One might even be obliged to conclude that Antigone is noble but imprudent, perhaps even unjust something one is not apt to conclude if one believes that there was a Greek response to the unburied corpse and that Antigone merely expressed that response in its most dramatic form.

What, then, did "the Greeks" believe about these matters? It is difficult to say. After all, even in the *Antigone*, as we have also seen, various positions are taken. Antigone herself seems to identify her compulsion to bury her brother with some kind of divine injunction. But the reader is led to wonder whether it is because of this, or because it is an affront to her pride or for some other reason, that she makes her desperate effort. Creon, on the other hand, insists that a refusal to bury a traitor is salutary, indeed even sanctified if not required by the gods, especially when that traitor would (as he evidently believes) have destroyed the temples of his city. In any event, Creon sees his decree as politically useful. Antigone's sister, Ismene, is somewhere between Antigone and Creon: she considers the denial of burial lamentable; but she (out of fear, at least) is somewhat respectful of the laws of the city.

What could Sophocles expect his original Athenian audience, in fifth century-B.C. Greece, to think about this? Were not quite varied responses to be found, even on this relatively simple issue, among the Athenians of Sophocles' generation? Consider what happened when the Athenian generals, after the naval Battle of Arginusae in 406 B.C., failed to recover the bodies of the dead from the water. (This was during the Peloponnesian War.) These generals, despite their victory at Arginusae, were condemned to death and executed by the Athenians.

This Athenian fervor, then, is one response, no doubt a widespread one, to the problem of proper treatment of corpses. It is a response that is reflected in an observation by a character, centuries later, in one of Cicero's dialogues: "[Men do not believe that] their interests end with their lives; hence the sanctity of burial is part of the pontifical law [in Rome]." On the other hand, there is the response of Socrates—not necessarily at the trial of the generals, since that could be understood as an insistence by him upon the procedural proprieties, but rather on the day of his death. Plato *Phaedo* records Socrates' counsel to Crito that no trouble need be taken with his (Socrates') corpse. It is indicated thereby, as we have seen, that Socrates does not seem concerned (so far as his own interests, as distinguished from the sensibilities of his family and other survivors are concerned) about what happens to his body after he dies.

No doubt, the prevailing beliefs with respect to burial (whether those of Antigone or those of Socrates) are likely to be keyed to opinions one has about the gods. In the Antigone itself, we see that the blind seer Tiresias supports

Antigone's position on the basis of considerations which can be considered more "theological" than are hers. In that play, we also hear Creon argue that the gods like law-abidingness and patriotism. Or, if we go on to a work such as Cicero *On the Nature of the Gods*, we can see the ancients' diversity of religious sentiment in full bloom. Various opinions are there indicated about the gods. There are no out-and-out atheists among the characters in this work of Cicero's—but then, atheism is very hard to find any time, whatever the form of words may be.

More immediately at hand is what is to be found in Plato himself about the divine and its relation to the lives of human beings. It should be instructive to consider here what is said in his Timaeus about these and other matters. (The Timaeus, it has been noticed, was the only Platonic dialogue available to the western world for most of its history.)

The divine, in perhaps its most nearly cosmic form, may be seen in the Timaeus, The ordering of the *cosmos* by divine power is related there, an ordering which ranges from the shaping of the heavens above and of various divinities to the emergence on earth of human beings and thereafter of the lowest living things. The range of "creation," as recapitulated by Timaeus, is extensive.

Precisely what Timaeus himself does say about these matters is a problem. Two responses, one ancient, the other modern, put us on our guard at the beginning of these investigations. An Epicurean, in Cicero's dialogue *On the Nature of the Gods*, opens his account of the divine with this disclaimer: "You are going to hear from me no fatuous and fanciful doctrines, such, for example, as that of the carpenter-architect god who put together the world, presented by Plato in his Timaeus."

The modern skeptical response is, it can be said, somewhat more respectful. Kenneth Clark has observed: *"As for the Timaeus, Clive Bell used to say that when he thought he understood the Timaeus it was a sure sign that he was drunk. I agree."*

Our awareness of such diverse responses, along with our realization of the considerable reputation enjoyed by the

Timaeus during the Middle Ages, puts us on notice that there is no settled opinion about the Timaeus and that, consequently, we must think for ourselves. On the other hand, since there is such diversity, whatever we dare say about this subject is not without some support in the literature.

What, then, is said in the Timaeus about "the carpenter-architect god who put together the world"? This overarching divinity this demiurge is seen, in this dialogue, as primarily a maker, not as contemplative. He works with pre-existing matter: the stuff from which everything visible is made is not itself made by the demiurge in the sequence described by Timaeus (whatever may have been the ultimate origin of that stuff). There does seem to have been a chaotic movement of visible bodies before the making (that is, the ordering?) of the cosmos by the demiurge.

The stuff, or material, from which everything visible is made seems to be keyed to four elements: earth, fire, air, and water. The proportions among these are critical in any enduring (not necessarily eternal?) combination of these elements. It is again and again indicated that the material from which these four elements were made had an existence and a decisive nature prior to the shaping of the cosmos by the demiurge (53A-C). When Timaeus turns to an account of this stuff, the probable (or tentative) nature of his account is emphasized (48D-E). It is not possible for him to speak here with the kind of certainty he had exhibited with respect to "the operations of reason," and which may be seen, for example, in his mathematics (47E-48A). In any event, one gets the impression that the preexistent nature of this stuff places limits on what the demiurge can do as creator. There are, for him, necessary limits; he is not omnipotent. Indeed, it can be said, there is something "perplexing and baffling" in the receptivity of the stuff which is very (but not infinitely) malleable. (If the stuff of the universe were infinitely malleable, would it not be as if there could be a creation from nothing as well as complete annihilation?)

In the sequence of creation, three stages are of particular

interest to us. There is the creation of the cosmos itself; there is the creation of certain unnamed gods who will, pursuant to the will of the demiurge, exist forever once created; and there is the emergence, through the agency in turn of the created gods, of human beings and other mortal things.

First, the cosmos is created, it seems. It is presented as a living creature, patterned on "that intelligible Creature which is fairest of all and in all ways most perfect" (30D). There can be, it is argued, only one such universe patterned on the eternal perfection, "one generated heaven, unique of its kind" (31B). This question is returned to later: an infinite number of "universes" is again ruled out. But the recourse, in the construction of things, to the five regular solids, raises the more plausible question, whether there are *not* an infinite number but rather five universes. Timaeus stands by the conclusion that there is only one, but he concedes the plausibility of the suggestion that there are five (55D). Is this left open? Does fiveness relate as well to the five participants originally scheduled for the conversation recorded in this dialogue? But only four showed up this day: one of the anticipated participants is ill. Are we meant to wonder whether fiveness *is* capable of sustained realization? (There *had* been five of them the day before?)

The dialogue concludes with a reaffirmation of the oneness of the universe (or cosmos): "And now at length we may say that our discourse concerning the Universe has reached its termination. For this our Cosmos has received the living creatures both mortal and immortal and been thereby fulfilled; it being itself a visible Living Creature embracing the visible creatures, a perceptible God made in the image of the Intelligible, most great and good and fair and perfect in its generation—even this one Heaven sole of its kind" (92C). This emphasis upon the one echoes, it can be said, the somewhat ostentatious counting of the others with which Socrates opens this dialogue (17A): "One, two, three—but where, my dear Timaeus, is the fourth of our guests of yesterday, our hosts of today?" Can things be grasped only in their oneness, in their unity? Is diversity essentially unknowable, unless one can bring it all together as a one, as a "fulfilled" one? Otherwise, can one know whether one has an "it" to grasp? That which has thus far escaped one's grasp might radically change one's view of what one has?

We must turn now, in the sequence of creation, to "the creatures both mortal and immortal." The immortal creatures–the gods made by the demiurge in turn create mortal creatures. These gods are instructed in their creation of mortal creatures by the demiurge; they model themselves in their creation upon what the demiurge has done.

Male human beings come first among mortal creatures. From them "evolve" women and the lower animals. There even seem to be natural laws (as we would call them) in accordance with which the various mortal creatures, because of their misconduct, pass into one another, evidently as a kind of degeneration, once man is created. This movement is not a matter of choice (unlike what may be seen in the Republic's Myth of Er). Nor is it a matter of chance (as is seen to some extent, it can be said, in the Darwinian scheme). Rather, there is a movement in the Timaeus from the highest to the lowest, in this effort to present a comprehensive account of the things that are. Yet that account concludes, as we have already seen, with an emphasis upon the one cosmos, "most great and good and fair and perfect in its generation". The universe, then, with all that is in it, is seen as eminently purposeful except that that purpose may be difficult for human beings to realize with respect to *the things that always are*, including the stuff out of which all (that is visible?) is made and the perfect being upon which the cosmos is patterned.

We began, it will be remembered, with a realization of the diversity of opinion among "the Greeks" with respect to matters of overriding importance, both practical (the problem of burial) and theoretical or at least theological (the nature of the gods).

We have seen that this diversity of opinion on such subjects may be found within the work of particular authors (such as Sophocles and Plato). One of their characters may hold one opinion, another character a different opinion. We have also seen, from our preliminary survey of the Timaeus, that a diversity of sorts may exist even within the opinions of a single character. That is, Timaeus' account presents somewhat diverse divinities.

There is the demiurge. He seems to be the supreme father. His powers, we have seen, are not absolute: he does not create from nothing, but rather "must" work with pre-existing stuff (whose origins are not indicated). In addition, his constant willing seems to be necessary if that which has been made by him is to retain its form and do what is intended. The elementary stuff shaped by the demiurge seems to have a "will" of its own: it will not stay put, it seems, without constant supervision.

Then there is the cosmos—that living, intelligent, and permanent being—which is either divine or is modelled on the divine.

Then there are the various subordinate deities who are entrusted with subordinate creating. These three sets of divinities are required, Timaeus seems to say, if one is to explain *the all*—if one is to be able to account for the existence of things both divine and earthly. No account is possible, he also seems to say, without invoking the divine, but the divine in rather complicated forms.

When one looks to Plato's other "characters," the diversity in the divine becomes even more marked. Consider what is indicated about the divine by others in the Timaeus. But, first, we must recall what the others have said. Among the things provided by Socrates is a summary of part of the conversation of the day before, recorded in the Republic, which is itself an account of what had taken place in the Piraeus the day before that. (This emphasis placed in this summary of the conversation of the Republic is upon the constitution in words of "the best city.") Then there is an anticipation by Critias of what he will relate in the dialogue that we know as the Critias about the ancient war between Atlantis and Athens. (That account will deal, he says, with the history of "the best city" as experienced in deed a regime which was not immune to catastrophic accident? What does *this* suggest about divinity and the governance of the world?)

One critical difference between the Republic and the *Critias* is that the named gods (Zeus and his colleagues, for example) figure hardly at all in the Republic but very much in the *Critias*: Athena and Hephaestus established Athens; Poseidon established Atlantis, because of his desire for a woman; and Zeus must finally bring Atlantis to its deserved ruin.

The named gods (including the Thracian goddess of the opening lines) figure so little in the Republic that they are not mentioned at all in the summary of that dialogue that Socrates provides in the Timaeus. (But, it should be noticed, neither is the philosopher-king mentioned in this summary. Is this partly because he is an image of the divine?) What is emphasized in the summary is that the institutions of "the best city" are arranged in accordance with nature (17C-D).

Not only are the named gods not mentioned in Socrates' summary, but if the teaching by Socrates in the Republic is taken seriously, then the conventional (largely poetic?) accounts of the gods are in need of considerable purgation. Thus, the gods must not be understood to change, to lust, etc. But this understanding of the divine would call for drastic reconsideration of what is depended upon in the *Critias*—where, as we have noticed, Poseidon's lust is critical to the founding of Atlantis.

Still, it can be said, the Republic can manage to do without the named gods for the most part (except, perhaps, in oaths) because it reports an ascetic gathering devoted to the discussion of that political asceticism which a truly just regime can be said to be. The regime described in the Republic is unresponsive to (or unconcerned with) *eros*, as conventionally understood. Since it is a city in words, it can be independent of the gods who minister to, and in various ways discipline, the passions (erotic and otherwise) of human beings.

On the other hand, named, involved, and hence somewhat passionate gods may be inevitable in a "working" city if it is not to become cruel or even monstrous. Does conventional piety tend to contain excessive pride? Do the involved gods tend to have a gentling, a civilizing, effect? Consider what happens in the *Critias* as the divine influence wears off: misbehaviour becomes rampant. (One is reminded of the accounts in the Hebrew Bible of the falling away of the Israelites when they forgot God. Is the God of the Israelites similar, in critical respects, to the named [properly purged] gods of the Platonic dialogues?) Compare Benardete, *"On Plato's Timaeus,"* pp. 30-31: "Critias all but says that the love of wisdom is due to nature and the love of war to the gods." Does this mean that the wise should be reluctant to embrace war?

Of course, a concern by the city for its gods can also have deleterious effects. This is reflected in Plato *Euthyphro* and *Apology*, where Socrates' vulnerability is evident because he does not acknowledge the gods that the city acknowledges. Although it is important to keep the condemnation of Socrates in mind, too much *can* be made of this (as may be seen in the modern Enlightenment?). In our times it is well to be reminded instead of the salutary influence of piety, however destructive of the familial and the natural an excess of piety can be (as may be seen in the *Euthyphro*). We can see in Plato *Phaedrus* Socrates' own use of the gods. He shows there what *he* can do with the named gods.

These diverse accounts of the divine prompt us to turn now to a question which is implicit in the Timaeus: What is the authority for the various opinions about the divine set forth by Timaeus himself? The reader is induced to wonder thus when he notices that the accounts of things provided in the dialogue by others (that is, by Socrates and by Critias) do have their immediate sources indicated. Socrates' account is, we have noticed, a summary of what he had related to them the day before (which, in turn, had been the report of a conversation of the day before that). Critias' account, about Atlantis and events of nine thousand years before, came (it is said by Critias) from the Egyptian records by way of Solon. (It is "a strange piece of fortune," Critias says, that Socrates' account of the best city fits in so well with Solon's account of the composition and activities of an ancient city [25E]. Is this like the fortune of the marriage lots earlier referred to [18E]? That is, is "fortune" here likewise contrived?)

Nothing is said, however, about where Timaeus gets his account of the demiurge and of all its doings. Nor is anything said about how long ago these things happened. (There is, unlike in the Hebrew Bible, no genealogy or other history since the creation.) Timaeus reports, in considerable detail, what no man could have seen. Consider in this respect the opening chapters of Genesis. Are we meant to understand that the word of God, there relied upon, came to mankind through the Biblical prophets?

What is the status of such revelation for Timaeus? The named gods, as we know them, may reflect divinities that appear here and there to men: for example, both in Egypt and in Greece, as Critias reports. Men who travel about encounter the same gods, under different names, in various places. Or rather, they encounter the effects or relics of such gods, in the forms of temples, priests, and rituals, as well as in the form of stories. Also, such gods instructed men in all manner of things "down to divination and the art of medicine" (24C). These gods, it is assumed, somehow manifested themselves in an authoritative fashion, usually "long ago."

But however the gods manifested themselves originally, and to whom, reports about them come down to us, it seems, primarily as the "discoveries" of the poets. It is those discoveries, it also seems, that Timaeus incorporates into his account of the emergence of the named or lesser gods. (Does he, in this respect, reconsider what Hesiod who is mentioned in the dialogue along with Homer had done in presenting the emergence of the named gods?) Is Timaeus, because of what he knows of *the* divinity behind the named gods, able to present directly what the poets could do no more than speak figuratively about? The poets cannot, or at least do not, explain what they say. The poets make much of particulars and of passions associated with those particulars. They shape thereby the passions and character of the people. But, it has been noticed, the poets in turn are somewhat shaped by the people. It is said in one of Cicero's dialogues, "By their clamorous approval and applause, the people mold the character of the poets according to their will—as if the public were some great and wise master whose praise is all-sufficient."

All this, then, can be seen to raise a question about the ultimate authority of the poets with respect to the named gods. Timaeus, because of what he has divined about the demiurge, has a model upon which to base these lesser gods. These gods copy the demiurge in their creations. The poets, it appears from this perspective, have at best a dim awareness of the divinities set forth by Timaeus. How does what the poets offer us compare with what the Biblical prophets and Biblical revelation offer us? Does the Bible provide us access to the divine—to the divine in its particular manifestations among men, to the divine in its "historical" significance that the poets simply do not provide us, or do not provide us in as reliable a form? Certainly, ancient Christian partisans rooted in the Bible claimed that their revelation was essentially different from what the pagan poets had provided. In some ways, it can be said, St. Augustine (in the opening chapters of *The City of God*) uses the teachings of the pagan philosophers against the gods of the pagan poets. Does he, while "using" the philosophers as he does, fail to exhibit the deference toward received opinion that philosophy tends to show? Does he, as a born-again rhetorician, take from philosophy only what is useful for him, thereby either undermining the cogency of that (philosophy) which he relies upon or calling into question the general position he is defending? Perhaps an analogy would be useful here. It is sometimes said, in support of a more or less skeptical position, "Words don't have meanings; it is people themselves who put meanings into words." Does not this statement presuppose that at least the words *people*, *meanings*, and *words* have comprehensible meanings in themselves? Perhaps one should approach Augustine's critique in the same fashion.

Timaeus concerned himself with the "revelations" then available to him. He suggested where the named or lesser gods came from, and how—the gods which the poets report. How has Timaeus learned what he knows, for example, about the demiurge? Does he not rely upon something other than what the poets and prophets, conventionally understood, drew upon? Is he not trying to do more than merely substitute his intuition or insight for theirs? Does he do anything other than propose a "revelation" of his own? How else, then, may the divine be ascertained?

Perhaps by working back from what one experiences: something has made all things, including the generated gods? A "theology" thus derived might be replaced in modernity by physics, evolutionary biology, psychology, and astronomy. Or perhaps the divine can be ascertained by going beyond experience by figuring out, on the basis of the very nature of things, what the divine must be like. In proceeding thus, does one work from what one observes, as well as from the ideas innate in human beings, or only from the ideas?

How, then, does Timaeus know what he reports about the demiurge and its doings? A clue is perhaps found in what Alfred North Whitehead says about Aristotle. (It is appropriate that Whitehead should be drawn upon here, since he, as a mathematician and scientist with philosophical interests, may be considered the modern equivalent of Timaeus.) Whitehead says, in *Science and the Modern World*:

> *Aristotle found it necessary to complete his metaphysics by the introduction of a Prime Mover—God. This, for two reasons, is an important fact in the history of metaphysics. In the first place if we are to accord to anyone the position of the greatest metaphysician, having regard to genius of insight, to general equipment in knowledge, and to the stimulus of his metaphysical ancestry, we must choose Aristotle. Secondly, in his consideration of this metaphysical question he was entirely dispassionate; and he is the last European metaphysician of first-rate importance for whom this claim can be made. After Aristotle, ethical and religious interests began to influence metaphysical conclusions.*

Thus, Whitehead seems to suggest, Aristotle was the last man to think clearly about God, using only nature and reason. I will have more to say later about what Whitehead calls "ethical and religious interests," which are touched upon in a Whitehead passage following upon the one I have just quoted:

> *The Greek gods who surrounded Aristotle were subordinate metaphysical entities, well within nature. [This, as we shall soon see, may be a Timaean view of things.] Accordingly on the subject of his Prime Mover, he would have no motive, except to follow his metaphysical train of thought whithersoever it led him. It did not lead him very far towards the production of a God available for religious purposes.* It may be doubted whether any properly general metaphysics can ever, without the illicit introduction of other considerations, get much further than Aristotle *licit introduction of other considerations, get much further than Aristotle. But his conclusion does represent a first step without which no evidence on a narrower experiential basis can be of much avail in shaping the conception.*

The phrase, Prime Mover, warns us that Aristotle's thought was enmeshed in the details of an erroneous physics and an erroneous cosmology. In Aristotle's physics special causes were required to sustain the motions of material things. These could easily be fitted into his system, provided that the general cosmic motions could be sustained. For then in relation to the general working system, each thing could be provided with its true end. Hence the necessity for a Prime Mover who sustains the motions of the spheres on which depend the adjustment of things.

I will have more to say further on also about the problem of what does sustain "the general cosmic motions." We need not concern ourselves here with whether modern physics is sound in its assumption that bodies once in motion need nothing to sustain their motion. Nor need we concern ourselves here with whether the statement I have just quoted from Whitehead is an adequate account of Aristotle's scheme of things. It suffices to notice that Whitehead's account of Aristotle is suggestive about the Timaean derivation of the demiurge.

Timaeus seems to derive much of what he says about the workings of the demiurge, and of other beings thereafter, from his studies of astronomy, physics, biology, etc. that is, from his studies of the things we see around us. His prowess as an astronomer is pointed up early in the dialogue. This had been preceded by an account, transmitted on this occasion by Critias, from an Egyptian priest who had said to Solon, an Athenian:

> *There have been and there will be many and diverse destructions of mankind, of which the greatest are by fire and water, and lesser ones by countless other means. For in truth the story that is told in your country [Athens? Greece?] as well as ours, how once upon a time Phaethon, son of Helios, yoked his father's chariot, and, because he was unable to drive it along the course taken by his father, burned up all that was upon the earth and himself perished by a thunderbolt,—that story, as it is told, has the fashion of a legend, but the truth of it lies in the occurrence of a shifting of the bodies in the heavens which move round the earth, and a destruction of the things on the earth by fierce fire, which recurs at long intervals.*

Thus, as we see here, dramatic stories about divinities, and about the offspring of divinities, can be said to have been derived from astronomical or from other natural movements. It might help, in order to understand such things, to have available to us the extensive records of the Egyptians.

Timaeus, in developing his derivations, must begin by distinguishing between that which is "existent always and has no becoming" and that which is "becoming always and never is existent" (27D). It is upon this fundamental distinction (between being and becoming) that such reasoning as his must rest. Also brought to bear upon his investigations are such things as opinions about the appropriate shapes for various objects, with the sphere being considered the best for the cosmos, which is a living creature (33A sq.). Also critical are his uses of mathematics, with quite elaborate proportions utilized in his speculations about the fabrication of the soul of the cosmos (35B-36E).

Does Timaeus' mathematics lead to what he has to say about the cosmos? Or does what he understands, somehow or other, about the cosmos lead to the mathematics he makes so much of here? Consider, in this connection, an observation made in a review of a memoir by Leopold Infeld, a longtime collaborator in physics of Einstein's:

> *Einstein's estrangement from the mainstream of physics and his opposition to quantum mechanics are a recurrent theme [in the Infeld book], but the puzzle remains. Perhaps Einstein felt that when he created general relativity he heard the voice of God and that he listened in vain for that voice in the noises of contemporary physics.*

We can see, in Timaeus' account, a shadowing over from the "supernatural" into the "natural." In large parts of the dialogue, it is difficult to distinguish between divine causes and nature. (One is reminded of the phrase in the Declaration of Independence, "the Laws of Nature and of Nature's God.") Thus, some things are said by Timaeus to come into existence through necessity (48A). We have noticed that no dates are provided by Timaeus: the developments seem timeless, as if in the very nature of things. (We have also noticed that this is to be contrasted to Critias' dates, vague though they may be. Perhaps this also indicates, still another way, the difference between a "practical" man like Critias and a more "theoretical" man like Timaeus. But Critias, it should be noticed, was not so practical that he could avoid the political, and perhaps also personal, unsavoriness of his career as one of the Thirty Tyrants.) Considerable emphasis is placed by Timaeus upon the likelihood, not the certainty, of his account. He alerts his listeners to this at the outset and repeats his disclaimer a dozen times. Does not this disclaimer reflect an effort to reason from what nature provides, rather than an effort to relate what has been definitively provided by some authority, divine or human? Must not any effort to reason from that which nature provides recognize that an infinite variety in things is possible? Until one can know all, we again wonder, is only probable reasoning possible with respect to nature?

Is the God of Nature still working, not only to keep things going but also to bring new things into existence? Or are all things, including the new things yet to manifest themselves, essentially there in the beginning? Nature does seem to be at the root of things. Is not what is said by Timaeus (e.g., 39D-E), about how all things mesh together, at the basis of physics, both modern and ancient? Is this not critical to an understanding of nature as authoritative? Nature, then, is at the root of things, just as it was (earlier in this dialogue) in Socrates' summary of the *Republic.* The question remains whether Timaeus' is the cosmology that fits in with Socrates' political thought. Is it consistent with this emphasis upon nature to see man as somehow keyed to the heavens? This keying may be seen in the fashioning of man by the star-like lesser gods (42D sq.). This is a natural view of man's emergence which accounts for the special character of man which recognizes the godlike qualities, or at least aspirations, in him. Is not this combination of the mundane and the heavenly in man the basis of the openness of mankind to poetry, to that fashioning of the concrete in the light of the eternal?

Why did not Timaeus suggest that the demiurge created directly the human beings of this world? For one thing, this suggestion would directly contradict the poetic tradition and thus would be, in a sense, wasteful if not even dangerous. Rather, Timaeus incorporates, in his account that which he considers essential or useful or at least acceptable in whatever the poets have provided. Besides, he senses that living (mortal) things operate differently from the other created things in the universe. A kind of natural order may be seen in the way living things operate. Does life on earth seem to have emerged in a way, somehow natural, that the use of the stories of the lesser gods reflects? (I notice in passing that there is in the account of the movement from the emergence of men to the emergence of the lower animals a "reverse Darwinism," just as Ptolemy is a "reverse Copernicus." But the direction of the movement may be secondary: the essential relations may be suggested, no matter which "direction" one considers things to move.)

Furthermore, Timaeus senses (like a careful scientist?) that the prevalence of the named gods reflects *something* which is available to mankind. Such gods are widely dispersed, although the names they go under differ from place to place. (The descendants of such gods, and the doings of such descendants, can be left to the poets to describe

[400].) Timaeus evidently cannot discount as being completely without significance the worldwide attempts to describe the gods in the terms that the poets have used. Certainly, the impersonal divinity of the metaphysicians does not, typically, inspire worship. Religious interests and instincts find expression in particular forms of divinity, revealed or otherwise tailored with view to local circumstances.

Since one can see in the Platonic corpus a variety of approaches to the divine, one may be moved to wonder:

1. What determines what one believes about the divine? Is not what one believes influenced, at least in part, by one's character? Just as Zeus is, in Plato *Phaedrus*, refashioned as the leading divinity to suit and minister to Phaedrus' inclinations, so the leading divinity is fashioned in the *Timaeus* to suit and minister to Timaeus' inclinations, if not with a view to Socrates' interests as well. Other views or aspects of divinity, appropriate to Socrates' interlocutors, may be seen in other Platonic dialogues—for example, in the *Euthyphro* and in the *Crito* (with its godlike laws). Consider, also, the *Republic*, where common notions about the gods are questioned. In that dialogue, where the doctrine of the ideas is developed, a kind of abstract divinity is taken for granted.
2. What are the uses of various beliefs about the divine? That is, what do these beliefs tend toward? Are not they likely to have corresponding effects? The beliefs espoused may depend, in part, upon one's circumstances, upon one's immediate purpose, or upon chance. But it is prudent to keep in mind here Cicero's warning, "Piety, like all the other virtues, cannot live on specious pretense and ostentation".
3. What is the relation between politics and religion? Much is made both of the appropriateness of a story associated with the divinity of one's city and of the appropriateness of telling such a story in the city on

> the feast day of that divinity. Even so, Timaeus' account of the gods is given by a stranger, about whom relatively little is told us. This is an outsider's, not an Athenian's, view of things: particular cities, or peoples, do not matter in *Timaeus*' account, whereas they do in Critias'. Timaeus' view of divinity is cosmopolitan, drawing.

And yet, however much one's opinion about the divine is influenced by one's character or by one's immediate purposes or by considerations which transcend the interests of particular cities, it seems suggested by the *Timaeus-Critias* exposition that even the most elevated cosmology is grounded in, or framed by, the city. Consider the frame provided for Timaeus' account: a city in words ("the best city") precedes Timaeus' account; a city in deeds (the best city in action) anticipates and then follows Timaeus' account. (Timaeus himself, although not an Athenian, is said to come from a well-ordered city.) Is not the political, or at least political philosophy, the setting in which such things as Timaeus' cosmology can exist? Timaeus' interest in political philosophy is limited. Does this mean that he cannot truly understand what he is doing—he cannot grasp the conditions of who he is and what he is doing—and hence he can have, at best, no more than a provisional account of the whole?

A key question remains: What may God be? Perhaps this is *the* question of all philosophy. Certainly, this question is implicit throughout the Platonic dialogues. Is there not an awareness of the divine which informs and shapes all of the opinions about the divine that we have begun to examine? Is there not some *one thing* which is manifested in the diverse opinions we have touched upon here? Consider, for example, what Socrates draws upon in the third book of the *Republic* and elsewhere in order to argue that certain common stories about the gods cannot be true, however they happened to have been developed once upon a time.

Is not the truly divine something that is one, unchanging, and hence anything but diverse? The diversity reflected in men's opinions about the divine reflects the differences among, and the varying limitations of, human beings rather than anything unsettled and variable in the "nature" of the divine itself. Is the divine—an eminently single thing—incomprehensible? Indeed, are there not for human beings three intrinsically incomprehensible things in the universe? (1) There is the demiurge (or overarching divinity, or divine "force"). (2) There is the model, including the unchanging truths of geometry, to which the demiurge looked in fashioning the world. (3) There is the stuff out of which all (visible?) things are made. We have already noticed that it is said by Timaeus that there is something "perplexing and baffling" in the receptivity of the stuff which is so malleable (51A). (Do the demiurge and the model somehow come together? Are they, in a sense, one?)

Why are these three things the demiurge, the model, and the stuff incomprehensible? Partly because we cannot know their origins. So far as we can tell, these three things have always been. There is no thing outside or before them, by which we can take our bearings in understanding the origins, or cause of the being, of these three things. Thus, it can be said by Timaeus, "Now to discover the Maker and Father of this Universe were a task indeed; and having discovered Him, to declare Him unto all men were a thing impossible" (28C). Or, as Whitehead says, "God is the ultimate limitation, and His existence is the ultimate irrationality. For no reason can be given for just that limitation which it stands in His nature to impose. God is not concrete, but He is the ground for concrete actuality. No reason can be given for the nature of God, because that nature is the ground of rationality."

It is no accident that Zeus is not quoted at the end of the *Critias*. The dialogue breaks off just as Zeus is about to speak. Critias, it seems, believed he knew what Zeus would (or did) say in particular circumstances. But, then, this Athenian had made early in the *Critias* a bold statement, that it is easier to speak about gods than about men because we are more familiar with men and can criticize more minutely whatever is said about men (107B-E). Critias presumes to report about Zeus (who was troubled by the misconduct of the people of Atlantis) that he called all the gods together, at the middle of the cosmos, to announce (it seems) what he proposed to do about Atlantis (121C). To place Zeus at the center of the cosmos may be to have Critias' gods (and especially Zeus as ruler) usurp the place of Timaeus' god (the demiurge, as creator).

Plato, it can be said, knew better than that—and so he breaks off the dialogue before Zeus can speak. "Zeus" is not permitted such a usurpation as Critias, a future tyrant, was about to "lead" in his name. (We are provided, in Critias' anticipation in the *Timaeus*, the end of the war between Atlantis and Athens. That is, we are told earlier what happens after Zeus speaks.) Besides, what Zeus does say to human beings is what all can hear and see especially if we consider that what Zeus "says" has to be evident primarily in what happens among men. This means, that there may be, in Plato's opinions, no special revelation of the divine will. It may also mean that the reports of the poets about the conversations among gods, such as may be seen in Homer *Iliad*, are implicitly called into question, especially if speaking (as well as other actions) requires bodies.

Still, we are given the direct discourse (in the Timaeus) of the demiurge to the lesser gods:

> *Gods of gods, those works whereof I am framer and father are indissoluble save by my will. For though all that is bound may be dissolved, yet to will to dissolve that which is fairly joined together and in good case were the deed of a wicked one. Wherefore ye also, seeing that ye were generated, are not wholly immortal or indissoluble, yet in no wise shall ye be dissolved nor incur the doom of death, seeing that in my will ye possess a bond greater and more sovereign than the bonds wherewith at your birth, ye were bound together. Now, therefore, what I manifest and declare unto you do ye learn. Three mortal kinds still remain ungenerated; but if these come not into being the Heaven will be imperfect; for it will not contain within itself the whole sum of the kinds of living creatures, yet contain them it must if it is to be fully*

> *perfect. But if by my doing these creatures came into existence and partook of life, they would be made equal unto gods; in order, therefore, that they may be mortal and that this World-all may be truly All, do ye turn yourselves, as Nature directs, to the work of fashioning these living creatures, imitating the power showed by me in my generating of you. Now so much of them as it is proper to designate "immortal," the part we call divine which rules supreme in those who are fain to follow justice always and yourselves, that part I will deliver unto you when I have sown it and given it origin. For the rest, do ye weave together the mortal with the immortal, and thereby fashion and generate living creatures, and give them food that they may grow, and when they waste away receive them to yourselves again.*

Is not this kind of discourse, of a general "philosophical" character, radically different from the sort of thing (the battle orders, so to speak) that Zeus was believed by Critias to have said on a special occasion? Has what the demiurge is reported by Timaeus to say always been said or ordained by that nature which images for us the doings and arrangements of the demiurge?

Three things the demiurge, the model, and the stuff—I have suggested, are in principle incomprehensible. All other things are subject to investigation to a degree or in ways that these three things are not. The origins of other things, for example, can be known (at least, in a probable sense). But even the other things we are familiar with are "secondarily" incomprehensible—in that they are made up of or have been modelled upon or have been made by things which are themselves intrinsically incomprehensible. For example, the motives of the demiurge must remain somewhat mysterious. It is said of him, by Timaeus, "He was good, and in him that is good no envy ariseth ever concerning anything; and being devoid of envy. He desired that all should be, so far as possible, like himself". This is, we are told, "the supreme originating principle of Becoming and the Cosmos," according to the wise. We are also told, "For God desired that, so far as possible, all things should be good and nothing evil" (30A). These motives, which remind us of the first chapter of *Genesis*, in which God is reported to have regarded various of His creations as "good," do remain somewhat mysterious. Did the demiurge need to create, based on an eternal model, in order to *possess* that which He can otherwise do "no more" than contemplate? Indeed, does the demiurge surpass His eternal model, in that the "working" model includes mortal beings and hence is complete in a way that the eternal model could not be? Such an ambition on the part of the demiurge would be mysterious indeed.

The divine itself is inevitably diverse in the opinions of men (just as justice is), in part because of men's varying talents in quite different circumstances. The divine, I have suggested, is so difficult to grasp that only diverse accounts of it can emerge and we need all of these accounts if we are to be able to have a reliable indication of how divine things and divine doings truly are.

Certainly, not every soul is capable of grasping all that can be said about the divine and so, mythology is made use of (28B-C). But what of Timaeus' account? Socrates gives his preliminary assessment of it at the beginning of the *Critias*, when he refers to it as theatrical (albeit theater on a grand scale?). Is Timaeus' account regarded by Socrates as a theatrical that is, fanciful and dramatic counterpart to what Socrates had said (two days before) about the Ideas in the *Republic*?

As a fanciful account it is entertaining (however difficult) and otherwise useful. But perhaps it does not suffice. Just as Plato knew better than Critias about what (and whether) Zeus speaks to men, so perhaps Plato knows better than Timaeus about what the divine can be said to be and to do. Why do I say" Plato" and not "Socrates" here? The fifth member of this party is missing, we notice at the outset of the *Timaeus*. And the missing fifth member (who would complete "the hand" that seeks to grasp these matters) is said to be ill. One is reminded of the *Phaedo*, the Platonic dialogue reporting Socrates' death, where it is said that Plato himself is missing because he is ill. For this and other reasons, perhaps, it has long been suggested by students of the *Timaeus* that Plato is the missing fifth member of this gathering. This "Plato" can be considered a Socrates who had had the advantage of being able to reflect upon what Socrates thought and heard and upon what had happened to him. And this observer is artist enough to be able to present these matters effectively in writing.

What would Plato have said when his time to speak came? Hermocrates is not recorded as giving an account either. But perhaps *he* can be understood as the most inarticulate member of this gathering, someone who contributes little in the way of opinions but is still useful almost as "matter"—perhaps like the stuff out of which the universe is made. But back to Plato: what *would* he have said? Do we not have his position in the view presented of all this together (including the doings of the various characters and what is done to them)? Does Plato have a comprehensive view of divinity which incorporates, one way or another, all the opinions men generate about the divine? It is this comprehensive view that Plato provides his readers an opportunity to secure for themselves. They are thus encouraged to aspire to a grasp of the one thing which unites and informs all these diverse opinions of the divine.

I return, then, to the familiar question, "What did 'the Greeks' believe about this or that?" Or, rather, I return to the question of what we should make of such a question. Recourse to such a question ("What did 'the Greeks' believe..?") is no substitute for thinking through problems. Are we not obliged to think about the things that the Greeks, including Plato's characters, thought about if we are to begin to understand them—or, at least, to begin to be clear about which questions matter? *To think* means, among other things, that one's city or one's character or other influences or factors cannot be ultimately decisive in determining what one opines. One should be aware of such things and how they affect one's opinions, but one must be able to look beyond above or beneath them if one is to understand how things truly are.

One is not thinking, or thinking for oneself, if the Greeks are used as authorities for the opinions one happens to have.

But neither should the Greeks be regarded of use only as authorities, and therefore to be rejected because we try to reject all authority as such. Rather, we must consider their arguments and assess their evidence, whether with respect to the divine or to the human.

4

Aeschylus in the History of Philosophy

Introduction

It is as if the playwright wished to make sure that each of the plays could stand alone, that the audience would not have to draw upon memory to follow the main lines of the action. In the sense, then, that we can more or less comprehend what is happening in each of the plays without reference to the other two, the plays are somewhat independent and autonomous.

Furthermore, the setting of each of the plays is distinctive. The Argos of the first play is not the Argos of the second; and, of course, the action is removed to Delphi and Athens in the third play. Several years separate the action of the second from the first play; a year or so separates the third from the second.

Additional indications of autonomy can be found. The objective of the principal character in each of the first two plays—the objective stated at the outset is carried through to the conclusion planned for it. We see preparations made for killings; we see the plans executed; and we then hear justifications for what has been done.

Consider also the lesson taught by each play. In the first, the arrogant leader meets his doom; in the second, an unfaithful wife is brought to justice; in the third, conventional or traditional justice is made to bow before the demands of comprehensive justice. Each of the plays has a problem to consider, a problem which it seems to dispose of.

These are the ways in which the three plays of the trilogy may be said to be somewhat independent and autonomous, a conclusion reinforced by the fact that single plays of the trilogy are routinely presented to modern audiences. In fact, it is now rare to have the entire trilogy presented at one sitting. But the criteria that I have mentioned thus far are not the vital ones. For despite all these factors, the plays are not truly independent and autonomous.

It is instructive to notice, therefore, how the character of each of the plays is altered because it is a part of the trilogy. The nature and degree of alteration that we find points up the interrelations among the plays. But before we come to that discussion, there are other considerations that also militate against a finding of autonomy.

Aristotle, in examining the requirements for tragedy, speaks in the *Poetics* of the forms of plot to be avoided. What he says of defective plots would seem to apply to any serious dramatic work by a responsible artist:

A good man must not be seen passing from happiness to misery, or a bad man from misery to happiness. The first situation is not fear-inspiring or piteous, but simply odious to us. The second is the most untragic that can be; it has no one of the requisites of tragedy; it does not appeal either to the human feeling in us, or to our pity, or to our fears.

The reasons Aristotle gives suggest why the Agamemnon and The Libation Bearers cannot really stand alone. There would be something offensive to our moral sensibilities if Clytemnestra were to be left as triumphant as she is at the end of the first play. Similarly, it would be odious if a desperate

Orestes should be last seen (as in The Libation Bearers) with the Furies in pursuit.

I must restate, therefore, what I have said. The Agamemnon is not simply the story of the arrogant leader who meets his doom. It is as much, if not more, the account of the success of a wicked woman. She is not merely the instrument of fate, an instrument that is insignificant compared to the fallen hero. If she were only that, it might not matter what happens to her thereafter. Despite the fact that the failings of Agamemnon are amply recalled, it is a questionable Clytemnestra who dominates the stage and is left triumphant. It is not right that this should be so, however much we may respect (if not admire) how she carries off her daring plot against the most powerful man in Greece.

Nor is The Libation Bearers simply the chronicle of the inevitable punishment of a treacherous wife. It is much more the drama of a young man who finds himself on a dreadful mission as the agent of Apollo. He is compelled to act; he acts with the highest motives. That a man executes, and executes in the proper spirit, the divine command would seem to be justification enough for any act. But the matricidal Orestes, despite the protection promised by an insistent Apollo, is endangered by the unrelenting Furies. There is a conflict here that cannot be left unresolved. The play cannot end at this point.

The care Aeschylus takes to establish Orestes' essential innocence is important. (The character of his Orestes is different in critical respects from Sophocles' and Euripides' versions.) It is not Orestes, but the Chorus and his sister, who talk of blood for blood and simple revenge. He is the only one who, after the momentous deed in either play, can make a sober appraisal of his act. Electra is much more like her mother, moved by passions which make her terribly singleminded. Orestes can hesitate; he has to be reminded of Apollo's command. He can wish Agamemnon had died at Troy not only, we suspect, because of the greater honour that would have come to his father from such a death but also because he dreads the duty before him. Not so with Electra: she can only wish that his murderers had been killed first by those they loved. It is no accident that nothing is seen of Electra after the meeting with Orestes at the tomb of Agamemnon: she takes no part in the slaying; she does not appear in The Eumenides. Clytemnestra's blood, Aeschylus wants to make sure, will be spilt in as guiltless a way as possible. For there is more to come; this is not the end.

Perhaps Clytemnestra has good reasons for killing her husband. Certainly, it cannot be said that his death is altogether unmerited. But here Aeschylus obscures the good and magnifies the bad motives. The sacrifice of Iphigenia is overshadowed in the Agamemnon by the adultery of Clytemnestra, by her implacable hatred, and by her ferocious delight in the accomplishment of a breathtaking deed. Besides, there is in her case no explicit divine decree but rather human passion directing events. At most, we have here the right thing being done for the wrong reason. She cannot be left in her prosperity.

We are given indications, as each of the first two plays draws to a close, not only of the fact that things cannot be left as they are but even of the direction from which correction will come. To be sure, these indications do not create the dominant impressions the immediate action is too strong for that. But they do provide grounds for supposing that accounts are not yet closed. Clytemnestra can, at the end of the *Agamemnon*, defy the horrified people of Argos and exult in her triumph. But there is talk of Orestes, so much so that he can even be regarded as a character in the first play. Aegisthus' poignant remark, "Exiles feed on empty dreams of hope. I know it. I was one," provides some indication of coming events. Orestes is an exile; Orestes hopes. Will that hope bear fruit? This question is left unanswered. But we do know that Aegisthus was an exile whose hopes were not empty.

At the end of The Libation Bearers, Orestes seems to be left to his punishment. But we cannot forget the command of Apollo. "[Loxias] declared I could do this and not be charged with wrong". Even the blood thirsty Chorus of foreign slave-women, it should be noted can wonder, "Where shall the fury of fate be stilled to sleep, be done with?". By indicating in these ways that there is more to come, that the future is already to be glimpsed in the present, Aeschylus closes the first and second plays in this trilogy. But he does not end them. The end, as Aristotle says, is something after which there is nothing.

I have already suggested important respects in which the character of the individual plays is altered by being a part of a trilogy. The plays do not stand alone partly because they need each other to bring out their full meaning.

In both the Agamemnon and The Libation Bearers, after their respective double killings, there is defiance expressed by those responsible for the bloody deaths. The opposing "factions" are brought together, elevated to the plane of abstract justice, and reconciled in The Eumenides. Orestes is acquitted and the Furies make their peace with Athena. Standing alone, the actions of the first two plays are exciting and gripping enough as actions.

Even The Eumenides is given, by its inclusion in a trilogy, a depth it would not otherwise have had. The issues may be adequately presented before the Temple of Athena. We are at least told enough to know what the problems are. But we run the kind of risk that comes in a Common Law jurisdiction from a reliance upon what the lawyers call "black-letter law." The law set forth in the summary of judicial opinions, even by the most competent compiler of decisions, simply may not tell us what the issues are really like until the facts of actual cases are before us. Similarly, in The Eumenides, there is not only a conflict of principles, but also of characters. To forget this is to ignore the dramatic element. It is in this way that the last play is illuminated, and in a sense altered, by the actions of the earlier plays, just as the earlier plays are reshaped by the last one.

I shall return to the level of the principles worked through in the plays after I consider other respects in which these plays affect and alter one another. Take, for example, the problem of Clytemnestra's true feelings upon hearing the report of Orestes' death in the second play. Her speech is sorrowful: "She put a sad face on before the servants to hide the smile inside her eyes," the nurse tells us. But we cannot be certain that the nurse's affection for Orestes and hatred for Clytemnestra do not make her unjustly attribute to the mother so unnatural a reaction. Even the divinely-directed Orestes, we see shortly thereafter, is made to hesitate, upon the threshold of another unnatural action, matricide. Cannot Clytemnestra be similarly restrained by natural sentiments? But we have been prepared by the Agamemnon to expect the worst from her in matters such as these. Her hypocrisy, we have learned, can be superb.

Consider also the change in how Clytemnestra's motivation is regarded from play to play. In the Agamemnon, the best case is presented for her, as the sacrifice of Iphigenia by her father is recounted and referred to several times. Other motives develop, but this seems to be the one that originally pointed Clytemnestra in the direction she has taken. But after the first play, there is no further mention in this connection of the slain daughter; she seems to drop out altogether from an appraisal of the forces that had moved Clytemnestra. Clytemnestra's position becomes more and more difficult to defend the further we are removed from the spell cast by her personality and by the power of her deeds.

The treatment of the Iphigenia episode indicates also a shift in the impression one has of Agamemnon as the trilogy develops. All of his shortcomings are marshaled against him in the first play. In the second, however, the grandeur of his kingly station comes to the fore. Iphigenia is referred to simply as the "pitilessly slaughtered sister" (not "daughter"), without explicit reference to the slaughterer. In The Eumenides, the final judgment on Agamemnon rendered by Apollo wrenches the first play out of the setting in which it had been left: "He had done [in his campaigning] better than worse, in the eyes of a fair judge."

Interpretations of other events and characters have to change as one play throws light upon another. The sending of the child Orestes away from Argos by his mother, the character of Aegisthus, and even the nature of retribution change in their appearances as we proceed from play to play. We learn, furthermore, that the involvement of the gods has been greater than even the claims of their earthly partisans had led us to expect. Finally, in The Eumenides, the powers that had previously lurked behind the human action, that had moved and guided it to some extent, meet face to face. When Apollo and the Furies do meet, the clash of principles dominates the stage and all previous action is thrown into a new light.

Before this The Libation Bearers had made necessary a reevaluation of the Agamemnon. What was the meaning of Clytemnestra's action if it required Orestes'? On the other hand, would the slain Clytemnestra have her avenger in turn? In The Eumenides the differences between the first two plays become crucial. We see in the Agamemnon the old pattern of blood for blood. To the casual observer the pattern in The Libation Bearers is substantially the same. The outrage expressed by Clytemnestra's ghost and by the Furies in The Eumenides is not altogether without justification. This is the way things are done, this is the way things, are responded to. It is the problem left by The Libation Bearers, not that left by the Agamemnon, however, that calls for the establishment of a higher standard than that by which Clytemnestra and her partisans had acted. This higher standard, according to which human beings can both judge and act, is arrived at in The Eumenides. Only then can we truly see what happened in the first two plays.

The Furies, it is suggested in the Agamemnon, are on the side of a rough kind of justice. But, as we proceed, we see that they do not discriminate, that they are somewhat arbitrary, if not even tyrannical. The claims of true justice, of justice approached in the proper spirit, are muffled in the first two plays. Only later do we see that things need not be the way they have long been, however noble certain blows struck in revenge may appear to be.

There is only a hint in The Libation Bearers of a clash of "right with right". Even Apollo has a limited view of what is right. He is far too scornful of the claims of the Furies, with their "ageold distributions of power". An impartial and disinterested tribunal must be established for all time. So impartial and fairminded is the Athenian tribunal, in fact, that it divides its vote evenly, recognizing thereby the justice of the fundamental claims on both sides.

Thus we see law and order where once there was either anarchy or tyranny. There are to be sanctions: "What man who fears nothing at all is ever righteous?". But these are to be sanctions regulated by law. Moreover, order is to be brought out of the relations among the gods; the old and new divinities must be reconciled. Just as there is a need for sanctions among men, so is there among the gods and other immortals. Athena must remind the Furies, in order to persuade them to accept their new status, that she has access to Zeus' thunderbolts. The chaos of what has gone before cannot be fully appreciated until a model of law and order, of reason and justice, is presented in The Eumenides. But the necessity for that model is not fully apparent to us without the experience of the Agamemnon and The Libation Bearers. Only then can we share the satisfaction of the goddess of reason when she proclaims that her "ambition for good wins out in the whole issue".

We can now return to the question about whether the Oresteia trilogy as a whole is truly a tragedy. There are two simple, but apparently conflicting, observations critical to this inquiry. The first is that since the change in the hero's fortunes is from misery to happiness, rather than from happiness to misery, the trilogy does not conform with what has been often said to be a crucial element of Aristotle's more or less authoritative test for tragedy. The second observation is that since Aeschylus is obviously a tragedian, his masterpiece is likely to be a tragedy. The form, means, and manner of imitation of the Oresteia seem to be those described by Aristotle as distinguishing tragedy from the other poetic forms.

The problem of whether a trilogy *can* be a tragedy should not detain us long. The Oresteia can be treated as an extended play, or at least as a series of plays with the effect of one long play. The length of such a play would be limited only by the competence of the author. The longer it is, consistent with its comprehensibility as a whole, the better it may be.

In the early days of poetry, we are told, the graver among the poets "would represent noble actions, and those of noble personages; and the meaner sort the actions of the ignoble". Then, as soon as tragedy and comedy appeared in the field, "those naturally drawn to the one line of poetry became writers of comedies instead of iambs, and those naturally drawn to the other, writers of tragedies instead of epics, because these new modes of art were grander and of more esteem than the old". On the basis of this passage, it would seem that what we know about Aeschylus, both with respect to the gravity of his character and the nobility of the actions and personages that he represents—what we know about him justifies considering the Oresteia a tragedy.

Aristotle's survey of the historical development of the tragedy reinforces this judgment. Tragedy attained its natural form only after a long series of changes. In the course of this development, two of the principal contributions were made by Aeschylus. The perfected form, however, seems to have come later. Aeschylus' work is probably ignored in the *Poetics* partly because Aristotle preferred to deal with the full natural form, and partly because Aeschylus' writing is so distinctive, both with respect to the other poets and from play to play. Nevertheless, Aeschylean drama has that "tone of dignity," that magnitude, which Aristotle considers to be found at a late point in the progress of the development of the tragic form. It is highly likely, therefore, that Aristotle regarded Aeschylus not only as a tragedian but as one of the outstanding tragedians.

The unity of a plot, to continue with a consideration of some of the points about which questions might be raised with respect to the Oresteia, does not consist in having one man as a subject. Rather, the emphasis should be placed upon the unity of action: "a complete whole, with its several incidents so closely connected that the transposal or withdrawal of any one of them will disjoin and dislocate the whole". My discussion and conclusions thus far speak to this point.

There remains to be considered the problem presented by the ending of the Oresteia. Aristotle's criterion here is of the same order as that limiting the action represented to one day. That is to say, it is not absolutely essential for a tragedy to have "the hero's fortunes [change] from happiness to misery," but rather it is something that is to be found in "the perfect plot". It is a caution worth emphasizing, considering the disposition of many authors to minister to the sentimentality of the audience (as we have seen with our soap operas). But it is not a caution or difficulty that is appropriate with respect to Aeschylus. My conclusion here is supported by other indications in the *Poetics*. At an earlier point, Aristotle even accepts tacitly the development from misery to happiness as one that is appropriate in tragedy. And, in the context in which is found the caution we are examining, he observes that the finest tragedies are always based upon the story of some few houses, that of Orestes being given as one such house. He adds, a little further on, that the original stories must be kept as they are. It should be noted that although we do not know exactly what version of the Orestes legend Aristotle referred to, it seems that the hero (albeit a matricide) is permitted eventual redemption in all of the legends that have come down to us.

Perhaps most important to any assessment of how the Oresteia should be regarded, there is in this trilogy the classic "tragic effect," the purgation of certain passions among the spectators. We see here, in fact, tragedy of the highest order, perhaps the greatest parable in the West, at least outside of the Bible (which it perhaps anticipates for Christians), of the human aspiration for law and justice (if not even personal salvation) in changing circumstances.

5

Gorgias in Philosophy

Introduction

Gorgias of Leontini in Sicily, Greek Sophist and rhetorician, was probably born before 480 B.C. and is known to have been alive in 399 B.C. He came to Athens on a diplomatic mission in 427 B.C. to seek help for his native city and subsequently travelled widely, giving public lectures and private instruction in many Greek cities, especially in Thessaly. Among his numerous pupils were Isocrates and perhaps Thucydides.

The encyclopedia entry continues:

> *Whether Gorgias should be classed as a Sophist has been much discussed. In Plato* Gorgias *he is described as a teacher of rhetoric, not as a Sophist, and in* Meno *we are told he refused to claim that he could teach virtue, as other Sophists claimed. On the other hand, Plato recognized Gorgias, together with Prodicus and Hippias, as a professional educator of men and he certainly taught the art of persuasion as a means to political success. Whatever was the precise content of his teaching, he must in a general sense be regarded as belonging to the sophistic movement.*

Philostratus, who wrote a *Lives of the Sophists* in antiquity, refers to Gorgias as "a man to whom as to a father we think it right to refer the art of the sophists". He explains:

For if we consider how much Aeschylus contributed to tragedy by adorning it with costume and the high buskin, and types of heroes, and messengers from abroad or from the house, and with the distinction between suitable onstage and offstage action, Gorgias would correspond to this in his contribution to his fellow artists.

Philostratus continues in his account of the originality of Gorgias:

> *For he was an example of forcefulness to the sophists and of unexpected expression and of inspiration and of the grand style for great subjects and of detached phrases and transitions, by which speech becomes sweeter than it has been and more impressive, and he also introduced poetic words for ornament and dignity.*

It is reported that Gorgias himself, perhaps after reading in his old age the Platonic dialogue that bears his name, said to his friends, "How well Plato knows how to satirize!".

The most effective satire draws upon something critical in the person satirized. We must wonder what the historical Gorgias was like.

It is obvious, from the way Gorgias is referred to in Plato *Meno* and even more from the way he is dealt with personally in Plato *Gorgias*, that Socrates respected the man. There *is* an affinity between philosophy and sophistry. Something of Gorgias' teachings can be garnered from the way he is spoken of in the Platonic dialogues.

What is likely thus to be saved may well *not* be the principal work of an author. That is, what is likely to be saved in this fashion is what is distinctive in his work (and hence is used to illustrate a point), even if that which is distinctive (as, for example, in the work of an El Greco, a Monet, or a Degas) may be a small part, and perhaps not even a representative part, of the whole.

The conventional parts of Gorgias' work may have been of no interest to those who drew upon him, especially if he should be quoted only to illustrate points for which no one else provides materials. The materials thus drawn upon may even have been used by Gorgias himself to develop points made by others. One of Gorgias' better known speeches, his encomium of Helen, can be described by a scholar as "a test speech," the work of "a pupil of Gorgias, neither very serious nor very intelligent, but acquainted with the current views of rhetoric and with a certain skill in the technique of the probability argument, a young man endowed with wit and a rather unscrupulous and materialistic outlook". Even so, we must make do with what has happened to come down to us as words from Gorgias' hand.

Chance can especially be seen in the Gorgian fragments that have been salvaged. We do not have the context for many of them. Nor can we be sure how the others were used, even when we happen to know the work in which they originally appeared. Rather, we have the fragments that happen to have been used by authors in works of their own which in turn happen to have survived.

The minor fragments can be conveniently allocated, for our purposes here, among a half-dozen categories. First, there are the indications in Plato's dialogues, especially the *Meno* and the *Gorgias*, of what Gorgias stood for. Thus, he is said in the *Meno* to have limited himself to enumerating the virtues, not attempting either to define or to inculcate them, an approach that is reflected in the way Meno (who had evidently studied with Gorgias) proceeds in talking with Socrates.

Then there are Gorgias' technical prescriptions. He was known in antiquity for his treatise on rhetoric, which seems to have been lost. This was evidently drawn upon by Aristotle in his own *Rhetoric*, when he reported, " Gorgias said that 'the opposition's seriousness is to be demolished by laughter, and laughter by seriousness,' in which statement he was correct". This leaves open the question of whether there are in our lives things that are intrinsically serious or intrinsically laughable.

Then there are Gorgias' scientific opinions. These include his account of what colour is (taken from Empedocles, and drawn upon in the *Meno*); his description of the power of the burning glass; and his opinion, if it was *his* opinion, that the sun is a molten mass. Plutarch draws upon a description of the tomb of Isocrates in reporting, "Near it was a tablet showing poets and his [Isocrates'?] teachers, among whom is Gorgias looking at an astronomical globe and Isocrates himself standing by".

Critical to Gorgias' reputation as an orator, or as a teacher of orators, was his ability to fashion vivid expressions which took the public fancy. Thus, he was known to have attempted to moderate struggles between the Greek cities with the observation, "Victories over the barbarians require hymns of celebration, over the Greeks lamentations". Related to this sentiment is the observation, "A friend will expect his friend to do only just actions in helping him; but he himself will serve his friend with many actions that belong to the category of unjust also". Similarly paradoxical (or is it "human"?) is what Gorgias had to say about tragedy: "Tragedy, by means of legends and emotions, creates a deception in which the deceiver is more honest than the non-deceiver, and the deceived is wiser than the non-deceived".

Of course, risks are run when one has recourse to vivid expressions. For one thing, the novelty can wear off and the expressions turn flat. Or particular images can be ill-conceived from their outset, as is argued in an ancient text reviewing the kinds of rhetoric:

> *The third kind of rhetoric that which is concerned with something ridiculous, awakening the guffaws of the young and being basically a shameless flattery. The circle of Thrasymachus and Gorgias practiced this in style and in their invalid arguments, making use of many equal clauses and failing to understand when this figure is appropriate. Many also have displayed it in figures of thought and tropes, but especially Gorgias, since he was the most affected, during the course of the very narrative in his* Funeral Oration, *not venturing to say "vultures" he spoke of "animate tombs."*

It is said that Gorgias was also laughed at for calling Xerxes "the Persians' Zeus".

Then there are fragments from Gorgias in which he exhorts his fellow Greeks. We have already noticed his efforts to discourage war among the Greek cities. Plutarch records this comment:

> *When Gorgias the orator read a speech at Olympia about concord among the Greeks, Melanthius said: "This fellow advises us about concord, though he has not persuaded himself and his wife and his maid, only three in number, to live in private concord." For it seems that Gorgias had a passion for the little maid and his wife was jealous.*

Of women generally, Gorgias could say, "Not the looks of a woman, but her good reputation should be known to many". His advice to his fellow Grccks included counsel relating to his long life, reputed by some to have been 108 years: "And when someone asked him what regimen he observed to live such a great length of life so pleasantly and with perception he said,

> *'By never doing anything for the sake of pleasure.'" His final lesson for the Greeks came from his deathbed:*

Gorgias of Leontini at the end of his life and in advanced old age, overtaken by a feeling of weakness, lay down and was gradually slipping off into sleep. When one of his friends came over to see him and asked what he was doing, Gorgias answered, "Sleep already begins to hand me over to his brother Death."

Finally, in this inventory of the minor fragments from Gorgias, there is the observation that "existence is not manifest if it does not involve opinion, and opinion is unreliable if it does not involve existence". Another translation of this passage reads, "Being is unrecognizable unless it succeeds in seeming, and seeming is weak unless it succeeds in being". Isocrates, perhaps Gorgias' most famous student, assesses his teacher's reflections upon *being* in this way:

> *For how could one outdo Gorgias who dared to say that of existing things none exists or Zeno who tried to prove the same things to be possible and again impossible? The theories of the early sophists [included one which] said that the number of existing things is limitless but Parmenides and Melissus said it is one and Gorgias none at all.*

We can turn now, from this inventory of the minor fragments, to the principal remains of Gorgias, beginning with the discourse in which he had dared to say "that of existing things none exists."

The most famous work we have from Gorgias is what was called by one writer in antiquity "an elegant treatise *On Nature*," written about 441 B.C. This treatise, with the full title of *On the Nonexistent or On Nature*, is summed up by another ancient writer in this fashion:

> *Gorgias proposes three successive headings: first and foremost, that nothing exists; second, that even if it exists it is inapprehensible to man; third, that even if it is apprehensible, still it is without a doubt incapable of being expressed or explained to the next man.*

A twentieth-century scholar identifies the major divisions of the treatise in these terms: "Nothing is; if it is, it is unknowable; if it is and is knowable, it cannot be communicated to others". This scholar observed that Gorgias' treatise had not received much attention in the first half of the twentieth century:

> *This is probably due mainly to two reasons the highly technical and indeed to many readers repulsive nature of its content, and the widely held view that it is not meant seriously but is simply a parody or joke against philosophers, or at least a purely rhetorical exercise.*

In response to these objections this scholar continues:

> *The first of these views [that it is a parody or joke] seems so obviously wrong that it is hardly necessary to devote much time to discussing it. The short answer must be that there is nothing humorous about the treatise and no indication that it was ever intended to be so. In this respect it is in exactly the same position as the second part of Plato's dialogue* Parmenides. *Its general thesis might conceivably amuse those to whom all attempts at philosophy are inherently absurd, but such persons could hardly be expected to work through the difficult arguments which make up the contents of the work. The view that it was purely a rhetorical exercise is no more plausible. The final answer to both views must consist in showing just what is the content of the treatise and the serious purposes to which it is directed.*

This scholar, like others before him since antiquity, subjected Gorgias' thesis to a searching, somewhat technical examination. It is not necessary to rehearse these arguments here. It is enough to notice that they are available, as are of course the extended arguments that Gorgias makes in support of his thesis.

It does seem to be assumed by Gorgias in his treatise that man is the measure of all things. It also seems that the existence of things depends upon the ability of the human mind to grasp and to communicate that existence, to grasp it by means of demonstration. In this respect, Gorgias stands with the famous Sophist, Protagoras. But he may be more radical than Protagoras, and perhaps in that way something more than a Sophist.

Socrates would recognize the problems in establishing existence, in reaching an understanding of things, and in communicating what one knows to others, even though he would be more likely to work in the order opposite to that of Gorgias: he would begin with the difficulties in a person's attempt to state what he believes himself to know, which could lead in turn to a consideration of what is and can be known. Then, with his more talented interlocutors, he would move to an awareness of what we would call the ineffableness of Being.

In any event, Socrates would not consider it either prudent or simply correct to argue as categorically as Gorgias does against the conventional positions here. Socrates understands those positions to rest upon a general human intuition and upon common sense.

It is difficult to escape the suspicion that there is, in Gorgias' performance, much of the *tour de force*, or exhibitionism. It often does seem that Gorgias argues primarily for the sake of argument. When he seems to be doing that, he can be impressive and admired without really being persuasive. Socrates, it is easier to believe, argues primarily for the sake of the truth.

Gorgias, that is, seems to be more interested than Socrates in success in argument. This is the way that he advances himself. However much he may argue against the existence of things, he does not seem to deny the existence of the money that he was so adept in earning during his long and profitable career, even though his reputed capacity in spending it as fast as he made it must have made him wonder sometimes whether money really existed.

How seriously is Gorgias' treatise on nature to be taken? Perhaps the most useful thing about it has been the array of arguments it has called forth explaining and reinforcing the conventional understandings of mankind threatened by Gorgias. This treatise does more, however, than deny one conventional position after another. It does affirm, if only implicitly, the power of words. Also assumed is the desirability of the ends served by a skillful use of words. Gorgias' argument assumes as well that both his argument and the minds between which it is passing exist. If his argument were taken in full seriousness, human beings would have to be regarded as completely isolated from one another intellectually, so much so that any attempt at communication and persuasion would be futile. Yet Gorgias tries to persuade others to accept something that he understands that understanding and communication are impossible. If one argues, in effect, that human beings do not exist, then anything seems to go; absurd arguments are not to be wondered at. Do they not become, in such circumstances, something to be played with rather than to be taken seriously?

Another way of putting this response is to say, with various of Gorgias' ancient critics (including, it seems, Aristotle), that Gorgias' approach means that "the criterion is destroyed" upon which understanding and discourse depend. "For there would be no criterion if nature neither exists nor can be understood nor conveyed to another". A modern scholar put it this way: "Such then being the difficulties raised in Gorgias, the criterion of truth is done away with, so far as they are concerned. For there would be no criterion of what does not exist and cannot be known and cannot be naturally passed on to another."

What is presupposed by Gorgias' treatise, its preparation and promulgation (to say nothing of its preservation over millennia)? To what extent, or in what way, do skeptical positions such as Gorgias' depend, for their effectiveness, upon criteria or standards that are generally appreciated, including standards about good and bad, right and wrong? Do not all skeptics, or relativists, work from or assume something stable, knowable, and permanent? All the fancy dancing is possible because of a fairly steady dance floor, as seen for example in the language that is provided them and the reasoning ability that language reflects. The dancer may become the dance and the dance floor as well or so it can seem to the self-centered thinker of Gorgias' persuasion.

Perhaps still another way of putting these observations is to say that human beings have an intuitive grasp of things (a *pistis*) which is not susceptible of demonstration in that it provides the starting point or premise of understanding. Gorgias himself seems to believe that words somehow exist independently of things. This permits him to argue (as if it mattered) that things do not exist.

There may be a sound intuition at the root of Gorgias' argument here, but an intuition which undermines his argument. His remarkable reliance upon words as independent of things may reflect, without his being aware of it, that state of things which found more plausible expression in the Platonic Doctrine of the Ideas.

The key, then, to Gorgias' position (and to that of someone such as Martin Heidegger, millennia later) is that an attempt is made to reason to, or to establish by reason, Being itself. But must not Being be grasped or intuited in that sense, it is incomprehensible? Its non-existence or our lack of certainty about its existence does not follow from the necessity of having something beyond which no argument can reach. However salutary it can be to call into question much that is conventionally accepted, especially when dubious cults and myths dominate the thought of one's day, it goes too far to insist that nothing that is conventionally accepted has any grounding in a sound intuition. Socratic sobriety is instructive here, which can include noticing the extent to which the argument in each of the three parts of Gorgias' treatise depends upon notions repudiated in the other two parts.

We must wonder what the condition was of the Greek cities that permitted Gorgias, with his somewhat nihilistic views, to be well received there for so many years among the political elites. Certainly, his ambitious students did not feel they would be discredited by associating with Gorgias, however much his art permitted, if it did not compel, one to challenge conventional opinions in the most comprehensive manner. But then, the eminently political Pericles risked associating with Anaxagoras, a thinker even more challenging in critical respects than Gorgias.

We can see in Gorgias' *Helen* speech what his skepticism can mean when put in the service of a defense argument. We can see there what a facility with words can mean, what it can mean to assume that speech can somehow rearrange everything.

Gorgias knows what everyone knows about Helen, that she ran off to Troy with her lover, and that a great war followed, which brought much destruction and suffering to Greeks and Trojans alike. But, he argues, she is to be excused, since she did what she did either by will of Fate and decisions of the gods and vote of Necessity or by force reduced or by words seduced or by love possessed.

To argue as Gorgias does on Helen's behalf is to deny ordinary experience, including experience about the workings of love. Does he not challenge what "everyone knows" about Helen and what she did? Is not the Homeric tradition itself called into question, and in a way different from that sometimes employed by Socrates or Euripides? How seriously is such an approach to be taken, whatever the facts happened to be in Helen's own case?

Gorgias' defense of Helen means, in effect, that no one is culpable. When he defends Helen, however, it is useful for him to condemn others, such as the man who either forced or seduced her. Would not the defense of Helen be ineffective, however, if all culpability all acknowledgement of good and bad were explicitly denied? It should be obvious that similar defenses could be made by Gorgias, in due course, on behalf of the man who forced or seduced her. Consider, for example, what could be said about how her beauty stripped others of all self-control.

This is not to deny that we are willing to hear Gorgias' defense of Helen herself. Do we not sense that she is special and therefore that ordinary rules may not apply to her? This would be to recognize and exalt *the noble* but there may be something too utilitarian, if not even prosaic, in Gorgias to leave much room for the noble. The noble does not permit itself to be diverted from its high purposes by mere words.

We see also in the *Palamedes* defense speech by Gorgias an approach which can lead to the effective denial of the guilt of any particular defendant, however much the defense exploits condemnations of others as guilty. We can see as well in the *Palamedes* the considerable reliance upon words alone that we have noticed elsewhere in Gorgias. What is the "reality" of the situation? Is it not impossible from such a presentation—without an independent access to the facts and without the counter-arguments to assess what "really happened"?

Is the audience supposed to know what happened? (See the end of Plato *Apology* for the problem of Palamedes.) Or is it that the facts do not matter for Gorgias' purpose? There *are* telling lines in the speech—such as, "The accusers cannot know for certain that I committed the crime, because I know for certain that I did not." But this and many other such lines can, unfortunately be voiced by guilty men as well as by innocent, especially if the guilty have had access to the counsel of advocates such as Gorgias.

This obliges us to consider, however briefly, why it is that Socrates' speeches in the *Apology* are persuasive *with us* standing alone. Or do they really stand alone? Perhaps important in the Socratic speech is a display of wisdom in a way that reflects a sound character. There are, as well, the many references by him to well-known episodes that an uninhibited audience could be expected to shout down if not accurately reported. Besides, we are shown the interventions of Socrates' supporters, the limitations of his accusers (upon cross-examination as well as in the form of their indictment), and the interventions of the crowd when stirred up by him. In the *Palamedes* speech, on the other hand, we have only a display of the power of words to shape all of the world that matters.

Do not all three of the major works we have from Gorgias depend in the final analysis not only upon his adroitness but perhaps as much, if not even more, upon the appearance of adroitness? It is the advocate that the audience is asked to vote for, less so for the client or cause of the advocate. The Sophist, with this approach, is essentially an actor and a teacher of actors. In these activities, novelty is often mistaken for that genuine originality which can present things for what they are.

Much, if not all, that Gorgias did was designed to win over multitudes, not to discourse seriously with those of genuine philosophical interests. This may help explain why Gorgias' work has survived only in fragments whereas that of Plato and Aristotle has been preserved and transmitted with obviously great care over millennia.

The preservation of the best work reflects an awareness of the good. Thus, it is Aristotle *Rhetoric* that comes down to us substantially as it was written, not Gorgias'. What Aristotle has to say about rhetoric is illuminated by, and must be in the service of, what he has to say elsewhere about ethics and politics. We can see among the accusers of Socrates a rhetorician who went wrong that is, a rhetorician who was merely a rhetorician and hence perhaps jealous of the deeper drawing power exercised by Socrates. Socrates was done in, to some extent, by men who considered him a political rival of sorts.

Gorgias, of course, would never be an accuser of Socrates. That may be partly due to his good-naturedness. But it may also be due to his having cut himself off, as a travelling teacher, from serious political life. Which came first, Gorgias' skepticism or his apolitical existence? He did begin his career abroad in the service of his city. But he eventually found himself both apolitical and aphilosophical (that is, professionally skeptical), however much what he had to say resembled at times either political speeches or philosophical discourse.

Gorgias may have come to sense that there was no firm foundation upon which he rested. His most positive endorsement of conventional virtues can be seen in the fragment we have of a funeral oration. On such an occasion, the principles and aspirations, as well as the very existence, of the community must be approached with deadly seriousness. That is not the occasion for playing games with words and even if that is what one "naturally" tries to do, the solemnity of the occasion invests one's words with all the seriousness which they are capable of reflecting. The community as community is naturally reaffirmed by any funeral oration, especially one for those who have fallen in battle.

What is common to the longer things we have from Gorgias (*Helen*, *On Nature*, and *Palamedes*) is an exhibition of, not necessarily a belief in, the power of argument. If one took Gorgias' arguments seriously, either one would not be able to condemn (or properly praise?) anyone or one would not be able to know anything or, at least, to communicate anything.

How seriously can such an approach be taken? Is its principal effect to legitimate self-interest, even as it makes one wonder whether any interest should be taken seriously? Many are likely to be taught by this approach that one can and should look out completely for oneself, perhaps even that "anything goes."

Gorgias obviously exhibited great skills, which were admired and imitated (and lavishly rewarded) by quite sophisticated audiences and cities. His were skills that Socrates evidently did not have, however useful they might have been for Socrates on occasion. There is an element of shamelessness in such skills as well as a sometimes silly willingness to believe things that may not be quite so. That is, one usually has to persuade oneself before one can persuade others. Another critical difference is that Gorgias would not have had the reservations Socrates exhibits in Plato *Crito* about fleeing Athens to save his life. Gorgias always knew how to take care of himself, from a conventional point of view.

The potential usefulness of Gorgias for the cause of philosophy is indicated in the Platonic dialogue named after him. After all, he reports, he is capable of persuading patients to undergo necessary but painful treatment which doctors cannot themselves persuade their patients to undergo. We see Gorgias in that dialogue as a man who somehow senses his limitations and who prudently leaves some of the more questionable implications of, if not departures from, his position to be developed by his less thoughtful imitators, and especially by an Athenian (Callicles) who is not as vulnerable as a visiting alien would be.

We also see Gorgias as in need of guidance as to the ends to which his considerable skills are to be directed, ends which are served by the enlistment of the rhetorician in the development of salutary stories about divine judgment. Gorgias could serve well in medicine so long as a competent physician directed him, just as he could serve well in diplomacy so long as a competent city directed him. A proper study of the Platonic dialogues, including the Gorgias, should help us discover both what the original Gorgias and the other Sophists were like and what could properly be done with and through them.

6

Medieval Discussion of Intentionality in Philosophy

Introduction

It may well appear equally out of place to bring into the picture such intentional entities as the senses of expressions; the sense of the term "horse" or "detective story" is assuredly not something whose possession would content a man when he is owed a horse or is looking for a detective story. All the same the sense, or as Buridan calls it the *ratio*, given us by an object expression really is somehow involved when the verbal is an intentional one; Buridan says the object expression *appellat suam rationem*, where we may perhaps render the verb *"appellat"* (perhaps the most obscurely and multifariously employed of all medieval semantic technicalities) by saying the expression "calls up" or "evokes" its own *ratio*. Buridan's main point is in any case clear: that the truth-value of a sentence whose verbal is an intentional one may be changed if we change the *ratio*, the sense, given in the object expression, even if this expression still relates to the same thing in the world. This point is clearly correct, as many of Buridan's examples show; thus, if a body is both white and sweet and I see it, I may truly say "I have discerned something white by my sense of sight," but not "I have discerned something sweet by my sense of sight."

Can't I, though, say I have discerned something sweet by my sense of sight, if the body I have discerned is in fact sweet? Well, it's better to say "There is something sweet that I have discerned by sight" if this is the case I have in mind. This means, according to Buridan, that the sweet thing is something which my sense of sight discerns under some *ratio* or other, not at all necessarily under the *ratio*: sweet—this *ratio* comes in only *sub disiunctione ad alias rationes*, as one possible alternative *ratio*.

Buridan here observes a tendency of Latin idiom, which comes out in much the same way in English: when a verbal is intentional, an object phrase is differently construed when it precedes the main verb that is a part or the whole of this verbal, and when it follows that verb. In general, taking "to *F*" as representative of an intentional verbal, we shall distinguish between the forms "b F's an *A*" and "There is an *A* that b F's." The latter form if construed in the spirit of Buridan will mean "There is some actual *A* of which it holds that b F's it under some *ratio* or other"—possibly, though, under some other *ratio* than that of being an *A*. (In Buridan's Latin examples there are no words corresponding to "there is" and "that" in the form "There is an *A* that b F's"; this difference between English and Latin idiom is obviously trivial.) Of course this distinction of word order is not *strictly* observed in ordinary English or Latin; we have to consider what is actually meant in the case under consideration. An instructive example, to which I shall presently return, is one I borrow with slight alteration from John Austin: "I saw a man born in Jerusalem" *versus* "I saw a man run over in Oxford." But we may very well decide for present purposes to stick to Buridan's convention of word order, as a way of marking the distinction he quite properly wishes to draw.

Buridan rightly regards the inference from "There is an *A* that b F'd" to "b F'd an *A*" as an invalid form; for if "There is an *A* that b F'd" is true, the general term represented by "*A*" need not give us the aspect of *ratio* under which such an *A* was the object of b's F'ing. Moreover, though Buridan himself does not consider (the Latin equivalent of) the verbal "was looking for," his machinery helps to clear up our puzzles about this verbal. We should use "There is a detective story Geach was looking for" for the case where one would say I was looking for "a particular" detective story, and reserve "Geach was looking for a detective story" rather for the case where I was "just" looking for a detective story. In the former case, if the book I was looking for was a book printed in Baskerville type, one might equally well say "There is a book printed in Baskerville type that Geach was looking for"; but one could not infer "Geach was looking for a book printed in Baskerville type," since the *ratio* under which I was looking for the book will have been the one expressed by "detective story," not the one expressed by "book printed in Baskerville type."

Buridan assumes that from "b F'd an *A*" we may infer "There is something that b F'd." In fact, as we shall presently see, he assumes more than this; and even this much is doubtful. But we may use this assumption to show how Buridan's theory looks in terms of modern quantification theory. The intentional verbal represented by "to F" would answer, not to a two-termed relation between a person and an object of his F'ing, but to a three-termed relation between a person, an object of F'ing, and a *ratio*; and the forms "b F's an *A*" and "There is an *A* that b F'd" would respectively come out as:

For some *z*, b F'd *z* under the *ratio: A*

For some *z*, and for some *w*, *z* is an *A*, and b F'd *z* under the ratio *w*.

It may be helpful to work out in this way the concrete example from John Austin that I mentioned just now. "I saw a man run over in Oxford" would come out as:

For some *z*, *z* is a man and I saw *z* in Oxford under the *ratio*: run over, and "I saw a man born in Jerusalem" would come out as:

For some *z*, *z* is a man and *z* was born in Jerusalem and, for some *w*, I saw *z* under the *ratio w*.

Buridan's analysis, seen in this light, already raises one severe difficulty. The form with the term preceding the intentional verbal essentially involves quantifying over *rationes*. Now I am not at all impressed by rhetoric about mysterious entities, by questions in the peculiar (anti-) metaphysical tone of voice "But what are they?"; it is all right to quantify over entities if you can supply a sharp criterion of identity for them. The paradigm of this is Frege's sharp criterion of identity for numbers. But for *rationes* we can get out of Buridan no hint of such a criterion. He gives us many examples of *rationes* he takes to be patently different, like the *ratio*: white and the ratio: sweet; but we have not even one example of the same *ratio* differently expressed, from which we might divine a criterion of identity. This lacuna makes Buridan's account schematic at best.

A more serious defect is Buridan's acceptance of the inference from "b F'd an *A*" to "There is an *A* that b F'd." Notice that this would still be unacceptable even if we let pass the inference to "There is something that b F'd"; for this does follow from:

For some *z*, b F'd *z* under the *ratio: A*

But there is still no obvious necessity that what is F'd under the *ratio*: *A* should in fact be an *A*. And in concrete examples Buridan's pattern of inference, from the form "with the term after" to the form "with the term before," often seems patently invalid. He himself chooses examples that look all right, e.g. from "I see something white" to "There is something white I see," or from "I recognize somebody coming" to "There is somebody coming whom I recognize." But of course we may not pass from "James is looking for a universal solvent" to "There is a universal solvent James is looking for"; we may not even pass from "Geach is looking for a detective story" to "There is a detective story Geach is looking for," because, as we saw, the premise is compatible with my not having been looking for "a particular" detective story.

Even among the examples Buridan himself supplies, there are some that hardly favour his thesis. Suppose poor old Socrates is a competent astronomer immured in a dungeon where he cannot tell night from day. Then Buridan is willing to pass from the premise "Socrates knows some stars are above the horizon" to the conclusion "There are some stars Socrates knows are above the horizon." You naturally ask which stars Socrates knows are above the horizon; Buridan has a ready answer—the ones that are. To be sure, it is in a rather attenuated sense that the constellation Aries (say) is then known by Socrates to be above the horizon: namely, not in respect of the complex *ratio* expressed by "Aries is above the horizon," but only in respect of the one expressed by "Some stars are above the horizon." But at least Buridan can hardly be forced to pass from premises that would in this case be true to a conclusion that would in this case be false. Although in his view *one* true answer to the question "Which stars does Socrates know are above the horizon?" might be "There is the constellation Aries that Socrates knows is above the horizon," he can on his own principles disallow the inference from this to "Socrates knows that the constellation Aries is above the horizon"; this shift of the term, *from* before the main-verb part of the verbal—knows that—is above the horizon *to* after that verb, is just what Buridan disallows, as we saw. And Buridan's motive for wishing to pass to the conclusion: "There are some stars that Socrates knows are above the horizon" is that even the abstract knowledge expressed in "Some stars are above the horizon" ought in his eyes to latch on to some actual, and therefore definitely specifiable, stars.

This example is rather a cheat, though, because Buridan is trading on a peculiarity of the verb "to know." What you know is so; if Socrates knows some stars are above the horizon, then some stars are above the horizon, and we may ask which ones are. But suppose Socrates believes some lizards breathe fire—not being so good a zoologist as an astronomer. May we pass to the conclusion "There are some lizards that Socrates believes breathe fire"? and if so, which lizards are these? Certainly not the ones that do breathe fire, for Socrates' belief is false. Moreover, it may be impossible to find any principle for picking out, from among actual lizards, the ones Socrates believes to breathe fire. Buridan often resorts, when faced by such an embarrassing choice, to a parity-of-reasoning argument; what is true of some so-and-so, if there is no reason to think it is true of one so-and-so rather than another, must be true of each and every so-and-so. We should then have to pass on from "There are some lizards that Socrates believes breathe fire," to the further conclusion "As regards each lizard, Socrates believes that it breathes fire." From this, indeed, we could on Buridan's principles not infer "Socrates believes that each lizard breathes fire"; Socrates' belief would latch on to each and every lizard, but only *via* the complex *ratio* expressed by "Some lizards breathe fire." Still, in Buridan's own words, *videtur durum*, it seems tough to swallow.

I now come to a similar puzzle of Buridan's own, in which his own principles raise severe difficulties. A horse dealer, he supposes, currently owns just three thoroughbreds, Brownie, Blackie, and Fallow. The customer accepts the dealer's promise "I will give you one of my thoroughbreds," but the dealer fails to deliver, and denies that he owes the purchaser anything. "If I owe you any horse," he argues, "I must owe you either Brownie or Blackie or Fallow; they're the only horses I have, and you can't say I owe you some other horse, let us say H.M. the King's charger. Now what I said didn't relate specially to Blackie rather than Fallow, or the other way round; what goes for one goes for the other; and similarly for Brownie. So either I owe you both Brownie and Blackie and Fallow, or I owe you not one of them. You'll surely not have the nerve to say I owe you all three, when I only said I'd let you have one; so I don't owe you even one. *Good* morning."

Part of the trouble Buridan has in saying what is wrong with the horse-coper's argument comes from his accepting the inference from "I owe you a horse" to "There is a horse I owe you"; and we have seen reason to doubt the validity of the rule by which Buridan has to allow this step. But even without this inferential move, Buridan can give the horse-coper a longer run for his (or rather his victim's) money. Even if in general we cannot validly pass from "b F's an *A*" to "There is an *A* that b F's," it seems plausible to accept this particular instance of a term-shifting inference: "I owe you something; *ergo*, there is something I owe you." And we can consistently accept it without accepting Buridan's invalid rule: many philosophers seem to think that any instance of an invalid form is an invalid argument, but this is a gross logical error. Let us then have our horse-coper arguing again, "If I owe you a horse, then I owe you something. And if I owe you something, then there is something I owe you. And this can only be a thoroughbred of mine; you aren't going to say that in virtue of what I said there's something else I owe you. Very well then: by your claim, there's one of my thoroughbreds I owe you. Please tell me which one it is."

Buridan has an ingenious way out of the difficulty. It can be said that x is owing by me to y if and only if by handing over *x* to *y* I should be quits with him (*essem quittus*). Now whichever thoroughbred (*bonus equus*) *x* may be, if the horse-coper hands over *x* to the purchaser then they are quits. Buridan concludes that, whichever thoroughbred *x* may be, the dealer owes *x* to the customer. This goes even for H.M. the King's charger; for if the horse-coper bought or were given this horse, he could be quits with his customer by handing it over, as he could not be if he had not handed over exactly what was owing.

We can now clear up the "parity of reasoning" argument about the three horses the dealer already has. It is true of Brownie, and it is true of Blackie, and it is also true of Fallow, that this is a horse the dealer owes his customer. So, considering just Brownie and Blackie, we may in a sense say these are two horses the dealer owes. But Buridan rightly warns us to avoid confusing collective and distributive predication; it is not that there are two horses together which the dealer owes, but that of each one of the two it holds good that he is a horse the dealer owes. Moreover, by Buridan's general principle we may not pass from "There are two horses the dealer owes" to "The dealer owes two horses"; that would call up the *ratio*: two horses, which did not come into the dealer's original promise. Similarly, from "Brownie is a horse the dealer owes" we may not infer "The dealer owes Brownie"; this would be true only if the dealer's original promise had called up the *ratio* expressed by the name "Brownie," as *ex hypothesi* it did not.

It is very reluctantly that one finds fault with Buridan's brilliant way of securing obvious justice for the customer without bending the laws of logic. All the same, the inference from "I owe you something" to "There is something I owe you" cannot be let pass unchallenged. No doubt many an investor in the Post Office Savings Bank has inferred from "The Post Office owes me something" to "There is something the Post Office owes me"; his thought is "The Post Office has it all stacked up somewhere—*aes alienum*, other people's brass—and some of it's mine." The inference is invalid, and the conclusion is false; and the mistake is far from trivial—as those unscrupulous politicians were well aware who made use of this false impression in their highly successful propaganda to the effect "The Socialists were going to take *your* money out of the Savings Bank and pay it over to the unemployed"!

This difficulty is not confined to the present example; there are, I think, very many instances in which from "b F's an *A*" or "b F's something or other" we may by no means infer that there is an identifiable something-or-other which b is F'ing. On this point Buridan's theory stands in need of radical reconstruction. I think I can see in part how such a reconstruction would be possible; but there are difficulties that still remain.

Let us take the example "Geach was looking for a detective story." On our former analysis, which closely followed Buridan, this would come out as:

For some x, Geach was looking for x under the *ratio*: detective story.

But this would have the unwelcome consequence that, even when I was "just" looking for *a* detective story, there was some identifiable *x*—not necessarily a detective story, to be sure—that I was looking for. We need rather a dyadic relation between Geach and a *ratio*: "Geach was-looking-for-something-under-the-*ratio*: detective story," where I have hyphenated the words of the verbal to show that logically it is just one indivisible relative term.

We may achieve considerable clarification if we expand this analysis to:

> *Geach was looking for something under the* ratio *evoked* (appellata) *by the expression "detective story," and then treat "was looking by" as a single relative term, which we may abbreviate to "was L'ing." We now have a verbal flanked by a name of a person and a quotation, rather than by a name of a person and a designation of a* ratio. *This dodge, suggested to me by Professor R. Montague, avoids our difficulties about quantifying over* rationes; *we may now analyse "There is a detective story Geach was looking for" as:*

For some x, x is a detective story, and, for some w, w is a description true just of x, and Geach was L'ing w (Geach was-looking-for-something-under-the-*ratio*-evoked-by the definite description *w*).

Here we quantify over forms of words, whose criterion of identity, if not completely clear, is a lot clearer than that of *rationes*.

A similar method suggests itself for dealing with problems of what may be called *intentional identity*. In a way parallel to the Buridan convention we may distinguish between "There is a poet whom both Smith and Brown admire" and "Smith and Brown both admire the same poet"; the latter would cover the case where both Smith and Brown are victims of the same literary fraud as to the existence of a poet, as well as the more normal case where they both admire (say) Wordsworth's poetry. Let us use the expression "AP" as short for "admire as a poet someone conceived under the *ratio* evoked by"; then "There is a poet whom both Smith and Brown admire" would come out as:

> *Unfortunately, the line of solution we have been following leads us into difficulties. Suppose we use "D'd" as short for the verbal "dreamed of someone under the* ratio *expressed by." Then in our present view we should have to paraphrase "There is a red-head Harris dreamed of" as:*

For some x, x is a red-head and, for some w, w is a description true just of x, and Harris D'd *w*.

Now suppose we take w to be the description "the fattest woman in the world." The paraphrase would be true if Harris dreamed of the fattest woman in the world and the fattest woman in the world is in fact a red-head; but the proposition paraphrased might then quite well be false, because in Harris's dream there may have been no red-head, and the fattest woman he saw in his dream may have been as bald as an egg. (I owe this counter-example to my pupil Mr. David Bird.) Similar difficulties arise for our account of intentional identity: for if c and d each worshipped something under the *ratio* expressed by "the deity of the Sun," it does not follow that c and d both worshipped the same deity c might be an ancient Egyptian worshipping the ancestor of Pharaoh, and d a Japanese worshipping the ancestress of the Mikado.

I hope this paper shows why modern logicians still need to take medieval logicians seriously. In great measure their problems are ours; while for some of them, like the problems of *suppositio*, modern logic provides adequate solutions, there are other problems, about modal and intentional contexts for example, that are still wide open; and the talent that was shown by medieval logicians in wrestling with their problems demands our deepest admiration.

Rule of Meaning for Religious Language

The theory has additional historical value as an example of a very common solution to the problem of informative theological language offered throughout the thirteenth century in Western philosophy. It is essentially a reply to the question: *"Can you show that theological statements are meaningful?"* A.N. Prior has remarked: *"The real intellectual difficulty of the believer or would-be believer is not the problem of proof but the problem of meaning."* It is worth noting that the same question was hotly and subtly discussed by most of the medieval writers and the most common conclusion was that a theory of analogy was required. Most recent writers in philosophical theology have made some reference to the theory of analogy current in medieval times, and almost universally these writers have judged it hopeless. As will appear in the course of this paper, authors like Flew and MacKinnon, Farrer, and Mascall have offered interpretations of the analogy doctrine considerably different from the one I shall propose. I consider their interpretations as seriously deficient and misleading, and I shall endeavour to show implicitly both how little they understood the complexity of the doctrine and how much more penetrating a language theory the analogy rules constitute than most modern writers have supposed.

St. Thomas Aquinas actually formulated four distinct but complementary analogy rules. In this essay I am concerned to analyze only the two most important of these, although the other two rules are stated in the list of definitions given below. This essay is divided into three main parts, the first two sections being summaries of the "exhibition analyses" by which the two rules in which we are interested are formulated. The third section is a brief sketch of how these rules were employed to solve the problems of informative discourse about God.

Before undertaking the analysis of analogy rules, I must make the following additional points of introduction:

1. The two rules of analogy herein discussed are concerned with the comparative meaning of two or more instances of the same term used as predicate in two or more statements of the form a ("X is T" and b) "Y is T."

2. As a result, we must distinguish between the *technical* sense of "analogy" which we shall use and at least one other ordinary language sense of "analogy."

When the word "analogous" occurs in ordinary language, there is usually a context of comparison: "Spanish is analogous to Portuguese"; "The navigator of a ship and the ruler of a state are analogous"; etc. *Things* are said to be analogous if they have common characteristics or similar relations. And the term "analogy" is often taken as a synonym of "similar" or "similarity."

We are not speaking of the analogy of things in this essay; we are speaking of the analogy of terms. And "being analogous" will signify a semantical property of a term in several of its instances. Which semantical property? The property of conforming in its employment to one of the analogy rules stated below. Hence, the analogy theory of St. Thomas is concerned with the similarity of meaning of instances of the same term not directly with the similarity of things. Of course, Aquinas argues that similarity of meaning is connected with the similarity of the things signified by the terms in question; but that comes much later and is not part of the meaning-theory itself.

3. St. Thomas' analogy rules are the results of a language analysis and are designed to solve specific language problems. The first of these is this: Aquinas, for theological reasons, was committed to accepting the traditional Christian language about God which is found in the liturgy and in the traditional catechetical instruction given children and converts, as being accurate, informative and true. This was "ordinary language" and was to be accepted as being applicable to God. But Aquinas has undertaken to solve the following problem: How could he show that this language (all of the terms, expressions and employments of which are learned from human experience) can be applied, without such equivocation as would render invalid all argument, to God, an entity which is so different from the objects of experience as to be "inexperienceable" in any of the ways common to ordinary human experience? Although the analogy theory I am treating as a whole was actually formulated piecemeal as problems arose over the applicability of "experience" predicates to God, the object of the whole theory is to preserve the literal sense of ordinary beliefs about God.

The second specific language problem St. Thomas was trying to solve is as follows: He accepted the Aristotelian theory of the categories as a classification of predicates such that entities denoted by the predicates in a given category, say "substance," were all those things denoted by all the terms in that category used *univocally*. As a result, transcategorial statements cannot have univocal predicates. An example of a transcategorial statement is: "Both trees and numbers exist"—where "trees" belongs to the category of substance and "numbers" to quantity. Aquinas would remark that the whole statement given is elliptical for two statements in which the predicate "exists" occurs twice and is used analogously. Hence, the theory of analogy was required to justify the meaningfulness of transcategorial statements. And, since metaphysical statements were by their very generality transcategorial, the theory of analogy was required as a justification of the metaphysician's claim to be uttering meaningful discourse.

Definitions

General Conditions:

1. (a) and (b) stand for sentences.
2. All definitions are for (a) and (b) in a language.

Def. I - 1: Verbal Symbol:

"'S' is a verbal symbol":

if "S" is a recognizable pattern of marks or of sounds used for the purpose of expression and communication. (What is regarded as the same pattern in difficult instances is partly a matter of physical similarity, and partly a matter of conventional understanding.) Two marks or two sounds having the same recognizable pattern are two instances of the same symbol, not two different symbols.

Def. I - 2: Linguistic Expression:

"'L' is a linguistic expression":

if "L" is a verbal symbol (S), and if S is associated with a fixed meaning either by convention or stipulation.

Def. I - 3: Same Expression:

"'L' in sentence (a) and 'L' in sentence (b) are the same expression":

if "L" in (a) and "L" in (b) are instances of the same symbol, and if the two instances are not totally equivocal.

Def. I - 4: Word:

"'W' is a word":

if "W" is a linguistic expression.

Def. I - 5: Same Word:

"'W' in sentence (a) and 'W' in sentence (b) are the same word":

if "W" in (a) and (b) respectively is a linguistic expression, and if (*according to Def. I* - 1) "W" in (a) and "W" in (b) are numerical instances of the same verbal symbol.

Note: "W" in (a) and "W" in (b) can be the same word without being the same expression.

Def. I - 6: Term:

"'T' is a term": if "T" is a word capable of naming or applying to a thing or things.

Note: All terms are words, but not all words are terms.

Def. I - 7: Same Term:

"'T' in (a) and 'T' in (b) are the same term": if in each case "T" is a term and if "T" in (a) and in (b) is the same word. *Note:* Sometimes "T" in (a) and "T" in (b) will be the same word *and* the same expression (*Def. I* - 3), and sometimes the same word but *not* the same expression. When "T" in (a) and "T" in (b) are the same term, they are "instances of term 'T.'" This is a departure from the practice of C. I. Lewis in *Knowledge and Valuation*, but it conforms to the practice of the Scholastics whom I am explaining, and using Lewis' definitions would require two parallel sets of definitions which would constantly require correlation.

Def. I - 8: Same Term and Same Expression:

"'T' in (a) and 'T' in (b) are the same term and the same expression":

if (1) "T" in (a) and "T" in (b) are the same word; and (2) if "T" in (a) and "T" in (b) are the same expression.

Def. I - 9: Same Meaning of Same Term:

"'T' in (a) and "T" in (b) have the same meaning)":

if (1) "T" in (a) and "T" in (b) are instances of the term "T",

i.e., are the same term; and (2) "T" in (a) and in (b) is used univocally (*Def. I* - 12).

Def. I - 10: Signification:

"Term 'T' signifies F":

if F is one of the properties which it is both necessary and sufficient for a thing to have in order to be denoted by "T."

Def. I - 11: Intention:

The intention of term "T" is the conjunction of all other terms each of which must be applicable to anything to which the term "T" is correctly applicable.

Def. I - 12: Univocity:

(a) "Term 'T' is used univocally in (a) and (b)": if "T" in (a) signifies the same property as "T" in (b).

(b) "Term 'T' is used univocally in (a) and (b)": if there is a one to one correspondence of the same terms in the intention of "T" in (a) and of "T" in (b).

Def. I - 13: Equivocity:

"Term 'T' is used equivocally in (a) and (b)": if "T" in (a) and "T" in (b) are not univocal.

Def. I - 14: Total Equivocation:

"Term 'T' is totally equivocal in (a) and (b)": if there is no property which is included both in the signification of "T" in (a) and in the signification of ""T" in (b).

Def. I - 15: Partial Equivocation:

"Term 'T' is partially equivocal in (a) and (b)": if "T" in (a) and "T" in (b) are used equivocally, but not totally equivocally.

Def. II - 1: Analogy of Inequality:

"Term 'T' is analogous by inequality in (a) and (b)": if 1. "T" in (a) and "T" in (b) are instances of the same term.

1. 2. "T" in (a) and "T" in (b) are univocal by *Def. I* - 12.

2. 3. The property F, signified by "T" in (a) and (b) is either:

1. not physically congruent, in the one case being a nonseparable part of the subject, and in the other, all of the subject; or

2. different in degree according to some standard; or

3. possessed by the subject in (a) in a different mode (necessity, contingency, etc.) from the subject in (b).

Def. III - 1: Analogy of Attribution:

"Term 'T' is analogous by attribution in (a) and (b)": if 1. "T" occurs as predicate in two or more indicative sentences: (a) "F is T" and (b) "G is T."

"T" in (a) signifies a property T of F.

"T" in (b) signifies a relation of G to F where G is either a cause of F's having property T or is in some respect an effect or affected causally by F's having property T.

Def. IV - 1: Sameness of Res Significata:

"The res *significata* of 'T' is the same in (a) and (b)": if 1. there are given at least two sentences (a) and (b) in which there is respectively a predicate term 'T.'

2. "T" in (a) and "T" in (b) are instances of the same term.

3. "T" signifies property T of X in (a) and T of Y in (b).

4. all the terms of the intention of "T" in (a) which specify the class of things to which property T belongs, occur in the intention of "T" in (b).

Def. IV - 2: Difference of Modus Significandi:

"The *modus significandi* of 'T' is different in (a) and (b)": if 1, 2, 3, and 4 of *Def. IV* - 1 hold.

5. for any thing Z, having the property T implies that Z can perform either actions (A) 1, 2, 3, - n; or (B) 2, 3, 4, - n and not 1; or (C) 3, 4, - n and not 1 and 2; or....; or n....

6. the intention of "T" in sentence (a) and in (b) is determined by the intention of the subject term "X" or "Y" in such a way that only one of the alternative groups of actions is signified.

7. the terms of the intention of "T" in (a) which specify which of the alternates (A), (B) or (C) is performed, are not the same as the terms in the intention of "T" in (b) which, consequently, specify a different alternative.

Def. IV - 3: Similar:

"A is similar to B": if 1. A and B are terms, things, properties, relations, or anything of any kind or kinds.

2. A and B are in some respect or respects identical.

3. A and B and the identical respect or respects are not numerically identical.

Def. IV - 4: Proportional Similarity:

"ATx and BTy are proportionally similar": if 1. A and B are things, x and y are properties, actions, etc.

2. there is a term "T", which signifies the two instances of relation T.

3. ATx and BTy are proportions: i.e., A is related to x by

T and B is related to y by T.

4. "T" when used in the statement "ATx is proportionally similar to BTy" is not univocal.

5. T in ATx and in BTy is not numerically identical.

6. T' in ATx and T' in BTy are similar.

Def. IV - 5: Analogy of Proper Proportionality:

"Term 'T' is used analogously by proper proportionality in (a) and (b)": if 1. "T" occurs as predicate in two or more sentences of the form (a) "A is (or has) T," and (b) "B is (or has) T," where "B" and "A" denote individual things A and B.

2. "T" signifies a relation T which holds between x (where x is a property, action, event, relation, etc.) and A; and between y (property, action, relation, etc.) and B.

3. ATx and BTy are proportionally similar.

Def. IV - 6: Similarity of Relations:

"Relation R is similar to relation R1": if 1. both are relations.2. they have common formal properties with respect to either a formal or merely linguistic set of axioms, the latter not being explicitly formulated in ordinary language.

Def. IV - 7: Analogy of Improper Proportionality:

"Term 'T' is analogous by improper proportionality in (a) and (b)": if A) alternative 1:

1. "T" is used as a predicate in a sentence (a), of the form "F is T."

2. the denotation of "T" is a class of objects Z having as members individuals w, y, z, according to the ordinary rule for its employment.

F is not a member of Z.

4. between F and the members of Z there is a proportional similarity with respect to relations R and R1 and the characteristic behaviour or other properties of F and the members of Z.

5. "T" is used as a predicate of F to call attention to the similar relations of F and the elements of Z.

6. "T" is equivocal with respect to its occurrence in (a) and in sentences where it denotes members of Z.

B. alternative 2:

1. "T" is used as predicate in two indicative sentences of the form (a) "x is T" and (b) "y is T," where "x" and "y" denote x and y, individual things.

2. term "T" is used as predicate of "x" with respect to a language rule R which determines the intention of "T" and x has the property signified by "T."

3. "T" cannot be used as predicate of "y" because y does not have the property signified by "T."

4. in terms of R, sentence (b) is incorrect.

5. "T" is equivocal with respect to (a) and (b).

6. there is a similarity between a relation of x to its characteristics and the relation of y to its characteristics.

7. "T" is used of y to call attention to the similarity.

5. In the sections of this essay where I summarize two of the exhibition analyses by which Aquinas developed the language rules of Analogy of Attribution, *Def. III* - 1, and Proper Proportionality, *Def. IV* - 5, there is a basic presumption that the cases of ordinary language which are taken for examination are in fact cases of *informative* language. And the rules which result are supposed to be recipes by which St. Thomas can construct, other parallel uses of language which will also be informative. These statements generated according to these rules will be applicable in arguments about God and in metaphysical contexts without further justification as to their meaningfulness, provided that St. Thomas' analysis of ordinary language has in fact produced the rules according to which the ordinary language employment of certain terms is rendered meaningful.

6. There is no direct argument for any philosophical point in what follows. But I suggest that the analogy theory here in discussed does offer evidence for the following two claims:

(a) a. If one regards talk of God as informative discourse (that is, the discourse of literal assertion) and employs the discourse of Christian tradition (the Creeds, etc.) one may appeal to an analogy theory something like that herein explained to account for the cognitive meaningfulness of such discourse.

(b) b. If one wishes to maintain that there are any exclusive categories (in Aristotle's sense) of things in the world and at the same time supposes that there can be any universally true metaphysical statements, he presupposes a meaning-theory fundamentally similar to the proportionality theory of St. Thomas.

Analogy of Attribution

The first of the analogy rules is called the rule of "attribution." We are concerned here with sets of two statements of the form (a) "F is T" and (b) "G is T." We shall take two examples of such pairs of statements:

1. (1) (a) Fido is healthy. (b) Fido's bark is healthy.
2. (2) (a) John is brilliant. (b) John's work is brilliant.

The first of these pairs is roughly the example used by St. Thomas. The other is contributed to push his analysis a little further than he did in his own desultory discussions of attribution. It might be useful to keep in mind that I am following St. Thomas' line of thought up to *Def. III* - 4 and its corollaries.

In his analysis of attribution, St. Thomas wishes to discuss the cases where a term occurs as the predicate of two statements with different subjects, only *one* of which subjects, by the usual rules governing the employment of predicate terms to signify properties of the subject, could have the property signified by the predicate term.

It is easy to see what Aquinas means from his example. Suppose we have two statements: (a) "The dog is healthy" and (b) "His bark is healthy." It is clear from conventional linguistic practice that both employments of the term are informative and proper in ordinary discourse. St. Thomas believed the property of "being healthy" to be compatible only with animals and plants as such, and he concludes rightly that at least part of what is signified by the term "healthy" in both these cases is numerically the same: the one state of affairs of the whole dog. In other words, the term "healthy" in sentence (b) does not signify some property numerically *different* from what "healthy" signifies in sentence (a); it does not signify a numerically *different instance* of health. Presuming that the "bark" in (b) belongs to the dog in (a), then the health in (b) is one and the same as the health in (a).

He says that the predicates of some sentences signify properties which *inhere* in what is denoted by the grammatical subject, e.g., sentence (a); and the predicates in *other* sentences, like (b), do not signify properties all of which *inhere* in the subject of that sentence, but rather partially specify that the subject of that sentence is related to the subject of that other sentence in which the same predicate does signify a property *inherent* in the subject. (I am using "subject" to stand for "what is *denoted* by the grammatical subject.") The predicate term in (b) *partially* specifies the relation of the secondary subject of (b) to the primary subject because the predicate term in such a sentence usually only tells us which of the properties of the primary subject we should look to if we wish to figure out the relation of the secondary subject to the primary subject. The other conditions which I shall cite for analogy of attribution will further specify the *kinds* of relations that may obtain between primary and secondary subjects. In any given use of ordinary language, reflection is expected to disclose the particular kind of relation which obtains. But when constructing philosophical instances of analogy of attribution, the philosopher will have to show the two subjects to be related in one or the other of the ways known from the forthcoming ordinary language exhibition to justify such uses of terms.

Before discussing the kinds of relations which are found to obtain in ordinary language instances, and before investigating the possibility and usefulness of philosophical constructions, it may be helpful to consider the following question. Given the sentences (a) and (b), above, and given that part of what is signified by "healthy" in (b) is numerically the same as that property signified by "healthy" in (a), and given further that there is only one health which is inherent in the dog, does sentence (b) say anything about the dog's *bark* or not? That is, sentences in general purport to say something about what the subject denotes (they do *not* say what the subject denotes, but only something about what the subject denotes). If "healthy" signifies a property of the dog, one might conclude that then the sentence (b) says nothing about the *bark*. However, Aquinas notes that if (b) is to function as sentences usually do, it will in fact 'say something about the dog's bark. St. Thomas' move was to say: "The sentence (b) says the dog's bark is related to the dog's health in a certain one of the specified kinds of ways in which a predicate of the 'dog' can be used of its 'bark' or of 'medicine'." This move is later found to be equivalent to saying: "Sentence (b) is a short-hand for the statement: 'The dog's bark is a sign that the dog is healthy." What is *said* is that the bark performs a signifying service with respect to the presence of an inhering property "health" in the dog. In summary, this analysis, so far, proposes that the statement (b) tells us *that* and *how* the subject either actually or potentially functions (i.e., is related) with respect to a certain property belonging to another subject. Most of the traditional Thomists, Cajetan and John of St. Thomas and many neo-Thomists, have expressly interpreted the "designation" of the analogous term with respect to the secondary subject (secondary analogate) to be merely "extrinsic," merely designating accidental (fortuitous, even though constant) relations. However, these writers cautiously add that this does not *exclude* the. "presence of the analogous property in the secondary analogates, although imperfectly." What they could mean by this is obscure and the fact that they place their emphasis on the extrinsic relations which they say are "designated" is the point I wish to emphasize. As far as I can see, what they are saying is exactly the analysis given above: that the sentence (b) tells us *that* and *how* the secondary subject either actually or potentially functions with respect to a certain property (signified by the predicate term) belonging to the primary subject in (a). For the authors mentioned, then, the initial conditions for an analogy of attribution are of two kinds: (1) The term is used at least once (in the two sentences under consideration) to signify a property inherent in a subject. (2) The term is used on other occasions of subjects which do not actually possess the property but are related in specified ways to the things which do have the property.

Many interpreters have claimed that the sentence containing the secondary use of an analogous term of this kind does not say anything about the nature or properties of its subject in itself, but only states facts about the relation of the subject to the primary subject with respect to the property signified by the analogous term. Contrary to this commonly accepted interpretation, I shall attempt to show that these secondary sentences *do* say something about the nature of the subject, even though it be very little and indirectly. A person who says "That's a healthy bark your dog's got" is saying something about the dog, to be sure, but he is also saying something about the bark. And when I tell you "This food is healthful," I am not *only* telling you something about the *relation* of the food to your health; I am telling you something about the food, which is additional to its relation as cause of health. It is true that you would not know very much about the food if you did not know what properties food would have to have in order to be healthful. But if you did, it would be legitimate for you to conclude that this food has those properties (or at least that I believed it had these properties) and thus I would have told you something about the food.

Another example: When we say that a student's work is brilliant, we are not only saying something about the fact that this work is a sign of the brilliance of the student who wrote it, we are saying something about the work itself. Even though the term "brilliant" appears to be applied primarily to students who can and habitually do produce work of a given quality, saying "The work is brilliant" tells a person who has some information about the standards for being called "brilliant" and the kind of work brilliant people produce, something about the work produced.

However, this brings up a further problem. For the sake of an example, I assumed that the *primary* sense of "brilliant" was the instance of the term signifying the intellectual prowess and creativity of the student and that the secondary sense has its application to the work produced. Actually, in re-examining certain terms functioning analogously it is sometimes difficult to say which is the primary instance of the term, although it is clear that the two instances are different but related.

Aquinas, preparing for philosophical employment of analogy, offers a rule for deciding which instance is primary. He distinguishes between the order of things and the order of knowledge. In effect, he says that the use of the term which is supposed by the other uses of the same term is the primary onc, the one which *must be known first* in order to use the term of the other cases. Thus, it seems that to be correct in calling a student "brilliant" we must have evidence of the high quality of his work, and since the potentiality of producing high quality work is what is meant by "brilliant" when applied to the student, just the opposite of my previous assumption is the case: the primary sense of the term on Aquinas' rule is to signify "high quality work" although the more frequent use of the term may be to signify a person's capacity for producing such work.

Aquinas points out that the order of things may be different from the order of knowledge. There can be times when the order of things is neither the same as the order of knowledge nor as the order of applying the terms which follows it. Our example of "brilliant" is a case in point. As a matter of fact, the student must have certain powers before he can produce high quality work; this is a causal and logical priority. But we do not *know* his powers until he has produced some high quality work; this is a psychological priority. Hence, we *describe* his powers in terms of the quality of his work, although he works in terms of his powers.

It is this fact which Aquinas cites as part of one of the arguments to show that we can "name" God from His effects, because even though we *know* God from His effects, the properties of the effects are derived from the powers of God.

St. Thomas says:

> Sometimes, indeed, that which is prior in nature is secondary regarding knowledge, and then among the analogues there is not the same order both regarding the things and the order of the term: thus the power of healing which is in medicines is naturally prior to the health which is in the animal, as cause to effect; *but because we know that power through its effect, we also name it from its effect.* And thus it happens that "healthful" is prior in order of nature, but the animal is called "healthy" with priority in the order of naming.

So far, the exposition of analogy of attribution has shown Aquinas to be exhibiting the following points about the function of certain words in ordinary language which are called "analogous by attribution":

1. The "analogy of attribution" is concerned with the comparative functions of two instances of the same term occurring as predicate in two sentences, one primary, the other secondary.
2. A term analogous in this way is used in at least one instance in a sentence as predicate where all the properties it signifies do not belong to the subject, but where it signifies a relation of that subject to another subject possessing the property normally signified by the term and related *via* that property.
3. These predicate terms always have a primary use where in some indicative sentence they signify a property inherent in the subject and have this property as their *definitive* property.
4. Irrespective of the fact that these secondary sentences do not signify a specific property of the entity denoted by the subject, they do give information about the properties of the subject.
5. The property signified by an analogous term in its primary and secondary occurrences is numerically one. That is, there is only one property of "health" which belongs to the dog, and the secondary sentence does *not* say it belongs to the bark.

The several other points so far made regarding (1) the kind of analysis Aquinas was doing, (2) the uses to which he would put the analysis, (3) the fact that the Thomists do not make much use of analogy of attribution in natural theology, and (4) the fact that there is a rule for deciding which of the terms, in doubtful cases, will be considered the primary one, are all points necessary in the exposition; however, they are not part of the special informations necessary for the analysis which will be developed.

Let us consider the other properties of analogy of attribution.

6. "The primary analogate is put into the definition of the others with respect to the analogous name." St. Thomas says:

It is necessary in all cases where terms are used analogously of several things, that they are all used with respect to one; and thus, that one use must be contained in the definition of all. And since the notion which the term signifies is its definition, as is said in the *Fourth Book of the Metaphysics*, it is necessary that that term be used primarily of that which is supposed in the definition of the others, and secondarily of the others, in the order by which they approach more or less to the primary term: thus "healthy" which is used of "animal" is part of the definition of "healthy" which is used of "medicine," which is called healthy in as much as it causes health in the animal; and of the definition of "healthy" which is used of "urine," which is called "healthy" inasmuch as it is a sign of the health of the animal.

Suppose we take "healthy" as used in the sentence—

(a) "My dog is healthy" to be defined as follows: "X is healthy" equals by definition: "X has a certain organic state characterized by properties a, b, c, ...n." We are not concerned that the assertion "X is healthy" is defeasible even though all the properties are present. By hypothesis, let us suppose it can be and is defined by a finite list of properties and degrees of properties. If we are going to define the term "healthy" in the following sentences, we shall have to appeal to the definitions already given of "healthy" in the sentence (a) above.

(b) "My dog's bark is healthy."

(c) "His pills and dog-food are healthy."

Sentence (b) can only mean something like this: "My dog's bark has those qualities which are signs to me that the dog is 'healthy,' that is, has the organic state characterized by a, b, c, ...n." Hence, I take it that Aquinas' point is clear: In all cases where a term is used as a predicate to attribute a relation to a subject with respect to a property possessed by a different subject, and where the term used normally signifies that property of the other subject, the definition of the term in its primary sense is part of the definition of the term in its secondary sense.

Aquinas does not try to rule out the possibility that two different people might disagree about which is the primary sense of the analogous term, nor does he deny that they might even disagree about when to use the term because of that. Suppose that someone has been reared bearing the word "healthy" applied only when a dog's or man's voice was loud and clear. The term "healthy" might thus be associated with the meaning of "loud and clear voice." When I say to him that the dog or man is healthy, he interprets this to mean "capable of a loud and clear vocal utterance." Thus his conception of the significance of both sentences (a) and (b) is different from mine. Another person might learn that the term "healthy" usually follows another set of rules which also reverse the relative priority of the "senses" of the analogous term. But neither event, his learning to apply the word by a different convention, nor his reversing the convention, would be an exception to the rule presupposed by Aquinas.

In any case where a term is neither univocal nor totally equivocal but occurs in several instances as predicate of indicative sentences, the meaning it has in at least one instance (supposing that we have at hand at least one each of every kind of instance in which the word can be used according to the conventional rules for its employment) must be entirely included in the meaning it has in every other instance.

In fact, on the definitions given of univocity and total

equivocity, the rule is a tautology. Cajetan, Penido, Aquinas and Aristotle (at least as Cajetan interprets him) all seem to imply that the secondary analogate can only be related to the primary analogate as efficient, final, material, or exemplary cause (which they extend to equal: sign and symptom). When we say that a man is charitable, Cajetan would say we are showing that he is dispositionally (at least) the efficient cause of charitable acts; when we say a given kind of action is charitable, we are saying that its performance is usually a sign of a charitable act. It functions as a sign because it is usually an effect of charity. Thus Aquinas' rule for analogy of attribution contains a provision that the secondary uses of the term will signify a causal relation of their subject to the normal subject of the property. By this he means that the subject of the secondary sentence must denote something which is either cause or effect (in the wide, Aristotelian sense of the four causes) of the property signified by the primary occurrence of the term, as belonging to the primary subject.

Hence, this is the seventh characteristic: The secondary analogate in its definition, in addition to the definitions of the term in its primary instance, will also contain a phrase specifying a causal relation to the signification of the primary term.

The eighth characteristic of this kind of analogy is that the "term does not have one definite meaning common to all its partial modes." There is nothing about the term itself as it occurs in various sentences which tells us that it is not being used "denominatively," to signify its definitive property as inherent in the subject; nor is there anything about the form of sentences which tells us that the term is not being used to signify its definitive property of the subject. When we formulate (1) "The dog is healthy" and (2) "The bark is healthy," they are both of the same form: X is F and Y is F. That the term "F" has not the same meaning in both sentences is only known from the "logical rules of ordinary language." Sometimes we are not sure whether a term indicates only a property of its subject or a relation to a property of another subject, as was shown by the example of "brilliant" when applied to the student and his work. However, Cajetan's point is clear enough. The term cannot possibly have exactly the same *meaning* in all its instances if we include as part of its meaning in some instances the *relationship* of the definitive property to the subject.

Some Scotists have said that what is analogous is not the property term but the copula. "The dog *is* healthy" means: The dog has the property "healthy"; "The bark *is* healthy" means: The bark is related to the health of the dog. But Aquinas' supposition seems to be recommended by its simplicity and by the fact that relevant questions and answers about the dog's bark being healthy would indicate that in ordinary discourse the speaker realizes he doesn't mean by "healthy" exactly the same thing in both cases.The analysis which St. Thomas suggests for the statement "Term 'T' is analogous by attribution in (a) and (b)" is as follows:

Def. III-1: Analogy of Attribution:

"Term 'T' is analogous by attribution in (a) and (b)": if

1. "T" occurs as predicate in two or more indicative sentences: (a) "F is T" and (b) "G is T."
2. "T" in (a) signifies a property T of F.
3. "T" in (b) signifies a relation of G to F where G is either a cause of F's having property T or is in some respect an effect or affected causally by F's having property T.

The following propositions are implied by the definition and are corollaries:

1. There is only one (numerically) instance of the property T of "T" in (a) and it belongs to subject F.

2. The term "T" in sentence (b) cannot be defined unless the entire definition of the term "T" in sentence (a) is made part of its definition; and still the definition will not be complete, because part of the intention must be a specification of the causal relation of G to F.

3. The term "T" does not have the same intention in both of its instances in (a) and (b): i.e., the term "T" is not formally univocal, *Def. I*-12; nor is it totally equivocal.

Terms are said to be analogous by attribution not because they attribute a property to subjects which logically cannot have that property, but because the sentences in which they are used in their secondary meanings ascribe a causal relation of their subjects to the thing having that property, and at the same time imply that the subject of the secondary sentence has whatever properties, relations, and dispositions are necessary in order to be related in that way to the subject of the primary analogate (the term used in its primary sense).

Analogy of Proper Proportionality

In looking at the language analysis by which this rule for Analogy of Proper Proportionality is generated, we are concerned with pairs of statements of the following forms:

1. (a) "A is (or has) T."

   b. "B is (or has) T."

2. (a) "ATx"

   b. "BTy"

And the supposition is that statements of the first form which fit the rule we are developing (*Def. IV*-5) are reducible in principle to statements of the second form. This supposition is not an integral part of the theory; and it seems to have independent justification. Examples of each form are:

1. (a) Fido has knowledge of his dog house.

   Plato has knowledge of philosophy, *or*

   Fido is the cause of his barking.

   Plato is the cause of his actions.

2. Fido knows his dog house.

   1. Plato knows philosophy, *or*

   Fido caused the barking.

   Plato caused the murderous shot.

1. Let us take it as given, by inspection of the examples, that the *predicates* "knows" and "causes" *are not univocal in (a) and (b) of each set.* This is *the first characteristic* of the language rule. Later paragraphs will justify this presumption,

if it should be in doubt here.

2. *The second characteristic* is that there are at least two instances of the property signified by "T."

On this condition rests the first and most important difference between Analogy of Proportionality and Attribution. In the latter case, there is numerically only one instance of the definitive property signified by both instances of the analogous term, whereas in this case there must be one instance of the property for each instance of the term as predicate of a sentence with a different subject.

A problem raised by this requirement can be phrased thus: if the term is equivocal, then the intention (or connotation) of the term must differ in its various instances; i.e., a sentence affirming and denying a term "T" of the same subject would be contradictory if the intention of the term was identical in each instance; and the term would not be equivocal by *Def. I-13.* If the intention of the term differs, then a criterion must be given of how far the intention of the term can vary in two instances of the term before a different property is signified. For if different properties are signified by a term in two of its instances, then the second condition of the analogy of proper proportionality is either unsatisfied or ambiguous. The second condition states, briefly, that the two things denoted by the term "T" must have the property signified by "T" and that the first condition must still be preserved: that the term is equivocal. On the assumption that "T" is equivocal, one might say, "Yes, the things denoted do have the property signified in each case, but the properties are not the same." And if "Term 'T' in its instances signifies the same property" equals by definition "Term 'T' in its instances has the same intention," then either the term is univocal or the second condition is unsatisfiable. Hence, we must demand some analysis from St. Thomas which will allow a term to be univocal in signification (*Def. I*-12-a) while being equivocal in not conforming to the rule for univocity in intention (*Def. I*-12-b).

St. Thomas claims to offer such an analysis; for he held the theory that the intention (*intentio*) of a term specifies not only the kind of property signified but the way the property is signified. And hence, "signification" has two senses: the *res significata* and the *modus significandi*. It was part of his theory that the linguistic rules which govern the use of a term, and thereby determine its intention, make into elements of the intention of a term those terms which specify the *modus significandi* (which I shall explain shortly). To our objection that when we define a term we cite the terms characteristic of its intention and we never find a term indicating the mode of signification, Aquinas would reply that most of our predicates signify in the *same* mode of signification, and that for ordinary purposes it is not necessary to make such a distinction. Furthermore, it is only a logical technique for one to distinguish between what is signified and how it is signified, because in every actual instance of discourse about the world of experience the mode of signification corresponds to the *mode of existence* which the property has, and, consequently, is implicit in the rule which governs the employment of a term.

Although every perfection which belongs to creatures is taken by exemplary causality from God, as from a principle having unified in itself all perfections, no creature can receive that perfection according to the same mode by which it is in God. So, the creature fails to be a perfect representation of the exemplar because of the different mode in which the perfections are received. And because of that (difference in the mode of receiving) there is a scale, as it were, among creatures according to which some creatures receive from God more and higher perfections and participate in His perfections more fully. And because of this there are two aspects of the terms to consider: the thing [*rem* which equals "what *kind* of thing"] signified and the mode of being signified. Therefore we must consider that when we, who know God only from creatures, employ a term, we always fall short of a representation of God with respect to the "mode of being signified": because the term signifies the divine perfections through the mode by which they are participated in by creatures.

If, however, we consider *what* is signified by the term, what the term is used to signify, we find that some terms are used primarily to signify the perfections exemplified in God alone, not being concerned with any mode in their signification; and that some terms are said to signify a perfection received according to a given mode of participation; for example, all knowing is an imitation of divine knowing, and all knowledge of divine knowledge. Therefore, the term "sense" is used to signify knowing through that mode by which knowledge is materially received through the power of the conjoined organ. But the term "knowledge" does not signify a particular mode of participating in its principal signification. Hence, it must be said that all those terms which are used to signify a perfection absolutely are properly used of God, and primarily are used of Him with respect to what is signified, even though not with respect to the mode of signification, such as "wisdom," "goodness," "essence," and others of this type.

I have used this passage to illustrate two things:

(1) that Aquinas understands a difference between what is signified (the kind of property signified) and what kinds of conditions are supposed as surrounding what is signified, even though both are signified simultaneously by any term given its use in a determinate context; and

(2) that Aquinas has two different uses of the phrase "*modus significandi*" which function in entirely different ways. First, there is the sense in which "knowledge" as used of a man and of a dog is understood to be different, not in what is meant by "knowledge," but in what *kind* of knowledge is possible. Since "knowing" is a property which admits of degrees according to the ability of the person, and of kinds according to the nature of the thing which knows, in the two sentences:

(a) "Fido knows his dog house" and

(b) "Plato knows philosophy," the term "knows" is different not as to *what* is signified but as to which *kind* of knowledge is signified. To avoid possible confusion, I point out that St. Thomas did not believe that sentence (a) is an anthropomorphic or metaphorical description of the dog's actions. He merely claimed that words like "knowing," "wise," "good" are vague with respect to classes of activity included in the signification of the term. He says the intention of "knows" is proportionally the same in sentence (a) and (b), but the mode in which the property is possessed makes entirely different the kinds of action which can be performed.

This allows the Thomist to construct a hierarchy of "powers" or "perfections" on the Neoplatonic assumption that

(1) being a man is better than being an animal and an animal better than a plant, etc.; and

(2) any other beings which know or will in a simpler (less complex), freer way and act more accurately to satisfy their desires are higher on the scale of perfection in beings. Those properties which belong to several levels of the hierarchy and which are named by a single term are said to be named by an analogous term. Thus in Thomist terms the foundation of this kind of analogy is the unequal and different-in-kind participation of different natures in the same property according to differing modes of being determined by their natures.

Divine knowing, human knowing, and animal knowing are all "knowing," but one is not the other; yet the term "knowing" (apart from any particular sentence) is neutral with respect to the three modes of knowing. An obvious objection is this: if the term "knowing" is neutral with respect to the three various modes, then why is the term not univocal? St. Thomas' answer is that terms are univocal or equivocal by comparison of their use in sentences, and "knowing" as used in a sentence with "dog" for a subject and in another sentence with "man" for a subject is not univocal, even though he would admit we may form a meta-language term "knowing" which is neutral with respect to all object-language senses of "know"; but then the meta-language sense of knowing will not be univocal with *any* object-language sense.

In considering this example, we must remember that St. Thomas' conception of knowing is considerably different from contemporary notions. He assumes

(1) that the man is more than quantitatively different from the dog; he is *essentially* different;

(2) the *possessio formae alterius ut alterius*, which constitutes knowing, is fundamentally known as a human activity involving abstraction and it is the mode of "abstraction" which is "cancelled out" as inapplicable when "knowing" is used in sentences about animals.

If, in attempting to criticize the Thomist claim that there is a foundation for the analogy of the term "knowing" in the unequal and disparate participations of things in the powers of knowing, we were to suggest that we could formulate three *different* concepts of knowing and terms for each, one for humans, animals, and God, St. Thomas would reply that the properties signified would have in common something which is the basis for an analogous term. (It is here that analogy becomes a theory about things, or at least supposes one.) For example, Aquinas could formulate a vague concept which would include the three concepts of knowing, as I said. To do this, let us accept Aquinas' technical and admittedly recondite partial definition of "knowing" as the *possessio formae alterius ut alterius*, "the possession of the form of another as belonging to another." For St. Thomas, however, this is not a complete definition, for he wishes to add the phrase: "according to one's natural mode of possession." So, "knowing" is "the possession of the form of another as belonging to another according to one's natural mode of possession." This concept is neutral with respect to the concepts of knowing. But it is not on the same level as the other three notions. It is a meta-language notion which includes the other three and which signifies all three equally and alternatively. In the sentences (a) "Sense knowing is the possession of the form of another as belonging to another according to one's natural mode of possession" and "Divine knowing is the possession etc.," the phrase "possession of the form etc." serves as a univocal term. It is a predicate in sentences about predicates of sentences used earlier as examples; hence, it is a predicate in meta-language sentences. But the fact that we can form a term in a meta-language whose intention will include the intentions of terms occurring in object-language statements and which are analogous, does not make the analogous terms univocal. In fact, the only reason our constructed term can include the intentions of the analogous terms is that we *constructed* it to signify the intentions of the analogous terms; and the only time it actually includes the intentions of the other terms is when it occurs in a meta-language sentence.

From this discussion, it should be clear why St. Thomas could say, "What is 'knowing' for a man is not what is 'knowing' for a dog, although both are properly called 'knowing'." There are some instances of terms used as predicates where they signify not only what property is possessed but *what kind of possession* the property is had by.

Moreover, the language rules which govern the employment of terms like "knowing" make the intention of the term (which has a section of its intention that, if imagined in C. I. Lewis' terms, *Def. I*-12, is a conjunction of other terms) *contain some conjoined disjunctions* of terms. When a term like "knows" is used in a given sentence (b), a context is established which cancels out the inapplicable elements of the intention of "knows" in (a), thus making the intention fixed in the sentence as a conjunction of terms. Aquinas would say that the elements cancelled out are the inapplicable modes of possession; i.e., from the intention of "knowing" in the sentence "Fido knows his dog house" there are cancelled out of the intention any terms like "abstractly," "by deduction," "by induction," etc.

The second sense of the phrase "*modus significandi*" refers to elements of the intention of a term which are derived from the *way we learn the term.* For, Aquinas says, many people do not understand the difference between the way a dog knows and the way a human knows (in fact, it is almost impossible to specify), chiefly because we apply "knowing" to dogs, having recognized the similarity of their actions to ours. Hence, for these people, in the connotation of the term "knowing" there are elements which are appropriate only to humans; and most times, even when they are consciously ruled out when the term is used in sentences about animals, they are not replaced by anything definite. That is, within the intention of the term applied to animals there is no term which specifies *how* the dog knows. This point is of considerable importance for Aquinas in his discussion of language about God. If the intentions of terms have as elements terms which express the mode by which the property signified by the term is possessed, and if all the modes of possession are determined by the nature of the thing which has the property, then the terms of our experience-language, if applied directly to God, would signify a way of having the property which is no more compatible with the nature of God than the elements of the intention of "knowing" which make it signify "knowing as humans know" would be compatible with the nature of the dog.

But if the sentence in which the term is used establishes for a person who understands the nature of the subject the context which "rules in" or "rules out" certain elements of the intention of a term, then some elements will not be common to the intention of the term "knows" in the sentences (a) "God knows" and (b) "A man knows." And St. Thomas' rule is: the nature of the thing denoted by the logical subject determines the modal elements of the intention of predicates which are applied to the subject.

This analysis has supplied the elements of Aquinas' answer to the problem proposed earlier: namely, if the analogous term signifies two different properties, it should be called "equivocal"; but Aquinas' second condition for analogy of proper proportionality is that the two things must have the property signified by the analogous term. Yet if the term signifies two instances of the same property, then there seems to be no reason why it should be called "equivocal," for it will be univocal on our definition of univocity I-12-a and not univocal on *Def. I*-12-b. However, in terms of *Def. I*-11: Intention, Aquinas would thus say that, in brief, the term is used univocally if it has the same intention in each instance, and the intention in two instances is the same if all elements of the intention in one instance are common to the intention of the term in the other. But he holds that the "mode of signification" is part of the intention of the term (wherever a mode of *possession* is relevant). Thus, if the "mode of signifying" is different, the intention of the term is different even though the property signified be the same; and hence the term is equivocal (*Def. I*-13). And, he would argue, there are cases where a term is univocal in signification but equivocal in intention, just because there are modes of signification. Although I have indicated that St. Thomas does not believe it possible to separate, more than logically and artificially, the *res significata* from the *modus significandi*, the example of "knowing" is some help in understanding what he means. The *res significata* is what is common to all activities which we can call "knowing." But what we call "knowing" admits of kinds and of degrees. There is no instance of knowing which is not one kind or another, and both the kind, "sense" or "abstract," and the metaphysical mode, "finite" or "infinite," are part of the meaning of "knowing" in any synthetic statement in which it occurs. This is what is meant by *modus significandi.*St. Thomas' two statements that the *modus significandi* differs and that the *res significata* is the same when some terms are applied to God can be defined as follows:

Def. IV - 1: Sameness of Res Significata:

"The res significata of 'T' is the same":

if 1. There are given at least two sentences (a) and (b) in which there is respectively a predicate term "T."

2. "T" in (a) and "T" in (b) are instances of the same term.

3. "T" signifies property T of X in (a) and T of Y in (b).

4. All the terms of the intention of "T" in (a) which specify the class of things to which property T belongs, occur in the intention of "T" in (b).

Def. IV - 2: Difference of Modus Significandi:

"The modus significandi of 'T' is different": if 1, 2, 3, and 4 of Def. IV - 1 hold.

5. For any thing Z, having the property T implies that Z can perform either actions (A) 1, 2, 3, - n; or (B) 2, 3, 4, - n and not 1; or (C) 3, 4, - n and not 1 and 2; or......; or n.....

6. The intention of "T" in sentence (a) and in (b) is determined by the intention of the subject term "X" or "Y" in such a way that only one of the alternative groups of actions is signified.

7. The terms of the intention of "T" in (a) which specify which of the alternates (A), (B), or (C) is performed, are not the same as the terms in the intention of "T" in (b) which, consequently, specify a different alternative.

Thus, St. Thomas could hold that a term which differs in *modus significandi* but is the same in *res significata* is equivocal, even though all things denoted by the term will have the same property signified. That there is at least one such term is evident from the example given: "knowing," provided we accept at least provisionally Aquinas' analysis of the nature of knowing.

One would be inclined to seek an easy formulation of the analogy of proper proportionality in terms of the points so far explained by saying that terms are analogous by proper proportionality if they differ in their respective instances in *modus significandi* but not with respect to *res significata.* However, this is *not* what Aquinas meant by analogy of proper proportionality. *This is merely the reason why certain terms cannot be used of God and creatures univocally and it is St. Thomas' explanation of how a term can in two instances signify the same property and yet be equivocal.* St. Thomas has merely explained how the first and second conditions of this analogy can be rendered compatible. He has yet to exhibit the other conditions of this analogy.

3. The third characteristic of terms analogous by proportionality is that there must be a proportional similarity between what is denoted by "T" in (a) and what is denoted by "T" in (b). I shall briefly explain what Aquinas meant by *similarity*, secondly what he meant by *proportion*, and thirdly, what he meant by *proportional similarity.*

(a) *Similarity*: Aquinas has four senses of "similarity"; since the explanation of these notions is not possible under the circumstances of this essay, let us, instead, take a very general definition of "similarity" as being sufficient for our purposes. "Two things are similar if they are in some respect or respects identical but never numerically identical." The "respect or respects" can be and must be specified, says Thomas, wherever a factual proposition "This A is similar to that B" is analyzed. This very general definition is what I have given as *Def. IV* - 3.

(b) *Proportion*: For Aquinas the term "proportion" (*not proportionality*, now) is a synonym of "relation." And a proportion obtains between A and X where a relation obtains between A and X.

Note: I stipulate that "property" is a one place predicate in object-language sentences; "relation" is a two or more place predicate.

(c) *Proportionality*: When Aquinas says: "A proportionality holds between A and B," he means: There is a *similarity in the proportions* (or relations) of A and B. That is, a relation R obtains between A and some property, thing or event, K, and a relation R^1 obtains between B and some property, thing or event, Y, and R and R^1 are similar.

Hence, a proportional similarity obtains between any two things, A and B, which have similar relations to some property, event, or thing. So, Aquinas would say that a proportional similarity obtains between *Plato* and *Fido* because the relations signified by "knowing" which obtain between Fido and his dog house and Plato and his philosophy are similar (that is, in its two instances the relation signified by the term "knows" has some common properties or relations).

4. Turning now to *Definitions IV* - 4, *Proportional Similarity*, and *IV* - 5, *Analogy of Proper Proportionality*, we observe that the latter is formulated in terms of the former. A term is analogous by proper proportionality if it signifies in both its instances relations of the respective subjects and if the subjects, in regard to these relations, are proportionally similar.

And the subjects are proportionally similar if there exist entities, relations, properties or events such that ATx and BTy are true or could be true, and term "T" used to refer to the two instances of T would not be univocal, and the relations T of ATx and BTy are similar.

5. *Similarity of Relations*: For the analogy of proportionality rule to be fully established, it must be possible to apply the definition of *proportional similarity* to things and to decide

whether or not two things are in fact proportionally similar. But to do this, we need a criterion for *similarity of relations.* That is, it is a necessary condition of this analogy that the things denoted by the predicate be proportionally similar and it is a necessary condition of proportional similarity that the *relations* of the things be similar. Hence to apply the rule confidently in crucial cases we should need a criterion of similarity of relations.

Now, St. Thomas had not the slightest doubt that with regard to most ordinary language uses of terms like "knows," "exists," etc., in senses which fulfill this rule of analogy (like the two paradigm sentences: (a) "Plato knows philosophy" and (b) "Fido knows his dog house"), the reason the term was extended to its analogical use about dogs by human convention in the first place was that men had *recognized* the similarity in the relations. And later, in talking about God, Aquinas points out that if one can establish that God has certain relations to the world (from empirical premises) then it will follow from the general form of language that the relations are similar to relations of our experience.

Taking account of what Bochenski has proposed and of what Aquinas seems to have had in mind, I suggest the following definition (*IV* - 6) of Similarity of Relations:

Def. IV - 6: Similarity of Relations:

"Relation R is similar to relation R^1": if

1. Both are relations.

2. They have common formal properties with respect to either a formal or merely linguistic set of axioms, the latter not being explicitly formulated in ordinary language, or, they have a common property.

The difficulties with this criterion of similarity are obvious; Bochenski's proposed criterion says relations are similar if they have common formal properties, i.e., common syntactical and semantical properties. This is obviously not a thought which St. Thomas might have had. Furthermore, while this offers some hope for a more careful development of the analogy theory, it means that a great deal of analysis would have to be done to see if the relations attributed to God do have common properties with relations in the world of experience. Such a criterion supposes a more extensive formalized language than seems practicable. The second alternative, the proposal that the relations have common properties with respect to linguistic axioms which are presupposed by implicit language rules governing the employment of the analogous term, is very similar to St. Thomas' assumption that if the relations are sufficiently similar we will recognize that fact and use the same term to signify the two relations. I am not really sure what such language rules would be like.

This deficiency in the analogy theory is serious, because it is so difficult to imagine a set of rules under which the necessary conditions for analogy of proper proportionality (that the relations be similar) could be determined to have been fulfilled. Yet, it would be an *ad ignorantiam* error to argue that no such criterion is possible. However, let us go on to see how this theory is applied to language about God. For I think it will be found that the difficulty I have just mentioned is not so prominent when the rule is used in practice, although it is clear that a fully accurate and adequate analogy theory will have to contain a practicable criterion of similarity of relations.

Application of the Analogy Rules to Language about God

(1) Aquinas argues that he needs a theory of analogy for language about God because:

(a) If the predicate terms in G-statements (statements with "God" or a synonym as the subject) are *totally equivocal* with respect to the occurrences of the same predicate terms in E-statements (with any object of ordinary, direct or indirect experience as subject), then all arguments with an E-statement in the premises and a G-statement as the conclusion will be invalid, committing the fallacy of equivocation; and all G-statements will be meaningless because none of human experience will count either as evidence for or as explications of those statements.

(b) If the predicates of G-statements are *univocal* with respect to instances of the same predicates in E-statements, then God will be anthropomorphic, since all predicates we have are derived from experience and are primarily used of limited or finite things. And it was a basic thesis among the medievals that our descriptive categories of the world are of "the world-as-experienced," are homocentric. The term "finite" or "dependent" refers for Thomas to a mode of existence, and he holds that the context of all our language supposes that part of the meaning of the predicate terms is the *mode* of existence of the entity to which the property is attributed. I made this point earlier in distinguishing the *modus significandi* from the *res significata*. He insists that if you do not make such a distinction of kind from mode, you will not be describing the Christian God, the transcendent God. Furthermore, he also argues that if God is to have such properties as self-existence and omnipotence, He must be a significantly different kind of thing from anything in our experience. So, the predicates attributed to Him cannot be univocal with any E-statement occurrences of the same terms.

(2) As a result, the terms in G-statements must be partially equivocal with respect to the same terms in E-statements. St. Thomas claims that he can show as a matter of empirical fact that if we use these analogy rules we can explain the way these predicates in G-statements are related to ordinary E-sentence occurrences of the same terms; *and*, moreover, if we do explain the theological language this way, we shall (1) preserve the transcendence of God; (2) preserve the intelligibility of theological language; (3) make sense of the claim that human experience can furnish some evidence for the truth of the theological beliefs. For, God will be *at most* proportionally similar to the world. That is, God's *operations* will have properties in common with some operations, like causing, which are internal to the world. And we will *name* God from his operations (in a way to be described). So, while all our natural knowledge of God's properties will be by

inference from His operations, what we do attribute to God will not be grossly anthropomorphic and will not be arrived at by invalid arguments. How, in outline, this application of the analogy rules is carried out, I shall now describe.

(1) Aquinas believes that he can show that between the world described in E-statements, the world of experience, and some entity not part of that world there obtain several relations: (1) "being moved by"; (2) "being efficiently caused by"; (3) "being conserved in existence by"; (4) "being excelled by"; (5) "being designed by" (each relation is established by one of the five existential arguments).

(2) A term which signifies these relations (let us take only one, for consideration, say, "being caused by") cannot be used in exactly the same way as it is used in a sentence like this: "My black eye was caused by John." For this latter is an E-statement and the fundamental assumption is that God won't have any properties or relations in the same way as any of His creatures. (This assumption is outside the purview of our analysis; let us take it as a supposition that all theologians would accept it.)

So, the argument is: God is at most proportionally similar to John (that is, is not *directly* similar) because the relation "being caused by" is similar (but not identical) in the statements of the form (a) wCg and (b) bCj. And the term "being caused by" is analogous by proportionality because in its two occurrences it is used equivocally but not totally equivocally. The reason why we cannot replace *this* term ("being caused by") with a univocal term is that in (a) the "mode of signification" which is proper to "C" in (b) has been cancelled out; and because we don't know the characteristics of the *mode of possession* by which God has His properties, we can't fill in the part of the signification which is cancelled out.

So, the term "being caused by," while having all elements of its intention present which are necessary to distinguish "being caused by" from any other relation, *still* does not have present the positive elements (elements not made up of negations of finite modes) by which to distinguish the divine mode of being from the finite mode. And yet, even if these latter modal elements *were* present, the term would still be equivocal because the modal elements of "C" in (a) and "C" in (b) would be different.

(3) All natural knowledge of God consists basically in showing that certain relationships with possible worlds actually obtain between things that exist and God.

(4) These relation terms, which are thus analogous by proper proportionality with instances of the same terms in statements about the world, are then transferred into *names* of the other relatum, "God." This transference of relation terms into names follows the rule of Analogy of Attribution, since you can call a person by the names of his actions, because he is the cause of his actions. Thus we call a man who smokes, a "smoker," and a man who judges, Judge, and a man who designs, a "designer." And transforming the name of an effect to become a name of the cause is an instance of analogy of attribution. So, the entity X which has the relation "being mediate or immediate cause" of all other entities and events is called "First Cause."

(5) Next, utilizing the fact that secondary employments of terms analogous by attribution still tell us something about the subject, St. Thomas proceeds to determine what properties God would have to have if He is the Cause, the Judge, the Conserver, etc. Thus He arrives at properties like: intelligence, free will, simplicity, etc. But *these* terms can all be turned into "relation predicates" and shown to be analogous by proportionality with respect to ordinary language occurrences of the same terms—occurrences which are psychologically prior.

(6) Hence, all statements about God employ terms which are analogous by proper proportionality with respect to psychologically prior instances of the same terms in ordinary experience describing statements. Thus analogy of proper proportionality is the general form of language about God.

In a word, Aquinas supposes that there are two basic sets of statements made in discussing the existence and nature of God.

(A) The statements which assert that some relation "R" obtains between entities of a certain kind (the things of the world) and some entity not a member of that kind.

(B) The statements which employ cognate forms of the relation term "R" as common nouns or adjectives to either name or describe the entity. An example of (A) is: "Every thing which has really distinct properties is causally dependent upon some entity which does not have distinct properties; and there are some entities which have distinct properties." An example of (B) is: "There exists a First Cause." It is immediately obvious that statements of set (B) logically presuppose both the truth and meaningfulness of statements of set (A). How set (B) is derived from (A) is described in the next section (7). The relation terms that occur in sentences of set (A) are said to be analogous by proper proportionality with ordinary language occurrences of the same term, or suppose statements where terms are employed in a manner according to that analogy rule.

(7) Some statements about God employ terms which, in addition to be being used analogously by proportionality with respect to E-statements, are also used analogously by attribution with respect to other and logically prior G-statements. That is, the statement "The world is caused by God" is logically prior to "God is the First Cause." The statements which attribute common names to God employ predicates analogous by attribution with respect to instances of the same predicates occurring in statements asserting that certain relations obtain between the world and God. Thus, to say "God is the artificer, the designer, the Judge," etc., is to employ as a common name a term which by both logical and psychological priority is employed in a statement which says "The world is made, planned, and judged by God."

In summary, having ruled out univocal language about God, Aquinas claims that his analogy rules offer a way of taking ordinary language literally in orthodox claims about God. Furthermore, he claims that he cannot be accused of accepting an inadequate kind of language about God, for no other language is *possible* given the Christian assumption that God is transcendent and different in kind from all other things.

Perhaps the sense of the claim I made at the outset, but did not directly support, is now clearer: if one wishes to render philosophically plausible the claim of most orthodox Christians that their traditional descriptive statements about God are both literally meaningful and true, one must employ an analogy theory fundamentally similar to that of St. Thomas; and, I might add, the existence of such a theory as that of Aquinas, even with its substantial defects, renders quite plausible the belief of many Christians that their theological utterances are indeed literally meaningful. It seems that the whole question of whether or not explicit rules can be developed to give a criterion for the meaningfulness of religious statements must be re-opened and re-examined in the light of the substantial progress that can be made toward such rules with a properly understood and developed theory of analogy.

7

Augustinian Argument for Philosophical Dialogues

Introduction

The emphasis on the primacy of Augustine's theological interests receives further justification from another source. In the Retractiones, as is well known, Augustine went to considerable effort to review his principal writings and to make whatever necessary corrections were required both of his statements on doctrine and on philosophy. Yet in all the Retractiones the emendations on philosophical issues are proportionately few and occur primarily where the consequences of Platonism conflict with Christian belief. Even in the De Libero Arbitrio Augustine's main concern in the Retractiones is with the problem of grace. No mention or supplementation is made of the philosophical issues. Generally, then it would seem that the absorbing interests and demands of theology, the polemics of the day, and the burdensome and ever increasing administrative duties left Augustine with little of the enthusiasm and the time with which he once engaged in philosophical argument. Also, it may be observed that there is nothing in the Retractiones comparable to the De Principiis of Origen, no great philosophical synthesis summing up his concluding opinions.

Above all, the basic motivation for Augustine's apparent unconcern with a more systematic exposition of an argument for God's existence than that found in the De Libero Arbitrio may be attributed to his more absorbing conviction that the approach to the existence of God must proceed always from faith, that without faith we cannot have understanding. His own experience as revealed in the Confessions an experience that might be described as an existential argument shows that the existence of God is not so much a matter of reason but rather of faith. The God of faith exists in our memory, He is ever present to our intellect, He is the source of our love and our life, a Being experienced rather than achieved through reason. The accomplishment of reason is to establish God as a transcendental being for the better understanding of the world and the place of man. But the actuality of God is more a matter of the religious experience of the individual than a matter of dialectic. And God's existence is so evident in faith that it may be said that this has the effect of rendering the argument of the De Libero Arbitrio more of an explication of the existence of God than a demonstration. Some would contend that the argument proceeds too easily and even rather naively from the existence of truth to Truth itself. But for Augustine this is not a deficiency in the argument nor an unwarranted inference; rather it is because in his eyes the identification of truth with Truth itself as God is so self-evident as to need little more justification or argument. Persuasion is not merely a matter of logic. Augustine does not feel called upon to go beyond what to him becomes merely a simple intuition of the existence of God. An intuition that actually stems from his faith and is made more apparent to reason through that faith. In a somewhat analogous fashion in one of his sermons on faith, he observes that nature itself is a miracle that constantly exemplifies the work of God. But the very evidence of God in nature becomes apparent only with the attainment of faith.

Men wondered that our Lord God Jesus Christ filled so many thousands with five loaves; and yet they do not wonder that through a few grains the whole earth is filled with crops. When the water was made wine, men saw it, and were amazed; what else takes place with the rain along the roof of the vine? He did the one, He does the other; the one that thou mayest be fed, the other that thou mayest wonder.

Rather than a belief in God following demonstratively or inferentially from the evidence of nature, the evidence of God in nature becomes evident and a source of wonder and conviction to the individual who first possesses faith. This is perhaps the principal reason for the rejection by Augustine of any approach to God from the empirical evidence of the external world. Such evidence, he feels, cannot lead through reason to faith nor to a knowledge of God's existence. For faith is grace and comes from God. Hence just as God first loves us, so that we may love Him; just as He first chooses us, so that we may choose Him; so, He first knows us and extends the grace and illumination of His knowledge to us, so that we may know Him. For Augustine, there is strictly speaking no teleological argument for God's existence, since our understanding of nature as teleological is consequent upon our faith and explicated in the light of that faith. The *crede ut intelligas* pervades the whole ontology and epistemology of Augustine.

Finally, since it is peculiarly the function of reason to explicate faith, any argument for the existence of God needs merely to clarify or to make more explicit what we already accept upon faith. To Augustine the argument of the *De Libero Arbitrio* accomplished just that; hence he felt no urgency to develop a more thoroughly demonstrative argument. Also, with his primary interest in theology, it becomes Augustine's purpose to explicate not merely the existence of God, but to employ reason for the explication of all the truths that God has revealed and to establish these truths against unbelievers and for the edification of the faithful. The revealed truths of God are manifold whereas the revealed truth that God exists is but one truth. In this connection it is relevant to note the observation of Grabowski that Augustine is really much more concerned with the need to clarify the nature of God rather than to prove His existence.

In all his proofs for God's existence from reason, Augustine presupposes that the mind already knows from faith what is examined by reason. Moreover, the principal purpose for the using of reason in probing into the concept of God is to bring out the purity and the excellence of the divine attributes rather than to demonstrate the actual existence of the Supreme Being.

And in any consideration of the requirements of demonstrative arguments, it is well to keep in mind that Augustine was by profession a rhetorician and that it is the function of the rhetorician to persuade rather than to demonstrate. Aside from an early interest in philosophical dialogue, Augustine's principal literary vehicle was to be the sermon, the letter, and the theological treatise.

Turning now to the structure of the argument in the *De Libero Arbitrio* a brief summary of the demonstration may be outlined. In refutation of the sceptics, Augustine begins by establishing the possibility of knowledge, initiating a method that was to be followed more narrowly later by Descartes. Analyzing next the nature of knowledge, Augustine proceeds from a consideration of the knowledge attained by the senses and the function of such knowledge to a consideration of the function of the intellect and the kinds of truths it attains. Describing the essential characteristics of both mathematical and moral truths he points out that they possess the characteristics of being eternal, immutable and necessary. From this the inference is then drawn that that which is eternal, immutable and necessary cannot be regarded either as created by the mind of man or as existing innately within the mind of man. This entails that such truths are objective intelligible realities transcendent to or "above" the human mind. As such they are dependent upon God and in some sense may be identified with God Himself as eternal, necessary and immutable truth. In a word, the existence of such truths as immutable, necessary and eternal leads to the intuition that God exists as truth itself.

Well, then, if we could find something which you not only do not doubt to be, but also to be more excellent than our reason itself, will you hesitate to call that, whatever it is, God?

To which Evodius assents:

> *It does not please me to name God that to which my reason is inferior, but rather than which nothing is superior.*

Sciacca gives the following summary of the argument:

> *Nous pouvons désormais donner la formule précise de la preuve: L'être intelligent connaît des vérités nécessaires, immuables, absolues; l'être intelligent, contingent et fini, ne peut créer, ni recevoir des choses, par le moyen des sens, les vérités absolues dont il a l'intuition; la Vérité en soi, nécessaire, immuable, absolue, q'ui est Dieu, existe donc. Ou bien, sous une autre forme (qui est plus proprement augustinienne): il n'y a rien en l'homme ou dans le monde qui soit au-dessus de l'esprit: or l'esprit a l'intuition des vérités immuables et absolues, qui sont au-dessus de lui; la Vérité immuable, absolue et transcendante, qui est Dieu, existe donc.*

Boyer puts the argument more succinctly:

> *Ainsi le raisonnement fondamental de saint Augustin revient à ce syllogisme; S'il est quelque chose au-dessus de notre raison, Dieu existe. Or, il est quelque chose au-dessus de notre raison.*

Boyer contends that Augustine establishes the major premise on the basis of the existence of degrees of being in nature and the minor premise in the following manner:

> *La vérité possède une réalité positive. Or cette réalité est, dans sa forme pure, supérieure à notre raison. Il y a donc une réalite supérieure à not're raison.*

That truth has such a positive reality is evident from Augustine's discussion of the nature of intelligible reality as exemplified especially in the truths of ideas and numbers.

Granting the existence and the reality of such immutable, necessary, and eternal truths and the ability of the individual to grasp such truths, just what does the argument actually prove? Has the transition from such truths to God as Truth itself been effectively demonstrated? Actually, there seems to be a missing premise here, a premise which would enable us to argue from such truths as effects to God as a cause. The use of a causal principle suggests the Cartesian argument that there is an idea of God in the mind and that the mind then infers from this idea of God as an effect the necessity of positing God as an existing being and the cause of such an idea. But Augustine does not suggest the use of the causal principle in this way. Furthermore, this line of argument makes a presupposition which is alien to the Augustinian approach and which Augustine rejected several times, namely, that the mind possesses innate ideas. Augustine will argue that God is certainly present to the mind and to the memory of man, but always present as "above" man, as a being whose existence is intuited or discovered with the truths that are present to the mind of man.

Implicit in the structure of this argument and stemming in good part from his Platonic background, there appears to be a kind of analogical argument. Augustine argues that just as there are common objects of sense perception, so there are common and universal truths present to the minds of all men. So, too, God in whom all these truths subsist as a common source is present to all men and the means by which man obtains a knowledge of truth. The analogy appears to proceed from the common objects of sense to the common intelligible objects to the common transcendent and super-intelligible object which is God. Putting the analogical character of the argument in another way, just as there is an interior sense which exercises a kind of regulative function over the individual senses, so there are the rules of number and wisdom which exercise a regulative function over mathematical and ethical knowledge. And transcending all forms of knowing will be God who illuminates all minds and is Truth itself in comparison to these lesser truths and forms of knowledge. In an analogous sense God might be considered to exercise a regulative function over all knowledge.

The Thomistic emphasis on the cosmological type of argument has led some commentators to discover more in the emphasis on causality in the writings of Augustine than is warranted. To this has been added some confusion or misconception as to the actual approach that Augustine takes to God, so that his theodicy is given a Thomistic cast. Certainly, the notion of causality appears frequently in the Augustinian quest for God, but this need not imply any explicit formulation by Augustine of a cosmological argument. Boyer seems to think differently and contends that "Saint Augustin*a done ramené l'argument cosmologique à l'argument ideologique.*" Many passages from Augustine are cited in support of this thesis. In the *City of God*, for example, Augustine declares:

> *Sans parler de la voix des prophéties, le monde lui-même par sa mutabilité, par sa mobilité admirablement ordonnées, et par les formes très belles de tout le visible, proclame silencieusement, en quelque sort, et qu'il a été fait, et qu'il n'a pu être fait que par Dieu ineffablement et invisiblement grand, ineffablement et invisiblement beau.*

Other passages of a similar nature may be readily discovered in Augustine, but it seems incorrect to interpret them as substantiating a cosmological type of argument. In the first place, they are not arguments and they are not demonstrative. Portalié's quotations from the *Confessions* represent more the testimony of nature rather than an argument. Secondly, as in the passage from the *City of God*, they frequently follow from some explication of faith or are clearly subordinated to such an explication. Thirdly, to discover causation in nature is one thing and to use it as a logical argument is another. Actually, it would be more in order for Augustine to arrive at a principle such as the uniformity of nature, more as a consequent of his faith than as any induction from experience. Also, the knowledge of causes and effects in nature is in the nature of *ratio scientiae* and such truths lack the marks of eternality, immutability and necessity. Hence, there can be no inference from such truths to the truths of *ratio sapientiae* to which "belongs the intellectual apprehension of the eternal." For Augustine the empirical approach never leads to the highest wisdom nor even to the highest form of knowledge. The orientation of Augustinian thought is always from a more strictly rationalistic or idealistic position in which sense knowledge is subordinated to reason. It is a mistake, therefore, to impose the Thomistic approach to God's existence upon the

Augustinian analysis. Augustine discovers God as present to the mind of man, but does not argue by means of a *demonstratio quia* from the effects in nature to God as the cause of those effects. Rather Augustine sees all things as images and vestiges of God after he has discovered God within and present to himself.

Observe that this is a discovery of God rather than a demonstration of His existence. In this way Augustine avoids a criticism that has always been directed against the empirical arguments for God's existence, namely, that they presuppose more in the conclusion than was contained in the premises. To the contention of Gilson, who seems to be in accord with Boyer on this point, that "*L'itineraire normal d'une preuve augustinienne va donc du monde à l'ame et de l'ame à Dieu,*" we might reply that the normal itinerary of the Augustinian approach to God's existence is from the soul to God and from God's presence to the soul to his discovery in nature. For how can I recognize the existence of God in nature unless He' had first revealed Himself to me? The Augustinian approach or "way" to God is primarily then an explication of what has already been achieved through faith. The identification of the eternal and immutable truths which we discover present to the mind with God is made possible only after God has first revealed Himself to us through faith. Strictly speaking, then, there is no cosmological argument for Augustine, but only the knowledge that creation is an effect of God, that the rules we find in nature have their origin in the rules of the mind, rules given to the mind by God. The order is from God to creation, from the discovery of God as present to the mind of man to the knowledge that God has ordered nature.

Although such a discovery of God cannot be attained by some form of cosmological proof, this does not mean that God is wholly inaccessible to man. Rather, it might be said somewhat paradoxically, that we can best discover God by first realizing that such a discovery is not a matter of reason or scientific knowledge. We discover God by apprehending Him as the source of all truth, but discovery does not mean the comprehension of God. Such a quest for God means that you must return unto yourself. The dwelling place of truth is the inner man. And if you discover your own nature as subject to change, then go beyond that nature. But remember that, when you thus go beyond it, it is the reasoning soul which you go beyond. Press on, therefore, toward the source from which the light of reason itself is kindled.

God thus becomes an object of discovery to the inner man, whereas the world of nature presents the *vestigia* or traces of God in the universe known only indirectly to the mind of the believer but apprehended directly in their manifestations to sense. For God is the source by which all knowledge is illuminated. Note that the injunction "to go beyond the reasoning soul," seems to emphasize that the activity of reason is restricted to this world, but that a kind of intuition takes us beyond any inferential stages to the discovery of God. Perhaps we might say that in the argument of the *De Libero Arbitrio*, the sensible world of contingent beings is the occasion for an intuition of the eternal truths, just as the intuition of such eternal and immutable truths becomes the occasion for the intuition of God as truth itself.

Yet what is the more precise relation of such truths to God? To what extent are such truths identifiable with the nature of God? If they are distinct from God and merely transcendent in the Augustinian sense of being above the human mind, then apparently we have not actually attained God Himself but merely the highest possible image of Him. On the other hand, to insist upon the identification of such truths with God as truth itself or as being in some sense contained within the divine mind can lead rather easily to an ontologism. This is certainly a debatable point in the Augustinian philosophy and it is possible on the basis of Augustinian texts to make out equally good cases for and against such a position. The solution of this problem as well as the exact status of such intelligible realities as the eternal and immutable truths would entail a comprehensive analysis of the Augustinian theory of the divine illumination. Such an analysis, however, would not lead to a definitive demonstration for the existence of God. The result of the argument seems to be, then, that we have an intuition or a discovery of God as present to the human mind, a presence reflected in or perhaps occasioned by the immutable truths of numbers and morals that we are capable of grasping through the medium of the divine illumination.

On the other hand, it has been argued that there are the elements of an ontological argument present in the writings of Augustine. In the argument of the *De Libero Arbitrio* it would be rather difficult to draw out anything very explicit. And that which is superior to every animating principle, we call that God. And whoever conceives it is united to it: because that which one conceives is true, while that which one believes is not (for that reason) true. Thus that which is true, without being present to the senses or the intellect, that can be but an object of faith and not of sensation or intelligence. Thus, the being who conceives God is united to God. Thus the rational soul conceives God, because it conceives that which is immutable and does not change. But both soul and body admit of change; thus that which is immutable is evidently superior to that which is not, and nothing is superior to the rational soul except God. If then it conceives something immutable, it is that without any doubt that it conceives. And it is Truth itself; and because the rational soul unites itself by knowledge, and this is the good of the soul, it is just to admit that this is the sense of the words: "But it is good for me to adhere to my God."

Parts of this statement seem close to Anselm without being explicitly the Anselmian argument. What Anselm shows is that if we conceive God in a certain way as a being than which nothing greater can be conceived that such a conception of God leads necessarily to His existence. The most that Augustine seems to bring out is that to conceive God is to be united to Him and that we do conceive Him as immutable and also as he says elsewhere as necessary and eternal. What seems to be lacking in the Augustinian statement is the Anselmian contention that to conceive of such a necessary being logically implies the existence of such a Being. Augustine may have considered such a logical step but certainly did not take it. He is more cautious and content simply to say that to conceive of such a necessary and immutable being (Truth) unites us with God or enables us to intuit or discover God.

Given certain expressions and statements in the writings of Augustine that seem to anticipate an ontological argument, we may well ask why a man of Augustine's intellectual genius apparently did not see the logical inference that might take him from the conception of a being exceeding all others in our understanding to the actual existence of such a being. In part the answer lies in what has already been brought out, namely, that for Augustine the existence of God is discovered or intuited by the individual rather than demonstrated. In other words for Augustine any formal demonstration or proof of God's existence is unnecessary for God already exists and is present to the individual. This point may be further elaborated in the light of a remark made by Augustine in reply to a letter from Bishop Evodius. The latter had asserted among other things in his letter that "reason itself demonstrates that God exists or must necessarily exist." On this point Augustine comments:

> *If you will recall points which you know well, or, if I mistake not, you once did know well, although you may have forgotten them, which I wrote after conferring and discussing with you in my treatises either on the greatness of the soul or on free will, you will find therein the answers to your problems, without help from me;*

that is, of course, if you apply the labor of your mind to draw the conclusions from the points which are there made clear and definite. You also have some help in the book on religion; if you would review it and look into it, you would never think that reason can prove the necessity of God's existence, or that by reasoning it can be established that God must necessarily exist. In the science of numbers, which we certainly make use of in every day life, if we say seven plus three ought to be ten, we do not speak exactly. It is not: they ought to be ten they are ten.

The necessity of God's existence for Augustine is a necessity that characterizes His existence but in no sense determines it. It is a necessity similar to that which characterizes the eternal and immutable truths of morals and mathematics. Such truths possess necessity as one of their attributes but they do not exist in virtue of any necessary inferential warrant on our part. To say, then, that God must exist or necessarily exists is to confuse necessity as an aspect of the divine nature with necessity as a modal function. For Augustine any statement that God ought to exist or must exist would appear to place a certain determination upon God's existence. But God's existence is such that it must be completely free from all determinations.

Furthermore, to assert that God must exist raises some possibility of a doubt regarding His existence, for modal judgments lack the certitude of assertoric judgments. In the eyes of Augustine there is nothing more certain than God's existence. Consequently, His existence is just as evidently and immediately known as are the eternal and immutable truths present to our minds. In neither case is any necessary inference required for the truth of their existence. Furthermore, the certitude of our belief in God's existence is the result of the grace of God and not of any inferential warrant. We believe that God exists so that we may understand that He exists. We do not understand or require the necessity of God's existence in order that we may believe in His existence.

Hence, any so-called "proof" of God's existence in Augustine should be regarded more as an explication of what is already true in fact and known as such through faith. The proof for the existence of God might be said to do little more than to confirm what we already know; it is reason's way of strengthening the conviction of faith. Restricting the meaning of proof to its older connotation of "testing," we could say that the function of any proof for the existence of God is that of confirming that which we hold on faith and through authority. The reference in Augustine's letter to the *De vera religione* should be interpreted in this light rather than in the notion that there is any foreshadowing in this work of the proof offered in the *De Libero Arbitrio. As an apologetic treatise the De vera religione is more concerned with the evidences for the true religion and as such is more a confirmation of God's existence than a demonstration of His existence.*

The development, then, of any form of ontological argument to prove the necessity of God's existence would have seemed almost redundant to Augustine. For God clearly and already exists and is present to the mind of man. The sole function of any so-called rational demonstration is merely the explication and confirmation of what is already known by faith and experience. That God is Truth itself is reason's way of explicating God's presence to the soul.

Finally, it appears to me that a part of the persuasiveness of the argument of Augustine stems from the use of certitude in its various forms and the analogies that might be elicited here. The highest certitude is that of faith. The discovery of other certitudes might be said to support in a lesser degree the highest certitude which we already possess in faith, just as the uses of reason and the acquisition of knowledge might be said to explicate and to support the truths of faith. Better, perhaps, the kind of assent we give to the truths of reason points the way to a need for a higher certitude. For no matter how firm the assent of the mind to the truths of reason, the mind remains restless in its certitude. The truths of faith, on the other hand, yield the firmest assent because that assent is caused by the will. The lesser forms of certitude merely reflect that quiet certitude based upon an adherence to the Truth which is God. Just as all knowledge finds its source in the divine illumination, so all certitude finds its source in the ultimate certitude of faith. Without his Christian faith, we might hazard the guess that Augustine would probably have become an Academician.

Of the various forms of certitude, the most familiar is the one Augustine uses at the outset of his demonstration in the *De Libero Arbitrio* and which follows upon the attempt to doubt our existence. Here Augustine argues not merely that man knows himself as a thinking being, but as a living, feeling, sensing being. The certitude in this case is not merely an intellectual one, but rather what might be termed an existential certitude. Such a certitude is basic to the other forms that we have indicated, namely, the certitude found in the truths of mathematics and morals. Also, we should not overlook another form of intellectual certitude—those exemplified in the disjunctives that Augustine is so fond of using in the *Contra Academicos*. After noting that differences among philosophers do not preclude wisdom and truth he declares:

> *I hold it to be truly certain that there is only one world or that there are many worlds: if more than one that their number is either finite or infinite. Likewise, I know that this world where we are owes its order either to the nature of bodies or to some providence; that it has always existed and will always exist; or that it had a beginning and will never end; or that it had no beginning in time and will have an end; or that it had a beginning and will not last forever. And I have much knowledge of similar problems of physics, for these disjunctives are true, and no one can confuse them with any likenesses to falsity.*

Long familiarity with the Cartesian approach should not deceive us here. For such intellectual truths to Augustine lack the fundamental content of an existential certitude, and they are not inferential steps leading to a proof of God's existence. Even though Augustine does not explicitly say so, such truths would be mere empty tautologies having their source in the wider certitude that is linked to the whole existence of man and not simply to one faculty of his being. Furthermore, they are subordinated to the certitude of moral truths and these in turn lack meaning unless integrated with the spiritual structure of man's being. Moral truths would have as little content as the will would have direction unless ordered to the grace of God.

The assertion that all such truths are immutable, eternal and necessary involves again the difficulty of relating such truths to a finite subject. How can man, as a finite being, subject to time and change, actually know of truths that are beyond time and change, unless in some way he has a prior knowledge of the meaning of eternity, immutability and necessity? Clearly, there seems to be no empirical way of arriving at truths with these characteristics. And since Platonic reminiscence must be rejected, it would appear that any recognition of such truths must be consequent upon some form of intellectual grace, such as faith and the divine illumination.

Hence, just as the forms of certitude converge on the highest certitude and through it take on meaning, so the various rational approaches converge upon that which is given and understood through faith. This explains perhaps why a person may follow the reasoning in an argument for God's existence, although he has not the faith which would enable him to establish the identity of the end of reasoning with the beginning of faith. He may even accept a proof for God's existence, and yet remain unpersuaded. As Fr. Luijpen expresses it:

> *we observe that it is impossible for man ever to recognize the validity of the proof of God, if he has not previously recognized his existence in its religious dimension, i.e., as directedness to God. Of this directedness the proof that there is a God is only the learned expression. The proof presupposes one's religiousness. It does not produce this disposition, but on the contrary is produced by it.*

It has been outside our purpose to pursue all the possible inquiries involved in Augustine's quest for God. Our analysis has been limited primarily to the argument from truth. It must be evident, however, that the inadequacies and difficulties of the argument are more than adequately supplemented by Augustine's profound conviction through faith that God exists. Actually the Augustinian approach to God rests far more upon an existential argument for God's existence rather than upon the limited demonstration of the De Libero Arbitrio. In fact, the whole life and doctrine of Augustine is representative of an existential argument which moves from that troubled and restless existence of Augustine to the moral demand and need for a God who would give meaning to his existence. The philosophical explication of the conversion is the achievement of God as that transcendental being who makes Himself known to us by what He does to us. It can never be overlooked in any interpretation of Augustine that God exists as a moral necessity for man—that to attain God we must first become moral. As Augustine himself puts it:

> *Oh God, whom no one finds unless he is first purified. And: It is certainly perverse and preposterous to desire to see the truth so that you may purify your soul, which should rather be purified that you may see.*

To conclude, an existential necessity rather than a logical necessity leads us to God. The attainment of God is dependent on our necessity of being good and to be good depends on God. The paradox of moral action leads more determinately than any proof to the necessity of God's existence. In part this is evident even in the very argument of the De Libero Arbitrio where the moral truths occupy a higher position than the mathematical truths. For Descartes, the mathematician, the highest certitude lies in mathematics and upon the paradigm of such ideas he moves to God. For Augustine, and his insight is greater, man is fundamentally a moral being and it is through the demands of such a nature that man moves with the grace of God to the existence of that Being in whom we live and move and have our being. God is not a problem to be solved by logical argument or scientific discovery. He is a mystery to be apprehended through faith.

8

Ockham and Textbooks on Scholastic Philosophy

Introduction

The problem discussed is this. Are things impossible because God cannot make them, or is it rather that God cannot make them because they are impossible? In this question, the conjunction "because" is intended to express some priority of nature. Whether Henry of Ghent was the first to formulate this particular problem or not, at least his question and the solution he gave to it became the starting point for a similar discussion by at least three of the later scholastics, Duns Scotus, William Ockham, and Peter Aureoli. The last two have developed their doctrines independently of each other, but both Ockham and Aureoli first give Henry's position and then Scotus' before presenting their own.

1. Solution of Henry of Ghent

Briefly, Henry's answer to the problem is this. The possibility of creatures has its origin in the omnipotence of God;

impossibility on the contrary originates with creatures. Hence, creatures are possible because God can make them, whereas God cannot make what is self-contradictory because it is impossible. In other words, we must attribute omnipotence to God before we can attribute possibility to a creature. But with impossibility, it is just the other way around. We do not attribute impossibility to a creature, Henry tells us, because we have first attributed some impotency to God, for impotency is not something real or positive in God; it is a negation.

The guiding principle for Henry's solution to this problem is one which Ockham quotes quite literally: "*Si veto illud quod attribuitur Deo secundum rationem sui nominis significat aliquid quod non est dignitatis simpliciter, etsi tale Deo attribuitur, hoc non est secundum se et primo, sed quia aliquid attribuitur creaturae et ex respectu ejus ad Deum, illud Deo attribuitur.*" Whatever is not purely and simply a perfection (*aliquid dignitatis simpliciter*) is not attributed to God primarily or as such. To this category belongs, first of all, every so-called relative perfection, for instance, the notions of creator, or cause, etc. which imply relations to creatures. Secondly, all privations or negations are included, such as God's impotence with regard to the impossible.

But is not omnipotence itself a relative perfection? Does it not imply a relation to creatures? Here Henry introduces a distinction. God's omnipotence or active possibility, he tells us, can be considered in two ways: subjectively, or in relation to the subject in which it is found; objectively, or in reference to the object or term which can be produced. The same is true of passive possibility. It may be considered subjectively, or in reference to the creature which is said to be possible; again, it may be considered objectively, or in reference to the active potency which is capable of producing it in being. Though only a conceptual distinction exists between the objective and subjective phase of any given potentiality, be it active or passive, still this suffices to speak of an order existing between the various phases of active and passive potentiality.

In general, the subjective phase has a priority over its

corresponding objective phase. Furthermore, whatever is of positive perfection in a creature is derived from the perfection of God. Hence, says Henry, the following order obtains. If we consider God's power or omnipotence subjectively, i.e. in relation to himself, we find that it involves no imperfection but is a perfection pure and simple. Therefore, according to the Ghentian norm, it must be attributed to God *"secundum se et primo."* Secondly, the passive potentiality or possibility of the creature, subjectively considered, is derived somehow from God's omnipotence. Thirdly, this same passive potentiality can be considered objectively, or in relation to God, as the active power or source of its possibility. This relation to God is real. But because of this real relation of the creature to God, we must attribute a corresponding relation in God towards the creature. The latter, however, will not be a real relation, but merely a conceptual one. This latter relation is God's omnipotence in so far as it implies a reference to creatures.

It is in this way, then, that Henry saves his principle that all so-called relative perfections, like privations or negations, are not attributed to God primarily or as such but only secondarily. That is to say, the correlative perfection is primarily attributed to creatures; but because these same creatures bear a real relation to God, God is given a new name to express his relation to creatures. Thus God is called "Lord" because creatures exist which are his servants.

Hence, Henry's conclusion is that, absolutely speaking, active possibility or omnipotence is attributed to God prior to attributing possibility to creatures; whereas impossibility is first attributed to such fanciful creatures as the chimera or other "impossibles" before attributing any impotency to God in their regard.

But as both Scotus and Aureoli have noted, Henry apparently retracted this opinion some two years after he had first proposed it. [5] For in his 8th Quodlibet Henry asserts that not only are things possible because God can do them, but what is impossible is so because God cannot do it. In other words, both active possibility and impossibility are prior in God to any corresponding passive possibility or impossibility in creatures. As Henry himself puts it: "*Non est verum dicere de impossibili simpliciter, quod Deus non potest illud facere, quia non potest fieri, sed potius non potest fieri quia Deus non potest facere, sicut et in affirmativa non dicitur Deum possibile aliquid facere, quia illud possibile est fieri, sed econverso quia Deus potest illud facere, ideo possibile est fieri aut objective aut subjective.*"

Here we have the opinion commonly attributed to Ockham as we shall see more in detail later. The fact that Ockham quotes Henry against Henry in his first argument against the Ghentian's earlier opinion, might lead one who did not bother to read this question of Ockham through to the end to believe that the Venerable Inceptor subscribed to the same opinion. Though even here it is difficult to see how this misinterpretation could arise, for the argument is clearly *ad hominem.* The point he wishes to make is, not that we must attribute to God's omnipotence a priority over intrinsic possibility, but that the principle used by Henry to reach his first position is false, namely that every relative attribute is affirmed of God only because we have previously affirmed a correlative attribute of creatures. Henry, Ockham insists, has already abandoned this principle, for on the basis of his second position, Henry would have to say that the contrary is true, namely that such relative terms are ascribed to creatures because their correlative terms have already been ascribed to God. And in this connection Ockham does not contend, as is patently evident to anyone who reads on to the end of the question, that either one of two such correlative terms, as active power and passive possibility, has any priority over the other. On the contrary, the very fact that Henry ascribes the priority at one moment to God and at another to the creature merely accentuates the truth that these notions are genuine correlatives; neither can be defined independently of the others; neither has any antecedence over the other. Hence, to put it positively, we have as much right to say that things are possible or impossible because God can or cannot do them as we have to say that God can or cannot do things because they are possible or impossible respectively. Or to put it more correctly in a negative formulation as Ockham himself does in his own solution to the problem, we have no right to say that either proposition is true if the conjunction "because" is intended to indicate some kind of ontological priority.

2. Solution of Duns Scotus

Like Aureoli, Ockham, after citing and criticizing Henry's opinion, presents that of Scotus. The solution of John Duns to this question is based upon his conception of the "creatural deas" in the mind of God. Unlike St. Thomas or Henry of Ghent, Scotus does not admit that the relationship of imitability of the divine essence *ad extra* in some specific way is by nature prior to the formal conception of the creature as a thought object. That is to say, he does not believe that the divine intellect is determined objectively to form the distinct idea of a creature because it sees that the divine essence can be imitated in such and such a way. This conception gives the creature some kind of fundamental existence in the divine essence as a *relatio rationis* which is by nature prior to, and is the ontological reason for, the divine knowledge. Scotus argues at great length against this thesis. While it is not our intention to give his arguments in detail, we might note that his position is dictated by these dominant thoughts. We cannot speak of a relation of imitability without first bringing in the two terms of the relation which are the divine essence and the creatures. If we insist with Scotus *"quod relatio non naturaliter cognoscitur nisi cognito termino,"* then to say that God sees his essence as imitable is to say that he already has a clear knowledge of both his essence and the creature which are the two terms of the relation. And since the terms are by nature prior to the relation, we cannot assign to the relation of imitability in a specific way an ontological priority over the formal knowledge of the creature, as the opinion of St. Thomas and Henry would have us do. Furthermore, since the creatural term, either in itself or in something that is not formally the divine essence as such, is required as an ontological determinant of the *"quasi-passivus"* divine intellect, *"hoc videtur vilificare intellectum divinum, quia tunc esset passivus respectu aliorum objectorum cognitorum."*

Scotus' own escape from this difficulty was to fall back on an idea that has appeared in various forms throughout the history of Christian philosophy, namely the conception that the creatural ideas are to be regarded as quasi-termini of the "creative" activity of the intellect of God. They are not actually created, for that would be to give them real or actual existence. No, the meaning here is that the divine intellect, by knowing a creature, gives that creature an *esse objectivum* or *esse intelligibile* so that the creature may be said to exist as a thought object.

It is this doctrine that Scotus introduces into his solution of the question at hand. Various *instantia naturae* can be distinguished. In the first instance of nature, Scotus tells us, the creature is produced in intelligible *esse* by the divine intellect. In virtue of this we may speak of the creature as having a certain whatness or quiddity. Now, because this quiddity is what it is, that is to say, because it possesses just this and no other formal nature, it is compatible with real existence, and yet does not actually require it. Hence, Scotus tells us, in this second instance of nature, the creature possesses of itself *esse possibile* or possibility.

With regard to impossibility, Scotus notes that the so-called "impossible" is a figment (*figmentum*) which consists of two or more positive entities, each of which is possible in itself but is of such a nature that it cannot be combined with the others in the unity of a single being. In a word, the impossible is an attempt to combine two incompatible notions. The result, according to Scotus, is not a true notion, but a figment that possesses a unity in name only. If we ask then for the ultimate reason for the impossibility of such a "thing," we shall find it formally in the nature of the two or more elements we are seeking to combine. He tells us: "Just as God, by his intellect, produces a possible in *esse possibili*, so he produces two formally different beings in *esse possibili* and these things produced are in themselves formally incompatible to the extent that they cannot exist simultaneously as one thing nor can a third something be composed of them. But this incompatibility which they possess formally, they have of themselves and they have it in some way from that which produced them as from a principle. And the impossibility of the figment as a whole follows from this incompatibility of these elements which it includes. And from this impossibility of the figment in itself and from the incompatibility of its parts, results its impossibility in relation to some agent."

Hence, for Scotus both possibility and impossibility are due (*ex se*) to the formal nature of the thing in question, yet if we reduce this inner or intrinsic possibility to its first extrinsic principle, we must admit, according to him, that the possible depends (*principiative*) upon the intellect as upon a principle. Hence the classic Scotist formula, that things are possible "formaliter" of themselves, but depend "principiative" on the divine intellect.

Ockham's first counter-argument to Scotus gives the clue to his fundamental criticism. The fact that something is known does not permit the converse inference, therefore, as known, it is or exists. Or to put it another way, the mere fact that a thing is known does not give the thing in question a new "existence" or *esse intelligible* within the knower. All that the known object acquires by being known is a certain extrinsic denomination.

Ockham at one time admitted such a "fictum theory" in regard to the human intellect, but later he abandoned the theory that the content of the concept is a quasientity within the accidental reality or quality of the concept itself. Consequently, if Ockham will not admit of such an intelligible *esse* as a diminutive sort of entity midway between nothingness and actual existence, then it follows that he will deny any kind of production in regard to such an *esse intelligible*. Hence, he denies all such productivity to the divine intellect as well. Whence his conclusion: "*Ergo creatura in tali esse intelligibili non producitur.*"

This fits into the pattern of his general criticism of Scotus' attempt to explain God's knowledge of creatures. Perhaps no scholastic has attempted such an elaborate divine psychology as has Duns Scotus. His distinction between God's manner of knowing his own essence and that of creatures, or between God's knowledge of what is contingent and what is necessary, has led Scotus to break down God's mental life, as it were, into so many formalities or rationes and then reconstruct these formally or conceptually distinct elements to establish a certain "ordo naturae." But as Vignaux has aptly expressed it: "*Si l'on entend par psychologie une décomposition de la pensée et une mise en ordre de ses éléments, le nominalisme exclut toute psychologie divine.*"

Ockham has emphasized the divine simplicity to such an extent that he refuses to have anything to do with Scotus' "instantia naturae," as though God's knowledge of his own essence were somehow prior by nature to God's knowledge of creature's. "*Talia instantia non sunt ponenda et ita impossibile est dari primo aliquod instans in quo prius intelligatur essentia quam creatura.*" Nor is there any point in establishing an order within God's knowledge of creatures, for instance between his knowledge of their necessary acts or their free or contingent acts, between their past, present, or future.

This knowledge of God is given with his essence; it is not something produced. *"Ipsa cognitio creaturae est omnino incausabilis imo etiam omnino improducibilis."* Consequently, Ockham abandons any attempt to explain how God knows things, particularly future contingents.

From all this it follows that Ockham's conception of the divine creatural ideas will differ radically from that of either Scotus or St. Thomas. To discuss his position on this point fully would unduly prolong this essay. Still we must give a brief summary at least if we would understand his notion of the possible.

3. Ockham's Conception of the Divine Ideas

As Vignaux has noted, Ockham's position in regard to the ideas or intelligibles represents a return to that of Peter Lombard. The saints indeed loved to speak of the creature's existence in God as an idea or intelligible. The Master of the Sentences already cautioned his readers that this expression must be correctly understood. Ockham quotes this passage, adding his own approval: "*Ex hoc ergo sensu omnia dicuntur esse in Deo et omne quod factum est dicitur esse vita in ipso, non ideo quia Creator sit creatura, vel quia ista temporalia essentialiter sunt in Deo, sed quia in eius semper sunt scientia quae vita est. Ecce hic habetur expresse quod creaturae non sunt in Deo essentialiter, sed sunt in Deo sicut obiecta cognita, et quod ipsa non sunt vita in Deo sed quod scientia in qua fuerunt tamquam obiecta cognita est in Deo vita.*"

In question five, distinction thirty-five of the first book of the Sentences, Ockham puts this query: "*Utrum [Deus] intelligat omnia alia a se per ideas eorum*?" His answer to this question indicates the fundamental divergence of his conception of the divine ideas from that of Aquinas for instance.

The divine ideas are not the *rationes cognoscendi ipsas creaturas. A ratio cognoscendi* is a general term for anything that is somehow necessarily required for a knowledge of something. Thus it could be that which moves the intellect as an efficient cause to the act of knowledge, or it could be the act of knowledge by which something is known, or it could be that which receives the knowledge subjectively, as for instance the created intellect or soul in man as the recipient of the ideas or concepts, or, finally, it could be some other necessary condition required for the knowledge of the thing in question.

Now, all of these possibilities are excluded in regard to God. First of all, God's knowledge of creatures is as uncaused as his essence itself. Hence, the ideas of creatures cannot effectively cause this knowledge. Neither can the ideas be the knowledge itself God has of the creatures, for God's knowledge, like his essence, is one, indivisible, simple; the ideas are many. Neither can it be the third, because the divine essence or intellect is not recipient of its knowledge but is formally its knowledge. Finally, if the ideas were a condition for the divine knowledge, they would have to be either the divine essence itself, which is impossible because the essence is one and simple while the ideas are multiple and divisible, or they would have to be something really distinct from God or some *entia rationis*. But God's knowledge is conditioned neither by anything really distinct from himself nor by any *entia rationis*. Hence, the ideas cannot be the *rationes cognoscendi creaturas.* God has but one *ratio cognoscendi,* his infinitely perfect and simple essence.

Neither are the ideas posited as some kind of creatural likenesses which represent creatures to the divine intellect, for this view falls heir to some of the same difficulties as the above. "*Dico quod non sunt ideae ponendae tamquam similitudines repraesentantes intellectui divino ipsas creaturas, quia illae similitudines non possunt esse divina essentia cum illa sit omnino implurificabilis. Nec est quod sint entia rationis quia nullum tale requiritur, nec ad producendum nec ad cognoscendum [creaturas].*"

Basing himself on St. Augustine, Ockham insists that the divine ideas are posited primarily as exemplars, to which God as it were looks in producing the particular creature in question. And the reason for requiring such an exemplar is that God is not a blind creator, but *rationabiliter operans.*

If then we were to give a strict logical description of the divine idea, how would we delineate it? Viewed precisely, Ockham tells us, the "idea" is not a thing as such, that is to say it does not possess a "quid rei." It is a term or concept which we employ to signify something. It is not an absolute but a connotative or relative term. In other words, it does not signify something only directly or *in recto,* but it directly signifies one thing and in addition connotes *in obliquo* the thing signified plus something else. As such it may be described as follows: *"Idea est aliquid cognitum a principio effectivo intellectuali ad quod activum aspiciens potest aliquid in esse reali producere."*

The idea then is something which an intellectual or rational efficient cause knows and to which he looks in producing it in actual existence. Now, such a notion or description does not designate directly or *in recto* the divine essence as such, for the things are many, whereas the divine essence is one and simple. Neither does it apply to any relation this divine essence might have towards creatures. No such real relation exists, for it is commonly admitted that while creatures may bear a real relation to God, God does not have any real relation to anything distinct from himself. Nor is there any conceptual relation that could be designated by this term. Hence, the only thing to which this term directly applies is the creature itself. *"Dico quod ista descriptio non convenit ipsi divinae essentiae nec alicui respectui rationis, sed ipsimet creaturae."*

It is the creature itself which God knows. He knows each and every creature that ever will exist or ever could exist. He knows it perfectly. He knows it individually. He knows it from all eternity, before it ever comes into existence. And before he actually creates it, he knows it, and knows it as non-existent. This knowledge is in no way dependent on the reality of the creature, but it is something God possesses in virtue of his divine essence. Hence, the only explanation we can give for it, and this is not properly an explanation, is that God is God. "*Ex hoc ipso quod Deus est Deus cognoscit-omnia.*"

Hence, it is the *"creatura producibilis"* that is designated by the term "idea." Or as Ockham puts it in logical language: *"Idea importat ipsammet creaturam in recto et etiam ipsammet in obliquo, et praeter hoc importat ipsam divinam cognitionem vel cognoscentem in obliquo; et ideo de ipsammet creatura est praedicabilis ut ipsa sit idea; sed non est praedicabilis de agente cognoscente vel cognitione quia nec cognitio nec cognoscens est idea sicut nec exemplar."*

As with the *esse intelligibile,* so with the *idea.* These terms designate the creatura itself. They are extrinsic denominations given to the creature by the fact that it is known by God from all eternity. But this does not give the creature some kind of real existence in God as in a subject; all we can say of the creature is that it is an object of divine knowledge. This does not say that it exists in God as an object but only that God knows it, and that from all eternity. *"Sequitur quod ideae non sunt in Deo subjective et realiter, sed tantum sunt in ipso obiective tamquam quaedam cognita ab ipso, quia ideae sunt ipsaemet res a Deo producibiles."*

It is the notion of Scotus, which gives the creatural idea an *esse obiectivum* or *esse intelligibile* as the quasi-product of the poetical activity of God's intellect, that Ockham is attacking in his first counter-argument. The other arguments of Ockham against specific points of Scotus' doctrine do not interest us, with the exception perhaps of the fourth. His criticism here of Scotus' distinction between the first instance of nature, where the creature is produced in *esse intelligibile*, and the second instance of nature, where the creature is said to be possible, is again indicative of Ockham's refusal to elaborate a divine psychology.

4. Ockham's Solution to the Question

Having criticized both Henry and Duns Scotus, Ockham can present his own solution to the original question very briefly. Correlative terms, like cause and effect, or active and passive potentiality, belong to the class of reciprocals which Aristotle says "come into existence simultaneously." That is to say, they are such by nature that we cannot define the one without defining at the same time the other. Hence Ockham's conclusion: since omnipotence in God implies, as its correlative, that something can be made, and conversely, since something can be made implies that God can make it, it follows that we cannot attribute active possibility to God before we attribute passive possibility to the creature, or vice versa. Active potency and passive possibility are by nature simultaneous; neither can be said to be the cause or the ontological antecedent of the other. "*In omnibus relativis quae vocantur relativa secundum potentiam activam et passivam vel causam et effectum, semper correlativa sunt simul natura. Et ideo quia sunt simul natura et mutuo se inferant, neutrum est magis causa alterius quam econverso. Et ita universaliter quando est aliqua consequentia mutua, tenens praecise per naturam correlativorum non est una propositio magis causa alterius quam econverso. Et quando quaeritur an primo conveniat Deo non posse facere impossibile quam conveniat impossibili non posse fieri a Deo, dico quod non prius convenit Deo non posse facere impossibile quam convenit impossibili non posse fieri a Deo. Nec etiam prius competit impossibili non posse fieri quam Deo non posse facere impossibile.*"

Ockham's answer to the question is clear. If we ask: Are things possible because God can create them, or can God create them because they are possible? Ockham replies that neither proposition is true if by "because" we understand some priority of nature. In short, it is a meaningless question.

II. OCKHAM OF THE TEXTBOOKS

If we compare Ockham's position as revealed in the text with that attributed to him by our neo-scholastic textbooks, we discover quite a contrast. In twelve of the thirteen textbooks we have examined, Ockham is presented as the defendant of the thesis that the internal possibility of a created being depends on the divine power. Thus, for instance in a recent edition of Hickey, we read: "*Occam et nonnulli alii intrinsecam rerum possibilitatem a divina potentia pendere autumarunt, ita ut res esse possibiles dixerint quia Deus potest eas producere.*"

Theoretically, Ockham's position is distinguished from that attributed to Descartes (rightly or wrongly, we do not wish to say), namely that the internal possibility depends on the free will of God in the sense that God could arbitrarily make what is possible–impossible and vice versa. Practically, however, the average student is left with the impression that there is but little difference between the two. This is brought out, for instance, by the following quotation: "Some philosophers, among them William of Ockham, defended the doctrine that intrinsic possibility depends ultimately on God's power. Why would things be intrinsically possible, i.e., why are their constitutive elements compatible and non-contradictory? Because God's omnipotence can produce them. And why are other things intrinsically impossible, i.e., why are their elements incompatible and contradictory? The only answer can be, because God's omnipotence cannot produce them. The ultimate ground for intrinsic impossibility would thus be the lack of power in God. If God had more power, the impossibles would also be intrinsically possible. But that, is patently false. God possesses power in an infinite degree; therefore, no things should be intrinsically impossible, if it were merely a question of God's power. In that case it should be within God's power to produce a being which is finite and infinite at the same time, which exists and does not exist at the same time, which is rational and irrational at the same time, which is living and dead at the same time. But to make an assertion like this, means to invalidate the Principle of Contradiction and that means to destroy the foundation of all being and knowledge; skepticism must follow such a view."

We have chosen this textbook for three reasons. First, it is a work that is enjoying a very great deal of popularity at the present time in Catholic colleges and universities of the United States, and some seminary professors have even suggested that it be translated into Latin for use in our seminaries. Secondly, it gives a fair summary of the arguments generally used by the other texts we have examined. Thirdly, it does what most of the other textbooks do not do; it gives the exact reference to the passage in Ockham where we are supposed to discover this doctrine, namely in the text we have analyzed and printed in full at the rear of this article. But when we turn to this text of Ockham, what do we find?

First of all, we discover the surprising fact that Ockham does not even discuss the problem of the source or priority of intrinsic possibility in this question. This becomes quite clear if we analyze what is meant by "intrinsic possibility." As Father Bittle is kind enough to explain to his readers, it consists in the compatibility or non-contradictory character of a thing's essential notes. In other words, it is what St. Thomas calls the absolute possibility of a thing, in contradistinction to relative possibility, which is commonly referred to as extrinsic possibility, i.e. the relationship a thing bears to that which can produce it. In some ways, this term "absolute possibility" is more exact, because "possible" as opposed to the "impossible" (i.e. what consists of self-contradictory or incompatible notions), as Aristotle tells us, involves no reference to an active power or potency.

Ockham, however, is clearly not speaking of absolute, but of relative possibility. This is evident from his own solution. He speaks of those relative notions *"quae vocantur relativa secundum potentiam activam et passivam,"* a clear reference to the second class of relative terms according to Aristotle's division. In fact even the example used by Ockham is borrowed from the Stagirite. Such notions, Ockham tells us, are correlatives according to Aristotle and as such are *"simul natura et mutuo se inferant."* Ockham goes further and explicitly refers us to Aristotle's discussion on the simultaneity of such correlative notions.

Further proof, if such were needed, that Ockham is not considering intrinsic or absolute possibility but extrinsic possibility is that he uses the term "factibile" rather than "'possibile" in discussing the problem of priority. In addition, if we read the text of his own solution carefully, do we not discover him making a distinction between what our neo-scholastics would call intrinsic possibility or impossibility and that which is extrinsic? Thus he writes: "*Et quando quacritur an primo conveniat Dco non possc facere impossibile quam conveniat impossibili non posse fieri a Deo, etc.*" The "impossibile" is regarded as the subject to which is attributed "*non posse fieri a Deo.*" But what is the "impossible" if not that which is intrinsically impossible, and the "*non posse fieri a Deo*" but the relative aspect we call extrinsic possibility? Now, the whole problem of priority or non-priority is discussed with regard to this relative aspect. And the same is true of the possible. "*Et eodem modo dico de affirmativis, quod non prius convenit Deo posse facere possibile vel creaturam quam creaturae posse fieri a Deo.*"

A second point generally made by the authors of our textbooks is that intrinsic possibility according to Ockham depends on the divine omnipotence as on its cause or ontological antecedent. Now, even if we ignore the failure to distinguish between intrinsic and extrinsic possibility and assume for the benefit of our neoscholastic authors that Ockham is speaking of the former instead of the latter, we still fail to see how they concluded that for him things are possible because God can cause them. It was Henry of Ghent, not Ockham, who espoused this theory. And in his second formulation, the Ghentian even went so far as to add that things are impossible because God cannot make them.

Could it be perhaps that someone read this text so hurriedly that he attributed Henry's opinion to Ockham?

Such a hypothesis hardly seems possible in view of Ockham's clear statement that absolutely no priority of nature exists between such correlative notions. They are "*simul natura . . . secundum Philosophum . . . Et ideo quia sun't simul natura et mutuo se inferant, neutrum est magis causa alterius quam econverso.*"

Another, and perhaps more plausible source of the error, is the assumption that the later authors instead of reading Ockham simply copied from the earlier writers without fully comprehending their various nuances of meaning. For in general, as we noted in the beginning, the older works contain less errors than the later ones. Liberatore, for instance, does not explicitly accuse Ockham of teaching that internal possibility depends on the omnipotence of God, but states simply that the Ven. Inceptor banishes internal possibility and leaves only external possibility. Urraburu, among the older authors, likewise does not specify which possibility depends on the omnipotence of God, but states simply that all possibility is to be traced back to this source according to a view "attributed" to Ockham. Schiffini, in explaining this "dependence," suggests two alternatives, namely: first, that the very possible is an effect of the divine power; and second, that the possible is called such in reference to the divine power. This last alternative would be closer to Ockham's opinion in the sense that correlatives mutually imply one another and, hence, cannot be defined independently of each other. But even such a statement is misleading on two counts: first, it does not restrict such a description to the extrinsic possibility or to what Ockham would call the "factibile"; second, it does not indicate that the converse statement is equally true, namely that the divine power is called omnipotence in reference to the possible.

But what interests us in Schiffini's statement is that he does make a distinction between what is (*esse*) and what is called (*dici*). Later works (e.g. Donat and Frick) simply combine the two. Donat tells us for instance that, according to Ockham, "*hoc solo, quod Deus aliquid facere possit, id dici et esse possibile.*" Still later works drop the *dici* entirely, as for instance, Coffey, Farges, and Bittle. It is this progressive misrepresentation that leads one to believe that later authors depended on the earlier for their interpretation of Ockham and made, no attempt to read the original text to which some at least referred their readers.

OCKHAM AND INTRINSIC POSSIBILITY

So far our analysis has been more or less negative. That is, we have shown that Ockham is not treating the problem of intrinsic possibility primarily. But the reader may ask: "What is Ockham's positive position? What does he hold regarding the source of intrinsic possibility?"

In answering this question, a few things should be borne in mind. First of all, as we noted before, St. Thomas prefers to use the term "absolutely possible" instead of intrinsically possible. In fact, as far as we can determine, Aquinas never seems to employ the terminology of "intrinsic" and "extrinsic" with regard to possibility. The closest he comes to "intrinsic" is to refer to the "absolute possibile" as that which is possible "secundum seipsum." In using this terminology, St. Thomas is following Aristotle, as he explicitly tells us.

Now, if we read Aristotle and St. Thomas, we discover a difference between their treatment of intrinsic possibility and that of the neo-scholastics. This difference, though slight, is not without significance. Where the neo-scholastics speak of the intrinsic possibility of a thing as a compatibility or lack of contradiction in its essential notes, St. Thomas and Aristotle speak of "absolute possibility" (or impossibility) only in connection with propositions. Thus Aquinas says: "*Dicitur autem aliquid possibile vel impossibile absolute, ex habitudine terminorum; possibile quidem quia praedicatum non repugnat subiecto, ut Socratem sedere; impossibile vero absolute quia praedicatum repugnat subiecto, ut hominem esse asinum.*"

This is not to imply that we cannot combine the subject and predicate of the proposition in a single concept, for the scholastics generally agree that where the elements combined do not mutually contradict each other they can be grasped by a simple act of apprehension. But the point we wish to make is that possibility and impossibility in this case are basically modalities of propositions about a given subject. Consequently, when we ask for the ontologic source of such a possibility, we should keep in mind that, formally speaking, we are inquiring after the source of a logical entity and not a real quality or perfection which inheres in the thing as such.

Secondly, we note that this intrinsic possibility or impossibility can be said to pertain to things of themselves. Thus St. Thomas says: "*Sciendum est ergo quod impossibile quod dicitur secundum nullam potentiam, sed secundum seipsum, dicitur ratione discohaerentiae terminorum.*"

Finally, we note that St. Thomas uses this notion of the "absolute possibile" to define God's omnipotence. In the *Summa Theologica*, for instance, he writes: "*Si quis recte consideret, cum potentia dicatur ad possibilia, cum Deus omnia posse dicitur, nihil rectius intelligitur quam quod possit omnia possibilia, et ob hoc omnipotens dicatur. Possibile autem dicitur dupliciter, secundum Philosophum in V Metaph. Uno modo per respectum ad aliquam potentiam; sicut quod subditur humanae potentiae, dicitur esse possibile homini. Non autem potest dici quod Deus dicatur omnipotens quia possit omnia quae sunt possibilia naturae creatae, quia divina potentia in plura extenditur. Si autem dicatur quod Deus sit omnipotens, quia potest omnia quae sunt possibilia suae potentiae, erit circulatio in manifestatione omnipotentiae; hoc enim non erit aliud quam dicere quod Deus est omnipotens, quia potest omnia quae potest. Relinquitur igitur quod Deus dicatur omnipotens, quia potest omnia possibilia absolute, quod est alter modus dicendi possibile. Dicitur autem aliquid possibile vel impossibile absolute, ex habitudine terminorum; possibile quidem, quia praedicatum non repugnat subiecto, ut Socratem sedere; impossibile vero absolute quia praedicatum repugnat subiecto, ut hominem esse asinum.*"

If we read Ockham, we find substantially the same position as that of St. Thomas. In answer to the objection that "esse possibile" is something that a creature has received from God, Ockham reminds his objector that possibility is not a real something which inheres in a creature. "To be possible" is something predicable of a creature; it is a logical modality that has been elevated to the status of a predicate. Hence we would be speaking more exactly if we said that a creature is possible not because "esse possibile" pertains to it, but because it can exist in the world of reality. "*Nec est proprius modus loquendi dicere quod esse possibile convenit creaturae, sed magis proprie debet dici quod creatura est possibilis non propter aliquid quod sibi conveniat sed quia potest esse in rerum natura.*"

While everything real which a creature has must be attributed to God as to a principle, this is not true of such logical entities as are predicated about them. Only in the sense that the rational creature, who formulates such propositions as "man is possible" or "it is impossible that man be a donkey," owes its total being, both substantial and accidental, to God as to a first principle, can we say that such predications are from God. "*Dicendum quod quidquid creatura habet reale tamquam aliquid sibi inhaerens, habet a Deo tamquam a principio; sed non quidquid convenit sibi in praedicatione habet principiative a Deo nisi illo modo quo Deus habet tales praedicationes a Deo, quia tales praedicationes quando sunt in actu et realiter, tunc sunt a Deo.*"

Properly speaking then, this absolute or intrinsic possibility is not something that a creature has by reason of some relation to an active potency in God. It is something which the creature has of itself. "*Et ideo esse possibile convenit creaturae ex se non realiter tamquam aliquid sibi inhaerens, sed vere est possibile ex se sicut homo ex se est non asinus.*" Not indeed that this "esse possibile" is something real pertaining to the creature, but in the sense that the creature can be. As Ockham put it in the quotation cited above: "*Nec est proprius modus loquendi dicere quod esse possibile convenit creaturae, sed magis proprie debet dici quod creatura est possibilis non propter aliquid quod sibi conveniat, sed quia potest esse in rerum natura.*"

Finally, Ockham, like St. Thomas, recognizes that to define omnipotence by the "factibilia" and the "factibilia" by omnipotence is a circle that explains nothing. Hence, he too defines the omnipotence of God in terms of what does not involve a manifest contradiction. "*Credo in Deum Patrem omnipotentem, quem sic intelligo, quod quodlibet est divinae potentiae attribuendum quod non includit manifestam contradictionem.*"

To conclude, we must confess that we find Ockham's notion of so-called intrinsic possibility in substantial conformity with St. Thomas' express statements on this point. Both are good Aristotelians.

But what of the ultimate origin of this intrinsic possibility? What of the formulation adopted by Thomists and found in our contemporary textbooks? "Possibilia fundantur in essentia *divina; sed constituuntur formaliter in ordine ideali per intellectum divinum,*" as one Thomist puts it.

Here we must confess that though we have read much in St. Thomas, we have been unable to discover any explicit text where he attempts to reduce "absolute possibility," as he calls it, formally to the divine intellect and fundamentally to the divine essence. In St. Thomas' own discussions, "absolute possibility" is treated as its name implies, namely as a logical entity, as something to be found formally in a proposition and not in God. Even when pressed to explain how the world was possible before its actual creation, he does not reduce its intrinsic possibility to something in God. Only on the ground of extrinsic possibility can we relate it to God. "*Dicendum quod antequam mundus esset, possibile erat mundum fieri, non quidem aliqua potentia passiva, sed solum per potentiam activam. Vel potest dici, quod fuit possibile non per aliquam potentiam, sed quia termini non sunt invicem discohaerentes, huiusmodi scilicet propositionis: 'Mundus est.' Sic enim dicitur esse aliquid possibile secundum nullam potentiam ut patet per Philosophum in 5 Metaph.*"

It is true that God knows all creatures from the beginning of the world and consequently prior to their actual creation. Hence, God knows what is possible and that from all eternity. But St. Thomas does not say that this knowledge formally constitutes the possible as possible; neither does he say that the divine essence, as imitable ad extra, is to be regarded as the ontologic foundation for the possible. What Thomists have done, rightly or wrongly, is to connect St. Thomas' teaching on the creatural ideas with the notion of intrinsic or absolute possibility. Now it was Scotus, not St. Thomas, who connected these two notions explicitly. And it was Scotus who gave to the possible sort of "existence" in God an "esse intelligibile" as we have seen. Is the present "Thomistic" tcaching on the origin of possibles another instance of the influence of Scotism on the doctrine of St. Thomas?

With Ockham, however, there is no possibility of tying up the teaching of the origin of the "divine ideas" with the absolute possible, for the "ideas" are not something found in God properly speaking. They are the creatures themselves and not the divine essence. They are objects of God's eternal knowledge, but this does not give them any "existence" in God. They are not the *ratio cognoscendi creaturas*, as they are for St. Thomas.

But in concluding, we might point out that if intrinsic possibility is a logical entity, we can say of the "possible" that, like the "idea," it is a connotative term which *in recto* signifies 'the creature itself and *in obliquo* connotes this same creature ash the subject of the predication "potest esse." If we ask, where is this fact that a given creature, say Peter, is possible, first recognized, Ockham would unhesitatingly answer: In God! For God knows every possible creature from all eternity. He knows it by an intuitive knowledge before he ever creates it. Furthermore, he tells us that only what is incapable of existing in the world of reality is not an object of this intuitive eternal knowledge. As he puts it: "*Dico quod contradictio est quod visio sit et quod illud quod videtur non sit in effectu, nec esse possit. Ideo contradictio est quod chimaera videatur intuitive; sed non est contradictio quod id quod videtur nihil sit in actu extra animam dummodo possit esse in effectu vel aliquando fuit in rerum natura. Sic est in proposito. Unde Deus vidit ab aeterno omnes res factibiles et tamen tunc nihil fuerunt.*"

In other words, anything that our modern neo-scholastics call intrinsically possible, i.e. anything whose being is such that it would imply no contradiction if it existed, is seen by God from all eternity as possible. This knowledge of God is absolutely one with his essence; hence, if we ask, why is it that God has this knowledge of the possibles? Ockham would answer: Because God is God. "*Ex hoc ipso quod Deus est Deus, cognoscit omnia.*"

9

Nicholas of Autrecourt to Bernard of Arezzo for Philosophy

Introduction

Nicholas of Autrecourt wrote nine letters to Bernard of Arezzo and one to a certain Egidius in a controversy concerning our alleged knowledge of causes and substances. The first two of these letters are extant in their complete form, and the letter to Egidius exists in an almost complete form.

First I shall make a few observations about Nicholas's thought which will aid in an understanding of my attempted reconstruction. In the first and second letters to Bernard of Arezzo, Nicholas laid it down that the sole sources of certitude are the immediate data of consciousness and the law of non-contradiction. Every logically necessitated inference must be guaranteed by the law of non-contradiction, and every certain conclusion must be deduced from principles firmly and exclusively based on evidence which only the immediate data of consciousness can supply. Since the conclusion of a logically necessitated inference must be identical with its premises or with part of what its premises signify (otherwise such an inference would not be formally certifiable by the law of non-contradiction), it is impossible to obtain existential knowledge in a conclusion which has not already been asserted in the premises. From this the following fundamental proposition is obtained: from the fact that one thing is known to exist or known not to exist it cannot be logically inferred that something else exists or does not exist. This being so, inference is powerless to provide any existential knowledge of causes or substances. Nor is this all. Not only are experience and logical inference unable to provide the knowledge that there are or are not causes or substances, but also not even the possibility of such connections or entities can be discerned in experience or obtained by logical inference.

The logical foundation of Nicholas's critique of Scholastic epistemology is simply his formulation of a strict conception of certitude. Historically, however, this critique appears to have arisen from theological discussions concerning the power of God. The fact that God was held to be absolutely omnipotent led to an important distinction between the *absolute* and the *ordinated* power of God. In virtue of His absolute power, God can do anything that does not involve a contradiction. Thus He can cause human beings to have experiences of objects which do not exist outside the mind. He can interrupt the general course of nature and so change ordinary causal routines. He can produce or conserve sensible accidents without their proper substrata, and all other things of this sort. If the existence of sensible data implied the existence of external objects, or if the existence of something alleged to be a cause necessarily entailed the existence of other things alleged to be its effects, it would be logically impossible for omnipotence to produce an intuition without its external cause or any so-called cause without its effect. But since it is plainly not a contradiction that one thing exists and that another and different thing does not exist, it is within God's absolute power to produce the one without the other. The *ordinated* power of God is subject to further restriction. Since God has made certain decisions about the construction of the universe and the general course of history, it would be a contradiction to say that He will not act in accordance with His own decisions. Our knowledge of such decisions, however, comes principally from revelation.

So far as natural knowledge is concerned, we are unable to know for certain either the general order of the world or the particular facts of a given occasion. It is useless to argue that, assuming that no miracle is taking place, the existence of one thing logically implies that of another. Thus we cannot logically infer that the object of our cognition implies the existence of something external to the mind if no miracle is taking place. Such an inference is open to two objections, either of which is fatal: we cannot *know* whether a miracle is taking place on a given occasion, and we do not *know* (aside from the consideration of miracles) that there is any connection between the object of cognition and anything else whatever. Such knowledge would be vouchsafed to us only if the law of non-contradiction manifestly guaranteed an inference from one thing to another, and no inference of this kind can be guaranteed in this way.

Nicholas seems to have employed two kinds of argument in his critique of the alleged knowledge of causes and substances. With regard to causes he argued (1) that they are not experientially discernible, and (2) that they are not apodictically demonstrable. (1) Experience and logical deduction are the sole sources of certitude. Therefore, if we had knowledge that a cause exists it would come from experience or from logical deduction. But it cannot come from experience, because experience of an object is either (a) exclusively of that object or (b) of that object with another object. If (a), it is impossible that the simple experience of one object could reveal more than precisely that object, so that whether that object is a cause or an effect of something else cannot be determined by the experience in question. If (b), we have the experience of at least two objects, but, since nothing but their conjunction is given, nothing in the nature of causal efficacy can be discerned. (2) It follows that if causes are knowable, they must be deducible from experience rather than immediately discerned. But as the premises of a certain conclusion must themselves be certain, the premises of a causal inference must be either propositions exclusively about experience or principles known *ex terminis*. We have already seen that experiential propositions cannot provide indubitable information about causes. Therefore, principles known *ex terminis* remain as the sole possibility. The question now arises whether the terms of such propositions have been defined nominally or whether they have a real definition. For example, if we define an agent as anything which acts on something else when it is brought into appropriate relation with that something else, it will follow from the premises "x is an agent and is brought into appropriate relations with y" that "y is affected." But whether x *is* an agent or is merely *called* an agent is not decided by such an inference. The fact that experience is noncommittal with regard to causes makes it impossible for logical inference to yield any causal information.

His argument against the alleged knowledge of substances is similar to the argument against causal knowledge. We cannot intuit substances because that which partially or wholly transcends the content of experience cannot be grasped in and through experience. We cannot deduce their existence from experience unless we apply to the items of experience nominal definitions whose appropriateness to those items must always remain an open question. If probable inference is based solely on experience, there is not even a probability that substances exist. For, if the premises of a probable inference are confined to the conjunctions observed in experience, no substance can be said probably to exist because no substance can be a member of a conjunction manifested in experience.

No one who has read these arguments can fail to notice that they anticipate Hume's negative critique even to the details of Hume's dialectic. There are also noticeable affinities between the philosophy of Nicholas and those of Leibniz and Kant. Yet, however interesting these parallels may be, I have found no conclusive evidence of any direct connection between Nicholas and the immediate predecessors or contemporaries of Leibniz and Hume. And since there are many differences between fourteenth century thought and the intellectual climate of modern opinion, it is best not to repose too much confidence in any analogies of this sort. This much will suffice for an introduction.

Lappe, Gilson and Vignaux have attempted to reconstruct the Fifth Letter of Nicholas to Bernard but without much success. As more fragments of this lost letter remain than of any of the other lost letters, the chances of its reconstruction are correspondingly greater, but the nature of the fragments makes any simple scheme of interpretation seemingly impossible.

As given in the so-called Articles of Cardinal Curty, the fragments of Letter Five are as follows (the numbering and grouping are my own. Their purpose will be presently explained):

I, 1 . . . haec con [sequentia non est evidens evi]dentia deducta ex primo principio: ignis est approx[imatus stupae et nullum e]st impedimentum: ergo stupa comburetur.

I, 2 . . . nescimus evidenter, quod ali[a a deo possint] esse causa alicuius effectus.

I, 3 . . . nescimus evidenter, quod aliqua causa causet efficienter quae non sit deus.

I, 4 . . . nescimus evidenter, quod aliqua causa efficiens naturalis sit vel esse possit.

I, 5 . . . nescimus evidenter, utrum aliquis effectus sit vel esse possit naturaliter productus.

I, 6 . . . quibuscumque acceptis, quae possunt esse causa alicuius effectus, nescimus evidenter quod ad positionem eorum sequatur effectus positio.

II, 1 . . . nescimus evidenter, quod in aliqua productione concurrat subjectum.

III, 1 . . . nulla potest esse simpliciter demonstratio, qua existentia causarum demonstretur existentia effectus.

III, 2 . . . non est nobis evidenter notum, quod possit esse aliqua demonstratio a priori differenti realiter.

IV, 1 . . . non potest evidenter ostendi nobilitas unius rei super aliam.

IV, 2 . . . quacunque re demonstrata nullus scit evidenter qui[n excedat no]bilitate omnes alias.

IV, 3 . . . [quacun]que re demonstrata nullus scit evidenter, quin ipsa sit d[eus, si per deum in]telligamus ens nobilissimum.

IV, 4 . . . aliquis nescit evidenter, quod una res sit finis a[lterius].

IV, 5 . . . [nu]llus scit evidenter qualibet re ostensa, quin sibi debea[t impendere maximum ho]norem.

IV, 6 . . . aliquis nescit evidenter, quin ista possit rationabiliter conce[di: si ali]qua res est producta, deus est productus.

The notice of John of Mirecourt on Nicholas's philosophy makes it plain that a theological principle is presupposed in fragments I, 1-6. God being the omnipotent Father. He can accomplish anything which does not involve a manifest contradiction. Hence, whatever God does with the cooperation of second causes He can accomplish without that cooperation. Because neither deductive inference nor direct experience can afford evident knowledge of the action of second causes, natural reason can find no impossibility in the supposition that God is the sole and immediate cause of everything. Moreover, reason and experience cannot discern causes or causal connections. This satisfactorily explains the import of, I, 1-6.

Since God preserves the species of bread and wine after the consecration of the Host has deprived these species of their proper and natural substrata, it follows that He can always separate accidents from substances and preserve the accidents supernaturally. The existence of a substratum cannot therefore be logically inferred from the perceived generation of accidents. It is possible that Nicholas at this point of the letter also repeated the argument that substances cannot be directly perceived. This explains the import of II, 1.

III, 1 and 2 may be easily understood in terms of the second letter to Bernard in which it is explained that because, in every logically necessary implication, the consequent must be identical with part or all of the antecedent, no logical inference is possible from the existence of one thing to the existence of another. Hence, causes cannot be inferred from effects nor effects from causes. This argument is intended to discredit both *demonstratio quia* and *demonstratio propter quid*, and so in a sense constitutes a criticism of any alleged cognition of the existence or nature of formal causes. Thus I, II, and III are criticisms respectively of our alleged knowledge of efficient, material, and formal causes.

It will be observed that thus far the argument of this letter has two aspects. The logic of the argument, it is true, does not require the theological context in which it is stated. The rhetorical advantage of such a context is plain, and it would be impossible to reconstruct this letter without keeping that context constantly in mind. Moreover, while there is reason to believe that Nicholas doubted that natural reason could have any knowledge even of divine causality, it was natural for him to put his philosophical argument in theological terms.

The IVth part of the letter, however, is difficult to reconstruct for several reasons:

(1) The theological premise of the argument ought to be the same as that of the earlier parts. It is not plain that this is the case.

(2) It is difficult to see how IV, 2-5 prove or elucidate IV, 1. Why is it the case that anything you may point out may be the noblest being? No reason is suggested in the fragments themselves, nor in the logic of the argument, nor even in the theological context as given thus far.

(3) Fragment IV, 6 seems almost meaningless in the context, and Vignaux remarks "*nous preferons abandonner la proposition au jeu des conjectures.*" Any tenable interpretation, however, must take account of this fragment.

I suggest that the fourth part of the letter can be given perfectly good sense in the light of a theological question which was much agitated in Nicholas's time. The advantage of my interpretation is that it not only takes account of all the fragments, but also allows that the theological principle underlying this part is, just as in the case of the earlier parts of the letter, the absolute power of God.

In the thirteenth and fourteenth centuries the problem of the Incarnation was much discussed. One of the questions, to put it briefly, was how Christ could be both God and man.

In discussions of this question by Ockham, Mitecourt and others it was pointed out that, in virtue of His absolute power, God could have united Himself with any finite being whatsoever had He chosen to do so. Hence, He could have assumed the form of a stone or of any animate creature. The fact that He elected to become man is known to us by revelation, but for natural reason there is nothing absurd in the proposition that God becomes a stone, a plant, or an animal.

In my judgment, this theological problem figured in Nicholas's argument that the nobility or perfection of one thing over another cannot be demonstrated by natural reason. Since, that is to say, it is logically and metaphysically possible for God by His absolute power to assume the form of anything that anyone might point out, it is impossible to prove by natural reason that that indicated thing is not God. Anything of the humblest appearance could, for all that natural reason can prove to the contrary, be God. Hence, natural reason cannot demonstrate that anything perceived by man is really nobler or more perfect than anything else so perceived. The doctrine of final causes is thus open to question because, by a similar argument, any attempted proof that one thing is the final cause of another can be successfully refuted. It is reasonable to suppose that at this point Nicholas used some other arguments of a non-theological character against the alleged knowledge of final causes and degrees of perfection. Although the theological argument was probably dominant, the other arguments would have been appropriate. For example, he may have also argued that the final cause of anything can neither be discerned in, nor deduced from, any of the early stages of its history, since this would be to deduce the existence of one thing from something different. He may also have argued that degrees of perfection could be proved only if causal efficacy could be proved. Since the latter is never evident, neither is the former.

If God and the creature with which He might elect to unite Himself truly constitute one individual with a dual nature, and if that creature begins to exist, it will be true to say that that creature is produced. Therefore, in the sense in which

God is unified with that creature it will be true to say that God is produced. This explains what is meant by the statement "*si aliqua res est producta deus est productus.*" It must be noted that a doubt is raised here whether anything is produced. Things might be eternal for all that natural reason can prove to the contrary. Nicholas is suggesting that if anything is produced and if God has united Himself with that thing, then in a sense God is produced. The argument that because a thing comes into being it is less noble than the thing which has produced it, therefore, turns out to be invalid, since in this particular case God would be both creator and creature. Hence, it is still true that the nobility of one thing over another is not evident to natural reason.

In an age in which Aristotelian philosophy and Christian theology were the principal contexts of learned discussion, it was not unusual that all the four causes should be discussed in succession, when our knowledge of causation was the question at issue. It will be noted then, that this letter successively discusses our alleged knowledge (1) of efficient causes, (2) of the material causc, (3) of the formal cause, and (4) of final causes. This interpretation is consistent with all of the extant fragments of the Fifth Letter.

In philosophy, systems theory, science, and art, emergence is the way complex systems and patterns arise out of a multiplicity of relatively simple interactions. Emergence is central to the theories of integrative levels and of complex systems.

In philosophy, emergence is often understood to be a much stronger claim about the etiology of a system's properties. An emergent property of a system, in this context, is one that is not a property of any component of that system, but is still a feature of the system as a whole. Nicolai Hartmann, one of the first modern philosophers to write on emergence, termed this categorial novum.

In religion, emergence grounds expressions of religious naturalism in which a sense of the sacred is perceived in the workings of entirely naturalistic processes by which more complex forms arise or evolve from simpler forms.

An emergent behaviour or emergent property can appear when a number of simple entities operate in an environment, forming more complex behaviours as a collective. If emergence happens over disparate size scales, then the reason is usually a causal relation across different scales. In other words there is often a form of top-down feedback in systems with emergent properties. The processes from which emergent properties result may occur in either the observed or observing system, and can commonly be identified by their patterns of accumulating change, most generally called 'growth'. Why emergent behaviours occur include: intricate causal relations across different scales and feedback, known as interconnectivity. The emergent property itself may be either very predictable or unpredictable and unprecedented, and represent a new level of the system's evolution. The complex behaviour or properties are not a property of any single such entity, nor can they easily be predicted or deduced from behaviour in the lower-level entities: they are irreducible. No physical property of an individual molecule of any gas would lead one to think that a large collection of them will transmit sound. The shape and behaviour of a flock of birds or shoal of fish are also good examples.

10

Rejection of Authority in Philosophy

Introduction

MACHIAVELLI

It will, of course, be observed that all authority cannot be dismissed if one is in search of certainty. Somewhere, it will be believed, there must be some knowledge which is firmly established and indeed indubitable. The Italians in whom we are specially interested displaced the center of authority from tradition to the individual. They differed largely in their opinion of the kind of knowledge that was most certain and in the fields of their major interest. Thus, Machiavelli (1469-1527) took as his main field that of political philosophy, and as a political philosopher his place is rightly in a history of that subject. But in his books appear some points which are of special interest to philosophers in general, regardless of their special studies. I refer to his creation of a sovereign on the model of Scotus' God and his descriptive method.

We pointed out that Scotus' God was essentially a will whose commands determined right and wrong, and we suggested that such a God alone was capable of dealing with a world made up of individual things and events. Machiavelli's Prince also makes right and wrong. There is no power above him to sway his will nor need he use his reason except in practical matters. For Machiavelli the word "ought" is strictly instrumental. It is the "ought" which we use when we inform others of how to obtain certain results. It is an "ought" which appears in laboratory manuals, cookbooks, and in general in all treatises which describe how to go about reaching certain ends. In *The Prince* Machiavelli expounds how to be a successful ruler. He rarely mentions the legitimacy of the ends, for he seems to believe that they are beyond discussion. If the sovereign knows what he wants, and that seems to be power, then Machiavelli's book is there to tell him how to get it. No prince wishes to lose his power. The very conception of personal sovereignty is based upon the wielding of power. One may discuss, to be sure, the relative desirability of republics and monarchies, but once one has chosen to write a guidebook for princes, it is irrelevant to include the government of other forms of state.

Consequently Machiavelli is interested both in how sovereigns lose their power, or weaken it, and how they retain it. He plunges immediately into the question by pointing out that it is easier for the heir of an ancient family to maintain his position because of what he might have called, but did not, the inertia of custom. What has been going on for ages takes on an air of necessity. People will believe that a king whose ancestors have ruled over them for centuries is almost self-justified. His will has the force of common law. It is the man who rises to new power who will find the problem of retaining his position more difficult. For, once the people have become used to the idea of change, they will accept his own downfall with equanimity as simply another change. One can see the effect of custom in the United States in the matter of presidential re-elections. The Constitution originally said nothing about limiting a president's terms to two. But Washington refused a third term and it became accepted as a matter of course that his successors would do the same. The three re-elections of Franklin Roosevelt were obviously not unconstitutional, but they violated custom and seemed monstrous to some of his adversaries.

When a ruler has conquered foreign territories, he does not ask whether he has any right to them. He has them in his power and his own problem is how to keep them. Machiavelli suggests, among other things, the planting of colonies in them, dispossessing the inhabitants, who will be few and poor. The remainder of the native population will not be injured in any way and will hesitate to rise up against their new ruler for fear of being treated like the inhabitants who have been dispossessed. Men, as he says, must be either caressed or annihilated. They will revenge themselves for small injuries but are powerless to do so for great ones. Hence why not be thorough about the matter? One could of course maintain an armed garrison instead of locating colonies in conquered territories. But in that event one would have to support the garrisons, which is needlessly expensive, and which injures everyone in the land. Here again there is no discussion of the rights and wrongs of colonizing other people's countries. The right of conquest is accepted as obvious. The question is simply the retention of the territory which has been won. Where Machiavelli suspects that such acts might be questioned, he is likely simply to state that it is a natural and ordinary thing, as he does of the desire to acquire possessions. The conjunction of "natural" and "ordinary" is not accidental. For Machiavelli's way of determining what is natural is to examine history, especially ancient Roman history and contemporary Italian history, and see what behavior prevails.

It is this feature of Machiavelli's thought which has proved so distasteful to later readers. When, for instance, he is discussing the best way of governing states that lived under their own laws before being occupied, he points out that one has a choice of despoiling them, of going and living in them in person, and of allowing them to keep their own laws while paying tribute, and setting up a government of a few who will keep the country friendly. This government, having been created by the conqueror, knows that it cannot exist without his protection. This technique is that of puppet governments. Machiavelli seemed to know what we have learned to our surprise, that it is always possible to find quislings. The puppets become despised by their own people and hence are all the fiercer, we have discovered, in protecting the interests of the conquerors of their own country. When this is not the case, and it will not be, he says, when states have been used to liberty, then the conqueror must lay waste the country. But when they are not used to liberty but have lived traditionally under a prince, the conqueror must kill the ruler and will then acquire the loyalty of his new subjects who have no prince of their own and cannot unite to choose a new one. Those of us who wonder at the success of the Communists in maintaining puppet governments in power have only to recall this item.

It is thus stupid to accuse Machiavelli of hypocrisy or even of satire, if the latter is accusatory. Often a straight descriptive account of human behaviour seems satirical for the simple reason that we overlook the facts for the intentions which lie behind them. Machiavelli, as is well known, was merely setting down the way princes both in the past and in his own times had succeeded in having their own way. That people were shocked may have been due not merely to their belief that their rulers were motivated by nobler aims but by their neglect of the real aims which lay open to any seeing eye. It is true that when he describes ancient usage, he has to rely on books. But when he is expounding contemporary history, his experience alone is sufficient. Were Talleyrand or Bismarck to have written a true and factual account of their negotiations, it too would have seemed so fantastic as to be satire. In fact, it still seems false to some Germans that Bismarck could have sent the famous Ems telegram. We probably find it hard to believe that we or our fathers have been fools, and we would seem to have been fools to allow ourselves to be governed by men who thought the end justified any means. We forget that in affairs of state it will be assumed that no nation will commit suicide and that the preservation of the group is a paramount interest. To Machiavelli the prince was the state. Nor did he have a satirical intention when he set forth the best means of preventing a ruler's loss of his kingdom.

There is, therefore, unless I have misread and misunderstood him, no reason to attribute hypocrisy to him. If a cookbook tells a woman how to make a chocolate cake, it does not tell her that she ought to make chocolate cakes, how often she ought to make them, for whom she ought to make them, on what occasions, or for what purposes. If the will of the sovereign, like that of God, is not subject to superior authority, we repeat, then the political philosopher must not attempt to criticize it except on the grounds of efficacy. And that is precisely what Machiavelli attempts to do. Thus when he urges a prince who has usurped power to commit all his villainies at once and get them over with, lest he have to live dagger in hand, he also argues that once the throne is seized, order should be restored, benefits conferred little by little, that they may be the better enjoyed. But the benefits and the order are not presented as terminal goods, but as instruments for the maintenance of rule. If a prince confers all his benefits at one time, the people will be disappointed when no more are forthcoming. And if order is not restored, neither harsh measures nor favours will do any good. The former will come too late; the latter will appear to have been forced from the prince.

It has not escaped the attention of the reader that Machiavelli is fully aware of the power of the governed. He sees them, too, wanting to have their own way, to fulfil their desires which they, too, will consider self-justified. If they are accustomed to liberty, they will not abandon it without a struggle. Their withdrawal of favor will mean abandonment, and it is they whom the ruler must woo by his constant protection of their interests. They are not rivals for the throne. Such rivals will be found among the nobles. The nobles therefore must be always kept under suspicion. But the populace, being the ruler's ultimate support, must be so treated that they will always and under all conditions remain faithful to him. He must make them want his rule. And this can be done only by protecting them against their enemies and giving them his friendship. And it is here that the ruler must exhibit those moral qualities which his people admire. Machiavelli points out that no one man can possess all the moral qualities, for otherwise he would not be human. What virtues he should constantly demonstrate by his acts and what he should be willing to dispense with are determined by the supreme end of maintaining his power. If certain vices would lose him the state, then he should avoid committing them. But if there are some which are necessary to save the state, then fear of scandal should not prevent his committing them. A ruler would do well to be liberal rather than niggardly; and yet if one is liberal in a modest manner, concealing his liberality, then no one will know of it and it will be ineffective. And if one is liberal ostentatiously, making a great display of one's magnificence, then it will be necessary to impose heavy taxes to pay for the show. Consequently it is better to be niggardly and run the risk of a bad name, for it will sooner or later appear that the ruler has saved enough money to pay for the defense of the state. When he is at the head of his armies and invading a hostile state, then he may indeed be liberal, for he is spending the wealth of others. Were he to spend his own money, which of course he would have acquired from his people, he would sooner or later become an object of hatred and lose the support of those whose backing is essential to his preservation. If one runs through the other virtues and vices listed by Machiavelli, one will see that in each case the effectiveness of the quality as a means of maintaining power is the final test. Since men must be ruled by fear, the ruler must be feared. It would be well if he could be also loved, but he cannot rule by love alone. He has it in his power to be feared but not to be loved. And he can rely only on what is in his power. Similarly, when it is a question of keeping faith, the ruler must have both the cunning of the fox and the courage of the lion. The fox cannot protect himself from wolves, but he can avoid traps. The lion can kill the wolves, but he cannot avoid traps. Therefore a ruler must be willing to break his word when it is to his interest to do so, especially since it is always easy to find a reason for failing to fulfil a promise. The outcome of Machiavelli's discussion of the virtues and vices is that a prince need not be virtuous but must seem to be so. The appearance will be accepted as the reality by the populace, and will keep them satisfied. And the reason why one should keep them satisfied is to help in preventing rebellion.

The *Discourses on Livy* are reflections on ancient history, the details of which do not concern us here. Though their influence was never so great as that of *The Prince*, they present a more complete political philosophy in which the state is the center of interest rather than its ruler. Machiavelli here seems to be more clearly aware that the fate of the governed is a matter of some importance, not merely insofar as it affects the success of their rulers, but in itself. But in drawing his conclusions, he has to assume that political problems have an essential homogeneity, that states have a common identity whatever their individual differences may be. That he accepts the truth of Livy's account of Roman history is obvious. However critical he may be of human behaviour, he is still not in a position to be critical of an ancient text. But even if he were, he would have had to have some exemplar about which to construct his argument, and the continuity of Italian history from the most ancient times to his own was no doubt sufficient justification for choosing Roman politics as that exemplar. The book is not, however, a simple discussion of antiquity. Roman history is treated as if it were contemporary history and the possibility that the problems of the times of Scipio were not identical with those of fifteenth- or sixteenth-century Italy is never faced. Again, in discussing the role of religion as an instrument in government, Machiavelli does not seem to see the great difference between a cluster of cults unorganized by an ecclesiastical hierarchy and Roman Catholicism. But this is the weakness of all political philosophies which are based on historical precedents. We can only learn from history when history repeats itself. And the fact that antiquity had rulers and the ruled is not evidence that the relations between the two were identical with those which obtained in contemporary Italy, or even highly similar to them. The analogies then are hardly close enough to be telling, but are made close by Machiavelli's imagination.

On the other hand, that the human race had certain traits which were pervasive was a fundamental assumption of the whole humanistic movement. That all men have certain basic desires or drives or instincts is undoubtedly true. But it is also true that the satisfaction of these desires is elaborately and usually rigidly controlled by the society in which they are expressed. Were Machiavelli resorting to antiquity simply because he was afraid to speak of his own contemporaries, this distortion would be understandable, if not very laudable. But, on the contrary, few men have been so outspoken about their contemporaries as he. There must then have existed in his mind an exaggerated notion of human homogeneity, a notion which was, of course, fostered by Christianity, which was a religion universal in scope and neither tribal nor local. To speak of Man in general or of Human Nature, rather than of this and that man and their individual natures, was Machiavelli's tie with tradition. Nor did he ever cut it. But submitting to the implications of this assumption might have led him to consider the interests of humanity as a whole rather than the interests of those who seek to manipulate humanity to their own individual ends. He is not above stating certain ethical dogmas—that, for instance, one's country must always be defended, that love of country should make a good citizen forget his private wrongs. Such dogmas are never defended by argument; they are simply stated. But in such statements Machiavelli overlooks the question of precisely what the country is. To all intents and purposes the country becomes identified with its ruler and his interests become paramount, just as they were in *The Prince*. The doctrine that there is a being called "The Nation," which is other than the sum or collection of people living in a given area under a given government, usually speaking the same language and believing in the same religion, a doctrine which is expressed in such terms as the *patria*, the *Vaterland*, *la nation*, and the like, may be justified and has certainly had beneficent results in practice. But it is also a doctrine which is far from being self-evidently true. In our own times it has been subjected to a modicum of analysis, but of that more later.

POMPONAZZI

If the interpretation of the Bible presented difficulties to the philosophers of the Middle Ages, so did the interpretation of Aristotle, whose prestige was so great that he was frequently simply referred to as The Philosopher. The nature of the Aristotelian corpus was such that special training was required in order to understand it. The problems were not simply matters of vocabulary. The text itself is disjointed, fragmentary, often corrupt, and if one were to use Aristotle as an unquestioned authority on matters which were of importance, then clearly it was essential that one know precisely what his opinions were. Unfortunately there were not merely several individual interpreters of his works, but also several schools of interpreters. Consequently one could not tell a student to go to the authorities in order to find out what the meaning of Aristotle's philosophy might be, for the authorities differed too widely.

Pietro Pomponazzi (1462-1525), almost a strict contemporary of Machiavelli, presented this problem in its clearest light. In his book, *A Treatise on the Immortality of the Soul*, published in 1516, he ostensibly is pointing out first that there are three different interpretations of Aristotle's ideas on immortality: that of Themistius and Averroës, that of Alexander of Aphrodisias, and that of St. Thomas Aquinas. The first of the commentators maintained that Aristotle believed the active intellect to be immortal in the sense that at death it became part of the Divine Intellect; the second, that he believed the whole soul to perish with the body; the third, that of St. Thomas, according to whom the soul is a unit, the form of the body, and is immortal. In the Preface to his book, Pomponazzi is careful to point out that he is merely interpreting Aristotle, not developing a theory of his own on the soul's immortality. He does not doubt that the Thomistic position is correct; he simply doubts that it agrees with

Aristotle's. But if none of these interpretations is sound, then of what use is it to go to authority to discover what Aristotle's real opinion was? Would it not be wiser to go to the author himself? And if one does, then what will be our conclusion?

Such a program would not seem revolutionary to us, but that it was even a possibility indicates the intellectual atmosphere of the time. Are we to conclude that the method of authority was so selfjustified that students automatically went to the books about books rather than to primary sources for their information? It cannot be denied that much medieval learning is second hand. Even St. Thomas himself goes to writers like Pliny and Aelian for facts about natural history. That he has recourse to the early Fathers for matters of theological interest is more understandable, for he had as one of his aims the establishment of a single and unified tradition. But the amount of simple quotation and paraphrasing of earlier writers, not for purposes of discussion but for those of determining the truth, was very great indeed, and one sometimes gets the impression that a philosopher believes something to be true simply because an authority says it is true. One can understand the importance of Pomponazzi's book only if one reads it in the light of this tradition. And its revolutionary character comes out in its author's disclaimer that he shares the opinions which he attributes to Aristotle. For that makes it appear that one must share Aristotle's opinion in this matter if one is to be orthodox. Was Aristotle, then, a father of the Church? Was one to believe, as Justin Martyr said of Socrates and Plato, that he had been illuminated by the Logos? Or was one to maintain, as Father Copleston maintains in his *History of Philosophy*, that ancient philosophy was a *praeparatio evangelica*?

Without running through Pomponazzi's arguments in detail, it suffices to say that he comes to the conclusion that Aristotle did not believe in immortality. This in itself might not have stirred up a tumult but there was good reason to believe that Pomponazzi shared the Stagirite's opinion. The thirteenth chapter of his book lists the arguments against the mortality of the soul, arguments which are not directed against Aristotle but against the idea when held by anyone. And the fourteenth then proceeds to demolish them, and again not merely by utilizing Aristotelian texts but by relying on inferences which are Pomponazzi's own. But worse than that, he then attempts to point out that whether the soul is mortal or not, man can live a virtuous life. For a virtuous life is a life lived so that each man can realize his potentialities. But no two men need have the same potentialities. Some are speculative, some practical, some given to artistry. We cannot all be philosophers or artisans, but we can all attain the kind of happiness which is reached through the perfection of our talents. "For farmer or smith, poor or rich, if he is moral, can be called happy, and is truly called so, and goes off content with his lot. In addition, even disregarding moral happiness, he can be called a happy farmer or a happy builder, if he works prosperously in agriculture or in building, although he is not so properly called happy on this account." But this comes down to an acceptance of Stoic ethics rather than Aristotelian, according to which every man is an organ of the great animal which is the cosmos and must perform his function as a part of a larger whole. This entire chapter reads like a plea for arranging one's life in harmony with one's abilities, never striving for a perfection which is beyond one's attainment. It is a purely terrestrial ethics in which man's celestial life is made to appear irrelevant. When the question is raised of whether this would not reduce man to a bestial level, Pomponazzi replies that no one would prefer to be a long-lived stag than a man. But is he then basing his moral code on man's general desires? Is he saying that one can find the good by discovering what man in general seeks? If so, then it is clear that, regardless of his air of merely expounding the doctrines of Aristotle, he is setting up an ethical system which runs in opposition to that of the Church.

It was supposed by Pomponazzi that his opponents would maintain that a mortal soul might just as well live as long as possible, since he has no future life of happiness to look forward to. Against this he maintains that even the beasts on certain occasions prefer death to life. They will die to protect their mates and, in the case of the bees, their state and ruler. Yet no one imagines that they have immortal souls which make certain acts sinful. We all know that they are mortal. Moreover death, even if the soul is mortal, is preferable to life under conditions in which one's country, one's friends, or one's virtue are at stake. When one dies for one one's country, one does it because such an act is right in itself and not because one's soul is immortal. Virtues, in other words, can be defined in humanistic terms and will have the same compelling power as they have when they are defined in superhuman terms. Are we always to be swayed by the anticipation of rewards and punishments? Such behaviour, he insists, is reprehensible. Virtue must be estimated at its intrinsic worth and that worth does not change because of what will be gained as its reward. A man may do good without reward and is not the less virtuous but rather the more so. If, then, rewards and punishments are given us in our afterlife for what we have done in this one, then they are not to be considered as more than nonessential consequences of our behaviour. This would certainly seem to put immortality in a domain which has nothing to do with virtue and vice.

Pomponazzi's conclusion is that the problem of immortality is neutral in the question of morality. But this does not entail the belief that the soul is indeed mortal, for we have the word of God that it is not. Therefore its immortality is to be accepted on faith and not by the light of natural reason. On this basis Pomponazzi is willing to assert the soul's immortality. On such a foundation all men can agree; on the foundation of reason they will be likely to disagree.

Before making up one's mind that Pomponazzi was insincere in this and merely attempting to save his skin, one should remember that even men like Pascal and Huet of Avranches were equally sceptical of rational proofs of religious dogmas. The seventeenth century was marked by philosophers who might be called pious sceptics, as we hope to point out later. The method of pious scepticism was not, however, acceptable to the Church. Pomponazzi's book was burned in Venice by order of the Doge, but he himself was unharmed.

I have not seen the decree, if it exists, which ordered the book burned, but one can easily understand why the doctrine of a twofold truth was distasteful to the Church. To teach that a doctrine might be irrational and yet acceptable was also to teach that the Church maintained irrational dogmas. But it had also been believed that man's resemblance to God lay precisely in the reason and if the reason turned out to be misleading when it directed its attention to the most important of our beliefs, then the image of God turned out to be a very faint image indeed. The distinction between the irrational and the nonrational or suprarational may be difficult, if possible, to make. But nevertheless it appeared more acceptable to the Church than the idea that truth might be twofold. Moreover the doctrine of the twofold truth could lead to abuses such as a person's maintaining the most anti-Christian notions under the guise of philosophy and at the same time maintaining their contradictories under the guise of faith. We may of course accept certain ideas as true which we ourselves have not demonstrated and which we are too ignorant to demonstrate. But that is quite another matter from maintaining that both of two contradictory propositions are true in the same sense. When we say that the world is flat to an architect and round to an astronomer we are not stating two contradictory propositions. But when we say that the soul is both mortal and immortal, then we are stating contradictory propositions. And hence if we have grounds for believing in its immortality, we are supposed to use our reasons to maintain that belief. If we fail, then we fail not because the reason proves its mortality, but because we either have no evidence of the soul's immortality, or we have used the word "immortality" in two or more senses, or because we have committed fallacies in reasoning. When, again, it is said that something might be true scientifically and false poetically, or the reverse, we are clearly using the word "true" in two different senses. But if that word is unambiguous, then clearly a statement cannot be both true and false and we may expect to suffer from asserting the contrary. We have no way now of judging Pomponazzi's sincerity, nor have we much need to. He succeeded in writing a book which demonstrated with some success that Aristotle did not believe in the immortality of the soul and that, furthermore, man could live a moral life with a soul which ceases to exist at death.

But regardless of the content of his major work, it was proof that one need not consult approved authorities to determine what an author taught; one had only to go to the author himself. This would lead, and in his case did lead, to conclusions which were not currently held. In choosing Aristotle as his target, Pomponazzi selected the one authority whose prestige was greatest and whose opinions were almost as widely accepted as those of Revelation. In the following century men were to use the same technique in reading the Bible, and there the results were to be equally upsetting.

TELESIO

When we come to Bernardino Telesio (1509-88) we see that the rejection of authority has gone so far that we have a man maintaining that sensory perception is the final source of truth beyond which there is no other. Few men have been more celebrated in their time and few more neglected by their successors. We all know that Bacon called him the first of the moderns, but what he contributed to modern philosophy is less well understood. That contribution, contained in his compendious work *De rerum natura*, first published in 1565, is not merely the setting forth of a new method of philosophizing but also the elaboration of a complete philosophy of nature based upon that method. It is the former that is of interest here.

For, by maintaining that sensory perception was sufficient for giving us premises so rich that we could deduce from them all we know on earth and all we need to know, Telesio would appear to be the initiator of the empirical method in philosophy. The empirical method requires presumably nothing more than a normal mind, a power of observation, and an ability to draw conclusions logically from what is observed. That observation requires elaborate controls, that its organization into a philosophical system requires certain fundamental patterns into which the substance of what we observe has to be arranged, that we cannot draw conclusions without some hypotheses about what we shall try to prove, do not seem to have occurred to Telesio. But since they seldom occur to more influential thinkers than he was, he may well be pardoned for the oversight. The pardon is the more deserved in that he was living in a time when philosophy was more likely to be practiced by the application of accepted rational dogmas to what might be called "the facts," than by the derivation of generalizations from the facts themselves. Thus Telesio in the first chapter of his book insists that one can discover the principles of natural philosophy only by perception and never by the reason, "as was done by the Ancients."

Like Pomponazzi before him, he indicates the conflicts in opinion which are exhibited in the works of the authorities, conflicts which would never have arisen if only they had followed their senses, for the senses would exhibit the true nature of the world, a nature which is always harmonious with itself, always the same, always operating in the same way and producing the same effects. This faith in what later was to be called the uniformity of nature is never questioned by him. And yet he, too, was aware that he might conclude to opinions which were contrary to the teachings of the Church. And he makes the usual disavowal of heresy or error, a disavowal which was phrased in the traditional manner, that if he has taught anything which is contrary to the Holy Scriptures or the teachings of the Catholic Church, he rejects it. His book is simply the statement of what would result from his method.

Now, of the millions of things which one might observe if one were to begin with sensory observation, Telesio observes that the sun is made up of heat, the earth of cold—two elementary qualities which had been established as such by Aristotle. But, in opposition to Aristotle, he insists that heat is the very being of the sun, cold of the earth. The four elements—fire, air, water, and earth—are reduced thus to two, and the four pairs of elementary qualities the hot-dry, the cold-dry, the hot-moist, and the cold-moist are similarly reduced. Moreover, both sun and earth, heat and cold, are perceptible to the senses. The world then is the product of the interplay of two opposite beings, for heat is observed to be by nature mobile, cold immobile; heat is tenuous and light, cold dense and heavy. But neither heat nor cold is corporeal, for each requires some body in which to reside, so that we can now observe three "principles." The body which is to sustain the two contrary properties takes the place of Aristotle's primary matter. It is something created by God whose inner nature is not observable by us. We know it only by its qualities. It is that which was to become material substance in the later history of philosophy, a being whose existence was required if the qualities were to be more than fleeting phenomena. The concept of an underlying substance which possessed qualities but which was not to be identified with them either individually or collectively has remained in some forms of philosophy to the present day. In the seventeenth and eighteenth centuries, it seems to have been taken for granted by many thinkers. And when it was not taken for granted its existence was asserted as an obvious necessity. At this point Telesio clearly goes beyond sensory perception. For if the material substratum cannot be observed, it is merely tautological to point out that its existence must be demonstrated by non-observational method. But Telesio does not object to argument as such. He objects simply to rational principles which dictate to the world what it ought to be before any observations are taken. If qualities are of such a nature that their being requires a substance to possess them, then he is willing to assert the existence of the substance.

He proceeds in a similar manner when he asserts that the sum total of matter can neither be increased nor diminished. It is obvious that perception could not establish the conservation of matter, and indeed it might be argued that we actually do perceive the destruction and creation of bits of matter. Telesio might have demonstrated his point by having recourse to the ancient principle, *ex nihilo nihil*, but on the contrary seems to have relied more on the principle of sufficient reason. For he argues that since all that is produced is produced by the action of heat and cold and these are incorporeal, there would be reason to believe that the amount of matter could be altered by the action of immaterial beings. Are we then to conclude that all change takes place on the level of perception and that the world is composed of an inalterable substratum overlaid with a shifting screen of immaterial phenomena? That would indeed seem to be appropriate, but it must be confessed that such an inference would be anachronistic. Telesio does, however, note the difficulty in attributing to a single subject contradictory properties and hence points out that matter must be broken up into particles that may individually possess the qualities in question. These particles, which perform the same function as the atoms of Democritus or the corpuscles of Hobbes, are referred to simply by the name of *entities* (beings), but they are granted the power of feeling so that they will know or feel heat and cold. If they did not have this power, there would be no accounting for their interactions. For were an entity to withdraw from its position, a vacuum would be created unless another entity took its place. And the former could not withdraw nor the latter find its place unless they both possessed at least a dim feeling. The dim feeling which characterizes the primordial entities is also needed since animals who are made up of matter do have feelings, and where would the animal mind have come from if it had not previously been in the hot and cold particles which compose the total beast? The question is a ticklish one, for if the animal soul is composed of the consciousness possessed by the material particles of which the animal is made, why not the human soul as well? Telesio does conclude that the human soul is material, made up of material particles, though more tenuous than the usual entities which we find in the inanimate world. The idea that by rarefying matter to a point where it is indistinguishable from what we would call a gas, we might reach something which would replace the immaterial soul and yet not be really immaterial gained credence, no doubt, from the old idea of spirits.

The spirits which are material are not identical with the whole soul of man. There is within him another soul which is incorporeal and immortal. It is this soul which inquires into eternal and divine matters and is put into the human body by God. No animal possesses one, which explains why animals do not reason. Our kinship with the animals resides in our spirits, then, not in our immortal soul. Since it is incorporeal, it cannot be observed by our senses and obviously cannot expand and contract. Have we then any right to assert its existence? Did Telesio bring it in simply to anticipate ecclesiastical objections? This is a question which no one can answer now. But the probability is that he believed in the existence of an immortal soul and did not see how a corporeal substance could know incorporeal things. But this problem ought not to arise if one was to be faithful to the method of observation initially posited. It may well be that Telesio was setting up the limits of philosophic inquiry and not asserting that Revelation was either unnecessary to man or false. It may also be true that he understood the limits of sensory observation, which he identified with philosophic method, and was merely expounding "the nature of things" as it appeared to sensation. In that case, however, it would have been more reasonable to say nothing of the supernatural at all. But it is perhaps best to seek no answer to a question which is no longer answerable.

CAMPANELLA

That Telesio's philosophy did not necessarily lead one into atheism or materialism is demonstrated by the opinions of his most illustrious disciple, Tommaso Campanella (1568-1639). Campanella, who entered a Dominican convent at the age of fourteen, soon tired of reading the works of the Aristotelian commentators and decided, as he says, "to read all the books of Plato, Pliny, Galen, the Stoics, and the Democriteans, and above all those of Telesio."

It was Telesio from whom he took the main tenets of his philosophy, Telesio, whose arrows, as he said in one of his sonnets, shot down the tyrant Aristotle. These fundamental tenets are:

(1) that all human knowledge is based upon sensation;

(2) that we do not know the real nature of things but only their sensory appearances; and

(3) that the intellect consummates the union between the knowledge which comes to us from the various senses and erects it into systematic form. But the idea that the senses bring us news only of heat and cold, of the sun and the earth has disappeared, as well it might, since Campanella was writing about sixty years later than Telesio and knew of the work of Copernicus and Galileo.

Though, as far as I know, he does not refer to St. Bonaventura, he arrives at a result which has at least logical relations to the beginnings of that writer's *The Mind's Road to God.* For he too maintains that the human mind, by contemplating the visible world, sees in it the reflection of God's mind. He begins one of his poems by saying,

The world is the book in which the eternal Wisdom has written his own thoughts; it is the living temple in which He, depicting His acts and His own image, has adorned with living statues its depths and its heights; hence each spirit should read and contemplate herein the art and governance, lest he fall into impiety, and may say, "I fill the universe by contemplating God, the heart of all things."

This is precisely a paradigm of the natural theology which may dispense with authority since the book of Nature can replace that of Revelation. For if the contemplation of the cosmos, its art and governance, is the contemplation of the eternal Wisdom, then why should a man avail himself of commentaries upon it, interpretations which are bound to be secondhand versions of what is open to all?

That the Heavens declare the glory of God and that it is possible to see, not merely to know about, His handiwork in Nature, was of course one of the principles of ancient Stoicism and in the Renaissance was restated by such men as Raimond Sebond, whose views were popularized by

Montaigne, and by the English Deists. In all cases it is a view which permits men to discover the truth without recourse to others, and neither tradition nor authority is needed to bolster it. When certain Protestant sects maintained that man had only to follow his inner light or the dictates of his conscience, they were in fundamental agreement about the authority of the individual mind, if not about method. But Campanella went even farther than this. For at times he speaks as if there were no difference between God and Nature, much as his predecessor Giordano Bruno did when he used the conjunction, *Deus sive natura*. But as a matter of fact, even a superficial reading of his remaining works will show that he erred more in phraseology than in thought. Thus toward the conclusion of the *City of the Sun* we find that the inhabitants of the City of the Sun have two metaphysical principles: Being and Non-Being, of which the first is "God Supreme." They worship God in Trinity, but they also maintain that God is the greatest Power, from which proceeds the Highest Wisdom, and from the two proceeds Love. This interpretation of the doctrine of the Trinity might have been acceptable as poetry, especially since Campanella had made it clear that the Solarians, if that is the proper word to give this imaginary people, had not had the benefit of Revelation; but unfortunately Campanella had frequently addressed God as Wisdom in his various works. Moreover, he had placed at the head of his Utopia *Metaphysicus*, and had given him as aides Power, Wisdom, and Love. Was one to see in civil government a replica of the cosmic rule? Was metaphysics to replace religion? And in that case, was reason to take the place of faith? Such questions were not directly answered in the *Civitas solis*, but who would have failed to notice that the very title of the work echoed that of St. Augustine's *Civitas Dei*? Metaphysics, moreover, is given an absolute rule over things both temporal and spiritual, "and after his judgment has been given, all controversy must cease." He is thus above the divine Trinity, as he is above the state. Perhaps, if he had named him *Religio* or even *Ecclesiasticus*, Campanella's fate would have been different.

For when Campanella came to discuss civil government in his political aphorisms, or in his *Political Discourses*, he was as ultramontane as Joseph de Maistre. The Pope was obviously supreme in all matters. Kings existed to execute his orders and to execute them, if need be, by force of arms. For Campanella had little confidence either in natural goodness or in the people, that *bestia varia e grossa*. The Church to him stood for wisdom; it was the representative on earth of what he so frequently called *il Senno supremo*. Consequently, it would be false to assert that he was either a pantheist or a materialist, whatever impression his metaphysical writings may make. One gathers the impression from surveying all his works which are available that he kept the two fields of philosophy and religion quite distinct and that his thought as a whole represents the twofold truth in action. Philosophically he was undoubtedly a disciple of Telesio, at least in his formative years; religiously he was a devout son of the Church. If the conflict seems irreconcilable to us, it is probably because we find it difficult to make so clean a separation between faith and reason.

But the same duality of "realms of truth" seems to have existed in his epistemology as a whole. Thus in his early years we find him writing a book entitled *Philosophy Demonstrated by the Senses*. Written under the direct influence of Telesio who, he says, was his delight (*Telesio me delectavit*), it attempted to expound a purely empirical metaphysics. Experience at this period of his life seems to have been thought of as a picture of the world, "God's book." But while asserting his fidelity to experience, he nevertheless—like Telesio for that matter—goes well beyond experience in his inferences. It will become increasingly clear, we hope, as this book progresses, that the ideal of believing in nothing but what experience tells one is impossible of achievement, for, after all, experience can only answer questions which are put to it by inquiring minds. The questions which Campanella put to it were, as all questions must be, inherited from his predecessors. Even Galileo, who prided himself on the acquisition of simple facts, was far from staying within the limits of the simple facts which he observed. As Campanella grew more mature and more independent of his master, he raised questions which he saw could not be answered by sensation. For sensations were produced in us by objects which essentially differed from us. If then we were to ask questions about the soul and God, questions which he could not resist asking while under torture, they must be answered by some source of truth adequate to their nature. He thus moved on to another theory of knowledge.

This theory had its origin in Telesio's notion that the ultimate particles of matter were dimly conscious. The degrees of consciousness were seen by Campanella to vary and to form a scale running up to that of the Soul of the World, a being which it is necessary to posit, he maintains, in order to make the interaction of things intelligible. But if knowledge always arises through the impact of external things upon us, then how could we know ourselves? And if the objects external to us are only perceived when their natures differ from ours, then how could we know other men's minds, the angels, and God? Campanella thus was forced to revise his theory of knowledge and to admit that each consciousness was self-conscious. This consciousness admits us into the very heart of things and no longer limits our knowledge to their outer natures. Their outer natures are their effects upon us; their inner are their consciousness. But how explain self-knowledge or, better, self-awareness if all knowledge arises through the action upon us of external things which are fundamentally different from us? Happily Telesio had seen that each particle and constellation of particles must desire self-preservation and no such desire could have arisen if they were not at least obscurely self-conscious. It required only a greater emphasis upon this aspect of Telesio's theories to build up a new theory of knowledge, and of metaphysics too, which in its full expression would be the antithesis of Telesio's.

For now self-awareness becomes the cardinal point of Campanella's epistemology, as it was of Descartes'. "Just as to know oneself," he says, "is essentially to be oneself, so to love oneself is to be oneself, but to know and to love oneself are distinct in origin and in relation, since self-love arises from self-knowledge." But if self-knowledge is identical with the self, then how about knowledge of other things? Obviously there must be a community of nature between what we are and what we know, and the problem of knowledge is the problem of identifying ourselves with our objects. This harks back to the ancient dispute, which Theophrastus records in his *De sensu*, about whether knowledge arises through the impact of similars or of opposites. When one asserts that knowledge is a relation between similars, one can easily develop an argument for mysticism at the conclusion of which one asserts that knowledge of God is absorption of the individual into God. One would imagine that knowledge of the beings lower in the scale of Being than God would also be absorption into them and that knowledge of Nature would be a loss of self-consciousness. But here Campanella, like many others who have followed the mystic way, appears to be so intent upon his goal that he does not see the logical difficulties of the road to that goal. Quite the contrary, knowledge of Nature is the absorption of Nature into us. For he both asserts that what we know of the external world is true, or can be true, of that world, and at the same time he also asserts that the occasion of our knowledge is always a change of ourselves into the things which we know. It is likely that he either was not aware of the obscurity of his solution or that he neglected to clarify it. Lest we seem too severe, let us restate the difficulty. If knowledge is always self-knowledge, then (1) the objects of knowledge must be absorbed into ourselves, or (2) we must be absorbed into them. In the former case, it would appear that, as the English Empiricists were going to say, we know only our own ideas. In the latter case, we lose our self-identity. The former alternative seems to be accepted by Campanella when it is a question of knowing the ordinary objects of experience, but the latter when it is a question of knowing God.

The precise meaning of the identity of self-knowledge

and self-existence is none too clear. The self in self-knowledge, according to Campanella, is not the object of knowledge, as an external thing might be an object of knowledge, for there is no separation between the self-as-knower and the self-as-known. So positive is Campanella of this, that he invents a new word for self-knowledge: *entitatis prae-eminentiam*, something he says which is far more divine than either action or passion. Pre-eminence of being is more divine, since God's self-knowledge must imply no separation in God's being. The Divine Mind must know itself as it is, must know itself while being itself. Self-knowledge in man must be of that sort too, otherwise one would run into the paradox of the retreating subject, a paradox of which the Post-Kantians were to make so much. We have here then two kinds of knowledge, one of which is innate, the other, namely knowledge of the external world, is acquired by "passion." The discrepancy between the two sorts was to arise again in the conflict between the English Empiricists and the Platonists. But the Platonists, while emphasizing the innateness of certain of our ideas, were clearer in their exposition of what those ideas were and why they must be innate. Before he terminates his meditations on this subject, Campanella reaches the point of maintaining that because of the homogeneity of all things, we can know all things; but also that since all things are in God, our meeting with them is but the occasion of our knowing them. As Blanchet points out in his beautiful exposition of Campanella's philosophy, this is not far from the seventeenth-century French doctrine known as Occasionalism, the doctrine whose main exponent was Malebranche.

In spite of the strong religious overtones of his philosophy, in spite of his mysticism, his belief in immortality, his ultramontane political philosophy, Campanella did not escape punishment. Twenty-seven years of his life were spent in jail and the tortures which he suffered were insufficient to make him recant. The whole horrible story is told not only by himself but also by Ancona, and its horror cannot be minimized. Fortunately in 1634 he was able to make his way to Paris where Richelieu took him under his protection. But it was not an experience to encourage other Italians to philosophize.

BRUNO

Meanwhile there had been born and had died a philosopher whose influence in the history of modern thought was at first obscured and later exaggerated: Giordano Bruno, born in Nola about the middle of the sixteenth century and burned at the stake for heresy in 1600, after seven years in prison. One has only to compare him with a man like John Locke to see how difficult it is to reconstruct from his bombastic, florid paragraphs anything resembling a system of philosophy. Fortunately that is not the problem which we have set before us. As a heretic he must have rejected authority, and no one who has read any of his works could doubt their heretical nature. What then did he substitute for authority?

The answer can only be found by an examination of his reasoning, and that his reasoning, like everyone's, starts from unproved premises is inevitable. But his premises, unlike those of earlier philosophers, do not come from the works of Aristotle, Plato, or the Pythagoreans, on whom he says all scholars are nourished, but apparently from self-evidence. And when they are stated, they are not made to harmonize by ingenious devices with those which he might have inherited from the masters. In the second of his dialogues on "The Cause, Principle, and One," he has his spokesman point out that there is a distinction between the development of a method and its application, that just as the sword maker need not know how to fence, so the methodologist need not know how to use his method. There is a distinction, he maintains, to be made between those first principles and causes which are, as it were, a revelation of God's nature, and the secondary causes which depend upon them. The source of our knowledge is God, but as God is infinite, we can know Him only by His works. But even then our knowledge of Him is imperfect, for He is so far above us and the world that we can never do more than approximate the truth about Him. Here Bruno follows a medieval tradition, whether he admits it or not, the tradition whose most obvious source is John Scotus Erigena.

In spite of the impossibility of knowing God, the philosopher must always attempt to proceed along the road to a knowledge of the divine, and that road, as in St. Bonaventura, begins with a contemplation of the natural world. Nature, then, will first show us a difference between principles and causes. The former are what one might call the necessary conditions for the existence or being of anything; the examples which Bruno gives are the beginnings of processes and the premises of an argument. Just as a seed may be the principle of a plant without germinating and becoming a plant, or a set of axioms may be stated without a mathematician's deriving any conclusions from them, so any principle may exist without any consequences following from it. Thus, he says, it is correct to speak of matter as the principle of the constitution of things, but it would be incorrect to speak of matter as the cause of things. Causes are always external to their effects, the agents which bring them into being and the purposes for which they come into being. Now all of this is as a priori as anything which the Scholastics ever propounded and, when Bruno proceeds to elaborate his argument, he does so exclusively by the dialectic method, which is more often the drawing of supposed implications out of the meanings of terms, than the observation, either controlled or uncontrolled, of natural things and events.

Thus he has his spokesman announce immediately that the "universal physical efficient cause" is the universal intellect, that the universal intellect is the first and principal faculty of the Soul of the World (the Neo-Platonic *anima mundi*), and that the world soul is the universal form of the world. This amazing proposition seems to be justified, and here we are freely interpreting Bruno from what he does, not from what he says he is doing, by abstracting from the various philosophies of the Ancients an idea which he believes to be common to them all. He thus goes back beyond the Middle

Ages and the philosophy of the schools to a more primitive kind of wisdom which he believes to be resident in their predecessors. But it is also interesting to observe that prominent among the absent is Aristotle. And indeed the opinions which he treats as those of the Greek philosophers are not merely those of Platonists, but those of the late Neo-Platonists, who were willing to expound the theories of Pythagoras, the Magi, and Orpheus, as they were those of Homer and Hesiod. He seems to have replaced one set of authorities by another.

His chosen authorities then tell him that just as man may through his intelligence make works of art and that works of art cannot be made without the use of our minds, so the universe and the things which occur in Nature must proceed from the operations of an intellect. But throughout the universe we find three kinds of intelligence: the divine "which is all things," the mundane "which makes all things," and the particular which "becomes all things." The divine is what in Aristotelian language would have been the form of the world; the mundane would have been its efficient cause; the particular would have been the actualities potential in individual events. This becomes clarified when we see him arguing that these particular causes are both extrinsic and intrinsic to the things which they cause. They are extrinsic since a growing thing is not what it will be until the process of growth has been terminated, and thus the cause which is fashioning it remains outside it. But they are intrinsic also because the formal cause is intrinsic to that which it forms; the formal cause remains, so to speak, within it until it is made. So Aristotle spoke of the psyche as resident within the living being, guiding its course of growth and at the same time being that which its growth would realize. Confronted with such paradoxes, the modern reader who, it may be assumed, is less friendly to mystic contradictions than was Bruno, will demand clarification. Bruno, however, as Professor A. O. Lovejoy has pointed out, thought no less of an idea because of its implicit inconsistencies. He had absorbed the *docta ignorantia* of Cusa and his predecessors, according to which the nature of the cosmos as a whole, or of God, must always be expressed in inconsistent terms since it is the nature of the whole to contain both the affirmative and the negative; and, since every adjective limits the nature of that which it qualifies, one must assert of the whole of being all adjectives.

Moreover, it was typical of philosophy up to the time of Hume at least to express all action in terms of an agent and its acts. Every act must have its agent, just as every attribute must have its underlying substance which it qualifies. Thus, if one observed a plant growing, there must be something that grew which was different from the growing. This practice is in accordance with our grammatical usage; whether it arose from that or not is something which we cannot determine. In any event it lies behind much of the explanatory technique of the classic thinkers and indeed gave rise to problems which would not have arisen had these thinkers been able to think in terms of functions, rather than in terms of substances. Thus, if there were such a thing as a universe which manifested order, there must be some being which was the principle of that order; and, if the order could be formulated in terms of some pattern or form, then the pattern or form must be something apart from that to which it gave form. But, since from the days of Aristotle down, the universal principle or cause or final goal was identified with what the Judeo-Christian tradition called "God"; though the two were in many ways quite different, it was almost impossible for Bruno to describe his first principle in terms other than those used to speak of the Judeo-Christian God. There is clearly no reason to ascribe human traits to what in the last analysis is a metaphysical principle, but Bruno cannot resist the temptation to speak of it as if it were really a more perfect kind of human mind. It has pleasure and delight in evoking all sorts of forms from matter; it cannot be envious of any possibility; it must be wise and good. It is within the world as the pilot is within the ship; it governs the world as the pilot governs the ship. Just as the pilot and his ship form a unit, for neither by itself can perform its appropriate function, so the world and its soul form a unit. At times he emphasizes the inseparability of the two; at times, the distinction between them. It is the former which leads him to speak of God or Nature as if there were no difference between them, except for purposes of conversation; and it is this which could lead men to denounce him as either atheist or pantheist. But at the same time he could focus his attention upon his first principle as if it existed apart from that which it was "informing," and at such times he speaks with the tongue of an angel.

Whatever the shortcomings of Bruno, and they can be exasperating, he never hesitated to follow an argument where logic seemed to take it. Thus he does not evade the conclusion that if the world as a whole has a soul, then all the things in the world have souls too. To the objection that this would imply that tables, shoes, and the like are animate, he replies that, since they have both matter and form, they must have some sort of spirit within them. Moreover, how could minerals and dead roots and herbs produce any effect upon the mind of man as they undoubtedly do when used medically—if there were not a community of nature between them and the mind? Could an entirely material thing affect a mental thing? That cause and effect must have a common nature was a principle so hallowed by tradition that it had become self-evident. It was to be used later by Spinoza in denying psychophysical interaction and by Berkeley in denying the material cause of our ideas. It is doubtful whether anyone before our own time would have thought to question it. Be that as it may, Bruno accepted the principle and thus was able to arrive at the conclusion that the whole universe was animate in varying degrees of animation and that its unity consisted precisely in the pervasive soul which was as unchangeable as matter, and hence eternal.

It followed from this that individual souls must also be immutable and that the souls of men were, as Christianity taught, immortal. But, again in accordance with tradition, Bruno distinguishes three kinds of soul:

(1) that which is never separate from its matter, and is

called a "material form";

(2) that which is not extended throughout the matter to which it gives form, but activates it without becoming identified with it;

(3) that which is not extended throughout its matter and is independent of it. His example of the first is fire; of the second, the vegetative and sensitive souls; of the third, the intellect. If one ask how he reaches this result, the answer is that he has taken the two terms, "dependent" and "extended," and has built up the following possible combinations of them: that which is dependent and extended, that which is dependent and inextended, that which is independent and inextended. The apparently fourth possibility, that which is independent and extended, is a contradiction in terms. This purely dialectical method permits him to give a kind of animation to all levels of being: the mineral, vegetable-animal, and human.

Another example of his dialectical method may be seen in his doctrine of matter. Matter, according to Aristotle, was the receptacle of the forms, being potentially everything but actually nothing. It was inert, simply the characterless stuff out of which everything was made or grew. But Bruno wishes to fuse the beings which are in the universe into a unity. He therefore insists that matter must somehow contain all the forms, as seeds might be said to contain plants, and as they were said to contain them only a bit later than Bruno's time by those biologists who believed in "preformationism." For if it did not contain the forms of things, how could they emerge from it? One typical answer was that the forms were ideas in the mind of God, who was thought of in this context as a great artificer who gave form to matter. But if that doctrine were held by Bruno there would be an irreconcilable duality in the universe, the duality of a creative, universal mind and the inert stuff without specific character which would be matter. Bruno simply neglects the former theory and instead cites that held "by Aristotle and his school" to the effect that the forms emerge from matter and are not put into it. Clearly, if they emerge out of it, they must have been in it, unless one wishes to violate the traditional dictum *ex nihilo nihil*, and Bruno had no such desire. But if matter is the source of all the forms, if they are contained in it and have only to develop under the influence of an efficient cause, then it would seem reasonable to believe that matter is but another name for the Soul of the World, or is the Soul of the World seen from below.

But the unification of Being was to continue still further and in the same manner. The universe as a whole is one, since as actuality it is one and as potency it is one; it is eternal, immobile, incorruptible, and in short has all the traits of the One of Parmenides. If one ask why it should have these traits, the answers are purely dialectical. It is immobile, for there is no place outside it in which it could move. It is everlasting as it is, since there is nothing into which it could be transformed it contains implicit within it all possibilities. It produces nothing, since there is nothing left for it to produce. And so it goes, proceeding on a path already laid down in the conception of the term "whole." Such arguments are always tautological, as perhaps all formal argument must be. For the same reasons it can be neither matter nor form. No particularization can be given of it, for to assert anything of it would be to deny something of it, on the principle that *omnis determinatio est negatio*. And consequently the universe as a whole must be supra-rational. This was the conclusion of Nicholas of Cusa, Bruno's immediate inspiration, and of most medieval mystics following in the footsteps of Erigena.

It is this being which is called The Infinite by Bruno. It is infinite in the sense of possessing all possible beings, not in the sense of extending outward into infinite space or having an infinite number of parts. It is true that Bruno believes the cosmos to be infinite in extent and to contain an infinite number of worlds. But the reason is that he sees no logical limitations to extension or number. One is supposed to envision it with the eyes of a logician or mathematician and, if one sees a possibility, to accept it as eventually realizable. This, in the last analysis, rests upon what Professor Lovejoy has called "the principle of plenitude," first announced by

Plato in the *Timaeus*. The principle gained its credibility from philosophers trying to answer the question of why God would not have permitted the existence of a possibility if He is perfect. The only plausible answer would seem to have been His "jealousy." In spite of testimony in the Old Testament to the contrary, it was maintained that God could not be jealous and must therefore permit all possibles to exist. The Infinite itself thus becomes the limit of all perfection and all degrees of perfection must exist within it. Clearly only a series of paradoxes could describe such a being, and Bruno, as we have said above, did not shrink from paradoxes.

The difficulty in the story of Bruno is why this appeared to be so heretical that it required purging by fire. Readers of medieval philosophy are used to such rhetorical devices and they appear in the most orthodox of philosophers. But there were two strains in Catholic philosophy, distinct logically though frequently fused. One is that deriving from the Bible according to which God must be conceived as a person, the creator and judge of the world. The other derives from Neo-Platonism in which God is the One, a simple metaphysical principle without personality but who may be talked about in personal terms. The two strains are to be found not only in mystics, like St. Bonaventura, but also in such rationalists as St. Thomas Aquinas. In the archives of Venice a French historian found a paper in which Bruno's misdemeanors were stated as follows: he was "imputed to have been not only a heretic, but also an heresiarch, having composed divers books in which he praised highly (*assai*) the Queen of England and other heretical princes, that he wrote certain things about religion which are not fitting, *even though he was speaking philosophically* (my italics), and that he was an apostate, having been first a Dominican brother, that he had lived many years in Geneva and in England, and that in Naples and other places he had been investigated on the same charges." Which of these charges was the gravest or whether the gravity lay in the combination, we cannot determine. But surely as far as his philosophic views were concerned, the Supreme Inquisitor, Santa Severina, could have found them anticipated in several of the most celebrated Catholic thinkers. The probability is that his extreme disdain for Aristotle and his complete neglect of St. Thomas were as much to blame as anything else.

GALILEO

The last of the philosophers whom we shall discuss in this chapter is the famous physicist and astronomer Galileo (1564-1642), whose attitude toward science is not unlike that of Campanella and the natural theologians: *"Philosophy is written in that very great book which continuously lies open before our very eyes (I am speaking of the universe), but which cannot be understood unless one first sets out to learn the language and to know the characters in which it is written."* This means that authority is rejected for direct observation; and, from what we know of Galileo's work as a whole, we can conclude that observation was not undirected or uncontrolled but was thought of as experimental. But furthermore, he seems to realize the need for knowing what the aim of observation must be; we are not simply to look, but to look *for something.* Following the sentence just quoted, appears the statement: "It is written in mathematical language, and its characters are triangles, circles, and other geometrical figures, without which means it is impossible to understand it in human terms; without which is to wander about vainly in a dark labyrinth." The dark labyrinth is the world of uncontrolled sensory impressions which tell us nothing until they are organized into general principles. These principles are then to be further organized into a mathematical system such as we find in geometry. What we are to look for, then, is some hint of mathematical order.

Now the senses may not give us quite so dark a labyrinth as Galileo seems to assert. But it is undoubtedly true that the very variety of what we see, hear, taste, smell, and touch is bewildering. It might have been easy enough to classify such impressions on the basis of the organs through which we perceive them and thus to speak of the traditional five senses. But this classification is not based on similarities in the qualities which we perceive at all, for in all groups of sensory impressions there are qualitative gaps. Thus there is no logical passage between the various colors. No one from the statement that we have eyes could infer that we should see red, yellow, blue, and so on. It might be inferred that visual impressions would vary in degree, from light to dark, from intense to less intense, from strong to weak; that is, from more to less; but that there should be discontinuous passages from one distinct quality to another (when it might be presumed that the same kind of cause was operating to produce them all) seems logically distressing. But the same is true of all our five senses. Tastes may be classified into bitter, sweet, sour, and salt, as has been done traditionally, but again there is no logical passage from bitter to sweet, or from sweet to sour, or from sour to salt, nor does one discover such a passage in any of the other directions. A little reflection will show that the same holds good for the other sensory qualities; in all there will be seen to be sharply differentiated qualitative discontinuities.

Moreover, there would be no predicting on the basis of having eyes, optic nerves, a brain, that the stimulation of this physiological apparatus should give us something so unlike it as colours. And who could have foretold that something so unlike a sound as the auditory apparatus could give us sounds, or that a chemical stimulation of olfactory end organs could give us something so evanescent and various as odors? If logic proceeds by explicating what is implicit in a set of verbal statements, then our sensory qualities, both in their variety and their discontinuity, present a logical puzzle.

Finally Galileo, like the Ancients, was aware of the individual differences in perception and of the illusions which we suffer when we rely on them. Thus for him the variety and the unreliability of perceptions made it imperative to discover some means of organizing and simplifying them. The simplification was produced not merely by the usual classification on the basis of the organs that transmitted them or produced them, but also by looking for characteristics of the world that would be the universal underlying source of them all. Are there then any properties which can be attributed to all material objects indifferently? The answer is given in Galilean physics. There is a set of properties which are sufficient and necessary to interpret dynamics, and that set will be given to the "real" world as distinguished from the "subjective" world.

The argument to the subjectivity of what John Locke was to call the secondary qualities, was set forth also in the *Saggiatore.* As soon as I attempt, says its author, to conceive of a material or corporeal substance, I find that it must have a certain shape; that it has a certain size in relation to other such substances; that it is in such and such a place, at such and such a time; that it moves or is at rest; that it is or is not in contact with another body; that it is one, little or big. These properties belong to any such substance, regardless of how I perceive it, whether with the eyes, ears, nose, or other sense organ. These properties are, then, universal in the world of matter. They may obviously be summed up as configuration, volume, location, date, motion, relative position, quantity. These are all properties which can be treated in, the "geometrical manner," and subjected to quantitative manipulation, in the literal sense of "quantitative." That is, the "more" and "less" can be submitted to actual measurement when they are applied to objects thus described; whereas when we speak of the qualities, such as red, sweet, and warm, as more or less, we have to measure their degree of intensity through the use of an instrument which will translate the quality into a quantity. In fact, it would be difficult, if possible, to assign a literal meaning to the statement that this is redder than that, in the way in which we say that this is larger than that. Of course if we mean by the former statement that this area was painted with more red pigment than that, the meaning is clear, but it is no longer qualitative.

Moreover, Galileo makes it plain that in his opinion there is no reason for attributing the qualities which Locke taught us to call "secondary" to the material world, since they could vary while the other properties remained constant. He could imagine a material object of a given size which might have a variety of colors, but he could not imagine a coloured object which did not have some size. All objects must have the dynamic properties which have been listed above, but they need not be either white or red, bitter or sweet, loud or soft, pleasing or displeasing to the nose. Such adjectives, he says, are mere words (*puri nomi*) when applied to the objective world; they have their seat only "in the sensitive body"; and hence, if the animate beings were removed from the world, they would carry with them all these qualities. He demonstrates his meaning by pointing out that even in touch, which may give one a perception of the physical and objective properties of an object, there may arise other perceptions, an excitation of the skin, a tickling sensation, which no one would attribute to the object. Moreover the same tickling sensation may be produced by a feather that is lightly moved over the human skin. We do not say that the sensation is in the feather but in us. It is this kind of existence, and no other, he concludes, that must be attributed to the many qualities that we call tastes, odors, colours, and others.

But none of this implies for Galileo the consequence that the various subjective qualities cannot be correlated with certain types of material objects. Thus a material object when it comes in contact with the human body "produces in me that sensation which we call touch," and which we locate for the most part in the palms of the hands or in the finger tips. Here we feel those differences that we call rough, smooth, hard, soft, of which some are pleasant, some unpleasant, "according to the different configurations of the tangible body," whether it be smooth or rough, sharp or dull, resistant or yielding. He correlates all these qualities of touch with the traditional element Earth. In fact, the theory of the four elements gives him a basis for classifying all the sensory qualities: tactile as arising from Earth, taste from Water, odor from Fire, and sound from Air. Since there are only four elements but five senses, he attributes sight to the influence of the Ether.

A little story in the *Saggiatore* relates how an investigator discovered the various ways in which sound could be produced. It looks as if Galileo believed one had only to look at "the facts," as they are called, and they would reveal their own nature. But as one reads his little story, one sees that not even his investigator approached the facts with an utterly unprejudiced mind. He first formed tentative hypotheses about how sound was produced and then looked to see whether or not they would be verified. Our reason for emphasizing this, which is perhaps obvious to one who has even a rudimentary knowledge of the history of thought, is that we are accustomed to speak and hear of the first steps in science as simple observation, to believe that scientists have only to look at the facts, as they are called, that these facts are perceptual data, and that they alone will tell their story. This tradition begins with Telesio in Italy, receives support from Campanella, and is reinforced by the work of Francis Bacon in England. Its philosophic development will be found in those British philosophers known as British Empiricists.

Pragmatists wanted to reform philosophy and bring it more in line with the scientific method as they understood it. They argued that idealist and realist philosophy had a tendency to present human knowledge as something beyond what science could grasp. These philosophies then resorted either to a phenomenology inspired by Kant or to correspondence theories of knowledge and truth. Pragmatists criticized the former for its a priorism, and the latter because it takes correspondence as an unanalyzable fact. Pragmatism instead tries to explain, psychologically and biologically, how the relation between knower and known 'works' in the world.

In "The Fixation of Belief" (1877), C.S. Peirce denied that introspection and intuition (staple philosophical tools at least since Descartes) were valid methods for philosophical investigation. He argued that intuition could lead to faulty reasoning, e.g. when we reason intuitively about infinity. Furthermore, introspection does not give privileged access to knowledge about the mind the self is a concept that is derived from our interaction with the external world and not the other way around. At the same time he held steadily that pragmatism and epistemology in general could not be derived from principles of psychology understood as a special science: what we do think is too different from what we should think. This is an important point of disagreement with most other pragmatists, who advocate a more thorough naturalism and psychologism.

Richard Rorty expanded on these and other arguments in Philosophy and the Mirror of Nature in which he criticized attempts by many philosophers of science to carve out a space for epistemology that is entirely unrelated to and sometimes thought of as superior to the empirical sciences. W.V. Quine, instrumental in bringing naturalized epistemology back into favour with his essay Epistemology Naturalized, also criticized 'traditional' epistemology and its "Cartesian dream" of absolute certainty. The dream, he argued, was impossible in practice as well as misguided in theory because it separates epistemology from scientific inquiry.

11

Emergence of Philosophy and its History

Introduction

The Hesiodic view of history was that of progressive moral degeneration; that of Lucretius was a theory of progressive improvement; that of St. Augustine was an attempt to attribute the fortunes of states to the moral character of the people who composed them. In general, from the time of St. Augustine up to and including that of Bossuet, Christians seemed committed to the view that obedience to God's commandments was the clue to a people's success or failure on earth. The City of God stood as a model for the City of Man, and the latter might either approach its model or swerve away from it as rulers and the governed were faithful to their divine King or faithless to Him.

Roughly speaking, history becomes a problem when the changes which obviously have occurred in human ways of living seem real rather than apparent. Hesiod, for instance, accepted the myth that in primordial times men were actually better morally than they were in his own time and that they had lived through a series of ages which, with one exception, were steadily worse, until his contemporaries had become as bad as men could be. What explanation could be given of this? Hesiod was far from being philosophic in his method of treatment; he was, as far as we can tell, simply relating a story in which he believed. In Aratus also, though the moral degradation of man is more clearly emphasized as the source of historical change, no reason is given why man should have fallen from his state of primitive felicity. In Lucretius, though the strains of primitivism and anti-primitivism are mixed, when he comes to his theory of progress, he mentions in some detail the steps in the amelioration of man's lot, attributing most of them to technological discoveries, but, again, giving no explanation of why man should either have made them or why, once made, he should have retained them. Fire was discovered by accident; but why should man have used it? Speech arose out of instinctive animal cries; but why did it not remain in the condition of animal cries? Similarly St. Augustine can give no satisfactory reason why our first parents should have fallen, why sin should have had more charm for them than virtue, nor why, when men had once seen the effects of sin, they should not have learned from experience that obedience to the divine law was better than disobedience to it. In the long run both the Hesiodic and the Augustinian philosophies of history are centered about a mystery, but in that they do not differ from the theories of progress. The basic fact which confronts all men interested in the subject is the difference between men and beasts in this respect. The beasts may be said to have had no history whatsoever; the bees of today are like those of ancient times; the ants still construct their anthills and the wasps their nests as they always have. But mankind has changed his ways of living in almost every field: his type of government, his cities, his arts, his language, his thoughts. If, on the one hand, we find living beings who do not change, and, on the other, those who do, then we can properly put the question of the cause of this strange difference.

Clearly the first step toward a philosophy of history is

plotting the changes; the second—though by no means a logical implication of the first the evaluation of the changes morally or otherwise; the third, detecting the cause of the changes. Such causes might be the intervention of some outside force, such as those disasters which are usually called with unconscious cynicism acts of God. Floods, earthquakes, droughts are external in the sense that man does not produce them, though an Agustinian would maintain that by his sins he did produce them indirectly. They are divine interventions in human affairs over which man does not seem to have control. If the climate changes, as it appears to have some millennia ago from a tropical warmth to polar cold, then obviously man must either meet the challenge of the elements or die. If, however, the cause of historical change lies within human nature itself, then no causal explanation in the strict sense of that term can be given; one can only trace the changes, see what order may be in them, and point out what feature of human life is itself responsible for the changes. Such features may be the steady and inexplicable increase in knowledge, both technological and scientific or their opposites; they may be the inevitable senescence of that happy invention, the Race or Nation itself. By thinking of Races or Nations as individuals, one can attribute to them the usual biological fortunes of birth, growth, senescence, and death. They may be simple animal impulses which orient man toward self-preservation, the need for which he does not question and which he satisfies at all costs. They may be inherent wickedness or inherent goodness, impelling men to satisfy their desires without criticism. But whatever the formula utilized by the philosopher, he will apply it only when he has become convinced that the changes in human history are so great that the homogeneity of the race can no longer be accepted. It would have been possible, to be sure and that possibility has occasionally been realized to deny the validity of any philosophy of history, and to maintain that however profound changes have been, they have never altered the universal nature of mankind. That theme has been echoed more often in aesthetic history rather than in social. The arts have frequently been said to be an expression of that which never changes, an expression of those inherently universal motives, desires, ambitions, hatreds, and loves of the human being as human. Almost any history of literature, for example, will speak of the unity of themes in poetry from Homer down to whoever is held to be the representative poet of the writer's time. In political and social affairs this is a harder thesis to justify. The modern state is identical with the ancient classical state, to say nothing of the states of so-called primitive communities, only in the trivial fact that in both there are individuals who govern and individuals who are governed. That the details of government and even the constitutions are sometimes called by modern names merely shows how poor our vocabulary is and how we have retained the names invented by Plato and Aristotle, usually by simple transliteration of the Greek, without stopping to think of the profound differences in their meanings.

By the middle of the eighteenth century there was too much evidence of novelty for it to be denied reality. The discovery of the New World with its strange peoples and civilizations, the growing knowledge of China, the revival of interest in classical historical texts, such as those of Thucydides, Polybius, and Livy, must have convinced many scholars that the homogeneity of mankind was an illusion. Technological inventions were too many to pass unnoticed and they were not unnoticed. Just as Lucretius and many of his predecessors gave long lists of those improvements in human fortune attributable to man's inventive ingenuity, so a writer like Agricola in his *De re metallica* could even extol the benefits of mining, a practice which was almost universally picked out by primitivists for condemnation. Louis Leroy, in his *De la vicissitude et variété des choses en l'univers*, where he actually is trying to illustrate the resemblance of the Moderns to the Ancients, gives long lists of inventions which have been made since the Renaissance. Scientific discoveries were beginning to accumulate, and by 1750 there was enough novelty in the sciences to make men question the authority of most traditional doctrines. The arts themselves, architecture, painting, sculpture, drama, and music, had all developed to a point where no man living in the thirteenth century would have been able to recognize them. Any history of science, the arts, or philosophy will provide striking illustrations of the difference between their subjects in the eighteenth and, let us say, fourteenth centuries. The question of the profundity of the changes could scarcely have been avoided. And whether anyone was prepared to explain why they had come about or not, the fact that they had come about could not be dodged.

1. VICO

The man usually credited with having introduced the philosophy of history into modern thought is Giambattista Vico (1668-1744). His *Principles of a New Science* did indeed present a novel outline of history to its readers, and though its author was more or less neglected until our own times, in spite of Michelet's efforts to popularize him in 1822, he was read by Montesquieu, Herder, Goethe, probably by Joseph de Maistre, certainly by Auguste Comte. Not only did the title of Vico's work indicate its supposed novelty, but he was fully conscious that his point of view and his conclusions were new.

One of the most interesting features of the *New Science* is Vico's attempt by means of a chart to make a comparative study of the development of the various people whom he knew: Hebrews, Chaldeans, Scythians, Phoenicians, Egyptians, Greeks, and Romans. It is obvious that he could find little recorded history of some of these peoples; the Scythians were, for instance, largely legendary figures. But the importance of the technique lay in its comparative method, by means of which he thought that he could disprove some of the generalizations and conclusions made by previous chronologists and historians. But it is also supposed to substantiate one of his cardinal principles: that the first age of history is that of religion or of the gods; the second, that of heroes; the third, that of men. The threefold division of ages runs parallel to three kinds of "natures," three kinds of customs, three kinds of natural law, three kinds of government, three kinds of language, of linguistic characters, of jurisprudence, of authority, of reason, of judgments, of cultural epochs (*sètte di tempi*). The parallelism is strained to fit the system, but Vico's purpose is to show that each age has what the Germans were later to call a *Zeitgeist*, which thoroughly permeates the works of those beings who were on their way to becoming human. We shall not follow the text thoroughly but simply illustrate Vico's doctrine with a few examples.

Thus the three kinds of natures, the religious, the heroic, and the human, are described as follows. The religious nature is strongest in those in whom reason is weakest; it was poetic or creative, and animated all things by spirits or gods. We find it in the "theological poets," who were the earliest pagans to express their wisdom at a time when each pagan nation had its own god. It was a fierce and cruel nature and the very gods who had been invented by these men were objects of terror. From this age two principles have survived: that "religion is the sole means powerful enough to check the ferocity of peoples," and that "religions prosper best when those who preside over them are themselves inwardly reverent." The principle that in the earliest period of history men were "theological" was to be revived by Comte in the early years of the nineteenth century, anticipated oddly enough by Turgot in 1750. The second nature, the heroic, was believed to have been conferred on men by the gods. The heroes thought themselves the children of Jupiter and, in contrast to their predecessors on this earth, saw in their heroic nature something of natural nobility. They were proud of this and rightly, since they had abandoned the bestial life of their predecessors. The third nature, the human, is intelligent and therefore modest, benign, and reasonable, recognizing the claims of conscience, reason, and duty. It is perhaps obvious that the three natures represent progress toward a better state of affairs and that the goal of progress is what Herder was to call "humanity." In other words, though the beings whose development Vico is tracing can only be called men, they are closest to animality in their primitive condition and are called human beings simply because there is no other name for them. There is a hint of this also in the three sentences that describe the three kinds of customs, wherein the third is inspired by a sense of duty, and the individuals are self-taught by their sense of duty; whereas the first kind of customs is that of people who are filled with religion and piety but a religion and a piety which come from without, presumably from the gods. This interpretation is strengthened by the description of the three kinds of natural law, the first of which is believed to be laid down by the gods and the last by human reason. Similarly the history of governments progresses from the original stage when all government is theocratic, to the second which is aristocratic, and the third which is human. In this third stage all men are equal before the law for the laws are an expression of the intelligent nature of man.

A second feature of Vico's scheme seems to provide for the survival into later stages of some of the characters of earlier. In the heroic age there are left survivals of the divine or religious age, as in the human age there are survivals of both the religious and the heroic. This is presented overtly in the section on "proofs taken from the determination of the character of commonwealths from the character of those preceding them." Thus in the heroic age, when aristocracies were the rule, the heads of families retained the power which they had in the religious period. This is an important qualification of the idea of a *Zeitgeist*, for if it is to be taken seriously, and unfortunately Vico did little with it, no age will be a pure form and the survivals of earlier ages may well be in conflict with the new conditions which are emerging. If this is general, then it is not the people as a mass who progress from bestiality into religion, from religion into heroism, from heroism into humanity, but certain individuals whose influence is great enough to spread throughout most of society and to give it its dominant traits. But the mechanism by which an age acquires a homogeneous character is not made clear by Vico, probably because he thought that the course of history was determined by God who for reasons unexplained laid down a law of historical development as fixed and immutable as the laws of physics. If there is any reason given by Vico why men were not established by their Creator in the human condition, I have failed to discover it. But we shall see that in this, as in many other details, Herder also agreed with his Italian precursor.

One of the most influential parts of Vico's philosophy of history was his idea that the first literature was poetry, as the first philosophy was mythology. Poetry and mythology become for him the initial stages of thought. Abstract thinking is a development out of poetry and mythology, and in this notion we see the beginnings of an idea which gained currency only in our own times: that the philosopher must pay as much attention to the basic metaphors which are used as a mold of thought and to the syntactical structure of our linguistic expressions as he would to the supposed substance abstracted from the form in which it is expressed. It would thus be possible for a single idea to be expressed in myth, in poetry, and in metaphysics. In discussing theology, for instance, Vico says that it is found in three forms:

(1) poetic theology, that of the theological poets "which was the civil theology of all the pagan nations";

(2) natural theology, which is that of the metaphysicians;

(3) Christian theology, "a mixture of civil and natural and of the highest revealed theology, and all three are conjoined in the contemplation of the divine Providence." The substance of all three is the same, but the first was discovered through sensible signs, "believed to be divine as sent from the gods to man," the second by eternal reasons which are not sensory, the third by force of a supernatural faith which is superior to both sensory perception and human reason. The immanence of all knowledge in even the earliest stage of human thought is shown in what he says of poetic wisdom. Out of it grew as from the trunk of a tree logic, ethics, household management (economics), and politics, which formed one branch; and physics, the mother of cosmography and thence of astronomy, chronology, and geography. Each of these branches flowered in metaphysical form and presumably, though the elaboration of the metaphor is ours, not Vico's, out of these metaphysical

flowers came the seeds of Christian thought. "In such a way this Science becomes at one and the same time a history of the ideas, customs, and deeds of the human race. And from all three we shall see emerging the principles of the history of human nature, and these are the principles of universal history which as yet has lacked its principles". That the same idea can be expressed in three ways was a notion which would not have been repugnant to anyone who had been educated in Christian exegesis, for as early as Clement of Alexandria, every biblical verse had several meanings. But whereas the exegetes who looked for literal, allegorical, and anagogical significance in their texts found three meanings for one set of words, Vico found one meaning for three sets of words. This meaning was but dimly seen by our primordial ancestors. For poetic wisdom was not reasoned and abstract, but felt and imagined. Yet these early poets believed literally in their poetry, and when they said that thunder was the voice of a god, they believed in and feared the god. The gods were the language is mine not Vico's a projection into external reality of men's poetic fantasies. The cosmos can be described only in a set of pathetic fallacies, but as soon as the mountain frowns and the brook babbles, the mountain and the brook are endowed with divine beings to do the frowning and the babbling. If this becomes a general way of thinking though "thinking" is hardly the precise name for it all things and events will be thought of in the same way and it will make little difference whether one is describing a landscape or inventing a political constitution.

In keeping with his idea of poetic wisdom, Vico asserts that writing came before speech, and since the first characters were hieroglyphics, or pictures, they were an exact counterpart of the images which the poetic spirit had already formed. It is a cardinal principle of the *Scienza Nuova* that the first men communicated with one another by means of gestures or material objects that might signify certain acts. (The example Vico gives is three ears of wheat or making the gesture of swinging a scythe three times to signify three years.) These primitive hieroglyphs took on symbolic meaning and thus could be used for communication in place of the things they symbolized. Articulated speech followed later and began with interjections, but this fantasy of Vico's will tell us little of his philosophy.

There is to be found in Vico's axioms, given in Book I, one which establishes a basis for his theory of human development. It runs, "Uniform ideas springing up among entire peoples unknown to one another must be based upon a general truth." This is a reproduction of the ancient Stoic idea of common sense, which was to reappear in the Scottish School at the end of the eighteenth century. If, then, several peoples isolated from one another have the same ideas, those ideas must be true. Vico applies this principle to "the natural law of peoples," not to matters of physical fact, but apparently there is no reason why it should not be universally applicable. Since ancient mythologies have certain common characteristics creation myths, myths of the origin of man, various metamorphoses, aetiological myths of all sorts one ought not only to discover the common nature of primitive man from a study of comparative mythology and language, but ought also to discover a residue of truth in what these myths and linguistic customs express.

And since Vico is above all interested in determining the spiritual character or the minds of such peoples, the study of mythology and philology seems to him of paramount importance. For it shows him the poetical and imaginative character of early peoples and, similarly, when their myths are similar also shows him what they believed to be true, and indeed what was true. Thus he can prove that there was a universal deluge, not merely on the basis of Genesis vii but also on that of the story of Deucalion and Pyrrha; and the existence of giants on similar evidence. It would seem to follow that, when a myth is found in only one region or among one population, it must be false, unless it could be demonstrated that previously it had been held by all or most peoples. Vico does not seem to have seen this consequence of his position and it is all the more interesting in that the form of monotheism which is expressed in the books of the Hebrew prophets was far from being universal and yet was, according to him, true. In fact, in his chapter on the general idea of his work he distinguishes between the natural law of the Hebrews and that of the pagans in that the former was revealed through the angels or prophets, whereas the latter was found in "sensible signs." The difference is certainly important, and just as certainly Vico believed in the Hebraic law rather than the pagan. Yet he fuses the two concepts together by pointing out that all primitive peoples believed natural law to come from a source which they called divine, meaning by this adjective something which could be foretold (*divinari*). In his anxiety to prove the universality of an idea, he rises to a level of abstraction in which what he himself calls a *fondamentale diversità* is overlooked.

The human mind, he says, is naturally given to delight in uniformity. This is perhaps the least disputable of all his axioms, but a little more resistance to the delight would have saved Vico himself from neglecting differences which might weaken his generalizations. He utilizes it to bring out the common significance of fables and, by his principle of the truth of common assent, to attribute to this common meaning absolute truth. Poetic truth thus becomes metaphysical truth and metaphysical truth becomes physical truth. He is clear in rejecting all supposed physical truth that is not harmonious with its two predecessors in time. A second axiom identifies primitive people with children who associate the names and ideas of the first people and things which they have encountered with everything encountered later which has any resemblance or relation to them. A third axiom notes that according to Iamblichus, the Egyptians attributed to Hermes Trismegistus "all discoveries useful or necessary to human life." These three axioms, he concludes, "give us the principle of poetic characters," that is, the poetic methods of communication. "The first demonstrates the natural inclination of the mass of people to invent [fables], and to invent them properly [*con decoro*]. The second demonstrates that the first men, the childhood of the human race, not being capable of forming intelligible genera of things, would naturally need to invent poetic characters which are genera or universals of fantasy, from which are derived, as from safe models or even ideal portraits, all the particular species resembling them in their generic traits. By means of that resemblance the ancient fables could be invented only properly. Thus the Egyptians reduced all their discoveries which were useful or necessary to humankind and which are the particular effects of civil wisdom to the genus 'civil wiseman,' whence the fancied image of Hermes Trismegistus, for they did not know how to abstract the intelligible genus of the 'civil wiseman,' to say nothing of the form of civil wisdom through which these Egyptians became wise. So remote were the Egyptians when they were enriching the world with discoveries necessary or useful to the human race from being philosophers and from understanding universals or intelligible genera". Thus we see that the identification of the human race with the growth of a human being lay behind Vico's thought, an identification, however figurative it might be, which has not as yet been abandoned by philosophers of history and which served Herder and Comte as well as their Italian predecessor. The notion that poetic characters were images probably is derived ultimately from Plotinus's famous passage in *Ennead VIII*, Bk. V, 7, in which he maintained the hieroglyphics to be concrete presentations of Platonic ideas. The attribution to individual human beings of all inventions was also the only way in the childhood of the race by which one could gather together under a single name a variety of things, and this was again analogous to Comte's theory that the child-mind, whether individual or social, could operate only in terms of human wills. Thus grain, for instance, becomes a *cereal*, that is, an invention of Ceres, and the art of sowing grain becomes an invention of Saturn, whose name, to be sure, has a resemblance to the Latin word for one who sows, *sator*.

Whatever the similarities between Vico's thoughts and Comte's, and they are very great, there are also important differences. For instance, the three stages of knowledge for Vico are expressed as follows in his Axiom 53: "Men first feel without observing [*avvertire*], then they observe with minds perturbed and stirred by emotion, and finally they reflect with pure minds".

The progress thus is from emotion to clarity of idea, not from clear notions of culture heroes or semidivine and divine wills, through metaphysical abstractions, to positivistic perceptual observations. The poetic character then, if Vico is consistent, must be essentially a conveyer of feeling. Yet out of this feeling comes factual truth. How this happens is not clarified by Vico, though he does say that the first languages dealt with bodies perceived by the senses, and that this kind of language was preceded by gestures. Words, since they arise after the language of gestures, are impregnated with feeling; but, since the men who invented them attached them to objects, they must also have had some perception of objects. One can, to be sure, be frightened or pleased without having anything like a clear perception of the object causing one's fright or pleasure, as when one is terrified of the dark or pleased by the fresh smell of dewy grass in the spring. Whether Vico observed the growth of a child's "ideas" or not, I do not know, but it is quite probable that children first are aware of their inner bodily states and of the feelings associated with them. But, that this is also true of the race as a whole no one knows, nor is there any way of finding out, since all human beings of whom we know anything have fully developed languages. One cannot repeat too frequently that the whole notion of racial cultural evolution with its assumption of primitive beings is but an assumption, an assumption which may have been justified in the nineteenth century but which can be accepted only with the greatest caution in the twentieth. In any event, Vico's axioms are about as consistent with his basic metaphor of growth as one could expect. He is willing not merely to assert the development of a people but also its decline. By Axioms 66 and 67 we find that "Men first feel needs, then look for the useful, then observe the fitting, then delight in pleasure, from which they become dissolute in luxury, and finally turn to folly and waste their substance"; and "The nature of people is first raw, then severe, then benign, then delicate, and finally dissolute." Each of the stages in the latter axiom corresponds to one in the former; rawness with necessities, severity with utility, benignity with the fitting, pleasure with delicacy or interest in *deliciae*, dissoluteness with luxury, after which comes madness. The final stage, we see, is far from being that happy period which more optimistic people such as Herder and Condorcet or even Comte were occupied with establishing.

Vico's account of human development bases its explanation of historical change on the natural growth of a people's collective mind. It is not divine interference or man's relation to God which clarifies the course of human events. What man does he does because of his knowledge of the world about him. The human mind itself, not the environment, changes by a natural development, just as an individual grows. No explanation is needed for its growth; that is simply the basic fact. That the human mind does not always operate in the same way, according to Vico, can be proved; that the changes move from worse to better is true only in the sense that clearness and distinctness of ideas, the formation of true ideas of a universal nature, and the derivation from them of philosophic laws are better than fables and myths. That human history is to be interpreted as mental evolution does not die out until the time of Karl Marx, to whom the material elements of culture are of primary importance, those elements being interpreted as the means of production. The second thinker in the Vichian line is Herder, who was born in the year that Vico died. His similarities and dissimilarities to Vico will be considered next.

HERDER

Vico's *Scienza Nuova*, in spite of its title, was less of a science than a rhapsody. Its basic data are often wrong, which was understandable in 1725; its organization was uneven; its demonstrations unconvincing; its leading ideas so vague that it is next to impossible to expound them and feel that one has done more than give one of many possible correct interpretations. The principle of common sense which is a test of truth, with its assumption that all men cannot be wrong even about matters of fact, would lead to the most fantastic geological and biological theories. The principle of poetic truth, though it has once more gained credence, is not for that reason any more plausible than it was in Vico's time. Neither its modern proponents nor its ancient have ever been able to set down clearly any test by which we may know whether or not we have the correct literal translation of its supposed ideas. As in allegorical interpretation, of which it seems to be a species, who knows when he has the right key? The principle of ages which are "spiritually" homogeneous admittedly has to be modified by recognizing that survivals of previous ages and anticipations of later are always to be found, and that their presence is not without influence on the ideas, arts, superstitions, goals, even linguistic habits of each period. These and other obvious objections can be made against not only Vico's philosophy of history but against its descendants as well. And yet it also conferred certain benefits upon modern thought. It suggested to human beings willing to read that each culture must be understood in its own terms and that there is no such thing as universal human culture good for all at all times. The variability of ideals, the variability of intellectual techniques, the variability of standards of right and wrong, beauty and ugliness, were all worth emphasizing at a time when universality was being accentuated in spite of growing evidence to the contrary. We may no longer feel easy in an evolutionistic social and cultural history, but the pattern that was being drawn by Vico seemed to many men of great intelligence to be the design which all history described.

The clarification of Vico's method and scheme was aided by the German Herder (1744-1803). Though he himself mentions Vico but late in his career, it is unlikely that he had not studied him closely, for the similarities between the two are too close to be accidental. Both believed in an early period of history when men expressed themselves poetically; both saw in the development of language one of the secrets of historical change; both saw history as "spiritual expression"; both believed, though in this Herder was clearer than Vico, that the history of each people moves in the direction of what they called Humanity.

One will find in Herder a constant emphasis upon the metaphor of growth, best exemplified in the growth of plants.

A plant at that time seemed to be the unfolding of potencies which were contained within the seed, and when Swammerdam, after studying the development of insects, formulated his theory of preformationism, it became normal for men to think of living beings as somehow growing by expressing outwardly that which was already contained within them. Certain external forces, such as food, were needed for this exfoliation to occur, but that which was exfoliated did not come from the external world at all. As a metaphor for man's spiritual life it thus gave room for dwelling on the richness of his inner nature; no mechanical causes for development were required; and a certain air of mystery was retained which was far from being displeasing to those men who hated the rationalism of the *philosophes.* The rationalist could not explain the constant pattern of each species' growth; he simply traced it and left it as a fact. He could give reasons for its failure to be realized but none for its success. The antirationalists needed no reason. The repeated patterns of growth became an expression of those inner natures which empirically minded philosophers frankly confessed they could never know. When Herder says, "Nations bloom and their blossoms wither away (*bluehen auf und ab*)," he can lay this down as an axiom since he has taken over bodily the metaphor of the life cycle. No dying nation ever gives birth to a new nation. "Culture moves forward, but it will never be completed; in new regions new capacities develop; the old capacities of the old regions disappear irretrievably." The continuity of history is thus broken, but in its place Herder places nations and what amounts to national souls each with its own inner determined character. He was thus able to envision classical civilization not as Civilization in itself, but as simply the culture of certain peoples who lived around the Mediterranean Basin. This being so, Germans owed it no allegiance and their own peculiar civilization was as inherently noble and worthy of cultivation as any other. As the plant unfolds its inner nature, exhibiting its own characteristic growth, leaves, and flowers, so each people must be allowed to do likewise and be appreciated on its own terms. Due allowance must be made for the influence of climate, food, and material resources we saw this in Montesquieu but beyond their influence is the peculiar nature of each people which is the dominant source of its development.

Moreover there seems to be no limit to the varieties of civilization beyond the law of contradiction. What Mr. Lovejoy has called the principle of plenitude operates in Herder's thinking as it did in Leibniz. "Nature has given the whole earth to her human offspring and has allowed to spring up on it whatever might spring up according to place, time, and force. Everything which can be, is; everything which can come into being, will, if not today, then tomorrow". But once the plant has bloomed, all is over and there will be no recurrence of the past. It is a universal law that everything will strive toward the point of its fulfilment, but the fulfilment is terminal in the absolute sense. This is the explanation of the death of nations and the course of empire. It is presumably the national spirit which dies, for new human beings may continue to inhabit the regions where it flourished. But at the same time there is a common goal to all human history: humanity. Humanity is one of these key terms that appear in philosophical writings and which are seldom clearly defined. Humanity to him is the idealization of that which distinguished the human race from all other things on earth. Our nature is organized to achieve this end; our finer senses and impulses, our reason and freedom, our health, our speech, art, and religion have been given to us for this purpose. But when one asks just what will be achieved when humanity is fulfilled, the only possible answer can be the complete actualization of whatever it is that makes man man. Humanity is not, however, simply the differentia of the human species as rational animality was held to be by Aristotle for men can be men and yet not human in Herder's sense. It is common to mankind (*Menschheit*) in the sense that all men are potentially human. The highest form of humanity is religion and all men have had some form of religion. But that does not mean that all men have attained the highest form of humanity. The puzzle lies in the hierarchy of values which

Herder fused with the cosmic hierarchy. We know that the end is good, that when attained men will be free, that each nation must develop toward it separately from external compulsions; but what the actual condition of human beings, as contrasted with that of subhuman men, would be, will be seen below. Herder was far from being a precise thinker and he seems to have been satisfied with emphasizing the inwardness of the stimulus to growth, the necessity for letting each people develop in its own way without forcing them to live up to foreign standards. And yet, along with his particularism or cultural pluralism, there was a strain of universalism as well, for when he approached the description of humanity, he could use only those adjectives which the Christian tradition had given him.

The argument for the ultimate achievement of humanity is not that of simple dogmatic anti-primitivism. The fourth book of Herder *Ideen zur Philosophie der Geschichte der Menschheit* is an attempt to present it as part and parcel of a universal purposive scheme. Man's organism is adapted for the realization of rational potentialities. One sees the gradual emergence of the human brain through comparative anatomy. No animal, however, below man has the power to reason. Others, such as the beaver, fabricate tools and shelters; the ape, however, has no determinate instinct; "his power of thought stands on the edge of reason, on the poor edge of mimicry. He mimics everything and thus a thousand combinations of sensory ideas must be conveyed to his brain, ideas of which no [other] beast is capable. Neither the wise elephant nor the trained dog does what he can do. *He wishes to perfect himself.* But he cannot; the door is shut. The combining of new ideas with those he already possesses and similarly the grasping of analogies is impossible for his brain." What then do the anthropoids lack? It is not speech or the appropriate organs of speech. It is erect posture and more complete integration of part to whole. Since, and this is one of Herder's capital assumptions, Nature works outwards from within, human anatomy must be adjusted to that for which humanity exists. The essential clue to animal anatomy lies in the way the head is related to the rest of the body, whether the eye can look upward, the head turn freely, whether it is above the rest of the body or a horizontal prolongation of it. Absurd as this may sound to biologists, it is nevertheless a principle that has guided certain forms of aesthetics in our own day, especially that form known as functionalism. When a critic of architecture says that one should build from the inside out or that form follows function, what is he saying other than what Herder said about the organic bodies? The difference, of course, is that the architect is making something to suit a definite and knowable end and is being urged not to limit that achievement by the material at his disposal or by historical forms. But the principle that the determination of a material structure will be beautiful in proportion to its suitability is inherent in Herder's law, and moreover the idea that living forms are determined by the functions which they are to perform integrates the world of life into that of artistry.

If the erect posture of man is his physical differentia from the other animals, it gives rise to other differentiae which are of psychological importance. Accompanying it goes the hand with its fingers playing freely and able to construct works of art. It is thanks to our hands that our artistic souls are able to gratify their desires. Apes can use stones to kill serpents, "their most severe enemies"; they can build houses and murder men. But they are not artists. We may have senses which are less acute than those of the beasts, but we have at least one sense, sight, which is finer than theirs and more suitable to the destiny of man. Moreover we are gifted with "the divine gift of speech." In speech our slumbering reason awakes, and through speech the data of all the senses are synthesized and man develops his sense of brotherhood with his kind. Though the animals make sounds and simple signals to one another, though birds sing and some can be taught to imitate human sounds, nevertheless they do not know what they are saying. Man takes the place of an inner impulse to reason when he teaches them to talk, but he cannot endow them with reason. Speech is the cornerstone of man's organism and soul. His reason and his culture are based on it. Ultimately it is responsible for his ability to form ideas.

How, then, does Herder conceive of reason?

Reason is far from being simple reasoning: the construction of consistent systems of propositions. It is not deduction, "an innate automatism". It is not the contemplation of Platonic essences, remote from life in a world of eternity. It is intimately associated with our powers of action. It judges not merely truth and falsehood, but also good and evil, fortune and misfortune. It is the name for human living as a whole, perhaps better translated by "intelligence." Reason and freedom go together, and it is thus that we specially differ from the beasts who are slaves to instinct. "Man is the first creature to be liberated". So free is he that he is apparently not even limited by external standards, for Herder says "The scales of good and evil, of falsity and truth depend on him; he can search, he must choose". This is so true that he might even be called "the very weights on the scales." Here is a kind of subjectivity which we have not met so far, but which we shall encounter in later German idealists. But it is not individualistic subjectivism, in accordance with which each man would make his own standards of truth and goodness. Quite the contrary, it is collective. "The cannibals of New Zealand and Fénelon, the abandoned natives of Tierra del Fuego and Newton are creatures of one and the same species". Yet one wonders why such different kinds of men, whose standards of goodness and truth seem to be so different when judged by the results of applying them, should be following the same faculty of reason. The answer is that Herder is speaking not of ends but of means. Reason as a tool is alike in all men, a way of living which struggles freely to attain certain purposes, even though the purposes themselves differ.

But man also is composed of a union of the greatest physical delicacy and the greatest longevity. Instead of furs and other natural coverings, he has made clothes, and these clothes enable him to withstand any climate. He is thus freed from any fixed abode; and, where the bear must have his cold and the ape his heat, man can roam as he will. "The closer to the beasts a nation is, the more tied is it to its land and climate by the bonds of flesh and spirit". And as if to give him time to wander—Herder believes that man is also the longest lived of all animals. "Oh what maternal care and wisdom was it of the divine economy, which determined the longevity and the duration of our kind! All living creatures of earth, which have soon to fulfil themselves, grow quickly too; they mature early and are quickly at the limit of their lives. Man, as a tree of heaven planted upright, grows slowly. He remains, like the elephant, longest in his mother's womb. The years of his youth last longer, uniquely longer than those of any beast". This gives him time to learn, to grow, and to enjoy life. He needs this much time to learn, to grow, and to enjoy life. He needs this much time because he has so much to learn.

Finally man is constructed for religion and humanity. Herder says, that he would like to use the word "humanity" to cover all the differentiae of man which he has so far listed: man's reason and freedom, his finer senses and impulses, his very delicate and yet strong healthiness, his covering of the earth, and his mastery of it. But all this is crowned with religion. "If the most desirable gift of man is understanding (*Verstand*), then it is the business of the understanding to observe carefully the interdependence of cause and effect and to suspect the same where he is not aware of them. Human understanding does this in all matters of fact, crafts, and arts". So we must turn our attention inward and see what is the inner cause of our outward effects. "This is the way of philosophy and the first and last philosophy has always been religion". As soon as he begins to ask this question, he will see that just as he is a being more powerful than the beasts, so there must be a being more powerful than he. Man is the visible God of the beasts. He does not know the source of his inner power. But he can understand that such a source must exist and that it is God. It is interesting to note that the proof of the cardinal religious principle is made by the understanding (*Verstand*) and not by the reason (*Vernunft*). That there is a non-rational source of knowledge which is superior to reason we have already seen in Pascal, and we shall see it again in Rousseau and Kant. But in both Pascal and Rousseau God's existence is proved by non-rational means. Herder in this passage seems to take the opposing method.

And yet when he comes to the question of man's hope of immortality, he turns away from the biological considerations which he has followed so far and introduces a metaphysical principle, that of the Great Chain of Being. "From the stone to the crystal, from the crystal to metals, from these to vegetables, from plants to animals, from these to men we have seen the ascending scale of the pattern of organization and with it the powers and impulses of creatures become manifold and finally are all united in the shape of man, so far as it can comprise them. In man the scale comes to an end; we know no creature above him which is organized with more complexity and artistry. He seems to be the highest in which a terrestrial organism could be fashioned". In him are joined rational capacities, freedom, and humanity; and all animate creation moves toward that end. We must assume, unless this scale of being is a simple *lusus naturae*, that there accompanies it a scale of invisible power incorporated in each creature. Now no power energy can be lost, for it would be meaningless to assert such a paradox. Just as nothing can come from nothing, so nothing can turn into nothing. The body may be decomposed, but the powers of which it is an indication—a material expression-can never suffer annihilation. There are three principles in accordance with which Nature operates:

(1) Powers and organs are indeed bound together internally but are not one and the same.

(2) Every power works harmoniously with its organ.

(3) When the husk falls away, the power remains. Now all powers go forward in continual progress and none comes to an end. Vegetables live on minerals, animals live on vegetables and other animals; man is the greatest murderer of all. But what dies in each case is the hull, the body; the powers of the lower orders pass into those of the higher. "The growth of a creature is nothing other than the continual effort itself of incorporating more organic powers into one's nature". The secret of Nature then is the order of spiritual forces, not of bodies. Here is the hope for immortality.

Thus Herder's philosophy of history is based not on historical data in the narrow sense but rather on a complete philosophy of nature. The laws that describe the interrelations of souls and bodies, the general drift of evolution, are to be found duplicated in the relations of the national soul to the history of the nation and to the general progress of cultural history. That the soul uses the body as the instrument for the achievement of its purposes is an idea as old as Plato, if not older, and that animate evolution is determined by the needs of the various animate beings and groups of beings was put to theoretical use by Lamarck, who was born in the same year as was Herder. The end of human history must lie within the human being himself, and is not to be determined by any external causes, though sometimes impeded by and also aided by them. Montesquieu's emphasis on the effect of climate is therefore discounted by Herder though, like many other readers of Montesquieu, he attributed more importance to the principle than its author did. Similarly materialistic theories, such as that of La Mettrie, had to be rejected.

Though Herder is firm in the belief that all men form one single species, yet he also insisted that each race or nation had its own peculiar soul and therefore its own destiny. He devotes a number of books to describing the various characteristics of the various peoples of the earth. Each tries to realize its human potentialities and each must be understood in its own terms. Each manifests a movement toward reason, toward speech and art, toward freedom or self-determination, toward religion, and toward realizing its hopes of immortality. It would be easy to find in Herder propaganda for strong nationalism or for equally strong internationalism. Since each people had its own soul, which in turn had its own purposes, speech, art, and religious ideals, so Germany, which, it must be remembered, was only a geographical name in 1784, had its own soul and had every right to actualize that soul's capacities and to liberate itself from the traditional domination of Mediterranean culture and Catholicism. Just how he defines a nation is far from clear, but he does emphasize that network of interdependence which binds people together and which is found in traditions, language, political constitution, and religion. It can scarcely be doubted that a group of human beings who speak some form of, let us say, Italian; who are baptized into the Catholic Church and believe in its doctrines; who live in the Italian peninsula; and who engage in the customary occupations of the Italian peasant are more closely alike than are the individuals who live in France and live like Frenchmen. This is very vague and inevitably remains vague. Yet the unity which appears in a national culture is not entirely illusory. Herder, like most people who believe in national souls and culture and traditions, failed to recognize the internal differences between members of a given nation differences which appear in social stratification, ways of earning one's living, naïveté or sophistication in matters of religion, degree of education, even speech. These differences lead to internal conflict, even if it is only a matter of the prestige and hence the influence which certain levels or kinds of culture exert on the others. We are more accustomed today to the complexity of the psyche, whether individual or collective, and more willing to admit the existence of ineradicable conflict as one of the major problems not only of the individual's biography but of his nation's history.

Like Vico, Herder thought of history as what he would have called spiritual history. Though the goal of humanity includes terrestrial domination, it is not the domination of one nation over all the others, but the domination of the human race over all the other animals and plants. That is involved in self-determination. When he points out that the people that is more closely tied to its land is the people closest to the beasts, he is not encouraging imperialism but cosmopolitanism. The environment is one of those things which the human spirit must conquer if it wishes ever to be free. He sees man as attempting to liberate his spirit from those very factors which others had maintained were its determinants. His distinction between *Vernunft* and *Verstand* and his appraisal of the former at the expense of the latter were, to be sure, an element in the growing anti-intellectualism of his time; but it was a useful challenge to those philosophers, like Voltaire, who had too narrow a conception of the function of reason. But here again he fell into a kind of vagueness which may have been unavoidable but was not for that reason any the less regrettable. One would imagine it to be the task of the philosopher to seek greater and greater clarity, rather than to pass on to others concepts which needed analysis. Yet the idea of *Vernunft*, though somewhat clarified by Kant, was left vague, and its overtones of mystery, which we have already seen in le coeur of Pascal and which were to reappear in Rousseau, failed to detract from its charm. The mystery could have been cleared up, had anyone desired to do so, by looking for those psychological causes which might determine our choice of premises, the direction of our deductions, the selection of our basic metaphors, our evaluation of problems. It may very well be true that ethical, aesthetic, and religious preoccupations, economic interests and emotional blocks perform these and analogous functions. But it is not enough to say so without any more ado and consider the problem solved. One sooner or later must face the problem of when and how and to what extent and under what conditions the course of thinking is so oriented.

CONDORCET

The third of our philosophers of history, Condorcet (1743-94), approaches his subject in a manner quite different from either Vico's or Herder's. His attitude is that of the group of *philosophes* to whom the reason meant reasoning and for whom mystery had no charms. Written while he was awaiting execution, the *Sketch of an Historical Picture of the Progress of the Human Mind* was published posthumously in 1795. It was a work which by the very nature of the circumstances under which it was written could not be heavily documented. But Condorcet had lived a life in the public service, had acquired a stock of knowledge which he had absorbed into his habitual ways of thinking, and was able to draw on his memory for what facts he needed. In common with Vico and Herder, he believes in ages, although his ages are ten in number instead of three, and the movement forward from age to age depends not on an inevitable propulsion, but upon human reason and technological ingenuity. It is the human mind which progresses, and by "mind" he means rational knowledge. But he also, in common with his fellows in Italy and Germany, makes an analogy between the development of the individual and that of the group, but the group has no collective mind of its own. It is simply a number of individuals united socially. Whatever community of thought there is in a society or an age is a statistical community, or, as one might say today, the modal ways of thinking.

Though Condorcet knew that the guillotine was waiting for his head, that this was the reward given to one of the most meritorious servants of the Republic in the age of enlightenment, no personal bitterness led him either to denounce the injustice of what he was suffering or to look forward to either further tyranny or degradation. On the contrary, he no sooner is launched upon his sketch than he announces a radical faith in increasing amelioration of the human lot. The outcome of his book, he says (*ibid.*, 4), "will be to show by reasoning and by fact, that no limit has been set to the perfecting of human faculties; that the perfectibility of man is really endless; that the progress of this perfectibility, from now on independent of all powers which might wish to stop it, has no termination other than the duration of the globe on which nature has set us. Probably this progress will proceed more or less rapidly, but it will never reverse its course, at least so long as the earth fills the same place in the cosmic system and the general laws of this system do not produce on this globe either a general upset or changes which make it impossible for the human race to preserve, to exhibit the same faculties upon it, and to find the same resources there."

In general, the social scene shows a drama in which there is always a struggle between the powerful: kings and priests who hold authority in their hands; and the weak: individuals. This struggle is unequal so long as the weak are prevented from acquiring knowledge, which itself, on the Baconian principle, is power. But since all men strive for enlightenment, the only sure hope of progress lies in the spread of education. *Les lumières*, knowledge, are the instruments of each man's perfectibility, and hence those who desire progress should do all in their power to further the extension of knowledge. But again knowledge is not intuition, insight, sympathy, the heart, or feeling; it is positive calculable science, the kind of knowledge which the *Encyclopedia* was attempting to popularize. It has two tools: experimental observation and calculation. But since Condorcet was a sensationalist in epistemology, he believed that observation should be helped by the analysis of ideas into those sensations from which they arose. It was beginning to be assumed by all members of this school that, if a composite idea could be found whose elements were not discoverable in sensory experience, it was a worthless phantom that ought to be discarded. Unfortunately, once a set of ideas has been accepted by men of any period, it is retained without examination or analysis. Thus there arise what Condorcet calls prejudices, but which might as well be called obsolete ideas, which linger on from one age into another. The task of the educated man is to rid society of the influence of these obsolete ideas. That Condorcet recognized the inertia of intellectual tradition is something which should be emphasized. Not only did he put his finger on a point of importance that is too often neglected, but he also illuminated one of the tenets of sensationalism which few seem to have recognized. From the Platonic or Aristotelian point of view, which was taken over by Scholasticism, knowledge cannot become obsolete. Ideas were by their very being supposed to be eternally true, inhabitants of a timeless world. How then could they ever become outdated? But if all ideas arise out of experience, then they will inevitably be conditioned and limited by the experience that gives rise to them. Such experience is always local and dated; conclusions drawn from it must necessarily be subject to correction, unless by happy chance and it could be only by chance one happened to hit upon a lasting truth; if the grounds for experience change, it might be expected that one's experience would also change and, if that occurred, then one's ideas would change too. The ideas of a man living on a seacoast in a mild climate insofar as they referred, let us say, to meteorology, would obviously be different from those of a man living on a mountain in Switzerland. And similarly those of a man living in a pastoral civilization would be different from those of a man who was a hunter; they would differ not only about the familiar objects of daily living: the animals, plants, the weather, but also about such matters as proper behaviour, the more important virtues and vices, and possibly even the gods. If this reasoning is correct, then ideas can become obsolete when that to which they are relevant no longer exists, or is passing away, or is overlaid with new conditions. Condorcet seems at least to have seen this possibility dimly and to have understood not only the existence of obsolete ideas but their influence on society.

The matter becomes of significance in his own meditations since he believes that all knowledge begins with the satisfaction of needs. These needs may be practical, such as deciding what to do about a surplus of property, or they may arise out of simple curiosity. Thus property first was limited to the possession of animals killed in the hunt and to the weapons used to kill them, along with household utensils. When a chief died, his property "naturally" was transferred to his family. Some of them own a superfluity capable of being preserved. If it is absolute, it creates new needs. If it is limited to one thing, while its owner needs others, the idea of barter arises. From that moment ethical relations become complicated and multiplied. Greater security and leisure induce meditation or at least "continued observation." Some individuals gave a part of their surplus for labour. Immediately there is created a class of men who have free time and "whose desires extend beyond their simple needs." Industry arises, the arts already known are extended and perfected, observations which "are presented to men by chance" make new arts blossom, the population increases as the means of living become more accessible, agriculture replaces other ways of providing food, and so it goes. Each change in the composition of society creates new needs which create new problems which create new needs. Society moves by the increase of knowledge, but knowledge does not increase

automatically. Sometimes men progress, sometimes they retrogress. Retrogression, as we have said above, arises from prejudice. Prejudice may be of various sorts, "according to the degree of education of the various classes of men, as well as according to their professions. If the prejudices of philosophers impede the new progress of truth, those of the less educated classes retard the propagation of the truths already acquired. Those of certain professions which have prestige or power present other obstacles. These are the three kinds of enemy which reason must combat unceasingly, and over which it usually cannot triumph unless it engages in a long and painful struggle". We cannot guide ourselves by the lessons of the past unless the past is repeated.

With this as his introduction Condorcet begins his description of the progress of the human mind from the first organization of men into hordes (peuplades) to the foundation of the French Republic. The divisions, when they concern historical times, are traditional and need not take up our space. But there are certain details of the dynamic process which may be of interest. Thus the first societies by their very union of several families created problems of industry, of food supply, and even of science. The fact that several families were living in close intimacy gave rise to a sense of common interest, for it was not long before they saw the necessity for protection against enemies and for co-operation in the chase, and thus they began to have feelings for justice and mutual affection which were later transformed into an attachment to the society itself. What Condorcet really meant was that he himself saw these needs and therefore that primitive men must have seen them. The war of all against all, which Hobbes with less affection for humanity had posited, did not occur to Condorcet, even though he had seen the Terror. The need for a chief "in order to act in common, either for self-defence or to procure a more certain and abundant subsistence," gave men their first idea of authority. And at this point Condorcet introduces a new element into his philosophy, the contribution of the genius. Language was the invention of society as a whole, the bow was that of a genius. But if it took a genius to invent so useful an instrument, the existence of a need is not itself sufficient to produce its satisfaction. It may well be true that some men are favoured by nature to produce new combinations of ideas through meditation, but if all ideas arise through the desire to satisfy our needs, then the genius, unless he had more acute needs than his fellows, would have no reason to exist. The determination of a need is usually made after the event; the historian, looking back on the history of an invention, may well declare that it arose out of the desire to fill a certain lack in society or in the life of an individual. But of two individuals, or for that matter two societies, one may feel a need which is common to both, and the other not. The need for good bowmen was as strong in France as in England, but the English and not the French developed the long bow. The need for printing was just as great before the fifteenth century as after. The need for a zero in the number system was as great in Rome as it was in the East, but the zero was not introduced into the West until sometime during the Middle Ages. It is, one suspects, the feeling of the need rather than the existence of the need which is the stimulus to invention, and the presence or absence of that feeling is not explained by Condorcet. A final peculiarity of this primitive period is the rise of a special social class in whose hands is kept all scientific knowledge. This class, "depositaries of the principles of the sciences or of artistry, of the mysteries and ceremonies of religion, of the practices of superstition, often even of the secrets of legislation and of politics," are the priests.

They are the teachers, their fellows are the pupils. They constitute organized authority and, though these words are not Condorcet's, it is they who preserve the obsolete ideas of the past and invest them with sanctity. It would not have been necessary to single out a special class of men to perform this role; the general run of human beings are only too ready to regard tradition as self-substantiated.

The second period of human history is called the Pastoral. The Pastoral Period arose because of the ease with which animals taken in the chase could be domesticated, because the land about the huts provided sufficient pasturage to nourish them, because the families had a surplus of meat, and could expect that bad seasons might produce famine. Hunting became unnecessary and was retained as a sport. And since the pastoral life is more sedentary than the life of hunters, men had more leisure and they "sought new sensations in the means of taking care of it". Slavery, then, was introduced through putting prisoners of war to work and hospitality became one of the cardinal virtues. Social stratification began with the recognition of the superiority of men of experience, and men in the upper strata became the first judges. "But at the same time the art of deceiving men in order to rob them became perfected, as that of controlling their opinions by authority founded on chimerical hopes and fears. There were established cults with more fixed rules, systems of belief less grossly organized. The ideas of supernatural powers were somewhat refined and alongside these opinions there appeared the establishment here of prince-pontiffs, there of priestly families or tribes, but at all times a class of individuals assuming insolent prerogatives, separating themselves off from men in order to make them more subservient, and seeking to take exclusively to themselves medicine and astronomy so as to unite in their own hands the subjugation of minds and to leave no means of unmasking their hypocrisy and breaking its chains". In passages such as this Condorcet utilizes his individualism to argue that in no society will all men be alike. Intellectually they might be expected to differ as their experiences differ. But if a special class, the priesthood, was able so to dominate the minds of their fellows, one might conclude reasonably enough that they felt the need to dominate while their inferior felt the need to be dominated. As long as no one rebelled, one might think that all were satisfied with what they had. One might also think that the separation of classes was itself a product of the ways of living. But Condorcet forgets his cardinal assumptions here and introduces a new element: the desire to retain power. We have now the following principles of historical change, either overtly stated or implied:

(1) changes in practical needs,

(2) curiosity about ideas and sensations,

(3) thc influcncc of geniuscs,

(4) the desire to retain power,

(5) the retention of obsolete ideas in the form of prejudices.

During the Pastoral Period men became attached to the soil and a division of labour had to be introduced. Some had to work the ground, others to make the instruments of agriculture, others to herd the animals. Soon five social classes developed: the landed proprietors, their servants, their slaves, labourers who owned no land, and merchants. It was in this period that writing was invented, beginning with hieroglyphics—as Vico and Herder also maintained. But here, too, the priestly class distinguished between two kinds of learning, one for themselves, the other for the people, the former expressed in the more ancient forms of language, the latter in demotic speech.

The priests in their meditations had almost universally created for themselves the metaphysical system of a great whole, immense, eternal, of which all beings were but the parts, of which all the changes observed in the universe were but diverse modifications. But their language and their monuments while expressing to them these metaphysical principles, these natural truths, presented to the eyes of the people a system of the most extravagant mythology, and became the foundation of the most absurd beliefs, the most insane cults, the most shameless and the most barbarous practices. Such is the origin of almost all the known religions.

Science at this time was entirely practical. There were a few moral and social maxims. Astronomy was as good as it could be without glasses. But until writing was developed no further progress could be made. In the fourth period, which runs from Greece to the time of the division of the sciences, about the time of Alexander, the Greeks, disgusted with kings, overthrew them, and in their overthrow they made it possible for all men to satisfy their curiosity individually. Every man had an equal right to know the truth and to communicate it. It was this, "even more than political liberty", which made the human mind independent and guaranteed the rapid extension of intellectual progress. But the Greek scientists became lost in too wide a speculation. "They wanted to penetrate into the nature of men and gods, the origin of the world and of the human race. They tried to reduce nature to a single principle and the phenomena of nature to a single law. They tried to enclose in one rule of conduct all the duties of ethics and the secret of true happiness". For that reason, instead of discovering truths, they forged systems, neglected observation, and, having no facts to guide them, engaged in subtle arguments as proofs of their speculations. Amid this nebulous mass of hypothetical and sophistical dreaming two figures shone out, that of Democritus, whose materialism "reappeared in more enlightened centuries," and that of Pythagoras, according to whom all phenomena were submissive to general law. Otherwise, Greek science was lost in verbal subtleties. But the priests nevertheless attacked it and accused the philosophers of impiety to the gods with the result that the philosophers themselves developed two kinds of doctrine, an esoteric for themselves and an exoteric for the public. By keeping out of politics and by retaining their complete freedom of opinion, the Greek philosophers were able to have a profound influence on the manners, laws, and government of their people. Their great weakness, especially in political philosophy, was to confuse men as they found them with natural men, and thus to base legislation upon men "corrupted by prejudices, by the interests of factitious passions, and by social habits". But although this was so, the Greeks nevertheless had a sense of their individual rights, whereas their Oriental forebears considered government as the protection of the rights of the prince. Their vices were remainders of more ancient times, their virtues their own contribution to progress. This passage was obviously a slap at Rousseau with his thesis that the progress of the arts and sciences was a detriment rather than a benefit to man.

From the time of the division of the sciences to their decadence forms the fifth period. Aristotle, who introduced it, was the first to universalize scientific method. He applied it not only to those disciplines which are habitually called science, but also to the arts. He was the first to see that intelligence could be applied to all fields of knowledge. He also separated the sciences from one another, and thus mathematics and physics were set up as separate fields apart from philosophy. Since the mathematician and physicist could retire into their studies and maintain their independence from the priesthood, they could develop calculation and observation. The other sciences also found a start in the works of Aristotle, but unfortunately their practitioners lacked the experimental method and the technique of analysis. But to Aristotle is due the primary law of epistemology: that "our ideas, even the most abstract, the most purely intellectual, so to speak, owe their origin to sensations". But the conquest of the civilized world by the Romans put an end to all that and, by attempting to amalgamate different peoples with conflicting ideas into a single nation, forced them to give all their attention and intelligence to the formation of law. They were entirely given over to practical matters, as indeed they had to be, and hence had no time for anything else. Had Condorcet forgotten at this point that all knowledge arises from practice? He argues as if the exclusive attention given by Rome to government, engineering, and problems involved in them, was the cause of the breakdown of ancient civilization and the subsequent triumph of Christianity. "The spirit of the new sect agreed better with a time of decadence and ill fortune. Its chiefs, in spite of their tricks and vices, were enthusiasts ready to perish for their doctrine. The religious zeal of the philosophers and upper classes was but devotion to a political system, and every religion which allows itself to be defended as a belief that it is useful to leave to the people, cannot hope to be more than a more or less prolonged death struggle". (It is unnecessary to do more than point out that the utility of religion to government was one of the most frequent arguments in its favour under the Old Regime.) The triumph of Christianity then was the signal for the complete degeneration of both science and philosophy. Its triumph was helped by the lack of printing, which permitted only the rich to gain knowledge. It was a triumph which ushered in the Dark Ages. Only Gibbon equaled Condorcet in his antipathy for the early Church and the Middle Ages. This antipathy on

Condorcet's part, if not on Gibbon's, must have been due to his ignorance of the technological inventions of that period and to his knowing nothing about it except the predominance of the Church and the rise of Scholastic philosophy. It should not be denied even by those who speak most enthusiastically of "the greatest of centuries," that Plato, Aristotle, and Plotinus need not yield to St. Thomas Aquinas or St. Bonaventura in either dialectical skill or metaphysical imagination, that the sculpture of ancient times was as beautiful as that of the Middle Ages, and that even the most eminent Christian philosophers repeated uncritically stories from Pliny and Aelian as well-founded scientific fact, that a comparison between Vergil and Prudentius would scarcely redound to the credit of the latter, and that the persistent use of Martianus Capella as a textbook, or even of the various works of Boethius, did not exhibit much rational insight. But at the same time, if one were interested in practical matters the satisfaction of vital needs the Middle Ages were far in advance of antiquity. One may praise or condemn periods, if one likes that sort of self-indulgence, but if one thinks that progress is based on technological advances, then it is strange to rank the Middle Ages below any preceding time.

The opening of Condorcet's discussion of this epoch of decadence, as he calls it, is typical of the opinions of those who so hated the Church that they were incapable of appreciating its real benefactions.

In this disastrous epoch we shall see the human mind rapidly fall from the heights to which it had been raised and ignorance drag behind it here ferocity, there a refinement of cruelty, in all places corruption and perfidy. Scarcely a few lightning flashes of talent, a few flashes of magnanimity or goodness, could pierce that nocturnal darkness. Theological daydreams, superstitious impostures, are the sole marks of human genius, religious intolerance their sole ethics; and Europe crushed between sacerdotal tyranny and military despotism, awaits in blood and tears the moment when new enlightenment shall permit it to be born again in liberty, humanity, and virtue.

Such a preamble will scarcely reassure the modern reader whose knowledge of this period of darkness is more detailed than Condorcet's. But it should be remembered that his own contemporaries had been hounded by the Sorbonne into anonymity, had been imprisoned for their opinions, and had little reason to think kindly of an institution organized to encourage the love of God and one's neighbor. The memory of Alexander VI and the Medici Popes, of the government of the Papal States and the Inquisition, was more lively in eighteenth-century France than it has been since the time of Leo XIII. This does not make Condorcet's opinion more valid, but it makes it more excusable. He is willing, however, to credit the Church with the condemnation of slavery. He sees the beneficent effects of the preaching of brotherly love. He recognizes that the Church's insistence on her independence from secular authority was a deterrent to despotism. But he believes that her own despotism was equally abhorrent in that it encouraged superstition and discouraged intellectual freedom. He admits that Christianity preached an ethics based on universal principles which no sect had ever denied, but it also created a host of purely religious duties and imaginary sins and thus departed from natural virtue. The only ray of light of which he is willing to grant the existence is the civilization of the Arabs, which "cultivated astronomy, optics, all parts of medicine, and enriched these sciences with some new truths".

Thanks to the intolerance of the priesthood, the viciousness of their private lives, their revolting hypocrisy, rebellion set in. Men began to see the inconsistencies of dogma and traditional maxims, the contradictions between Christian preaching and practice, and it was not long before the rebels were successful. Free thought manifested itself in political circles in Frederick II; in literary, with Boccaccio, in military, with the Crusades. People began to have some knowledge of ideas other than those which the Church had been willing to grant them. Free cities and city-states arose. In England Magna Carta set the example of a declaration of rights which the continental communes were to copy. These charters "were the origin of those declarations of rights regarded nowadays by all enlightened men as the basis of liberty, and of which the Ancients had no conception, could not have any idea, because domestic slavery had sullied their constitutions; because in their case the right of citizenship had been hereditary, or conferred by voluntary adoption; and because they had not been reared in the knowledge of those rights inherent in the human race and belonging to all men with complete equality". Thanks to Europe's increasing knowledge of Asia, mechanical arts had begun to be known; silk culture, windmills, papermaking, chronology, the compass, gunpowder, armor, all aided the progress of civilization. In Italy there was a revival of letters in Dante and Boccaccio. But all this was but germinal and happier times had to be awaited before the germs could grow. When printing was invented, bit by bit freedom of thought could spread, for knowledge could be had more cheaply in printed books than in manuscripts. This technological invention, then, is to be credited with the introduction of enlightenment, for it was no longer possible to control the spread of ideas. Then came Luther and the Reformation, and the absolute tyranny of the Church was broken. Unfortunately princes took over the power which Popes had exercised, and a new tyranny was established. All authority ranged itself against freedom of thought. But since princes had allied themselves with the various Protestant sects, they were forced to admit a certain freedom of thought, at least freedom to depart from the traditional thoughts of the Papacy. Only Christians enjoyed this and Condorcet has no illusions about the bigotry and intolerance of the new masters of men. But this very intolerance was a stimulus to rebellion and it was not too long before "this great truth" was pronounced, "that freedom is an inalienable good". "Popular movements, the revolutions which had stirred up Italy, England, and France, were to attract the attention of philosophers to that part of politics which consists of observing and predicting the effects which constitutions, laws, political institutions can have on the freedom of peoples, on prosperity, on the power of states, on the preservation of the independence, and on the form of their government". Copernicus and Galileo, Bacon and

Descartes were the founders of the new science. Whenever science touched upon political matters, those in authority attempted to suppress it, but where its contact was less evident, it retained its freedom and was permitted to advance. Bacon's contribution was the revelation of the true method of discovery: observation, experimentation, and calculation. But he lacked scientific knowledge at first hand. Galileo freed science from superstition, prejudice, and authority, utilizing the experimental and mathematical method to prove his points. But he restricted his investigations to mathematics and physics. It was left to Descartes to universalize a method which could be applied either to the physical or the moral sciences. "If in physical science his procedure is less secure than that of Galileo, if his philosophy is less wise than that of Bacon, if he can be reproached for having learned too little from the lessons of the one and the example of the other: to be suspicious of his imagination, to put only experimental questions to nature, to believe in nothing but calculation, to observe the universe instead of constructing it, to study man instead of making guesses about him; yet the very audacity of his errors served the progress of the human mind. He stimulated minds which the wisdom of his rivals had not been able to awaken. He told men to shake off the yoke of authority, to recognize only the authority admitted by reason".

After this period came the one between Descartes and the French Revolution. Nation after nation, the Dutch provinces and then England, freed themselves from both political and sacerdotal tyranny, and the epoch of human freedom was ushered in. Its birth was painful and slow, but finally it became clear that man "is a sensible being, capable of reasoning and of acquiring moral ideas." That is his nature, and states are formed to guarantee the exercise and expression of that nature. There was no social contract, for a contract can preserve only those rights one wants at the date of its completion. Following Locke, French philosophers such as Bayle, Fontenelle, Voltaire, Montesquieu, and their disciples fought for the truth. To them are due our freedom from despots in both the state and the church, the recognition of the independence of reason, freedom of speech and the press. Their war cry was Reason, Tolerance, and Humanity. As a final result of their doctrines the French revolted, and their revolution "embraced the entire economy of society, changed all social relations, and penetrated to the last links in the political chain". All this was attributable to the extension of rational science, which in turn could never have been realized without freedom of thought. Condorcet briefly traces at this point the progress of the various scientific disciplines, and it is especially noteworthy that he spends several pages on the benefits that the statistical method and the calculus of probabilities were to confer on scientific method. It is not yet time, however, to proclaim a complete victory over superstition and tyranny. "We still see that enlightenment is to be found in only a small part of the globe, that the number of those who enjoy it disappears before the great mass of men given over to prejudice and ignorance. We see vast areas groaning under slavery, and showing us only nations here degraded by the vices of a civilization whose corruption slows up progress, there vegetating still in the infancy of the first historical periods. We see that the work of these last ages has done much for the progress of the mind of man, but little for the perfection of the human race itself; much for man's glory, something for his freedom, almost nothing for his happiness. At some points we are dazzled by a blinding light; but thick shadows still cover an immense horizon. The philosopher's soul rests in consolation when it surveys a small number of objects; but the spectacle of stupidity, of slavery, of wild fantasies [*extravagance*], of barbarism afflict it much more often; and the friend of humanity can take no unmixed pleasure except in abandoning himself to the sweet hopes of the future".

They rest upon the following three propositions:

(1) the destruction of inequality among nations;

(2) the progress of equality in each people;

(3) the real perfection of man.

All nations in time will reach the same point of civilization, for it cannot be believed that nature has condemned one people to ignorance and barbarism and another to enlightenment. Within each nation education will be made more common, and the intellectual and moral inequalities of their members will inevitably diminish. And finally the very increase in knowledge will lead to the perfection of the race Condorcet seems to believe that men will always use their knowledge in the best fashion. We of the middle twentieth century are apparently living in a time of disillusion and downright despair.

12

Anti-Cartesianism of Philosophy

Introduction

The earliest of the Anti-Cartesians whom we shall discuss is Gassendi (1592-1655). Gassendi was a determined opponent of what he believed to be Aristotelianism, a disciple of Epicurus, and a priest. The combination was somewhat peculiar and for that, if for no other reason, might attract attention to him. His objections to Descartes arose primarily, one suspects, from his general anti-rationalism. This appears clearly in his arguments against the Aristotelians, which first appeared in 1624. Like so much of Gassendi's writings, the *Exercitationes* lists pretty nearly every argument which its author can either think up for himself or find in other men's works bearing upon his subject, and though much of what he has to say seems superficial and sometimes beside the point, his books are of inestimable value to the historian who is interested in the general state of opinion. Thus we should probably not feel that because Aristotle was neither a Jew nor a Christian, his ideas were of any less importance philosophically. But Gassendi feels that not enough attention has been paid to the fact that he was a pagan. He could not be said to have written under the inspiration of a divinity, but by the orders of an oracle. But oracles were conducted by demons, and what would be the greater profit of a demon, or *the* Demon, than to propagate the philosophy of a pagan and insinuate it into the minds of Christians? Had not Lactantius said, "Aristotle neither worshipped God nor even took thought of Him"? In fact, he believed the world to be eternal, not created, and probably thought the soul to be mortal. It is perhaps odd for a man who was to revive the philosophy of another pagan, Epicurus, to be so squeamish about Aristotle. But on the other hand, it was quite to the point to emphasize those elements in Aristotelianism which could not be reconciled with Christianity. For it had been the custom to select from the corpus those details which could be given a Christian dress and to omit the rest, a procedure which was also used in the reading of Plato.

But Gassendi's objections to Aristotelianism are not all so thin. His objection to the syllogism is, though in no way original, one which was to be repeated well into the nineteenth century. It is the objection that a syllogism is always a begging of the question. By the admission of all, there is nothing in the conclusion which was not previously in the premises. If we conclude from the premises (1) "All men are mortal" and (2) "Socrates is a man," that therefore Socrates is mortal," we must have already known that he was mortal when we framed the major premise, for we should have had to include Socrates in our survey of all men. Whether this objection is fatal or not, and it probably is not, it was one in which Gassendi had great confidence, and in view of the strong opposition to Aristotelianism as filtered through the Scholastics, which was manifested by others in the seventeenth century, it is at least worth recording here.

More basic than his objections to the syllogism is his theory that organized science is always misleading. Science can, in the last resort, deal only with appearances, not with the inner and necessary causes. The retention of the distinction between the sensory appearances of things and their inner natures gave him room for God, the mysteries of religion, and possibly miracles. Man wishes to know things which are beyond the reach of science, things which are open only to faith. We can argue about rational matters, but the things of faith are accepted without question. Science is a sort of empirical knowledge; such as, that I am sitting rather than standing, that it is now daytime rather than nighttime, that honey is sweet and not bitter, that fire is hot and not cold. But if one ask whether honey is sweet in its own nature and not simply sweet to the human tongue, then science has and can have no answer. Here we can say that we have no knowledge, that we are totally ignorant of anything "according to its own nature and how it is through its inner, necessary, and infallible causes." Such knowledge as we have comes from the senses or is of the present sensory moment. But unfortunately the senses do not always tell the same story. Sensory knowledge varies from animal to animal, from man to man, and within the experience of a single man. Are we to institute a court of judges who will declare what the universal truth is? That truth must be universal, Gassendi never doubts. That one could set up systems of relation in which certain statements would be true which would not be true outside of the system may have occurred to him but, if it did, he found it unsatisfactory. For the variation within individual experiences concerning sensory data is enough to prove to him that sensory statements are misleading. It should be clear that if one is careful enough of the way in which one expresses one's sensory experiences, one will not inevitably be wrong. Thus if for some reason or other a man pronounces honey to be bitter and there may be men who find it bitter then they are not in error when they say that they find it bitter. The trouble clearly arises when they leave out that part of the statement which says, "*I find it* so and so," and substitute for it, "*It is* so and so," meaning presumably that all men will find it so. But that was precisely what Gassendi and most people of his time desired. The result of this will appear later in this book.

Moreover the assumption of a distinction between inner

and outer natures was one which was to prove embarrassing to later thinkers. These *causae intimae* had to be unknowable for the very reason that if they were observable, they would fall under the suspicion that all observation fell under. If all knowledge comes from sensation, then one might have been asked why non-sensory statements should ever be made. The distinction between what a thing seems to be and what it is is an old and useful one. But when a thing is what it can never be observed to be under any circumstances whatsoever, or when it is what can never be inferred from anything observable, then the distinction does more harm than good. For the inner natures can be anything whatsoever; there is no way of verifying anything that may be said about them. In our own days such statements have been called meaningless. It would be wiser to maintain that they are simply unverifiable, for if they were meaningless, one would never know whether they could be verified or not. Moreover, one cannot tell whether a sentence is nonsense or not unless one knows what it is supposed to mean, what its framer thinks he means, what he intends by it. What justification was there then for Gassendi, since we are dealing with him, to make the distinction?

In the main the reason was the necessity for finding some basis for universally true statements. If any sentence is to be universally true, it would seem to be true of something and consequently that something must have exactly the nature which it is described as having in the sentence in question. Therefore one must find an object or set of objects which does have a single and unchanging character. Such objects do not exist on the plane of sensation, for the reasons already stated; namely, that sensory experience varies from individual to individual and from species to species and within the life of a single individual. But if all knowledge is either sensory or derived from sensation, then one must either conclude that there is no such object and that the world is a flux of sensations; or, that if there is, then it is unknowable. Galileo's technique was to make a distinction between those sensory qualities which varied with the observer and those which presumably did not. The latter constituted the world of physics. Descartes made a similar distinction. But Descartes' method was not to base all knowledge on sensation, as we have seen, but on certain irrefragable truths whose evidence was the impossibility of denying them without reasserting them. Gassendi wished to retain the traditional empirical method and yet have inner natures too.

He is convinced that there are inner natures, and he is also convinced that men can never know them. Knowledge of them pertains to the angelic, or rather to the divine, nature than to human. "Our intellect knows about or knows many appearances by experience". From such appearances only other appearances may be inferred. But one cannot by inference move from the sphere of appearance to that of inner natures, which by definition do not appear. Gassendi could have concluded that since we can have no knowledge of inner natures, we had best stop talking about them. And in a letter written later to Lord Herbert of Cherbury he points out that appearances are good enough for all practical purposes. If, however, we wish to go beyond the sensory appearances of things, to inquire into the nature of substances and principles, of formal and eminent causes, we shall never discover the answer. But we need not blame God or Nature for this; we should blame only our own idle curiosity. The fact that we cannot answer these questions is proof that God wanted the answer kept for Himself and has granted us whatever bits of information are needed for our guidance through Revelation. And the field of revealed knowledge is accessible to us only through faith.

Just as Gassendi attacked the remnants of Scholasticism, he attacked Descartes. So firmly convinced an anti-rationalist was bound to object to any philosophy guided by the principles of mathematical reasoning. Though his objections to Descartes; include almost everything that philosopher espoused, we must limit ourselves here to a few of his objections.

The most important of these is directed against the central Cartesian principle of the indubitability of self-knowledge. The natural light would suffice, he maintains, to prove one's self-existence; one need not have recourse to what is involved in thinking. Any act which we perform involves an agent, and that agent is ourselves. Why then all this extraordinary apparatus of doubting what we need not doubt? Descartes' reply is that all such acts occur as much in dreams as in waking life and hence, for metaphysical purposes, will not lead us to certainty. Whereas wherever thinking occurs, a subject of thinking is found. If one says, "I walk, therefore I am," the certainty of self-existence arises in the consciousness of walking, not in the act of walking. Descartes' reply would seem conclusive, given his definition of thinking, and, since one could walk and presumably perform most of the acts mentioned by Gassendi without being conscious of them, they in themselves would not produce the certainty required. But Gassendi, though weak in this objection, is stronger in his rejoinder when he points out that behind all this search for unity is the acceptance of the logical processes of inference as leading from true premise to true conclusion. The geometrical method was indeed accepted by Descartes without question as the soundest method and, though it may have been in fact the soundest, it was not self-evidently so. On the other hand Gassendi was wrong when he maintained that it was employed in deducing self-existence from thinking. "I think, therefore I am" was not held by Descartes to be a syllogism or any other form of inference. It was stated in inferential form, to be sure, but to Descartes, as appeared in his correspondence, the form of verbal expression was misleading. One knows oneself immediately in the act of thinking and that act is unique in this respect. Hence Gassendi's elaborate proof that the *cogito* was an incorrect syllogism was beside the point, however sound he may have been in his charge that Descartes had no absolutely certain proof of the value of the geometrical method.

As for the complete separation of the mind and the body, based on the clear and distinct idea of the soul in which there is no evidence of a corporeal nature, Gassendi maintains that his opponent had not considered his entire being, but only a sort of internal "somewhat more occult part," which he chose to call his soul. Could he not just as well have thought of his soul as a sort of sublimated spirit which has bodily and spatial existence? Was he bound to conceive it as immaterial? Does the concept of thinking entail immateriality? Descartes' answer to this will be judged differently by different critics. If one read Descartes as maintaining that since thinking does not in itself entail extension, one can conclude that its agent is inextended, thus agreeing that Gassendi's arrow falls far short of the target. But if one read Gassendi as maintaining that there is no more reason to assert inextension of the soul than there is to assert extension, the objection seems more telling. For if one should argue, for example, that one's evidence concerning some argument or other does not permit one to conclude that a certain statement is true or false, one must not conclude that its contradictory is true. Thus if one is arguing to a man's guilt and finds that he could not have been present when the crime of which he is charged took place, one has no evidence of where he actually was at the time of the crime. One has simply evidence of where he was not. Descartes to this could have replied that only two possibilities existed: immateriality and materiality. If then there is no reason to believe that a thing is material, one must conclude that it is immaterial. But again, where did Descartes get the premise that matter and mind sum up all possible kinds of being? Descartes did not bring this up and, it must be confessed, treated the whole matter somewhat cavalierly. Yet when one is building a new method, one might be expected to examine it for all its possible weaknesses. And, if one wishes to interpret his adversary in as sympathetic a manner as possible, one must admit that more was taken for granted by Descartes in this case then he was willing to confess. It is true that at the time no one would have felt the force of this objection very deeply, for the custom of dividing all existence into the material and the incorporeal was firmly established. The question was, however, one of technique, not of fact, and the technique was supposed to produce unquestionable conclusions, unquestionable because indubitable by the very nature of the method.

Another of Gassendi's objections to Cartesianism concerns the souls of the beasts. Descartes had identified thinking with doubting, understanding, affirming, denying, wishing, imagining, and feeling. But how could he deny that the beasts imagined and felt? They have organs similar to ours and therefore one might well argue that these organs serve the same purpose as ours. Moreover, though Descartes maintained that beasts do not choose and exercise volition, nevertheless he merely asserted this, since their behaviour would show the same characteristics as ours does when we choose and make decisions. But here Gassendi did not understand that Descartes' method did not permit him to grant anything which did not follow logically from his clear and distinct premises. The rules of the game would not allow him to make observations of the type which Gassendi demanded. Gassendi's objection was consequently really directed to the method itself rather than to its conclusions. And herein he could defend himself well enough. The idea of thinking might imply that of sensing, but it does not imply that of having sense organs. They are observed to exist but only as extended matter. Gassendi might at this point have said that so do other people, and the only evidence which we have of their minds is what is conveyed to us by their bodily actions, including speech.

There is no need to take up each of Gassendi's objections in detail in a work of the size of this one, for what we are describing is his general difference from his adversary. Briefly it can be said either that Gassendi did not understand the nature of Descartes' method or that he himself refused to use it. And in fact, when we turn to his own philosophy, we see that he is less avid of absolute certainty than Descartes and also more given to observation. The opening words of his best known work, the *Philosophiae epicuri syntagma (Outline of Epicureanism)*, makes it clear that in his eyes the aim of philosophy is to prepare one for a happy life. Since happiness consists in tranquillity and lack of bodily pain, philosophy is a kind of psychotherapy. This was quite in keeping with the Epicurean tradition and, as far as appearances went, quite out of keeping with the Christian tradition. For Gassendi says nothing about the philosopher's task including that of preparing man for his celestial life, or for that matter of preventing his descending to an infernal one. The major theme of his work is the elimination of fear, as it was of the *De rerum natura* of Lucretius, and it was natural that a man who strove for tranquillity, and thought he could find it in philosophy, should turn to the tradition which Lucretius was held to exemplify.

If Descartes is to be called an idealist, in the sense that he found the most certain truth in ideas, then Gassendi might be called a sensationalist, in that he believed the source of all our ideas to be in sensation or to arise out of sensation. Truth is of two sorts, the truth of existential statements and that of judgments. Existential sensory statements are bound to be true, for they simply express that which is. Judicial statements, however, must conform to existential statements, and consequently may be either true or false. Moreover judgments may deal with future conditions or with alternatives, and hence the mind when it is engaged in this exercise must have before it not simply a sensory presentation of colors, sounds, and other affections, but also what Gassendi, in keeping with tradition, called a *praenotio* or preconception. And since there are also judgments of value, of good and bad, of useful and harmful, of what we should do and what we should not do, it is necessary also to consider the criteria of the truth and falsity of such assertions. Hence truth really falls into three categories: truth of immediate experiences, truth of reasoning, truth of valuations.

The senses then can never lie. The notion of sensory deception should be transferred to the judgments which we make about what the senses themselves tell us. The senses are not judicial; the mind is. The mind can and does make judgments about sensory data, but the sense data themselves are simply what they are. They are the confirmation of judgments and in fact the best confirmation of them. But in themselves they are not assertions about anything. When one sees a color, one cannot be mistaken about what colour one sees, even if others see it differently. And so with the other sensory properties of things. When one makes a judgment about the matters of sense, then one is subject to error, as when one says that a red spot is an apple, or a real rather than imaginary apple. Yet each of these judgments must be tested by some evidence and the evidence is always either a sensation which is immediately given to one or which has been given to one. Such a concordance of opinion and sensory experience is verification. And obviously when the concordance cannot be discovered, then our judgments must be false. So far we are in the realm of common sense which demands that direct testimony, as it is called in the courts, be preferred to indirect or circumstantial. It is assumed by Gassendi that all statements of present existence are of the same sort and can be derived ultimately from the testimony of the senses. Yet he also believes that the mind can by the processes of composition, amplification, diminution, translation, and comparison build up complex or derivative ideas from such testimony. We shall see a similar theory in John Locke, who also maintained that our whole stock of ideas came from sensation or "reflection." Both men have been called empiricists and both agreed that raw experience had to be organized before it could be transmuted into knowledge. These procedures themselves which contribute preconceptions, in the technical sense of that word, to knowledge also depend upon sensation. Though Gassendi does not employ the term, they are what give structure to sensory material. We amplify a set of sensations when we imagine a giant, and diminish them when we imagine a pygmy. We compose a set when we imagine such a thing as a centaur, and we compare a set when we note certain similarities between it and another set. But more than that, a preconception gives; us our notions of classes of things, gives us our definitions. For all sensation is of particulars. We build up our universals by the process of diminution through which we are able to discard those characteristics of a particular which differentiate it from other similar particulars. Since we reason by using universals, the whole structure of logic is a contribution made by the operations of the mind to the material furnished us by the senses.

In matters of policy, where valuation is involved, pleasure and pain are the two passions which determine whether we approve or disapprove of anything. Pleasure which is entirely free from pain should be embraced; pain which is entirely free from pleasure should be avoided. The greater pleasure should be preferred to the lesser; the lesser pain should be preferred to the greater. This is the sum total of all ethics. It is an ethics which is clearly contrary to the Christian tradition and has its roots, as have his logic and physics, in what he believed to be the philosophy of Epicurus. But it must not be imagined that Gassendi was willing to content himself with so simple a formula. He knew very well that most men are not happy and also that most pursue pleasure and avoid pain. He knew also that pleasures seldom if ever come unmixed with pain and that often they are followed by pain. Hence the voluptuary is not his ideal man. Yet he insists that happiness is empty without pleasure, for happiness, as he never tires of repeating, consists ultimately in a painless bodily state and a tranquil mind. It is not to be found in the lives of the dissolute or sensual, in banquets and erotic pleasures. For such pleasures are disturbing to both body and mind. The use of reason is essential to the making of our choices, and it is also essential that we have the free power to choose. And both experience and common sense prove that we have them both.

The final question is that of the kind of universe in which we are to achieve our happiness. In answer Gassendi returns to the metaphysics of Epicurus, for like most philosophers he wishes to harmonize his cosmology with his ethics. The cosmos is composed of tiny particles of matter moving in the void. These particles, or atoms, are of a certain magnitude, shape, solidity, and weight. In other words, they have the primary qualities. The void, he believes, is needed to provide space in which they may move. This would seem to imply the materiality of the soul also, and he does in fact believe that matter exists in various degrees of materiality; the plants having a soul closer to pure matter, the animals having souls made of attenuated material parts. This notion of degrees of materiality was more easily accepted by seventeenth-century scientists than by us, for they already believed in the existence of animal spirits which, though material, nevertheless were extremely subtle and, as we have seen, could even be acted upon directly by the soul according to Descartes. Gassendi compares the animal soul to the "bouquet of wine," or the perfume of an unguent, as in La Fontaine we hear of animal souls as *la fleur de la matiere*. Since he follows the Aristotelian psychology in expounding a tripartite human soul composed of sensation, imagination, and understanding and recapitulating the vegetable, animal, and human kingdoms, it is possible that he also made a correlation between each of these sets of psychic powers with each of three degrees of materiality. But it should also be observed that not even his detailed description of the soul is supposed to give us an idea of its "inner nature." All we know is how it manifests itself in activity.

If Descartes can be said to have appeared in literary form in Racine, Gassendi can with equal justice be said to reappear in Molière. Neither playwright was a disciple of either philosopher, but the two currents of thought rose out of the schoolrooms into the salons and were as much part of the intellectual atmosphere of the time as Freudianism and the theory of relativity are of our time.

The *Femmes Savantes* of Molière is not an espousal of everything that Gassendi taught by any means, but the philosophical satire in that play is certainly directed toward the Cartesians. The complete separation between the life of the mind and that of the body, the insistence to the point of absurdity upon precision of statement, the hints that the erotic passions are utterly evil, may be either satires of the Jansenists or of the Cartesians, though it was difficult during the third quarter of the seventeenth century to tell which was which. Men of letters are often influenced by philosophic and scientific currents of thought without being fully aware of their implications and even in ignorance of their sources. It is only in that vague sense of the word that one can speak of Molière as being a Gassendian.

PASCAL

Though much of the opposition to Descartes came from men who followed Gassendi, there was some dissension within his own camp. His method had been adopted by some of his most serious adversaries, like the great Arnauld, who, while rejecting some of his conclusions, nevertheless, as in the *Logique de Port-Royal*, did much to popularize the technique of reaching them. The most important of such men was undoubtedly Blaise Pascal (1623-62). Pascal's claims to fame rest upon a solider foundation than his opposition to Cartesianism, for he was both a mathematician and physicist as well as one of the most forceful writers whom France has produced. Nevertheless, for our purposes he stands as one who saw some of the weaknesses of the regnant philosophy of his times, and consequently we shall make no attempt to give a complete picture or even synopsis of all his philosophic works.

In the famous amulet or *memorial* which Pascal had sewn into his doublet and which is now printed at the beginning of the *Pensées* [6] occurs the line, "God of Abraham, God of Isaac, God of Jacob, not of the philosophers and scholars." This was a reminder to him of the distinction between philosophy and religion, between the metaphysical God and the religious God, between, if one will, the Unmoved Mover of Aristotle and Jehovah. The former was a deduction from certain observations of self-evident propositions about the universe; the latter, an immediate certainty of what he was to call the Heart. The distinction between reasoning and intuition was expressed in the famous paragraph which Brunschvicg put at the opening of his edition of the *Pensées*, in the words, *esprit de géométrie* and *esprit de finesse.* Though no translation of these terms will prove satisfactory to everyone, I shall call the former "deductive reasoning" and the latter "insight." Deductive reasoning was, of course, the method used by Descartes, and Pascal's emphasis upon insight is made in criticism of his predecessor's exclusive use of reasoning. Yet it might be replied that even the *Discourse on Method* admitted the necessity of relying on the natural light, and the discovery of the clear and distinct ideas was not made by deductive reasoning. Pascal, however, maintains not that insight is confined to the discovery of premises from which all else must flow by deductive processes, but that in any sphere of discourse insight may be called into action. There is a moment even in a series of theorems linked together by logical necessity when a man sees what follows in a flash and has no further need to proceed step by step. One might find an analogy to this when one is adding a column of figures or reading a sentence or hearing a melody. One need not add each unit to the one above it or below it; one apprehends in what appears to be a single moment the sum implied. One need not read word by word and spell out each word letter by letter to see the meaning of the sentence; one grasps it as a whole. One does not add note to note, at least in classical composition, but hears the melodic phrase as a single musical figure. So there are minds which can both reason and also see results in a flash of insight. Those men, says Pascal, who are simply geometrical require that they have explained to them definitions and first principles; they are incapable of understanding anything whatsoever unless such clarification be provided. Those who have only insight and no rational powers have not the patience to go back to first principles. But it must not be imagined that insight was to be reserved for religious, aesthetic, or moral problems, and rational deduction for scientific. Such a division would be tempting; but Pascal himself believed that both faculties were necessary in all fields, as far as one can judge from the fragmentary condition of his *Thoughts*.

Apparently—and in the case of Pascal one can never be sure he was impressed by the nonrational factors in all knowledge. We should be likely to call such factors psychological rather than logical. When we assent to a statement, believe in what it says, agree that the facts are as stated, we have done more than analyze its supposed premises and drawn it from them as a necessary conclusion. The sources of belief are never purely logical and sometimes may even run counter to logic. Yet we have to act on our beliefs, not on our deductions until the deductions have been accepted by us as beliefs.

As Pascal says in his most famous sentence, "The heart has its reasons which the reason knows not." But he does not say that such reasons are irrational or cannot be explicated by the reason. He is pointing either to the natural light (the *lumen naturale*), to what Spinoza called intuition, what some of the English Platonists called an active sagacity of the mind, or what others have called common sense. Or he may be indicating the actual fact that reasoning requires orientation and can only justify what from some cause or other we believe. The reasons of the heart may be upset by deductive reasoning but they are not derived from its operations. It is in his insistence upon insight that Pascal is farthest removed from Descartes, though Descartes would have done well to emphasize its contribution to rcasoning itself, if necessary as a set of innate ideas.

It may well be Pascal's interest in the *esprit de finesse* which led to his well-known deprecation of philosophizing: "The true philosopher makes light of philosophy" (*Se moquer de la philosophic, c'est vraiment philosopher*). Here he follows Montaigne, as Brunschvicg points out, for Montaigne also recognized the importance of insight in all matters of reflection. But neither Pascal nor Montaigne seemed to feel the need of clarifying this difficult concept. Montaigne is too slippery a mind to capture; his readers are supposed to have enough wit to grasp the full meaning of his thoughts as they glide by. But unfortunately the philosopher conceives his problem as that of making precise ideas which sometimes by their very nature must remain a hint, a suggestion, a tantalizing glimpse of something which lies behind the horizon of precision. Pascal has to be treated, at least in a history of philosophy, as if he were pushing back those frontiers to their limit. Did he then mean that insight was a special faculty of the human mind, like Bergson's intuition, or did he understand the possibility that what we call insight is the fruit of long study as well as of experience? Is it not at least possible that when a man has lived with an idea long enough, he can grasp its implications as well as its presuppositions without analyzing it? A rapid calculator in arithmctic scldom knows how he reaches his conclusions; he apparently sees them in a glance. A beginner sometimes has to count on his fingers. Any type of behaviour which has to be learned, like walking or writing or speaking, begins by learning a series of steps, which a psychologist would be able to detail one by one. But as soon as the process is learned, the steps drop out of consciousness and the agent performs them without thought. The *esprit de finesse* may well be acquired through long study; yet when acquired it will seem to its possessor to have been always there. Just as few, if any, of us know how we grew out of baby talk into the traditional manner of adult speech, so the philosopher may forget how he developed those fundamental ideas and rules of procedure which either lie behind his thinking or guide it.

Since Pascal's writings on this subject are disconnected and seldom developed at any length, his readers need as much insight as he had himself to understand them. It would be agreeable to be able to say flatly that the *esprit de finesse* was, for instance, faith, or that it had its own subject matter, like the arts, or that it was given to us at birth, or that it was none of these things but something else. There is unfortunately no sound evidence in the *Pensées* from which one can reach any of these or similar conclusions. And yet if one is willing not to analyze too far, one can construct for himself a theory of the interrelations of the two kinds of thinking. Pascal, in opposition to Descartes, can be at the least credited with having pointed out that the geometrical method will not suffice for reaching the truth. For reasoning will neither give one a set of premises nor tell one what to do with them once given. The reason moves in a circle. It is an instrument for exposition, not for discovery. The heart is the discoverer and no one yet has found out its technique. When Pascal says that the more insight one has, the more differences one perceives amongst men, he is certainly speaking in praise of insight. And in such passages as this he is indicating that reason abstracts and finds general truths, certainly a commonplace, but that insight finds the peculiarities of the existent. But he is also saying that to recognize these peculiarities is to come closer to the truth about the world. He is both insisting upon the gap between logic and experience, essence and existence, reason and insight, and upon the greater importance of the latter members of each pair of terms. The word "importance," however, must also be interpreted. And for Pascal we suggest that the truths of insight were both closer to reality than the deductions of the rationalist and for that very reason were of moral and religious value. That they were closer to reality appears in another maxim to the effect that nature established her truths in separation from one another, whereas art, that is, philosophy, has enclosed them one in another. In other words the picture which geometry gives us of inferences being contained in their premises is untrue to the natural order. The world then is a set of individual things each of which is describable in its own terms, very much like a picture gallery in which there is no logical connection between one painting and another, and each is, moreover, isolated from its neighbors by a frame. That this kind of knowledge is of greater moral and religious importance appears in many maxims, of which one of the most striking is that in which he points out that the man of good taste reading a book hopes to find a man and discovers an author, whereas when a writer writes in natural style, the reader expecting to find an author, discovers a man. It is precisely such writers, those who use *le style naturel*, who "teach nature that she can speak of all things, and even of theology". To demonstrate the moral and religious importance of this kind of knowledge requires simply a reading of almost any page of the *Pensées* taken at random. For surely the basic anxiety of Pascal demands no proof today.

Pascal's logical skill taught him that if the world is one, there is no rational description of the whole. The reason must by its very nature classify its subjects; it deals with common nouns, universals, and it is only insofar as a thing exemplifies a universal that we can discuss it rationally. The world as a whole can be given a name: Nature, the Cosmos, Creation. Its parts can be described by comparison with other parts. But just as a man or a work of art or a historical event is more than what it can be described as being, so is the world as a whole. The famous passage on the relative scale of human affairs is based upon this incapacity of ours to grasp the whole of things otherwise than by insight. Man in the natural order is "a zero from the point of view of infinity, a whole from the point of view of zero, a mid-point between nothing and the whole." He can know appearances from his own point of view but must despair of knowing the beginning and the end of things. The one mind which can understand this is its author. The end of knowledge then is ignorance. But our ignorance will give us a proper sense of humility. We are suspended between the two infinites: the infinitely great and the infinitely small, and both seemed incomprehensible at this time. Curiously enough, a rational method of dealing with the latter was developed by Newton and Leibniz shortly after this time, and in the nineteenth century Cantor developed a rational definition of the former. But one is seriously deceived if one concludes that Pascal's situation would have been alleviated by these tools. For at this point he was dealing not merely with knowledge but with feeling. His knowledge, even if perfected by mathematics, would have reinforced his feeling of helplessness. Like Bruno he saw himself caught between two extremes over which he could have no control. This vision, which he so often expressed in thoughts of terror, was a vision, not a philosophic theory. With an imagination equalled only by Dante's he visualized himself, as Whitman was to say, "seeking the spheres to connect them" and knew that only prayer and self-abasement would enlighten him. His philosophy leads him immediately into religion and rational knowledge to a comprehension of its ultimate worthlessness. "Here is our true condition: We are incapable of certain knowledge and of absolute ignorance. We drift along on a vast plane pushed from one end to the other. Whatsoever mooring we think of tying up to and making secure, tosses about and drifts away. And if we follow it, it escapes our grasp, slips away from under, and moves off in an unending flight. Nothing stops for us. We have a burning desire for a strong support and a final foundation on which to build a tower reaching into infinite heights. But our whole foundation cracks beneath us and the earth opens down to the abyss."

With this attitude toward knowledge, it was natural enough for him to give as one of his aims opposition to those who made science supreme, such as Descartes. For Descartes, as he says, gave God only the function of setting the world in motion and then withdrawing from the scene. Such philosophy is both useless and dubitable, useless since it does not lead to God, dubitable because even its first principles are uncertain. It would perhaps be sounder criticism to say that Descartes had never reached his first principles, since he utilized methods which he had never completely analyzed. We have ourselves pointed out above that there were several ideas of which he had no doubt whatsoever, in spite of his pretensions to universal doubt, amongst which was his belief in the natural light and the complete efficacy of the geometrical method. Since the natural light varied from individual to individual and the reason relegated God to the position of First Mover, it was clear that neither was a satisfactory basis for philosophy. But here it must be said, in defense of Descartes, that Pascal laid down as one of his basic principles the independence of love and reason. When he says that the heart, not the reason, feels God, that the heart's feelings are not prompted by the reason, he was in effect attributing to what Descartes would have called a passion a cognitive power. So Rousseau in the *Profession of Faith of the Savoyard Vicar* was to insist that in religious and moral matters a non-rational power within us was supreme, and in fact even Kant in the *Critique of Practical Reason* was not far from the same position when he insisted that our moral needs could dictate conclusions to the reason. For Pascal the first principles of any truth could be discovered only by the heart. He cites as his examples our knowledge that space, time, motion, and numbers exist. We do not know such fundamental ideas by reasoning. We grasp them by means of the natural light or what later was to be called common sense. "First principles," he says, "are felt; theorems are deduced." It makes very little difference what name one gives to our apprehension of these principles, except when it is a question of their connotations. Unless logicians find some way of proving that only a given set of premises will imply a given theorem—and no such way has been discovered to date—no logical method of establishing them will be at our disposal. Here Pascal, whether one feels the force of his religious debates or not, is on the firmest ground. But it must also be granted that there is no sound way of arguing about first principles if they have no logical basis. If Pascal's feelings demand miracles and paradoxes as evidence for God's existence, that turns out to be his affair, not that of his opponents. But though his opponents may disagree about what their feelings demand, that they must have recourse to feeling, instinct, intuition, conjecture, or what is sometimes called experience, or common sense, will always be true. Pascal does not hesitate to admit that his heart and that of his fellow Christians are not like those of everyone. They have been touched by grace; their adversaries can only wait and hope for the same illumination. There is no point in reasoning with them, for reason is incapable of demonstrating the undemonstrable. This position which seemed so impregnable to its architect turned out, unhappily for him, to be unacceptable by that institution for whose sake and protection he had built it. Not only was Jansenism as a whole condemned, but the idea that faith could be used to prove God's existence was specifically condemned as late as 1840 when Bautain subscribed to the thesis that "Reasoning can with certainty prove the existence of God and the infinity of His perfections. Faith, a heavenly gift, is posterior to revelation; hence it cannot be adduced against an atheist for proving God's existence."

HUET

A third member of the anti-Cartesian circle was Pierre Daniel Huet (1630-1721). Huet, who was one of the most renowned scholars of his day, in his youth became an enthusiastic student of Descartes' philosophy, but bit by bit was not only convinced of the unsoundness of the Cartesian method but was also converted to a Pyrrhonic scepticism. His scepticism, like that of Pascal, was developed in the interests of religion, as was that of Montaigne, Charron, and La Mothe le Vayer.

Since his attack on Descartes preceded the publication of his book in defense of scepticism by over thirty years, we shall discuss them in that order.

Huet's leading objection to Cartesianism was what he believed to be the weakness of the principle of methodical doubt. For Descartes does not merely suspend judgment about the existence of an external world, the truths of mathematics, and, in short, of all our knowledge; his doubt amounts to the assertion of their falsity. But to believe in the falsity of an assertion is not to doubt; it is to believe. But equally shaky is the *cogito*. For if he were going to doubt everything, he ought also to have doubted his own existence, even when he knew that he doubted. For what is this *ego* which thinks? Has Descartes, in announcing that he is when he thinks, doing more than saying that he is when he is? Has he been able to distinguish between his existence and his thinking? Huet maintains that the reply is in the negative and that, by Descartes' own admission, the existence of the *ego* consists precisely in its thinking. He also assumes that he as a thinking being is the agent of thinking. This amounts to assuming without proof that the act of thought requires an agent, which if he had really wanted to doubt, he could well have doubted. The distinction between an act and its agent is, it cannot be denied, made by Descartes, and it is made without any suspicion on his part that it is an important distinction. Here Huet would seem to have put his finger on a weakness in the *Method* which has seldom been seen. When, however, he adds that a man who could doubt of his own existence could also doubt that he is thinking, he clearly missed the point. For since thinking and doubting were equivalent, in that doubting was a species of thinking, all Descartes could be said to have maintained was that when we doubt, we cannot doubt that we are doubting. That, it is obvious, would not have carried him very far along his road to the construction of a philosophy, but regardless of that, he should not be accused of errors which he did not make. Similarly when Huet interprets the *cogito* as if it were a syllogism, he is also beside the mark, for Descartes never maintained that it was one.

Among the things which Descartes might have doubted were the rules of logic. And Huet is right again when he points out that he took them for granted. We have pointed out above that Descartes' belief in the natural light was suspended, and it was probably the natural light which led him to the acceptance of these rules. When Descartes insists that "it is self-contradictory that that which is thinking should not exist while it is thinking," the self-contradiction appears only in the illumination of the natural light. Why then was he willing to accept some things according to the natural light and not others? Why was the existence of a thinking agent necessary and not the truth of such an axiom as that the whole is greater than any of its parts? Both turn out to be justified only by the natural light and Descartes gives us no principle by means of which we can accept some of its discoveries and reject others.

There is, furthermore, a threefold ambiguity, says Huet, in the word "thinking." There are the thinking mind, the subject matter of thought, and the action of the thinking mind upon that about which it is thinking. This is not merely a lexicographical exercise on Huet's part, for he points out that since the word "thinking" is used by Descartes to name all the mental faculties, it must also name the affections, in which it is assumed that something is done to the mind, that is, the mind is not purely active. If that is the case, then it must be of a nature capable of receiving influences from without and is not merely the thinking subject. But that in itself seems to imply that there is a world of things external to the mind and one need not have recourse to the veracity of God in presenting us with a world of possible experiences. This, as readers of nineteenth-century philosophy will observe, is a curious anticipation of later dialectical proofs, proofs which depend upon the supposed implications of ideas, or better, the implications of the sentences which express such ideas. Whether one has confidence in this manner of reasoning or not, it became one which was to be dominant in the German idealistic tradition and in fact has intimate relations to the Cartesian method itself insofar as the *cogito* is concerned. Huet, then, is attempting to use Descartes' own first principle as the initial premise of a philosophy and to draw out of it implications which were not seen by its author.

Again, Huet maintains that if the *cogito* is both thinking and the awareness that one is thinking, two mental acts are involved, and the second really is a matter of memory. For one cannot at the same time have an idea and the idea of that idea. Therefore, he says, since "I think" and "to think" are two separate ideas, the former does not mean and cannot mean, "I am aware that I have been thinking." If then memory is called upon to assert that one has been thinking, there is always a theoretical possibility of error when one asserts, "I am aware that I have been thinking." There is no more certainty in this assertion than in the assertion that I am aware of having walked or eaten or slept. Hence, he concludes that the proof of one's existence from the *cogito* is far from indubitable. And if one maintains that, regardless of the laws of logic, I am aware of myself in the act of thinking, then one relies upon the natural light, and why restrict its operations to self-consciousness? Why not continue and maintain that we also know the axioms of arithmetic in the same manner? How can one doubt that equals added to equals give equals, and yet not doubt that one is aware of oneself thinking? Huet here is insisting on the necessity of more assumptions than Descartes was willing to make. And his insistence arises from his observation that Descartes makes more assumptions than he is aware of. Again, when Descartes says that God cannot be a deceiver, Huet is only too happy to agree, for he is a Christian. But, he says, "We are arguing here from reason, not from faith, from philosophical, not from theological principles." And from such principles we have no way of knowing whether God is a deceiver or not. "As a philosopher, you do not know what God is, what He can do, what He wishes." On the other hand, even if God is not a deceiver, can we argue that He must have made us so that we cannot be deceived? For we are often deceived in fact.

Huet now turns to the followers of Descartes, *recentiores quidam Cartesianae doctrinae patroni*, who say that though we may be deceived when we reason, yet we could not have been made by God such that we would be deceived in the apprehension of simple ideas. Such apprehension is vision. But they give no reason why the vision of a simple truth, such an arithmetical axiom or the *cogito*, should be any more veridical than reasoning. Why should they be so doubtful of their premises and so certain of their conclusions? Such men are sceptics in their beginnings, dogmatists in their conclusions (*Pyrrhones in aditu, in exitu meri Pythagorae*). For if even the principles of mathematics can be doubted, and they are doubted by such Cartesians though apprehended as clear and distinct ideas, then we can be deceived by direct vision as well as by reasoning. The upshot of all this is that Cartesianism stops doubting at precisely the point at which doubt should arise, and no certain criterion of truth is given us beyond the faith which is required by religion. If this is so, then why not start with religion and admit the vanity of all philosophizing? We are not far here from Pascal's thought that to ridicule philosophy is to philosophize.

Huet's critique of Cartesianism is extended to cover the theory of the criteria of truth, clear and distinct ideas, the proofs of the existence of God, and the duality of mind and body. Briefly, he attacks the doctrine of the absolute truth of clear and distinct ideas on the ground that it amounts to nothing more than faith in the natural light and in God's unswerving veracity. For some ideas which seem clear and distinct to some people turn out to be false, some true ideas seem clearer and more distinct than others, and no idea is so false as not to have some clarity and distinctness. (He might have added that if one had a completely obscure idea, one would never know whether it was true or false since one would not presumably know what it meant.) In short, Descartes is simply saying that a true idea is true and gives us no real criterion of truth. The criticism here has a certain sting. But when Huet attacks Descartes' dualism, his criticism, though full of common sense, fails to understand the method by which the doctrine is reached. Huet maintains that though Descartes first is aware of himself thinking, yet he could not think unless he had a body. That in fact may be true, but it is beside the point. For Descartes was looking for what was implied in the concept of a mind, that is, thinking, not what was believed to be necessary in order for a mind to think. It is very strange that so acute a critic as Huet did not see this. But in it he was not alone, for Gassendi had also assumed much the same attitude.

It will be recalled that one of Descartes' main theories concerned the existence of innate ideas. Certain ideas which he believed could not have come into our minds from perceptual experience, such as the idea of God, must have been expressions of innate thoughts. "When Descartes writes that those eternal ideas, for instance, the axioms of geometry, have been written into our minds by God, as laws are given by the King to the minds of those who obey his rule, he confesses that there is a distinction to be made between ideas and the faculty of thinking. Nevertheless let us thank Descartes, and so we may interpret his opinion conveniently, that an innate idea, for instance, that of God, is a mental faculty of thinking generated within us in a certain sure manner; wherefore every time that the mind thinks, the idea of God will arise in it." But how does such an idea differ from any other? Even a fiction will arise every time the mind thinks of it. We form an idea of Alexander, and every time we think of Alexander the idea of that king will arise before us. But in the latter case we know the source of the idea in experience. In the former we do not. But we do not find the ideas themselves in experience; we find only the things which give rise to the ideas. Thus we may form universal ideas from our knowledge of particulars; but no particular actually has the character of a universal. Just as in Peter and John and other individual men we apprehend that they are animals furnished with reason, yet by the inspection of neither Peter nor John nor any other individual man can we educe this and compose into a unity that which was multiple, to say nothing of constructing and erecting that general and universal idea, and asserting that every man is a rational animal. We must therefore conclude that any universal is as innate as any other and that the idea of God or of the mathematical axioms is no more innate than others. But we know that such universals as the rationality of man are not innate, nor does Descartes say they are. But if they are not, how does he justify the distinction between those that are and those that are not?

So much is sufficient to indicate roughly Huet's objections to Cartesianism. But his own philosophy is to be found in the posthumous *Philosophical Treatise of the Weakness of the Human Mind.* This book, probably composed about 1690, was kept in manuscript and shown only to a few intimate friends during its author's lifetime. The reason for this can only be guessed, but guessing is not difficult once one has read the volume. For Huet in it tries to demonstrate the weakness of the reason and the necessity of faith which is suprarational. Though this might appear to bolster the cause of religion, actually the ecclesiastical authorities have never been willing to accept a doctrine which did not grant certainty to the reason within its own sphere. Huet, however, was unwilling to grant it even limited sovereignty. His motivation, as he gives it in his introductory chapter, is the familiar one of many a pious sceptic: that no certainty is to be found in philosophy, as is proved by the dissensions not only amongst philosophers of various schools but also amongst those of a single school. He concluded from his reading that philosophy "was not so much a search for the Truth, as the philosophers boasted, as a method of clever chicanery and subtle disputation." He then turned, he says, to Diogenes Laertius and found in the accounts of the sceptics what he was looking for. Though he could not agree to all their opinions, yet he could agree that the human mind by itself could not attain certainty and that the source of all our errors was the precipitation of our minds, "which makes us give our faith too lightly to the opinions which have been proposed to us." In that spirit of scepticism he breaks up his study into three parts: the weakness of the human reason, the best method of philosophizing, and answers to objections.

In order to analyze the procedures of the reason, Huet opens his discussion by an exposition of the nature of the understanding. The understanding is the reception of impressions made upon the brain by nervous currents stimulated by external objects. This is briefly, and in its general features, the thesis of the empirical tradition in philosophy, whether it is expressed in terms of atoms and eidola by Democritus; or of air waves, auditory end organs, afferent nerves, and the cortex. The details are, to be sure, entirely different, but it is important to note that Huet expressly points out that he is not continuing the Scholastic tradition of sensible species, in accordance with which the mind received qualitative duplicates of the various sensory data, colors, sounds, and the like. Thus, for him an idea is not an image or duplicate or anything in the external world, but an effect made upon the soul by a disturbance in the brain. These effects of cerebral events are then acted upon by the understanding to the end that they are compared and judged. Distinguishing between truth of existence and truth of judgment, Huet asserts that a judgment is true when the understanding relates the ideas "which are in us" with the objects from which they ultimately arise. Since the understanding must make the comparison between the two beings, the idea and that of which it is the idea, it is clear that difficulties will arise in being certain of the truth of any judgment. One might expect that a philosopher who had begun with an empiricist technique might continue with it. It would be normal for him to point out the difficulty, if not the impossibility, of comparing an idea with that of which it is the idea, since, as every Freshman learns, if we know only through ideas, we cannot grasp their subject matters directly.

But Huet begins by pointing out that there are some things which we know with the highest certitude, namely the truths of religion, of which we can have no rational knowledge. In other words, he does not reject ideas which cannot be known rationally; he rejects rationality. The truths of revelation are no less true for being non-rational and non-empirical. The Bible is full of passages which demonstrate our intellectual weakness; and as Huet was an erudite bishop, he could put his hands on page after page of scriptural texts to fortify his statement. St. Paul, Arnobius, Lactantius, St. Gregory Nazianzen, St. Augustine, and other fathers and ecclesiastical writers are called upon to testify to the fallibility of the human reason in questions of dogma; and the use of dialectic to prove the certitudes of faith is ridiculed. Now the only way open to the critic of Huet at this point was that of denying the truths of faith. But that way was too rocky for most men to follow. Either, then, an idea could be true and yet nonrational or it must be false if non-rational. Huet may have thought that he was defeating the rationalist by his insistence upon the nonrationality of dogma. In reality he was clearing the road for such people as Bayle and the anti-Christians of the eighteenth century. In order to fortify faith he attacked reason.

Having disposed of dogma, which has the highest certainty and yet is not open to rational justification, Huet turns to more earthly matters. To demonstrate, he says, that any empirical proposition is true, one must be sure that the idea one has of an object resembles the object itself. But that is impossible, for the effect upon the nervous system of the object may modify to some extent the appearance of the object, and usually does. This is easily demonstrated, as it was to be over and over again in later years, by pointing out that if one has an idea of, let us say, a tree, the tree is visible, immobile, and solid; its image is invisible, is not solid, and is "very mobile, very thin, and very fluid." The reason why it is invisible is, Huet believes, that though it stimulates in us the judgment which we make of its object, we see the object, not its image. Just how this occurs is left unexplained, as if Huet did not see the problem involved in the situation. If the image is actually the impression made upon the brain, then of course it is invisible; but if it is invisible, then there is no way of knowing what it looks like and its very existence is asserted by inference. The term "image" in that case is justified only by tradition, according to which physical objects emitted "sensible species" of themselves which entered the mind in various ways which do not concern us here. Certainly Huet may be said to have thought of them as a psychologist today would think of whatever happens in the visual area of the cortex when an afferent nerve current from the eye reaches it. For his argument continues to show how various accidents might modify the image to the point where its resemblance with the object to which it refers was extremely attenuated. It has, for instance, to traverse a medium which may distort it; if visual, it will vary with illumination; if distant, its size will be much smaller than that of the object from which it emanates; regardless of its sensory organ, it will vary with our state of health, age, fatigue. In short, Huet here revives the tropes of Aenesidemus which he found in Sextus Empiricus and which were constantly introduced to weaken men's faith in sensory knowledge.

To such objections are added the difficulty of knowing things which are in a constant state of flux, of attaining over-individual knowledge in view of the individual differences in men and the interconnections between things which makes the universe a network of related things which stretches well beyond our intellectual grasp. If one wishes to know what a man is, one has to know all about his soul and his body. But if one begin with the body, one will have to know all about the four elements which, compose it. And to know the elements one will have to ascend to the first causes of things, which are unknowable. If one start with the soul, one will have to inquire "what it is, where it is, how it acts, what is the effect of its action, how it is joined to the body. When all that is learned, one will have to ask what the reason is, what is its right use, what are its effects. This study will lead you into the study of all of dialectic. The matter will proceed *ad infinitum.*" Life is too short to permit us to attain such wisdom. After similar arguments about the inefficacy of the reason, and an appeal to all the various philosophers of the past who have maintained similar theses, Huet concludes that neither perception nor reason are reliable guides to truth. Thus the only philosophers who can never be deceived are those who assert nothing. This amounts to saying that if one keeps silent, one will never be contradicted. But that both he and his fellow sceptics use perceptual and rational evidence to prove their points seems of little importance to him.

The outcome of this is that one must turn to faith to provide us with that truth which reason cannot find. We have to live in accordance with some ideas which we will accept as true, and if such ideas are probable, that ought to be enough.

Such probability is not that of the statistician; it is not calculable. It is rather the psychological probability of ideas that are tested by that vague criterion known as experience. In ethical matters the precepts revealed by God will guide us, and, just as true happiness cannot be attained on this earth, so ultimate truth must always escape us.

Yet we can always manage our lives without philosophy; the proof is that most of us do so. So the man innocent of science can still believe in God and does, can run his business without philosophy and does. If the traditional argument against scepticism, that it is a self-refuting theory, is raised, Huet replies that he does not assert that all knowledge is always vain, but that, on the contrary, some ideas are true and some false, and that, other than those which are based upon faith in revelation, we have no certain way of distinguishing between them. We can, however, test some of them by what we know through faith, and if they are in agreement with faith, then we can accept them as true. This is the outcome of Huet's scepticism. The whole book is an apology for the program "I believe in order to understand." As such, it will be the target of ridicule by rationalists and empiricists as well. But Huet, whatever his weaknesses may be, realizes that formal reasoning must have a program. It is for him the art of substantiating ideas which one is already entertaining, or, if one prefer, the art of achieving consistency. Faith and common sense give us that which we wish to prove. It will not be any the less certain if unproved, but we will feel more comfortable if we can give demonstrations of our beliefs. That is justifiable, he believes, but we must not take it too seriously. As Bradley was to say in the nineteenth century, metaphysics is the giving of bad reasons for what we believe on instinct.

The technique of Huet was not very different from that of Bayle, his more famous contemporary. We shall, however, postpone our discussion of Bayle until we shall have treated philosophers in other countries and of other tendencies preceding him.

Idealism is the philosophical theory which maintains that

the ultimate nature of reality is based on the mind or ideas. In the philosophy of perception, idealism is contrasted with realism in which the external world is said to have an apparent absolute existence. Epistemological idealists (such as Kant) claim that the only things which can be directly known for certain are just ideas.

In the philosophy of mind, idealism is the opposite of materialism, in which the ultimate nature of reality is based on physical substances. Idealism and materialism are both theories of monism as opposed to dualism and pluralism. Idealism sometimes refers to a tradition in thought that represents things of a perfect form, as in the fields of ethics, morality, aesthetics, and value. In this way, it represents a human perfect being or circumstance. In the ancient philosophy of the Vedas, idealism refers to the dynamic consciousness of living beings that emanates from the divine cosmic source. Individual societies have inspired and grown their own specific set of idealism, but they all have these generalities in common.

Idealism is a philosophical movement in Western thought, and names a number of philosophical positions with sometimes quite different tendencies and implications in politics and ethics; for instance, at least in popular culture, philosophical idealism is associated with Plato and the school of platonism.

British idealism enjoyed ascendancy in English-speaking philosophy in the later part of the 19th century. F. H. Bradley of Merton College, Oxford, saw reality as a monistic whole, which is apprehended through "feeling", a state in which there is no distinction between the perception and the thing perceived. Like Berkeley, Bradley thought that nothing can be known to exist unless it is known by a mind.

13

Les Philosophes in Philosophy

Introduction

Renaissance, men like Telesio, Bacon, Montaigne and Descartes, were all eager to find a new method of inquiry which would supersede the supposed method of Aristotle, these men were as eager to draw up compendiums of information which would be reliable and which might serve as a foundation for human education. These compendiums were to contain the facts, and to show what supposed facts part of traditional beliefs were unwarranted. To do this, tradition had to be examined with the same impartiality as contemporary beliefs. The principle of authority as a test for truth had to be rejected and its place taken by the laws of evidence. The laws of evidence, as distinguished from the laws of logic, were practical rules for ascertaining what ideas could be accepted as they were pronounced by their adherents and what must be rejected. Thus in general we find these men maintaining that a witness who contradicts himself is unreliable. A book, usually thought of as authoritative, must bc held in suspicion if it states one opinion in one place and another in another when both are about the same subject. Such a book may be right in one of its opinions or wrong in both; but it cannot be right in both. Since the book which was most frequently used as a source of ideas on both history and philosophy was the Bible, the Bible was submitted to the same type of scrutiny as any other writing. It had been pointed out as early as Philo Judaeus that the Bible contained inconsistencies; but those who maintained it to be a work of revelation, given to us by God "who is neither deceived nor capable of deception," also maintained that the inconsistencies could all be eliminated if one would interpret it allegorically. In the second place, a witness is unreliable if he has something to gain by his testimony and, contrariwise, his reliability is less suspect if he has something to lose by his testimony. A man, for instance, who is named as heir to an estate in a will and who testifies that the deceased was insane at the time he made the will, is normally considered to have less prejudice than if he were to testify that the deceased had never been so clear-minded as when he wrote his testament. When a scientist advances evidence against his own theories, we tend to have greater respect for his word than when he neglects such evidence. Protestants who defend the burning of Servetus and Catholics who defend that of Bruno are not the best historians of either event, though as a matter of fact they may have been able to lay aside their personal interests in these cases and discuss them with complete objectivity. Finally, a witness is considered more reliable when he has first-hand knowledge of what he is talking about than when he is talking from hearsay. In scholarly matters one is supposed to use as far as possible primary sources. If one is writing about the opinions of Bacon or Locke, it is usually considered proper to go to their books for one's information rather than to books about them. Hence in religious matters it was believed by *Les Philosophes* that the Bible itself was better evidence about its teachings than commentaries on the Bible, though it must be admitted that the knowledge of Hebrew and Greek which is required to read it is not a common accomplishment. To examine original sources, to look for prejudice in authorities, to dig out inconsistencies was the proposed technique of these men. I am not saying that they were always successful in applying it.

Enlightenment, what the French of those days called *les lumières*, was what was needed if the human lot was ever to be improved. Give men the facts and they will use them properly. Teach them to reason correctly and they will avoid error and ignorance. Since truth is homogeneous, discord will be eliminated once all men possess the truth. Men disagree because of ignorance, false information, false inferences. Such seems to have been the general program of these reformers.

Beneath all this there appears to be an assumption that men really want knowledge and prefer the naked truth to the embellishments of superstition. But where a Milton writes "How charming is divine Philosophy", Keats writes, "Do not all charms fly at the mere touch of cold Philosophy?" The charm resides apparently in the applied ornaments, the metaphors and similes, the rhetoric, the emotional overtones which Plato satirized in the *Phaedrus*. A survey of human tastes will show that some men prefer the charms to that which is beneath them; others prefer the substratum to the charms; and a third find the simple and clear statement of the truth charming enough. There is to be sure a fourth group, and not the least influential, who maintain that the beliefs of their fathers suffice and that examination of what common sense or tradition propounds is sacrilege. They want the comfortable assurance that what has always been believed is unquestioned. Nothing, of course, has always been believed, but it is true that there is a body of opinion, usually uncriticized, which is upheld by the great mass of mankind, which gives stability to society, and which is believed automatically, or, as it is more commonly expressed, instinctively. By the eighteenth century this mass of popular doctrine had been shaken by the Protestant Reformation, the spread of free inquiry in the northern countries, the actual discoveries and inventions which had been made in increasing numbers during the previous three centuries.

It requires no great analytical skill to see that a second

presupposition was guiding these men: the presupposition that the frontiers of knowledge had not been reached and that no body of writings contained all possible truth. The demand for freedom of research was foolish if all was known and nothing new was to be discovered. There were several attitudes toward this question. On the one hand, there were men just as honest as their opponents who believed that all knowledge was already discovered, at least implicitly, and that a philosopher had only to explicate the ideas resident in the traditional beliefs. On the other hand, there were men, like those whom we are to examine in this chapter, who maintained and sought to prove that really new ideas, ideas which did not follow logically from traditional beliefs, could be proved and had been proved. But again some of the former could maintain that knowledge had to be appraised; that some knowledge was important and some unimportant, as Socrates has been reported to believe that astronomical subjects were of less interest than moral. But the latter group would reply that the implications of, let us say, astronomy gave man a new sense of his place in the universe and hence could not be separated from such a subject as ethics. All truth was frequently held to be of equal interest since one could not foretell the implications which any given idea or theory might have for human life. And, finally, if man is a rational animal, then he becomes less of a man when his reason is not allowed full play.

A program such as this demands first a compilation of what is really known, and the period which we are discussing the last few years of the seventeenth century and the first half of the eighteenth was famous for several such compilations. Of these the two most important are Bayle *Dictionnaire* and the *Encyclopédie* of Diderot and d'Alembert.

MORERI AND BAYLE

An encyclopedia is etymologically the whole circle of subjects necessary for education. Pliny *Natural History*, the works of Isidore of Seville and Cassiodorus, the *Specula* of Vincent de Beauvais are commonly cited as forerunners of our modern encyclopedias. But in 1674 appeared a *Grand Dictionnaire Historique*, by Louis Moreri which is the grandfather of modern works of this sort. Moreri organized his articles in alphabetical order, which he thought was an innovation, covered a very wide range of subjects, and thus provided his readers with easily found information on matters which he at least believed to be important. He has been criticized for his bias and did indeed spend a good bit of space refuting the ideas of some of the men he was writing about. He was more vulnerable to the charge of lack of judgment, for his credulity in using ancient sources was very great, though no greater than that of some of our contemporaries who pillage Diogenes Laertius for facts about the biographies of the ancient philosophers.

It was Moréri who gave Bayle the idea of writing his famous *Dictionnaire historique et critique*. Pierre Bayle (1647-1706), born a Protestant, converted to Catholicism for a short time as a schoolboy, and relapsing into Protestantism in which he died, was a man of enormous erudition who, without the benefit of modern libraries with their subject indexes or bibliographies, managed to read pretty nearly everything in French and Latin which was pertinent to his subjects. Like Spinoza, of whom he thoroughly disapproved, he found relative safety in the Netherlands and consistently refused positions which would tie him to a school or faction. His Protestantism, though fervent, never reached the fanaticism of his coreligionist Jurieu, and he found himself able to maintain as objective an attitude to his own sect as to others. He had had the advantage of Jesuit schooling, so that when he wrote of Catholic doctrine it was from first-hand knowledge. And like all scholars of his day, he was well trained in the classics. His lack of knowledge of German and English was of little importance since most learned works were written in French or Latin. It was, however, not merely the facts which Bayle presented which were of significance, but his method of criticism. His article on David will serve as a fair sample, and since it was one of those which laid him open to harsh criticism from Protestants as well as Catholics, it may be well to say a few words about it.

After giving the usual account of the story of King David with copious references to the Bible, Bayle says, "He was a radiant center of holiness in the Church; he sheds a light of fertile consolation and piety on it which it would be impossible to sufficiently admire; but he had his faults and even in his last words will be found the obliquities of politics. Holy Scripture reports them merely as history; that is why each of us is permitted to judge them. Let us end by saying that the story of King David could reassure crowned heads against the fears which stern casuists might arouse in them by maintaining that it is almost impossible for a king to be saved." Thanks to the activities of the Censors, Bayle changed this to read, "He was a radiant center of holiness in the Church; he sheds a light of fertile consolation and piety on it; but he had his faults." The rest of the passage which I have translated is omitted. But it was probably not so much the body of the article as the commentaries which caused the greatest trouble. As a note to the question of Saul, "Abner, whose son is this youth?", Bayle writes:

It is somewhat strange that Saul should not have known David on that day, seeing that the young man had played instruments several times in his presence, to calm the dark vapors which tormented him. If a story such as this appeared in Thucydides or Livy, every critic would conclude unanimously that the copyists had transposed some pages, published something in one place, repeated something in another, or inserted passages which were inauthentic in the author's work. But one must be careful of such suspicions as far as the Bible is concerned. There have been nevertheless people bold enough to maintain that all the chapters or all the verses of the Book of Samuel no longer have their original place. The Abbé de Choisi had solved the difficulty, it seems to me, in a better way. " David," he says, "was brought to Saul: first he did not recognize him, though he had seen him several times when he used to come to play the harp for him; but as several years had passed, as David at that time was very young, as he had come to the Court in the role of a musician, and as he then saw him clothed as a shepherd, there is no wonder that a King, burdened with business, whose mind was sick, should have forgotten the face of a young man in which there was nothing extraordinary." I should only have liked him not to say:

(1) there had been several years that Saul had not seen David;

(2) that David was very young when he came to the Court as a musician. There is no evidence that he was much less young when he killed Goliath, than when he came to Saul's Court for the first time; for at the time of his first trip, he "was a mighty valiant man, and a man of war, and prudent in matters, and a comely person"; he was only thirty years old, when after the death of Saul, he was elected King; and many years must have passed between the death of Goliath and that of Saul.

Though Bayle prefaced all this with the caution that one should not treat sacred history as one does profane, nevertheless he himself is obviously using exactly the same technique on both. The conclusion which the reader of his note was forced to draw was evident.

Nor does Bayle hesitate to expatiate on the faults of the great prophet and sage. Relating David's request of the King of Gath (I Sam. 27:5) for a city in which he might live and the grant of Ziklag, Bayle adds the following comment:

David took himself there with his soldiers and did not let their swords rust. He led them frequently on raids and killed men and women without pity; he merely let the cattle live; they were the only booty with which he returned; he was afraid that prisoners would reveal the whole mystery to King Achish; that is why he took no prisoners but slew all of both sexes. The mystery which he did not want revealed is that these ravages took place not on the lands of the Israelites, as he maintained to the King of Gath, but on the lands of the former people of Palestine. Frankly this conduct was pretty bad: to cover a fault a greater fault is committed. A king to whom obligations are owed is deceived; prodigious cruelty is committed in order to conceal this deceit. If David had been asked, "By what authority do you do these things?" what could he have replied? A private personage as he was, a fugitive who had found asylum in the land of a neighbouring prince, has he the right to wage war on his own account and without any commission emanating from the ruling sovereign of the country? Did David have such a commission? Did he not on the contrary abandon both the intentions and the interests of the King of Gath? It is certain that if today a private person of any birth whatsoever, should act as David did on this occasion, he could hardly avoid being called names bearing very little honour. I realize that the most illustrious heroes and the most famous prophets of the Old Testament sometimes approved of putting all life to the sword; and therefore I should hesitate to call what David did inhumane if he had been authorized to do so by the orders of a prophet, or if God by inspiration had commanded him to act in this way: but it is manifest by the very silence of Scripture on this point that he did it all by his own decision.

There is no need to quote his long disquisition of David's behaviour toward Uriah and the treachery which he plotted with Abner, but it is important to quote his justification for his comments on the King's behaviour.

Those who may find it strange that I should speak my feelings on these acts of David, compared with natural ethics, are asked to consider three things—

(1) That they must themselves confess that the conduct of this prince toward Uriah is one of the greatest crimes which can be committed. Between them and me there is but a difference of degree; for I recognize with them that the faults of this Prophet did not prevent his being filled with piety and with a great zeal for the glory of the Eternal. He was subject to waves of passion and of grace. This is a fate attached to our nature since the sin of Adam. God's grace led him frequently, but on various occasions his passions got the upper hand: politics imposed silence on Religion.

(2) That it is quite permissible for a private person like me to judge of facts contained in the Scriptures when they are not expressly qualified as coming from the Holy Spirit. If Scripture when reporting an act blames it or praises it, no one is permitted to appeal from this judgment; each must

base his approbation or blame on the model of Scripture. I have not been false to this duty: the facts on which I have tendered my small opinion are reported in Holy Scripture with no comments by the Holy Spirit, no trait of approbation.

(3) One would do great harm to the eternal Laws and consequently to true Religion, if one gave ground to the profane to object that, as soon as a man shared in God's inspiration, we should look upon his conduct as a rule of morals; so that we should not dare condemn the acts of people most opposed to the notions of equity, when it is he who has committed them. There is no middle point whatsoever; either these acts are worthless or acts similar to them are not evil; but since one must choose one or the other of these alternatives, is it not better to save the interests of morality than the glory of an individual? Otherwise, would one not bear witness to his preference for accusing the honour of God than that of a mortal?

What this amounts to is more than a denunciation of certain acts of David. It is a profession of principle: that one is free to interpret the Bible as one would any other book and that, in the second place, we know what is moral and immoral without the study of instances. Bayle has been accused of hypocrisy in maintaining that he would follow the Bible when the Bible definitely and overtly states a moral principle. But I see nothing either hypocritical or evasive in his attitude. A careful reading of the text will indeed show that David is not praised for the acts which Bayle finds reprehensible. Whether it was prudent for a man to state his opinion about so eminent a personage is another question and a question which was solved for Bayle by the persecution to which he was submitted. As a matter of fact, both versions of the article were printed in the edition of 1720, so that the reader could take his choice and also compare the two. But it must also be pointed out that in his book on comets, that morals had nothing to do with belief in God and that a society of atheists could be quite as moral as a society of theists. Atheism to him was no worse than idolatry and Bayle had plenty of evidence drawn from the Ancients to show that men who were pagans were as noble as Christians and frequently nobler. This was a fearful blow to his associates, both Catholic and Protestant, and opened the way to rational ethics based on natural law, *la bonté naturelle,* the law of progress, and other similar notions. It was a theme to be developed later by Voltaire and was in the same line of reasoning as that of the theistic hedonists, who, though believing in God, nevertheless defined good and evil in terms of pleasure and pain.

In metaphysical matters Bayle was a follower of Montaigne and La Mothe le Vayer. He believed, as many of his contemporaries did, including as we have seen so pious a man as Huet, that there are certain questions which the human reason is simply incapable of solving. On such matters he advocated the suspension of judgment. What made him suspect, when others were not, was his dwelling on the arguments in favour of scepticism, as well as his frequent obscenities. Most commentators on Bayle seem agreed that his taste for the obscene was greater than normal, though his master Montaigne was certainly as interested in such things as he was. He himself disliked Rabelais whom he considered to be a mere imitator of Lucian, and he defended himself vigorously against the charge of pornography. It is true that part of his defense consisted in pointing out that he had to do something to attract frivolous readers, a defense which will leave many of our contemporaries cold. On the other hand, he wished to present men of the past as they actually were and to rob them of the fake haloes which had been painted round their heads. By dwelling upon their vices, he was attempting to show that they were neither better nor worse than the common run of mortals; and in an age when it was still possible, indeed usual, to represent the lords of the earth as made of finer clay than their subjects, he performed a valuable service. If a man of his day wished to wallow in the muck of real pornography, he had no need to read Bayle's folios. The writings of the Libertines were numerous and readily available.

Bayle's contribution to philosophy, then, was not that of a great system builder, nor did he have much that was original to say on the sort of problems which have been presented so far in this book. But it cannot be denied that he was a great educational force in developing a historical sense, a historical technique of criticism, and in gathering together in one place a mass of information which up to his time had been scattered about on library shelves.

MONTESQUIEU

About half a century intervened between the publication of the first edition of Bayle *Dictionnaire* and the appearance of the first volume of Diderot *Encyclopédie*. Meanwhile new interests were capturing the attention of French philosophers. The seventeenth century thinkers, Descartes, Malebranche, Pascal, and their fellows, developed philosophies dominated by religious problems. One finds Descartes overtly accepting the authority of the Church and attempting to prove the existence of God as He was described in Scholastic texts. The duality of mind and body, which was a cardinal principle of Catholicism, was also one of his fundamental tenets, as we have seen. In Malebranche the characteristic doctrines are those of the primacy of faith over reason, man's vision in God, and God's constant presence in causation. In Pascal metaphysics is located on a plane distinctly lower than that of religion, and his depreciation of reason in favour of "the heart" is a commonplace. One has only to run over the list of those philosophers whose thoughts we have attempted to expound to see that their problems arose out of the field of religious ideas.

The growth of interest in secular matters is attested not only by the progress of natural science but also by the foundation of the various academies. The Académie Française dates from 1635, the Académie des Beaux-Arts from 1648, the Académie des Inscriptions et Belles Lettres from 1663, and the Académie des Sciences from 1666. This was in principle a recognition of the separateness of religious and secular studies, for though many of the members of the various academies were, to be sure, ecclesiastics, nevertheless their investigations were only occasionally supervised by the Church. The Church still had a monopoly on education, a monopoly which it was not to lose until the Revolution. But at the same time groups of scholars were meeting and reporting their findings to one another in relative freedom from religious censorship. The adjective "relative" must be emphasized here, for in comparison with the Royal Society, which existed in fact, if not in theory, from the middle of the century, its freedom was far from complete. It will be noticed that there was nothing corresponding to an Academy of Social Studies.

Four men will be mentioned here as precursors of the Encyclopedists: Montesquieu (1689-1755), Voltaire (1694-1778), d'Holbach (1723-89), and La Mettrie (1709-51). We select these on the basis of their influence on subsequent thinkers as well as on that of their actual contributions to philosophy.

In 1721 Montesquieu published his *Lettres Persanes*, surely one of the most delightful satires of French society ever written by a Frenchman. Through the devices of imagining two Persian travellers writing home about France, Montesquieu was able to take a more detached view of things than would have been possible had he written in his own person. The device was simply the reverse of that of the various Utopias which had been written. Instead of contrasting one's society with that of an imaginary ideal society, one introduced into it exotic visitors and recorded their supposed impressions. The importance of the vogue for this sort of writing, a vogue which lasted into our own times, was the suggestion that Occidental institutions and manners were not an expression of universal human nature at all but were provincial customs peculiar to one part of the globe. Once this way of looking at human affairs became habitual, the way was open for cultural relativism and ultimately for the apparently revolutionary idea that even moral standards are peculiar to the societies in which they arise. It should not be forgotten that Europeans had been accustomed to think of occidental history as universal history. St. Augustine's *City of God* is at most a history of Mediterranean man, but its author thought of it as a history of mankind. Its seventeenth-century replica, Bossuet *Discourse on Universal History*, first published in 1681, extends the tale into northern Europe. One would never know from this way of writing history that anything had happened east of Suez. And yet, if the French ever needed information about the ways in which other people lived, it was at a time when their empire was spreading over the globe. One might have thought that at least the Dauphin, for whose enlightenment Bossuet wrote his history and into whose hands it was expected to entrust the future of the empire, might have been given some consciousness of the kinds of problems which his proconsuls would have to face. But such knowledge was to come not from the official tutors of princes but either from secular scholars or Jesuit missionaries.

Montesquieu most famous work is the *Spirit of the Laws* (1748). The title of this work is not without importance, for it is in itself a concise statement of a philosophy of human nature. It runs, "The Spirit of the Laws, or the relation which laws must have with the constitution of each government, customs, climate, religion, commerce, etc." Though the anti-Platonic slant of this may be obvious, it should not be forgotten. Montesquieu is discussing laws, not the law. He is exploring their variations, not their homogeneity. He is attempting to show how they vary; that is, with what. If they vary with climate, commerce, customs, and so on, then the implication would seem to follow that our own laws are no different from any other and that the value of a constitution can only be measured in terms of the total situation in which it arose. That is perhaps why certain critics, like Dupin, feared that the book would have a bad effect on the loyalty of the French. For if one is educated to believe that one's king rules by divine right and that the Divinity always commands the same things everywhere, then one should not fall into the trap of believing that the theory of divine right is peculiar to Frenchmen or, at most, Europeans. In spite of his implicit relativism, Montesquieu believed that there were certain laws governing human behavior which were universal. These he called, as Hobbes and most philosophers did, the laws of nature. The laws of nature are those universal principles descriptive of human nature in general. To discover them one must attempt to imagine mankind living outside of society or, as was the custom at the time, before the formation of societies.

The laws of nature, for Montesquieu, can be found through an examination of man's essential being, that which distinguishes him from all other creatures. The first of these laws is man's sentiment of weakness, of his inferiority to all that surrounds him, his desire for tranquillity. Here Montesquieu is clear that his main opponent is Hobbes. The desire for domination arises only after man lives in the company of others; by which is meant that one has to have someone to dominate before one can have the desire for domination. The word "before" must not be taken in a chronological sense. Montesquieu knows perfectly well that he is not writing the history of the human race; he is simply trying to deduce human desires and acts. The priority suggested is logical. This is to be justified by pointing out the varieties of social organization. If all societies were alike, then it might be possible to derive from their structure some idea of what the human race essentially was. But since they all differ to some degree and since the differences can be explained, universal human nature must be logically prior to human nature as found in society. A second law of nature would be the desire for food. A third would arise from the desire for sexual union, a fourth is that for living together in social union. As soon as men live in society, their natural equality disappears and the state of war begins. It is because of this condition of inequality that special laws for maintaining peace and decency are required. Such laws must, by the very nature of the environments in which societies are to be found, differ from one another. Reason, which is their origin, demands this. For if there is a difference in climate, in the quality of the soil, in the economic life of a people that is, the way they earn their livings, in their religion, in the sizes of their population, and the like then reason must deduce special laws to fit these circumstances. One cannot expect an Eskimo to live like a Hottentot, nor a Frenchman to live like a Chinese. They are all human, to be sure, but the expression of their humanity cannot be found in a cultural vacuum. All men wish to eat; but they do not all find the same foods, do not all have the same soil to raise them in, do not all have the same climate to permit them to eat or raise what others eat and raise. The same argument can be applied to the other three natural laws, and in all cases it will be seen that civil and political laws are bound to differ if they are to be rational.

In accordance with this reasoning Montesquieu begins by differentiating the kinds of government, a distinction which superficially appears to be that of the Aristotelian tradition, but, as has been seen by other commentators, in reality was not. The republican, the monarchical, and the despotic constitutions are, to be sure, distinguished partly on the basis of the number of individuals who are sovereign, though Montesquieu does not include aristocracy or oligarchy among the types of government; but one also sees that the distinction between monarchy and despotism, in his opinion, is the fixity of the laws in the former and their capriciousness in the latter. In a republic, he says, the people or a part of the people is sovereign; when the whole people rule, one has a democracy; when part, an aristocracy. The people "are admirable in their choices of those to whom they will entrust some part of their authority. They have but to decide by means of those things which they cannot help knowing and which are part of their everyday experience, but they are too slow when speed is needed and too fast when deliberation counts". The people are too likely to act according to their emotions. Hence Athens and Rome were right in electing a group, which Montesquieu calls a senate, to act as a brake on their passions. One sees at this point how he makes use of his laws of nature. It will be recalled that the first law is man's feeling of his own weakness, not a sense of reason. We are primordially governed, then, by a feeling; and, when we are entrusted with the rule of society, we shall revert to our primordial nature. Feelings will not provide food for all nor peace for all, nor will they maintain a just and tranquil community. Feelings demand the correction of reason, and that correction cannot spontaneously arise from popular emotion.

One might imagine that a monarch, governing according to fixed laws which he could not change, would serve as this corrective. Such a monarch was exemplified by the King of England, who had a parliament in whose hands was the great obstacle to despotism: a set of fixed laws. Neither the nobility nor the King's Privy Council will perform this function, for the former pays little if any attention to the civil government and the latter are too susceptible to change. Montesquieu might have added, since he was thinking of his own country, that both groups have no basic interests in safeguarding the rights of the governed. But these rights are not natural rights in the customary sense of the word. For those rights which are implied in the laws of nature are irrelevant to organized society. They are presocial, as we have seen. Society does not exist to preserve them nor can it be criticized for not preserving them. Thus freedom, which we are likely to think of as a natural right, is restricted by Montesquieu to doing whatever the law permits and is by no means doing whatever one wishes. Every state has the same object in view self-perpetuation; and it is not to be expected that a state should grant to its subjects the right to destroy itself. But each state also has objects: aggrandizement was that of Rome; war, that of Sparta; religion, that of Judea; commerce, that of Marseilles; public tranquillity, that of China; navigation, that of Rhodes; natural liberty, that of the savages. One nation, England, has for its special object political liberty. But, whether Montesquieu is camouflaging his real purpose or not, his ostensible purpose is to show that even this object is peculiar to one kind of state.

Following John Locke, he proceeds to analyze the government of England in his famous chapter on the division of powers into legislative, executive, and judiciary. Based on his theory that societies are formed, in part, because of fear, he tries to show that no Englishman need ever fear his fellow citizen, since each set of powers is balanced and checked by the other two. If the executive is also the legislative, he can pass laws which suit his own purposes and then carry them out. If the judicial power is joined with the legislative, the judge would not only decide how the law applies but make it;

and, if it were joined to the executive, the judge would become a tyrant. "All would be lost if the same man, or the same body of agents, either of nobles or of the people, exercised the three powers". In the Italian republics, freedom is less than in the monarchies, for the simple reason that the three powers are united in one body. One need not read this chapter with a microscope to see that Montesquieu has no great admiration for human nature in the raw. On the other hand, though he laid the foundations for the modern theory of an organismic state, he did not believe that the state was an end in itself. He does not lose sight of his basic fact that citizens or subjects are individual people and that their governments are organized not merely to protect them and whatever rights they may be supposed to have, but also in accordance with certain natural conditions over which they have no control whatsoever. It is curious that this last point is one which is seldom emphasized in discussions of this philosopher. One should have inferred from the whole structure of his book that it was not the nature of Man which determined his form of government, but external causes which varied from society to society. If there was one extension of this principle which might have been expected from his followers, it was an ethical (and possibly aesthetic) relativism. But one does not find such an inference even in d'Alembert's eulogy of him which prefaces the fifth volume of the *Encyclopedie.*

Montesquieu's discussion of freedom is almost entirely limited to freedom from unjust prosecution. He was well aware of the growth of this type of liberty in England, and it is the English example which undoubtedly inspired his chapters on the subject. What he calls "philosophic liberty" is of little interest to him, and indeed he seems none too sure of whether it exists. "Philosophic liberty," he says, "consists in the exercise of one's will, or at least in the opinion one has that one is exercising it." He thus does not commit himself to the reality of the will's freedom nor does he seem to think that it matters for his purposes. "Political liberty," he continues, "consists in security or at least in the opinion one has of his security." The citizen's freedom then depends, above all, on the goodness of the criminal laws. When the relatives of an accuser could be witnesses against the accused, when a man could be accused without being heard, when false witness could be accepted, when only one witness was required, then the citizen was not free. Furthermore, penalties must be fixed by law so that caprice may be avoided. His hope is that in this way there will be uniform laws throughout the state and that the uniformity itself will be a guarantee of justice. In the second place, he insists on the necessity of preventing crimes as well as punishing them, for some crimes are committed because decency is too difficult, if not impossible. Finally, one should be punished only for one's "external acts," not for one's thoughts. In a state in which heresy, *lese-majesté*, books, and speeches could be severely punished, such comments must have seemed pretty revolutionary. To us who have seen the revival of these practices, they may seem so too. But from the philosophic point of view, not from the political, their burden is that of the natural equality of all men who have formed societies not because they are good in themselves, but because they serve useful purposes. Their utility must be directed toward those whom they serve, not toward those who administer them. It is no longer Zeus who has given the scepter to the ruler, but the governed.

It is Montesquieu's chapters on the influence of climate which have caused most stir among his readers; for here he emphasized something that was relatively novel. For centuries men had believed that physical things so remote as the planets might determine the course of individual lives, while others had maintained that all men were doomed to perdition because of Adam's fall, though a few might be saved by God's incomprehensible grace. The notion, then, that people had little personal control over their lives was not, in itself, new. What seems to have shocked people was that an external force of which they had not previously thought was the determinant. Montesquieu's idea of what a climate was is much too superficial to bear scientific scrutiny. That there are cold and warm climates obviously cannot be doubted; but, as Volney was to point out in his *Leçons d'Histoire* and elsewhere, no country has but one climate; and in countries of similar climates, the soil, the moisture, the winds, all may differ. That our author thought that men living in cold climates were vigorous and men living in warm were more passionate, more lecherous, less vigorous, is no longer of much interest. But what is of the greatest interest is his basing psychological traits not on the constitution of men as men, but on the environment in which they live. For, since the customs of a country are to be derived from the character of its inhabitants, and that ultimately from the climate, no way is left for judging all customs without regard for their causes. Moreover, the system provides a rule for so reforming customs that they will be harmonious with the environment. For instance, in discussing landownership in India, he says that since the land is entirely in the hands of the princes, the people have no way of avoiding the natural effects of the climate which in itself inclines them to laziness. Were the land in the hands of the peasants, they would have to work it, and thus the evil effect of the climate could be corrected. If Montesquieu had said that climate was the only factor determining character, he could not have argued also that its effects could be corrected by law. But he was, of course, far from maintaining such a monistic position. The impression that he is really talking about Europe, where the remnants of feudalism and the monasteries kept large acreages out of the hands of the peasants, is irresistible, especially when one reads his brief chapter on monasticism. It is perhaps unnecessary to insist that he expected his book to be read by Frenchmen.

The pluralism of Montesquieu appears overtly in Book XIX, chapter iv. There, raising the question of what produces a general spirit or mind of a people, he answers: "the climate, the religion, the laws, constitutional precedents [*les maximes du gouvernement*], customs, manners." "In proportion as in each nation one of these causes acts with greater force, the others give way to it to that extent. Nature and the climate almost alone dominate the savages; manners govern the Chinese; laws tyrannize over Japan; customs used to set the tone in Lacedemonia; precedents and antique customs set it in Rome". So convinced is he of the "naturalness" of a nation's character, that he urges his readers not to interfere with that character even though it appear distasteful to them. People should be let to develop in peace. There is, to be sure, a wide gap between virtue and vice; but moral vices are not always political vices nor are all political vices moral as well. This approximation to what was to be the doctrine of *laisser faire* is fundamental in Montesquieu. His purpose is merely to indicate where man-made laws have contravened those of nature, meaning by "nature" here those forces which come from acts of God. Might he not have thought that the climate could be changed, the soil made more fertile, new land dredged up from the sea, deserts watered, populations kept stable, manual labour reduced. In any event, to him the separation between Man and Nature was almost absolute almost, since he knew that men had in actuality interfered with Nature. But that there was, or could be, a constant interaction between the two does not seem to have made much impression upon him. He was writing, to be sure, before the development of steam power and electricity and cannot be properly criticized for not having anticipated their discovery. But he was also living at a time when, at least in his own country, civilization had become top-heavy. It was to take only a generation before the balance would be shifted and the superstructure overturned. His main argument, in the final analysis, turns out to be that laws have attempted to do too much, inasmuch as they had reached the point where they were in conflict with the very things with which they should be in harmony. These things could be grouped together under the general label *Nature*. Though this word has been abused and has become so ambiguous that it has ceased to have any utility in discourse, Montesquieu was assuming and tried to justify his assumption that a people is what it is because of factors that existed prior to the laws. One may influence these factors to a certain degree, but the moment always comes when failure will make itself manifest by signs that the primitive nature of men is violated. Their primitive nature is presocial and expresses itself in their passions, their weakness, their need for sustenance and mates. It is on this basis that his French disciples built their more extreme platforms.

LA METTRIE

If Montesquieu's philosophy made plausible that there were no eternal standards of law, no nonhistorical bases of government, good or bad, except insofar as the laws of nature were involved, La Mettrie (1709-51) increased the number of variables which could be functions of human ideals. The former had, as we have seen, related the forms of government to a set of factors which might vary independently of one another, so that there was little sense in comparing the government of an oriental country like China with that of an occidental country like France. If he was willing to use the constitution of England as a standard by means of which he might evaluate that of France, it was because both nations had about the same climate, the same religious traditions, and the same economic pursuits. But, to the extent that other determining factors differed, to that extent it was absurd to judge one constitution by the other. As far as individuals were concerned similar things might be said. The occidental religious tradition had upheld a psychophysical dualism according to which the soul might inhabit a body and might indeed become enslaved by that body. But there was always the possibility that a man escape his corporeal entanglements and liberate himself from the demands of the flesh. The possibility, though seldom realized, was in fact the goal of all good men. The Pauline battle between the flesh and the spirit was accepted as a fact, and for it to be a fact required a strict duality between the two hostile elements. If it turned out that the body was but a figment of the soul's ideas or that the soul was an effect of certain bodily changes, then the whole religious tradition collapsed.

La Mettrie's *l'Homme-Machine*, first printed in 1748, attempted to show, by the same arguments which proved that animals were merely machines without souls an argument which is usually attributed to Descartes that one could prove that men were also machines. The proof consists in pointing out that all psychic events are caused by physiological events. To maintain that something is caused by something else does not of course prove that it does not exist. One might as well argue that since no language exists that is not spoken by human beings, languages do not exist. This should not be taken to entail the idea that it is of no importance to discover general causes of things that are not known to have them. But it goes without saying that one should not assert more than one has demonstrated. What La Mettrie was probably driving at was the inefficacy of the soul, rather than its nonexistence. But in 1748 that was enough to classify him with the materialists and to horrify those readers who demanded a soul capable of doing; things in its own right.

La Mettrie, who was a pupil of the Dutch physician Boerhaave, prided himself not only on the results of his investigations but also on his method. Experience and observation alone were to be his guides, and only the experiments and observations of a physician were worthy of citation. Physicians will tell one that each man differs from his fellows through his temperament, which in turn is determined by the peculiar combination of his four humors: the black bile, yellow bile, phlegm, and blood. The imagination can be aroused by purely physical causes, such as fatigue or lack of sleep; drugs, such as opium or even coffee, can induce psychic states which could not arise without them; without food the soul "pines away, goes mad, and dies exhausted"; the kind of food determines whether a man will be savage or gentle; old age weakens the reason; even one's physical appearance indicates the quality of one's mind. "Look at the portraits of Locke, of Steele, of Boerhaave, of Maupertuis, and the rest, and you will not be surprised to find strong faces and eagles' eyes. Look over the multitude of others, and you can always distinguish the man of talent from the man of genius, and often even an honest man from a scoundrel". Temperature may turn a gentle and indulgent man into a passionate one. Climate determines the character of the people who live in it. And the possession of a brain determines whether an animal be intelligent or act only through instinct.

In the nineteenth century such philosophers as Schopenhauer were to use similar arguments in reverse to prove that the soul was autonomous. One had only to indicate the utility of these various material substances drugs, foods, and organic instruments to maintain that man's will sought them out in order to achieve certain ends. Does opium produce dreams or does a man take opium in order to escape reality? Does the brain determine thinking or does the animal that wishes to think develop a brain? We know that muscles can be developed by exercise, which in turn is undertaken because of an individual's desire to perform certain acts, not simply acrobatics; but also playing on musical instruments requires the most delicate adjustments of eye and muscle. One could as well insist that people have overcome almost all physical handicaps, substituting one sense for another, using artificial limbs, using toes in place of fingers, increasing the perceptual acuity of their sense organs through practice; and the desire to overcome these handicaps cannot, it might be argued, arise from the physiological equipment of the person. A person born without arms may use his feet and legs for those purposes which arms and hands usually attain. But the training comes from other human beings and the willingness to undergo the training must come from the individual's own will, not from the lack of the proper instruments in itself. But this reaction to the kind of materialism preached by La Mettrie, which was to be developed in much greater detail by Cabanis at the end of the century, did not appear, as we have said, until the nineteenth century.

The argument thus expounded was bolstered by arguments from comparative anatomy. La Mettrie seems to have believed that if he could show the similarities between the human and the animal organisms, he would have strengthened his position, for in general no one was anxious to prove the psychophysical duality of the beasts. La Mettrie was a great believer in the gradual transition from animal to human form, running through the apes. Man's intelligence has come about through speech, and before the invention of speech man was as much like a beast as an ape is. But speech is simply sounds or shapes, both arbitrary, and hence our intelligence itself depends on material causes. The origin of language was a problem that was to annoy almost all of the philosophers of the time. Roughly speaking, it may be said that those who inclined toward some form of materialism maintained that it had been invented; but others, of whom Rousseau was to be the leader, argued that inventions require intelligence and that, since man must have been intelligent before he could have invented language, language could not be the source of his intelligence. La Mettrie did not foresee this rejoinder and since words, whether spoken or printed, were physical beings and since these physical beings were of such a nature that they could produce physical effects on the brain through the visual and auditory nerves, and since these physical effects could be identified with the elements of the imagination, it could be maintained that all the processes of reason could be reduced to a sequence of images. These images are clearly of different sorts, depending upon the sensory apparatus through which they arise, and therefore the simplicity of the soul is destroyed at one blow. Yet the simplicity of the soul was an essential belief of Christianity. It was fairly generally believed that animals had images and that their apparent rationality was an effect of their recalling past images and acting in accordance with them. If the human soul also was simply a collection of images, then it, too, would be no more than the very complicated animal mind was said to be. La Mettrie accordingly devotes a long paragraph to the role that the human imagination plays in what we normally think of as rationality. "Imagination," he says, "is the soul, since it plays all the roles of the soul." "By the imagination, by its flattering brush, the cold skeleton of reason takes on living and ruddy flesh; by the imagination the sciences flourish, the arts are adorned, the wood speaks, the echoes sigh, the rocks weep, marble breathes, and all inanimate objects gain life". No psychic agent is needed to guide it; it operates under its own power. Its power, however, may vary from man to man, but its variations, again, depend on the physical organism which can be educated to perform intellectual marvels. These marvels will be found not only in the field of the arts but also in that of the sciences.

We are then admittedly animals, akin to all the others, more gifted in some ways, less in others. If this is so, then it becomes incumbent on La Mettrie to give some explanation of the moral laws which appear to distinguish us from the beasts. Here he revives some of the classical stories about animal gratitude and human bestiality and concludes that the natural law rules the beasts as it does us. The natural law is "a feeling that teaches us what we should not do, because we would not wish it to be done to us". As one of the most sacred commands of Christianity, the socalled Golden Rule was turned by La Mettrie into a universal psychological principle based upon fear. The beasts can fear as well as man and, if fear of reprisals is the one universal stimulus to doing right and avoiding wrong, then clearly, as he says himself, it does not require education, revelation, nor legislation to make it effective. What then of the Supreme Being, one of Whose functions had always been to reveal the right which frequently was in contradiction to our natural, as opposed to our supernatural, inclinations? La Mettrie has no hesitation in saying that he believes His existence to be probable, but he also has no hesitation in saying that it is irrelevant to morality. Reverting to Bayle, he asserts that an atheistic society could be as moral as a Christian society. Atheists have certainly lived noble lives and Christians have led ignoble ones. The existence of God is probable but irrelevant to the conduct of life. The soul then loses its position as a substance contained within, or living alongside, the body. At most the name should be reserved for the part of us that thinks. Animate bodies need but the possibility of motion, that is, self-originated motion, to manifest all the physical and mental traits which we discover in ourselves.

There are several inferences which could be drawn from this philosophy that would prove of great influence in subsequent years. (1) If the human being could be explained entirely through physical law, so perhaps could the universe. This deduction was made by d'Holbach. (2) If individuals were differentiated from one another by their original physical equipment, which could be corrected only by education, then either the attempt to produce a uniform human nature must be abandoned, or a new system of education must be introduced. The latter was the goal of the *Encyclopedia.* (3) If man were essentially a higher animal, then it was necessary to find out as much about the animal side of our nature as possible. This was to be the task of Cabanis.

D'HOLBACH

If La Mettrie demonstrated the superfluity of a soul in explaining human conduct, the Baron d'Holbach (1723-89) turned his attention to God, and attempted to show that the world was a machine without a machinist. La Mettrie was willing to admit God's existence as a plausible belief; d'Holbach could see no plausibility in it. Though his books were printed pseudonymously or in some cases anonymously this was the only concession he made to the censor. He may be justly criticized for his reasoning, but certainly no one could justly criticize him for hypocrisy. He was an atheist; he admitted it; he defended his atheism. His metaphysics is materialistic; his ethics hedonistic; his epistemology sensationalistic. Few people in his time were willing to follow him to the conclusion of his arguments; many nevertheless profited from some of them and shared some of them. His attacks on Christianity were as outspoken as his attacks on metaphysical spiritualism. To him it was a collection of superstitions fostered by a priesthood intent on keeping power in its own hands and reducing the human race to intellectual slavery. Its beneficial results, when they existed, could be had by purely rationalistic science; the rest had best be done away with. Like La Mettrie, he does not occupy much space in the traditional histories of philosophy. Yet his reasoning was clear and concise, and most of the attacks upon him were not based on fallacies that he had committed but on the horror which his conclusions stimulated. Much the same could have been said of *ce misérable Spinoza,* whose *Ethics* seems seldom to have been studied carefully in his time. But he, too, preached doctrines which were repulsive to the dominant classes in intellectual Europe, and since they were repulsive, they must also be false.

D'Holbach's main work is to be found in his *Système de la Nature*, first published in 1770. This work was preceded by his anonymous *Le Christianisme Devoile* (1767), in which he attempted to show the evils that organized Christianity had brought to the world. Since his attack on religion was similar to others which were to be made later in the nineteenth century, and since it is of interest in itself, we shall introduce our discussion of d'Holbach with it. His main argument against Christianity, other than the falsity of its beliefs, is its bad effect on the political life of a nation. When one remembers the intimate relations between Church and State in eighteenth century France, the target of his arrows becomes unmistakable. Christianity to him is the Gallican Church. Its purpose is to render the King's subjects loyal through fear. It preaches the virtues of submission to power, of renunciation, and of austerity, and it practices none of them. Its technique is based on seizing the minds of men while they are children: "Amongst almost all modern peoples education seems to have as its sole purpose the making of fanatics, bigots, monks, that is to say, men harmful or useless to society; no one gives a thought to forming citizens; princes themselves are generally victims of the superstitious bringing up which they are given, remain throughout their lives in the deepest ignorance of their duties and the true interests of their states; they imagine that they have done all that is needed for their subjects if they have their minds filled with religious ideas which take the place of good laws, and which spare their masters the painful trouble of good government." That the Church in France had privileges that were unique needs no proof here. That its privileges were often used badly is also well demonstrated. In fact, it was so closely intertwined with the State that any attack against it, any reform, would have entailed an attack against the State. The Pauline injunction to accept the government that God has given us must have prevented many devout Catholics from indulging in political reformation. And many of the outright abuses of power, such as the treatment of Protestants, which can be shown to have been disastrous even from the economic point of view, could be laid to the door of the clergy. The French saw their neighbours in England and Germany enjoying the fruits of philosophy and science; they saw their own people deprived of such benefits as might come from enlightenment or pushed into hypocrisy. D'Holbach's weakness lay in his attribution of the evils of the Gallican Church to Christianity itself. But the definition of Christianity was no easier then than it is now. Was it to be found in the four Gospels or in the Synoptic Gospels alone? Was it to be found exclusively in the words of Christ? Was one to include the Acts of the Apostles and the Epistles? Was Holy Scripture enough to establish Christian doctrine or must it be supplemented by the decisions of the Councils? And must these decisions be also supplemented by tradition? And if one or a group of these questions were to be answered in the affirmative, who was to be the interpreter of the texts involved? It is doubtful whether any reader of d'Holbach brought up in a Protestant country would accept his version of the tenets of Christianity. But d'Holbach was writing not only for Catholics but for French Catholics.

"The Christian religion," he says, "which prides itself on giving an unshakable support to morality and on giving men the strongest motives for urging them to lead a life of virtue, has been on the contrary a source of divisions, of fury, and of crime. Under the pretext of bringing men peace, it has brought them only madness, hatred, discord, and war. It has provided a thousand ingenious means of torturing them. It has spread amongst them plagues unknown to their fathers, and the Christian, had he been in his right mind, would have regretted over and over again the peaceful ignorance of his idolatrous ancestors." Not even the kings, whose powers were supposed to be bolstered by this religion, have succeeded in their purpose. For they have developed alongside of their own power a second sovereignty, that of the organized Church. And whenever the question has arisen of to which of the two, State or Church, was the subject's loyalty due, it was the second sovereign which won out. That the Church also had been the means of correcting the abuses of princes is not mentioned by d'Holbach. He can find nothing in its history but its failures. It must, of course, be admitted that

Christianity, however defined, did not succeed in bringing peace on earth or goodwill to men, or even peace to men of goodwill. It did not succeed as an organization in eliminating idolatry and superstition. D'Holbach was not unique in pointing out that even those individuals who had been officially charged with ministering to the needs of Christians failed often to lead Christian lives. He was not unique in indicating the irreconcilable conflicts in Christian teaching between, as he says himself, the God of vengeance, the God of mercy, the God of armies, the God of peace. But he might have been expected to see that the collection of beliefs and practices that were given the sacred name had been perpetuated and increased not out of the wickedness of a small group of ecclesiastics but by the great mass of suffering Europeans. He might also have asked himself whether he was not demanding of the Church something which it was not prepared to give. Pascal would probably have been willing to grant the truth of most of his criticisms. And at the same time he would have expressed his faith in those mysteries whose truth he was sure of. To this d'Holbach was ready to reply that "a revelation which would be true, which would come from a just and good God and which would be necessary for all men, ought to be clear enough to be understood by all mankind. Is the revelation on which Judaism and Christianity are founded of such a kind? Euclid *Elements* are intelligible to all who want to understand them; this work arouses no disputes among geometers. Is the Bible as clear, and do revealed truths give rise to no disputes among the theologians who proclaim them? By what fatality have the Scriptures, revealed by Divinity itself, still need of commentary and why do they need enlightenment from on high to be believed and understood?"

D'Holbach clearly belonged to that group of philosophers who maintain that everything in the universe is intelligible. By "intelligible" he seems to have meant "rational," and by "rational" to have meant "susceptible of scientific corroboration." But it could not be denied by a Christian that the very essence of his religion was the reality of mysteries, miracles, in short, unintelligibles. It should have been obvious, but unfortunately was not and presumably still is not that if all beliefs must be capable of statement in factual form, then mysteries have no claim on our faith. But if the mysteries cannot be framed in rational sentences, then it would be the better part of wisdom not to attempt to so frame them. A mystic could smile at d'Holbach's naiveté in assuming as a first principle something that would make his beliefs impossible and then in asking him to abandon them. A rational theologian was not in such a position. The mystic could keep a stubborn silence when asked to state his beliefs or at most if he felt impelled to speak could pour out the traditional paradoxes of his school. But a rational theologian was not in so fortunate a situation. And the overwhelming majority of Christians had been given to developing their religious and theological ideas in what they thought was rational discourse.

When d'Holbach comes to the question of ethics, he may be said to be on firmer ground. For whether his readers could define satisfactorily what they meant by such terms as "justice," "temperance," "equity," "clemency," they had to admit that even before the appearance of Christianity on earth there had been just, temperate, equitable, clement men. This had indeed been admitted by some of the early Fathers. But if this were so, then Christianity was not needed to propagate such virtues. Yet here, too, it could have been replied that though there were virtuous pagans, paganism in itself was not a body of beliefs fortified by an ecclesiastical institution which maintained that the very constitution of the universe was to be identified with the will of a just and benevolent God. Stoicism had been an approach to that goal, and again some of the early Fathers had maintained that philosophies of this sort were a preparation for Christianity. If the Church had taught that before the coming of Christ there had been no just and otherwise virtuous men on earth, it would have had to repudiate even the prophets and wise men of the Old Testament. But it had never turned its back on history to that extent. Yet if one were to believe, as d'Holbach did, that the theological doctrines of Christianity were absurd, nothing was left of its teachings except ethics; and he could with reason insist, as Bayle had done before him, that pagans and other non-Christians were as virtuous as Christians. Therefore he could conclude that the teachings of the Church were not even needed for the purposes of ethics. D'Holbach goes further than this. He attempts to demonstrate the absurdity even of the ethics of Christianity. Love thy neighbour as thyself is nonsensical because "every man by his very nature, loves himself in preference to all others; he loves his neighbours only because they contribute to his own happiness; he is virtuous insofar as he does good to his neighbour; he is generous when he sacrifices his own self-love to him; but he never loves him except for the useful qualities which he finds in him; he can love him only when he knows him, and his love for him is bound to be based upon the benefits which he receives from him". But the Christian could easily reply to this that so far, so good; it is precisely to correct this point of view that the Church spreads its teachings. Without the illumination of religion one cannot love one's neighbour as oneself; but once that illumination has been received, then a diviner ethics has been instituted in the human heart. I say that a Christian could easily have made this reply; but unfortunately there were too few Christians of this stripe in eighteenth-century France to do so with sincerity.

There is no need to outline the entire attack which d'Holbach made upon the Church as both a moral and political teacher. The question now arises of what he would have put in its place. And the answer was Nature. The command to follow Nature was as old as the fifth century B.C., if not older, and by d'Holbach's time the sacred word had become almost as saturated with ambiguities as it is today. One thing can be said with certainty: to d'Holbach the word named something opposed to the supernatural. He was talking about Nature as the subject matter of science, describable in terms of rational law, always obedient to such law. And his avowed purpose in expounding what he called his "System of Nature" was to free men from religious superstition which was, he believed, the origin of our inveterate hatred of others, our barbarous persecutions, our continual massacres which have so often appeared on the theatre of this globe. He hoped to "inspire man with courage and respect for reason; to teach him to know his essence and his legitimate rights; to consult experience and not imagination led astray by authority; to renounce the prejudices of childhood; to base his morality on nature, on his needs, on the real advantages which society procures for him; to dare to love himself; to work for his happiness while producing that of others; in a word, to be reasonable and virtuous in order to be happy here below; and to give up his daydreams which are either dangerous or useless."

The first step forward to this goal consists in abandoning the distinction between the physical and the mental. Man is a purely physical being and the mental is simply "this physical being considered from a certain point of view, that is, relative to some of his ways of behaving, due to his peculiar organization". D'Holbach in this sentence can be seen as one of the ancestors of what in our own time has been called behaviourism. There is no spiritual substance; what is called by the name of mind or soul is nothing more than special ways of bodily action. But these ways of acting are themselves determined by natural law just as everything else in the universe is. Natural law is simple, uniform, invariable; it is known by experience; and experience is always derived from our senses. If we could only remember this fundamental fact, then we would never fall into the errors that have caused so much harm in human history. But when we ask, as we inevitably do, what natural law causes men to fall into these errors, to follow prejudice and authority rather than experience, d'Holbach has no answer. The duality, which he asserts does not exist, reappears in another form. The purely material world, that is, the world admitted by all to be purely material, does not commit these errors. Falling bodies, gravitating planets, chemical elements and compounds always seem to follow the laws that Nature has assigned to them. But man, though essentially also a natural object and subject to exactly the same laws, is seen at once to act in an unnatural fashion. D'Holbach may attribute this to laziness or fear, but either it is as the result of natural law that we become lazy or afraid, in which case these emotional states are an integral part of our nature, or they point to elements in our being which are antinatural. Lest this seem to be a pedantic and sophistic complaint, let it be pointed out that no theory of human nature has been devised to date in which something analogous to the Fall of Man has not been invented. The chronological primitivist, for instance, who believes in something like the Golden Age, a time when men were living in a state of happiness, however his happiness may be described, is forced to admit that man's primordial nature has either been annihilated or has been seriously weakened. He is then obliged to account for the degeneration in question. The man who argues to the original goodness of man has to admit that he is no longer uniformly good and then has to account for his lapse from goodness. The spokesman for moral progress has to admit that in man's first stage on earth he was wicked or ignorant or cruel or dirty, or otherwise distasteful, and then has to explain why and how he ever rose from that condition. Oddly enough, the solution to the dilemma was easily found though few if any found it: it was the admission that human nature was not homogeneous but heterogeneous and that no uniform set of laws would describe it. But obviously if one begins one's work by assuming that natural law is fixed and uniform, then everything describable in its terms must be equally fixed and uniform. Though it is not our conscious purpose to quarrel with the men whose ideas we are expounding, this one is of such importance, even today, that we yield to the temptation of criticizing it.

Returning now to d'Holbach, we find that he not only believed that all knowledge was sensory in origin and thus inseparable from corporeal behaviour, but that natural law was synonymous with the laws of matter in motion. Thus Nature became a system of material particles operating in accordance with the laws of motion, and anything that might seem to be in conflict with this view must be erroneous. Sensation, thought, and all action must be interpreted as forms of motion and not merely as static effects of moving particles. Interpreted strictly this would imply that a sensation, such as a color or sound, an idea, as well as muscular displacements, must have all the characteristics of matter, be in space, and in fact even be ponderable. Neither d'Holbach nor any other materialist of his time ever did interpret materialism so strictly; on the contrary, all were satisfied if they could give reason to believe such events to be the effects of moving material particles. When d'Holbach defines what he means by "cause" and "effect," he does not evade the consequence of his view of Nature, but when he speaks of the effects in what is normally called the mind, he overlooks the consequences of his materialism. Thus, in discussing those motions which common sense would call sensations or volitions, he maintains that they are hidden from view and must be inferred to exist from their perceptual effects. But they could be inferred in this manner only if one had already assumed the very conclusion which he is attempting to demonstrate. One may rightly infer, to use his own example, that when we see a man running away from something, he is agitated by the passion of fear; but we could not infer that the passion of fear was itself a motion of material particles simply by seeing a man running away. It might be either material or spiritual or whatever third thing might be possible.

One might guess from what has been said that d'Holbach would accept the homogeneity of all things since they are material. But, on the contrary, he cites *le profond et subtil Leibnitz* to show that every particle of matter is an individual with its own peculiarities. Each particle differs from every other in all ways: in activities, motions, velocity, depending on the amount of material substance that is in them. There is nothing in this which would contradict anything that he has said about the homogeneity of matter itself, since experience shows that different portions of matter do differ in these measurable ways. The general qualities of all matter are extension, divisibility, impenetrability, configuration, mobility, but each of the qualities may obviously vary in degree, so that one can accept the homogeneity of matter while also accepting the principle of variety in its qualities. The list of these qualities clearly is that of Locke which, as we suggested, is the list of those properties which are sufficient and necessary for the construction of Galilean physics. By arguing to the possibility of various combinations of elements which in 1770 were still the four classical elements—d'Holbach was able to explain the existence of the so-called three kingdoms; and, since matter itself is indestructible, he concludes that there is a cyclical process continually going on in the universe, running from composition to decomposition. If this were not so, there would be the possibility of one kingdom's taking over the whole cosmos; that is, for instance, of all matter turning into animate matter or vegetable matter. "Movement brings to birth, conserves for some time, and destroys successively the various parts of the universe one by the other, while the sum of existence remains always the same. Nature by her combinations gives birth to suns, which proceed to become the centers of so many systems; she produces planets which by their own essence gravitate and describe their orbits about these suns; little by little the motion of each dies down; it will one day perhaps scatter the parts of which it has composed these wonderful masses, which man in the short space of his existence glimpses but for a moment in passing". But nevertheless each body has also the property of self-preservation. "Newton calls it the *force of inertia;* the moralists have called it in man *self-love;* which is nothing but the tendency to preserve oneself, the desire for happiness, the love of well-being and of pleasure, the promptitude of grasping everything which appears favourable to one's being, and the marked aversion for all that upsets or threatens it: primitive feelings common to all members of the human race which all their faculties strive to satisfy, and which all their passions, their volitions, their acts have as their continual object and end". And, since all this is part and parcel of the natural order, everything in it must be determined by the laws of that order. Hence the universe, whether that part which is human or that which is non-human, is ruled by Necessity. When we maintain that something happens by chance, we do so simply because we are in ignorance of its cause. And, when we see the order in accordance with which events occur, that is, their causes, then we conclude that this order is intelligent, a fallacious conclusion, a projection of our own nature and not an observation. It is one of our weaknesses to project our nature into Nature itself, but we must resist it. The order that is in the cosmos is the causal order and there is no reason whatsoever, he argues, to maintain that it is in itself or is the result of cosmic intelligence. Intelligence discovers the order of Nature, but it is not that order. This is d'Holbach's reply to the cosmological argument for the existence of God.

It follows automatically from the principle of universal necessity and from what might be called the naturalness of man, that no man can initiate action, and that hence free will is an illusion. As soon as one examines one's thoughts, says d'Holbach, it becomes obvious that nothing arises spontaneously, but that, on the contrary, everything that takes place in one's mind is caused by external forces. Man observes that he is part of the universal network of material particles colliding with one another and that even those psychical effects that appear to be most personal and secret are really tied in with motions external to the human being. He is, in other words, what La Mettrie described him as being, a machine. But the question arises here of whether d'Holbach has not proved too much. For even if man is a machine, composed of the same kind of matter as all other machines, he is, as an individual machine, capable of contributing something to the events in which he participates. A stone falling off a roof and crushing the skull of a man walking on the pavement below is responsible for crushing that skull, even though it does fall in accordance with the law of falling bodies. Had the stone been lighter, the accident might not have been so grave. Had it fallen a moment sooner or later, the accident might not have happened at all. The stone, it is true, did not determine its own weight or the moment of its release from the roof. But its peculiar characteristics must be taken into account when the event is described. Neither d'Holbach nor any other materialist ever thought of explaining admittedly material events without taking into account the peculiar natures of their component parts. Why human beings should form the one exception to this technique of explanation would seem explicable only as the materialist's anxiety to reduce the human mind to impotency. Whether a volition is material or immaterial is irrelevant to the point at issue. If a man's determination to do something is the immediate cause of his doing it, the materiality of his determination or the simple fact that it, too, was caused by something antecedent to its occurrence has nothing whatsoever to do with the case. It would be an interesting fact, to be sure, should our minds turn out to be material and that hence our volitions should be also material. But a man's responsibility, in the sense that he himself contributes something to the events of which he is a part, cannot be settled on the basis of his materiality or spirituality.

We can, in spite of such criticisms, follow d'Holbach in saying that man has no reason to consider himself to be one of Nature's darlings, a privileged person. He may still be said to be "subject to the same vicissitudes as all her other productions. Let him raise himself in thought above the globe which he inhabits and he will see his species with the same eye as he sees all other beings: he will see that, just as each tree produces fruit according to its kind, so each man acts according to his special energy and produces fruit, acts, and works that are similarly necessary. He will feel that the illusion which prejudices him in favour of himself arises out of his being both spectator and part of the universe. He will recognize that the idea of excellence which he attaches to his being has no other foundation than his own self-interest and predilection". Self-interest therefore has to become the ground of his ethical system. Self-interest is what Nature teaches and, since we should follow Nature, we should seek self-interest. The child when born has no other values; education supplies them and renders them compulsive through the force of habit. It is consequently the task of education to make virtue serve self-interest and vice prevent its satisfaction.

Here it would appear that d'Holbach switches his ground. For at this point he argues that education should make virtue advantageous and that public opinion and the state should co-operate in this program. But, he asks: "Are the examples which we see daily likely to make us respect decency, probity, good faith, equity, moral innocence, conjugal fidelity, constancy in the performance of duty?" Is it not true that religion, which is the main support of morals, does not make us sociable, peaceful, and humane? Are those who serve their country rewarded more than those who pillage it and ruin it? These are, of course, purely rhetorical questions. But an opponent of d'Holbach's might well reply that if these things are so, then self-interest demands that we follow along with custom and that what he condemns is, in accordance with his own principles, virtue. The answer is that d'Holbach has in the back of his mind, as we all have, a set of virtues and vices which he does not question. These virtues and vices are traditional: patriotism, conjugal fidelity, etc., and their opposites. His problem ought not to be that of urging people to make the practice of the virtues rewarding, but to show that the virtues themselves do serve the interests of the individual.

Happiness, he maintains, is nothing more than uninterrupted pleasure. "But that an object should give us pleasure, demands that the impressions which it makes on us, the perceptions which it gives us, the ideas which it leaves with us, in a word the acts which it stimulates in us, be analogous to our constitution, our temperament, our individual nature, modified by habit and an infinity of circumstances or causes which give us more or less permanent or temporary ways of existing; it demands that the acts which the object excites in us or that of which the idea remains with us, far from weakening or destroying us, move steadily in the direction of increase; it demands that without tiring, exhausting or alienating our organs, this object give our mechanism the degree of activity of which it is constantly in need". A healthy, well-adjusted organism is thus the first prerequisite for happiness. We return here obviously to the reconstruction of an ethics that has at least the appearance of being founded on his naturalistic principles. But when he moves beyond this point he strays once more from his path. Since he has already admitted that no two men are alike, he is also forced to admit that no two men have the same interests and that, because of this, education must step in to harmonize those that are in conflict. Education once more is called upon to demonstrate to its subjects that virtue is more useful than vice, but when he resorts to education he has abandoned his initial postulate. I am far from saying that, in fact, education is not needed to make a man moral; I am merely saying that if it is needed, then spontaneous self-interest or pleasure will not do the job. It is probable that d'Holbach thought that the practice of the virtues was actually more pleasant than the practice of the vices, much as the traditional hedonists frequently argue that some pleasures generate subsequent pains. As an empirical statement of fact, few would be willing to dispute it. But if one accepts it, then one also rejects the thesis that Nature is alone sufficient to establish a system of morality. And if by Nature we mean Nature corrected by art, then we are in a position identical with that of the antinaturalists.

Though d'Holbach wobbles between these two points of view, he shares the *Philosophes*' common enthusiasm for education. He admits only too vividly that though Nature sometimes gives an individual a constitution such that morality is easy and pleasant for him, she also sometimes endows a man with a constitution which leads to disaster. "Nature has made us a baneful gift when she gives us blood which boils over, a too active imagination, impetuous desires for objects that our circumstances do not permit us to obtain, or, at any rate, which we can procure only with incredible effort, capable of endangering our well being and troubling the calm of society." Evil therefore is as rooted in the natural order as good and one emerges from the *Systeme de la Nature* with a more healthy respect for its author's honesty than for his logic. Whether the system permits it or not, he will not accept men as his beloved Nature creates them, but is as fierce in his condemnation of some as he is eloquent in his praise of others. The value of his work as a whole lies in its straightforward and uncompromising exposition of a naturalistic ethics, so straightforward and uncompromising that all its inherent weaknesses show up. If one omit the theological virtues, one will find him in agreement with most of what his opponents also say. And neither they nor he can justify their initial assumptions. To say that obedience to the commands of God is the basis of all goodness is no more logical than to say that the basis of all goodness is to obey the commands of Nature. These statements turn into postulates, and the Naturalists' polemic against traditional Christianity rests on their refusal to accept their opponents' assumptions. No assumptions can be proved; if they could, they would not be assumptions. That the practice of the theological virtues leads to unhappiness may or may not be true; but when the naturalist insists that they do, he is offering a definition of unhappiness which the Christian would not accept. When he points to the irrefutable evidences of vice among Christians, from Popes to catechumens, the Christian replies that such men are not real Christians. One cannot maintain, in fairness to d'Holbach, that he has not made a valiant effort to infer a set of values from a set of facts or that the application of his theory to life would make it vicious even in the traditional sense of that adjective. If one could make the effort to forget the theological virtues for a moment, one would see that he is striving to give good grounds for practicing the others. But what religious man would be capable of that effort or capable of even entertaining the possibility of making it?

VOLTAIRE

One of the thinkers most difficult to fit into any historical pattern is Voltaire (1694–1778), for he can scarcely be said to belong to any philosophical group or school; he contributed no original ideas to the development of philosophy, and lived so long that his interests as well as his convictions changed steadily. The early Voltaire was a literary, rather than a philosophical, figure, and was a conventional dramatic and satirical poet. More or less of a sycophant, like the general run of *littérateurs* of that time, one never knows how much of what he said was sincere and how much ritualistic bootlicking. Yet, as he grew older and aligned himself with that group known as *philosophes*, it became clearer that he stood on the popular side of the barricades, on the side that was fighting for freedom of speech and conscience, for political reforms, and for anticlericalism. There are, in spite of the confusion and multiplicity of his views, certain ideas which later made him the idol of the revolutionary party, though he was scarcely to be considered a revolutionary himself.

One of these ideas was his pronounced antagonism to atheism. Much as he detested the organization of the Church and the domination which the clergy, especially the Jesuits, exercised over education and public opinion, he did believe in the existence of God, but it was not the God of Catholicism. It was the God of the Deists, the creator and governor of the natural and moral world. He did not believe that the idea of God was innate, for, as he pointed out, following Locke, innate ideas ought to be discoverable in all peoples and there are some, like the Hottentots, who have no such idea. The belief in God's existence must be founded on reason, not on its universality or even its necessity. Reason then will show us that there is an order in the universe and a relation which each individual thing maintains to that order. All cosmological arguments, he says, reduce to this: "When I see a watch the hands of which mark the hours, I conclude that an intelligent being has arranged this machine so that the hands will mark the hours. Thus, when I see the springs of the human body, I conclude that an intelligent being has arranged these organs to be received and nourished for nine months in the womb; that the eyes would be made for seeing, the hands for grasping, etc." But this argument, he continues, does not prove that the intelligent being created the universe out of nothing and is infinite in every way. Hence the cosmological argument must be reinforced by a second argument, which turns out to be that of the necessity of a first cause. The need for a first cause rests on the impossibility of an infinite series of causes running back into the endless past. There must, then, be some being "which necessarily exists through itself from all eternity, and which is the origin of all other beings. From this it follows essentially that this being is infinite in duration, in extent (immensité), in power; for what could limit it?" If it is replied that matter is precisely such a being, then how could one explain the existence of change? Voltaire believed that change introduces absolute novelty into the world and that a self-enclosed and self-limited material world would be incapable of changing. If change occurs, there must be some cause of the change; and a cause, he assumes, is always external to that upon which it exerts its influence. He thus retains the explanatory technique of the physicists of his time, which runs back at least to Empedocles, and which may be phrased in popular language as the principle that nothing changes of its own accord. It should be observed that Malebranche and Hume, the latter following the former, had already criticized this idea of causation by pointing out that we can never observe more than the change and that hence causation itself as a process is something added to our experience. But in this, as in so many other philosophical problems, Voltaire was to take over the traditional point of view. A material universe which simply had orderly change as one of its essential characteristics seemed absurd to him.

Nevertheless Voltaire did not adventure far on the theological path. When it came to describing the nature of this universal governor, he abstained. He admits that he does not know how God created the universe or how He operates. "His existence has been demonstrated to me; but as for His attributes and His essence, it has been demonstrated to me, I think, that I am not made to understand them." Similarly in regard to the purposes of existence: the cosmos is purposeful but I cannot pretend to knowing what the purposes are. Again, whether God be just or unjust, cruel or kindly, cannot be adjudicated, since those adjectives apply only to human beings and not to the Creator. "It is quite as absurd to say that God, in this sense, is just or unjust, as to say that God is blue or square". Oddly enough, in view of Voltaire's having written in Candide the most acid satire of Leibniz' Theodicy penned to date, he follows this statement with words that might have been written by Pangloss, if Pangloss had had the gift. "It is therefore insane to reproach God because flies are eaten by spiders, and that men live only eighty years, that they abuse their freedom to destroy each other, that they suffer illnesses, cruel passions, etc. For we certainly have no idea that flies and men should live forever. To be firmly assured that a thing is evil, we must be able to perceive at the same time that we could have done better. We surely cannot judge that a machine is imperfect if we do not have an idea of the perfection that. is missing. We cannot, for instance, judge that the three angles of a triangle are unequal, if we do not have the idea of an equilateral triangle. We cannot say that a watch is bad, if we have no distinct idea of a certain number of equal spaces which the hands of this watch must pass through in equal times. But who will have an idea in accordance with which this world detracts from the divine wisdom?"

The answer to this rhetorical question might be suspected to have been framed in Voltaire's own work, the *Poem on the Disaster of Lisbon,* with the subtitle, "Examination of This Axiom: Whatever Is, Is Right." [14] Instead of replying to the English poet that whatever is, simply is, and neither right nor wrong, since these terms apply only to human judgments, Voltaire in his preface to the poem flatly asserts that some things that are, are wrong. And one of the things that are wrong is disasters such as the Lisbon earthquake of 1755. He does not maintain that he can explain the origin of evil; on the contrary, it remains a mystery. "Revelation alone can untie this tight knot which all the philosophers have tangled; the hope of a development of our being, in a new order of things, can alone console us for our present sorrows, the goodness of Providence is the sole refuge to which man can have recourse in the shadows of his reason and in the calamities of his feeble and mortal nature." How to explain, then, the horrors of so great a catastrophe is the problem. Is one to lay it to the effects of eternal laws pronounced by a God Who is free and good? Can so many thousands of innocent people be accused of expiating crimes? Would the cosmos have been any the worse if this earthquake had not taken place? But the most cruel of all the explanations seems to be that of the good which will result from the disaster. People say to the stricken: Have courage, other hands than yours will rebuild your homes; others will be born in your ruined houses; the North will be enriched by your losses; your sufferings are but a necessary part in the general harmony of the eternal laws.

A des infortunes quel horrible langage! Cruels, à mes douleurs n'ajoutez point l'outrage.

The usual victims of eternal law have no feelings and do not cry out to their heavenly Father for comfort. But man is in a different situation. He finds no help in the idea that his body will at least nourish the worms who have to eat something. From that point of view all life forms a chain of destruction; all prey on all. Are we to construct a system of universal happiness out of mutual hostility? How are we to conceive of a God, goodness itself, a loving father, who pours out evil upon us with full hands?

Either man is born guilty and God is punishing us for our innate guilt, or this absolute master of all beings, without pity and indifferent to His creatures, has laid down laws of which the horrible consequences follow without interruption; or unformed matter, rebellious to its master, bears within itself its necessary evil consequences; or this disastrous and terrible life on earth is but a passage to an eternal world and death will put an end to our miseries. Whatever possibility we choose, we are in fundamental ignorance and nature gives us no solution to our doubts and fears. And though Voltaire had in his *Traité* maintained that no one could presume to judge the world without having an idea of a better one, he now believes that it is God's task to enlighten us.

On a besoin d'un Dieu qui parle au genre humain. Il n'appartient qu'à lui d'expliquer son ouvrage, De consoler le faible, et d'éclairer le sage. L'homme au doute, à l'erreur, abandonné sans lui, Cherche en vain des roseaux qui lui servent d'appui.

The solution to all this is Montaigne's question "*Que sçais-je?*" We do not know what we are, where we are, where we are going, nor whence we came. One cannot rebel against the laws of God—and Nature; one can only be resigned. But, one might add, our resignation does not prevent our writing poems eloquently giving the reasons for our resignation.

To leave a question unsettled, to maintain that one cannot settle it by rational means, is not to preserve a neutral attitude toward it. The Christian demanded an answer and, if one replied that no answer was possible, one was in the position of denying the affirmative as well as the negative. How sincere, for example, Voltaire was in maintaining in his *Traité* that one had no more reason to believe the soul to be immortal than to believe it mortal, I cannot presume to say. But all the arguments which he produces on this question are against immortality. He was obviously shifting the burden of proof to those who believed in it. On the other hand, when he is discussing the existence of God, he gives at length both the affirmative and negative, and gives them at some length, whereas when he brings up the question of immortality he acts as if everyone knew the arguments *pro* and devotes himself to the arguments con. His conclusion, moreover, stated in one sentence, seems evidence of mortality. "We must take care of those minds which believe that the mortality of the soul is contrary to the welfare of society, and remind them that the ancient Jews, whose laws they admire, believed that the soul was material and mortal, without mentioning the great sects of philosophers who were well worth the Jews and were very decent people [*honnêtes gens*]".

Voltaire also had a definite opinion on the question of free will, a question which many religious people believed had to be settled in favor of freedom if arguments for morality were to be settled properly. He states the problem in the *Traite* as simply as it has ever been stated. "Freedom is solely the power to act. If a stone moved by its own choice, it would be free; animals and men have this power; therefore they are free." One can doubt the freedom of the beasts, since one can observe them only externally; but in the case of man, one can introspect and introspection will prove that one has this power. This cannot be an illusion similar to sensory illusions, for they can all be explained by definite laws. But if the feeling of freedom of choice which we all have is deceptive, then God would certainly have deceived us without purpose. If there is no God and we are nothing but material objects, then we could not have the feeling of freedom; if God exists, and He does, then our feeling of freedom must be veridical. Freedom is not complete; there are certain obvious limits to what we can do. But there is a real area within which we can make our own choices and we do not require the freedom of God to be free. Voltaire still retains the definition of freedom which d'Holbach had laid down; he still believes that a being is not free if his choices are determined by antecedent causes. Consequently he might have been expected to explain more precisely just how anything could act without some motivation which would turn him in one direction rather than another. He admits that our choices can be guided by the reason, that we act often in the pursuit of pleasure. But he also thinks, or says he thinks, that the pursuit of pleasure is identical with freedom. But if pleasure is the same to all men which it probably is not-then man is not free to choose whatever he will, but is bound to choose the common pleasures of his species, whatever he may think. But if, for instance, what one chooses freely seems pleasurable—which it probably does for the very reason that one has chosen it, then one man's meat may still be another's poison and the choices be free.

Voltaire, as is perhaps well known, was far from holding to his belief in freedom. The article "Destin" in the *Dictionnaire Philosophique* is a complete reversal of the position which its author took in the *Traite.* Natural laws, he argues there, are immutable; there are no exceptions to them; and hence everything is necessary. Chance is an illusion. Therefore our decisions are as inevitable as material events. In the article "Franc Arbitre" we find the matter of choice presented to us as itself determined by the purpose which one has in mind. This purpose, or idea, dominates one's action, and once it is formed cannot be rejected. How such purposes or ideas arise within the mind, Voltaire does not pretend to know, but on the contrary asserts vigorously the impossibility of knowing it. Freedom of the will is circumscribed within the limits of what one call will. But once the purpose has been formed, the will is no longer free to resist its accomplishment. "Freedom therefore is not and cannot be anything other than the power to do what one wishes." But what one wishes to do is determined by ideas or passions or purposes that arise in the human mind from causes over which one has no control. This conception of freedom is repeated in the article "Liberte."

There is always something ironical in a determinist's writing propaganda, for if he is a determinist of Voltaire's kind, one might think that exhortation could have no effect on its hearers' wills. But it should be remembered that Voltaire did think that there was a small area within which man was free to choose, the area in which his ideas might determine his choices. There was thus no contradiction between his arguing that absolute freedom of the will was an impossibility and yet insisting on freedom of speech and conscience. His insistence, which was expressed in dozens of articles and pamphlets, appears also in the *Dictionnaire Philosophique* and presumably his intention was to supply those ideas which might be accepted by his readers as valid and would, when once accepted, become the determinants of their behaviour. One might ask what would determine the acceptance of such ideas, and in that case Voltaire would have no reply. How much faith he had in ideas is itself questionable, for in his article on freedom of the press "*Liberté d'imprimer*" he maintains that it is not books but acts that conquer men. "Rome was not conquered by books: she was conquered because she had revolted Europe by her rapine, by the public sale of indulgences; she was conquered because; she had insulted mankind, had wished to govern them like domestic beasts, had abused her power to such an extent that it is astonishing to find a single village remaining in her hands. Henry VIII, Elizabeth, the Duke of Saxony, the Landgrave of Hesse, the Princes of Orange, the Conde, the Coligny did everything, books nothing. Trumpets have never won battles and the only walls they have ever overthrown are those of Jericho." Could it be that since books in themselves are impotent, one may as well let them all be printed? This would be a strange defense of freedom of thought and speech.

We shall not attempt to expound all of Voltaire's philosophic ideas since we are doing no more than drawing an outline of the whole philosophic movement of the French Enlightenment. To be thorough one should include an exposition of the French atheism as it appeared in Naigeon, of the ethicists like Helvétius who followed the naturalism of d'Holbach, and of the many themes which were enunciated by Diderot. But our purpose in this book is simply to describe the major traditions as they developed in modern Europe and to include under each philosopher's name only his most conspicuous contributions to them. As the nineteenth century drew nearer, it was not so much Voltaire as Condillac who became the source of the leading ideas of that time, not so much the rationalism of Voltaire as what was sometimes called the sentimentalism of Rousseau.

14

Idealist Tradition in England for Philosophy

Introduction

The Democritean principle in the seventeenth century was given a precise meaning by Galileo: only those properties which are sufficient and necessary for building a theory of dynamics are "real"; all others are added to reality. Among these others are not only the ordinary sensory qualities of colours, sounds, and the like, but also whatever is named by general, abstract terms and the framework itself of knowledge, what Kant was to call its form. The sensory qualities were, in general, explained either as effects made upon us by physical objects or as effects similarly produced by ideas in the mind of God. Whatever their primordial source, they turned into our contribution to the natural world and, if the human race were to disappear, these qualities would disappear with it. In Hume these sources of ideas, for they were called ideas, were unknown and unknowable. But that they must exist somehow and somewhere, Hume never denied. To such philosophers the existence of general ideas, as well as the structure of knowledge, became a problem, especially since all of them, at least in England, were convinced that ideas were particular beings which might point to or represent, in Hume's terminology, the abstract ideas. As for the form of knowledge, that admittedly was not absorbed from sensation, since sensory data came into the mind individually and unorganized. The construction of groups of them into things, and the construction of things into patterns of occurrence from which general natural laws might be drawn off, was at least in Locke a creative act of the mind, which for reasons which he did not expound seemed to give us some clue to the real organization of the external world. But almost everyone believed that we had certain ideas, such as those of Revelation and of mathematics, which did not come to us from experience defined as sensory. Both were believed to be not only certain but the most certain parts of our knowledge. No one could deny that the ideas of Revelation did not arise from sensation; some, like Berkeley, maintained that mathematics did. But the laws of logic, which were incorporated into mathematical thinking, were either known intuitively or were simply the ways in which we inevitably thought when we did any thinking. The question therefore of the nature of knowledge could still be argued, as if the empiricists had by no means proved their point. The opposing tradition I have called Platonistic, since many of its adherents were directly inspired by Plato or his disciples, though the term, like most doctrinal names in the history of philosophy, is far from accurate.

Lord Herbert of Cherbury

The first member of this school whom we shall discuss is Lord Herbert of Cherbury (1583-1648), a younger contemporary of Bacon and of about the same generation as Hobbes. As famous for his influence on Deism as for his contributions to epistemology, he has certainly been too neglected by historians of philosophy. The work that is of interest to us was entitled "On Truth, in Distinction from Revelation, Probability, Possibility, and Error", and appeared in its first edition in Paris in 1624 and in its third in London in 1645, both editions being in Latin.

Herbert, like so many of the seventeenth-century philosophers whom we have been discussing, was troubled by the disagreements common to men who all seemed to be in the pursuit of truth. He believed that a single and universal set of ideas could be found which would be true for mankind in general, that there was such a thing as *The Truth,* and that men were not forced to be satisfied with a variety of personal interpretations of the laws of nature. What might be called the lyrical element in philosophy was rejected by him, as it is by most scientists. One ought to be able to discover some road that would lead one out of the morass of conflicting opinions to a field in which all would be in agreement. Whereas Bacon had maintained that the experimental method would reach this result, Herbert insisted that only a full knowledge of what truth consisted in would do so. Neither scepticism nor the division of the mind's truths into those held by reason and those held by faith would suffice. That man can attain to some truth he accepts as an axiom, for he cannot believe that God would have created man as His image and yet doomed him to err. But truth itself can be found in four areas of man's experience. (1) There is a truth of things. This appears in statements concerning existence or nonexistence, reality and unreality. It is the truth of facts. It is revealed to us by the presence of the thing about which we are making a judgment. (2) There is a truth of appearances. This arises, or may arise, when we are distinguishing the way things appear from the way they are. Yet, even when we confine ourselves to appearances, we may tell the truth about them. We are frequently deceived by appearances, but nevertheless we are not always deceived by them. The conditions under which we may reach the truth about them can be known and analyzed, and consequently we can, at least in theory, prevent ourselves from being misled by appearances and taking them for reality. (3) There is a truth of concepts. This truth recognizes the distinctions of classes of things, and the interrelations of species and genera, the place of an individual in a class. It is not, like the two former kinds of truth, dependent upon experience at all. It "belongs entirely to us". Since we are all individuals with prejudices or sense organs of varying degrees of acuity, the truth of concepts requires correction and the corrections are made by (4) the truth of intellect. The intellect "alone is able to decide in virtue of its inborn capacity or its Common Notions whether our subjective faculties have exercised their perceptions well or ill". Truth of the intellect requires not only knowledge of the preceding three truths, but also the organization of them into a consistent system, a consistency which Herbert calls conformity with the faculties, external and internal. This means that though there are four kinds of truth, there is a common truth which unites them all, which arises, as it were, out of a purgation of each of those elements which would prove an obstacle to their union. Conformity is a concept of which Herbert makes much use. He uses it to describe the uniform character of individual things through time, believing apparently that each thing, in spite of occasional variations, has a nature which does not change. Truth of things expresses that uniform nature. Truth of appearance "consists in the conditional conformity with the thing," so that whatever appears to be true of a thing will be only apparently true if it is not consistent with statements that are always true of the thing. Thus, if something now is red, now blue, now green, these colours are not part of the thing's constant nature and any descriptions of the thing in terms of its colour have only the truth of appearance. The truth of concepts is also conditional, but resides in conformity between "our subjective faculties and the thing as it appears". Our subjective faculties involved here are our powers of classification, and it is clear that for Herbert a classification may be made either on the basis of apparent or real similarities. The truth of intellect occurs when the three other truths are made to conform to one another, and this seems to be brought about by the intellect itself. We shall now see how much the mind itself contributes to knowledge of the truth.

The faculties by which we obtain knowledge are four in number. They are called by Herbert *Natural Instinct*, which gives us common notions; *Internal Apprehension*, which is analogous to Locke's ideas of reflection; *External Apprehension*, or what is more commonly called sensory perception; and *Discursive Thought*, or reasoning. It will appear, before Herbert has concluded his investigation, that they are arranged in order of decreasing reliability.

Natural Instinct is found in us all, and its objects are affirmed by common consent. "Whatever is believed by universal assent must be true," he says. Natural Instinct is the one faculty which cannot vary from man to man. It reveals to us those Common Notions which the human mind as human must employ in knowing. It is analogous to the common natures and habits of the animals and plants which all after their kinds preserve precisely similar habits of growth, appetite, and form. Herbert cannot believe that mankind is the only group of creatures which God has made heterogeneous. They must have somewhere within them a unifying principle which makes them all men and not simply this and that man. He realizes that we all show a large extent of diversity, but within the diversities of tastes, judgments, habits, and customs, there are some things upon which we are all agreed, and these he calls the Common Notions. This term, which was taken over from the Stoics, denotes man's differentia more than reason does. And whether one agrees or not with Herbert's list of Common Notions, his argument for their existence is not to be lightly rejected. The two Common Notions which he cites are religion and law and though he admits that there are various religions and various laws, he insists that all peoples have some religion and some idea of law. Hence to point out that the religion of one tribe is monotheistic and of another polytheistic would not be a disproof of his thesis, unless one could further demonstrate that one or the other was not really religion. Similarly to point out that one tribe permits polygamy and another forbids it does not in itself prove that both tribes do not have an idea of law. The problem, according to Herbert, is to discover as far as possible just what the Common Notions are, the primordial ideas shared by all mankind, and on them to erect a universal religion and a universal law. That under the heading of religion one might find some beliefs which were in absolute contradiction with all the other beliefs, so that one religion completely negated the other, does not seem likely to him, since he firmly believes that men could not be so at variance with one another and still be men.

Natural Instinct is given to us by God and is His instrument. But as we see it in operation, it is the expression of those faculties which are found in every normal man, "through which the Common Notions touching the internal conformity of things, such as the cause, means and purpose of things, the good, bad, beautiful, pleasing, etc., especially those Notions which tend towards the preservation of the individual, of species, of kinds, and of the universe, are brought into conformity independently of discursive thought". There are several details of this description which should be emphasized. One is that the principles of explanation are Common Notions. The next is that ethical and aesthetic terms are Common Notions. The third is that the Common Notions maintain the order and stability of the Cosmos, the Stoics' Great Animal, as animal instinct is supposed to make for the beasts' preservation. Finally, discursive thought, reasoning, has no part to play in the operations of Natural Instinct. We use certain Common Notions instinctively, as birds migrate or build nests. The Natural Instincts, then, are an expression in action of our humanity. The Common Notions are "inscribed within us" by Nature. "No one, however wild his views, imagines that they are conveyed by objects themselves". They are "not so much the outcome of experience as principles without which we should have no experience at all". This is what is meant by calling the Common Notions innate. Locke must have been a very careless reader of Herbert when he attacked him as he did, for Herbert was insistent that the Common Notions, though latent in all, appeared overtly not in children and madmen but only in normal people. Because the Natural Instinct is part and parcel of our human nature, it is prior not only to experience, in the Lockean sense of that term, but also to reasoning. For the laws of thought are part of our Common Notions and determine the course of correct reasoning. Finally all Common Notions are absolutely prior to and independent of evidence, and are universal, certain, and necessary.

Against any form of empiricism Herbert is arguing that the structure of knowledge is determined by the mind itself and not by its objects. This structure may be expressed in a series of statements which are incontrovertibly true and in accordance with which all true knowledge will ultimately be tested. But next in order of certainty comes the knowledge which we derive from the internal senses. Just as Natural Instinct seems to be analogous to the whole order of nature, so internal senses seem to be found in living beings which have no sense organs, the corals and shellfish being cited as examples. The examples of internal sense which Herbert gives are love, hope, and conscience, which he maintains are as universal as the Common Notions. Yet they differ from them in that they are directed to particular objects. We do not simply love; we love individuals. Hence the truth which comes from internal sense may be either general or particular. But they do not emerge out of the contemplation of general or particular objects. On the contrary, we direct them to the objects in question and thus we have some power over what is presented to us in experience. In that way we are able to make our whole inner life a harmony in accordance with the Common Notions. It is through this harmony that we reach blessedness, for through it we approach the condition of God's harmonious nature. There is a noticeable similarity here between the views of Herbert and Spinoza in that both men agreed that happiness was the fulfilment of our eternal nature and that it could be reached only through an awareness of the absolutely true. "We must not imagine," says Herbert, "we have reached the summit of perfection until we are genuinely filled with devotion and honour towards the divine justice; until we prefer to be chastised rather than evade the destiny. He has prepared for us." The end of life for both is to live in accordance with God and Nature, and for both there is a possible agreement between our nature and that of God.

Spinoza, to be sure, differs from Herbert in more ways than he agrees with him. But oddly enough the Stoic strain which is in both emerges at times to make the resemblance seem greater than the difference.

The external senses are those which put us in contact with the external world. But they are not simply recipients of material impressions; nor are our sensations simply "modifications" of the soul produced in us by external causes. On the contrary, by analogy with the process of cosmic emanation, according to which the cosmic hierarchy flows out of God's being as light issues from a candle, so the lower orders of knowledge proceed from the higher. Herbert never loses sight of his basic method, which is to derive all knowledge from the mind's own activity as far as possible. It is for that reason that he can say, when speaking of the external senses, "We possess a vague premonition, which anticipates the actual realisation of perception". We do not clearly know what we are going to see or hear, but we do suspect it as the internal sense in company with Natural Instinct prepares to guide and form our perceptions. The expression "the actual realisation of perception" must be taken literally. Perception is potentially in the mind; it is latent, waiting only to be actualized. The physical object which we may be observing is only the occasion of its actualization. He is so convinced of this that he abandons the traditional theory of the five senses, maintaining on the contrary that there are as many senses as there are differences between objects. Strange as this may seem to us who are accustomed to what might be called a receptive theory of sensation, it is no stranger than our belief that a nerve current explodes into a sensory quality when it reaches an appropriate area of the cortex. There is a discontinuity between the psychic event and the nervous event that is presumably its cause. I am not saying that the customary theory is incorrect, for that would be presumptuous. But Herbert's theory that our souls on certain occasions produce perceptions is no less logical. For if the percept is itself psychical and we know what we mean by "psychical," the puzzling discontinuity has been eliminated, though the duality of mind and body has not. Unfortunately, when Herbert comes to the point of explaining how the perception becomes actualized on the occasion of meeting an external object, he can produce merely the idea of conformity. So Leibniz, though with more candor, was to produce his concept of preestablished harmony when he met a similar problem. If it be assumed that Herbert was forced to maintain that external sense could never err, since the perceptive faculty would always be actualized in the same way on identical occasions, it must not be forgotten that no knowledge would be had at all unless the internal sense and Natural Instinct were operating along with external sense. And since we are free to follow the guidance of our Common Notions as we will, so we are free to err in ordinary sensory experience. The perceiver, if he "leaves the high road and wanders among by-paths must return to the Common Notions which are alone able to correct his mistakes. The external modes of experience are completely trustworthy when their proper conditions are present; when they are absent, truth itself is in default. For of what use is the eye when light, or appropriate distance or span of time are absent? We are free within ourselves to shut our eyes, stop up our ears, so long as all the conditions are present. It is the same with the Common Notions. Freedom reigns supreme within us, finding constraint only at one point, namely, in that it is compelled always to pursue its eternal happiness; though it may do so foolishly and sometimes in vain".

Discursive Thought, the fourth of our cognitive faculties, is the most subject to error. It is superfluous when we have Common Notions or when the internal or external senses are testifying. Moreover, it is the least disciplined of our faculties. Through its exercise men have been given over to wild theories, the fruit of which can never be anything other than evil. It sets itself above the Common Notions. Herbert's eloquence when he inveighs against it is that of the great moralists. Nevertheless he has to grant that when we cannot find any better means of reaching the truth, we are reduced to its exercise. Without it we cannot draw inferences nor connect general statements together. Moreover, it spots contradictions in terms and distinguishes the Common Notions. Its special province is analogy between things. But when it attempts to rise beyond the world of things, it is helpless without Common Notions. It is not the instrument of philosophy proper, since for Herbert that discipline can succeed by Natural Instinct alone. It can, however, develop logic whose purpose is the untangling of the Common Notions from "the cloud of words". Otherwise we would do well to reduce it to its own narrow province and never let it escape.

There lies behind all this a mass of presuppositions which are probably the chief justification for calling this epistemology Platonistic. They are:

(1) the idea that knowledge is essentially contemplation, rather than action;

(2) that there is a correspondence between all parts of the universe and the universe as a whole;

(3) that the technique of philosophy is the uncovering of that correspondence;

(4) that truth may be discovered through the consistency between ideas and the Common Notions;

(5) that on the analogy of emanation, reality is the ideal from which all else proceeds;

(6) that sensory experience is the occasion for the actualization of perception rather than its cause;

(7) that the Natural Instinct reveals the true nature of mankind.

On the other hand, there are certain Platonistic ideas which are not present in Herbert. (1) He says nothing about the theory of reminiscence, according to which we recall the knowledge which we had before birth on certain occasions. (2) If he suspects that we are reincarnated in other bodies, he does not say so. (3) There is little if any echo of the more famous Platonic myths, such as that of the Charioteer in the *Phaedrus* or that of Eros in the *Symposium* or that of the Cave in the *Republic*. (4) There is no mention of an intelligible world as distinct from a sensible world. In fact, he shows a closer resemblance to the Stoics than to the Platonists in his acceptance of the idea of common notions which are found in universal assent, in his belief that human happiness arrives when an individual lives in harmony with cosmic law, and in his religious doctrines, upon which we did not touch.

Henry More and Cudworth

The second generation of Platonists were largely men connected with Cambridge, and from them the misnomer "Cambridge Platonists" has come to be used for the tradition in general. Of this group we shall deal in detail only with Henry More (1614-87) and his friend Ralph Cudworth (1617-88), considering especially their contribution to epistemology and ethics respectively.

More's early interest in philosophy seems to have been stimulated by Descartes. But Descartes' psychophysical dualism left him unsatisfied, though he never denied a difference between the two substances. Yet, in order to make interaction between mind and body more plausible, he attempted to reduce that difference to what one can only call a difference of degree rather than of kind. This, it will be seen, was also the ambition of Leibniz, but both men failed to see that the two ends of a scale are still two and not one. It has been popular to believe that the difference between sanity and insanity is also only one of degree, but nevertheless those who are on one end of the scale cannot function in a world inhabited by those on the other, cannot understand their reasoning processes, and must undergo a course of therapeutic treatment before they can move comfortably in the society of the other. Mores material world is not to be described in purely mechanical terms and is indeed permeated with a "plastic spirit" which determines its behaviour. But nevertheless it is not a mind or a set of ideas or "spiritual" in the sense that the human soul is supposed to be spiritual.

It would probably be best to begin with a description of

what More means by "spiritual." In his *Antidote against Atheism* he lists those qualities which distinguish spirit from matter as follows: self-penetration, self-motion, self-contraction and dilatation, indivisibility, to which are added the power of penetrating, moving, and altering matter. In the *True Notion of a Spirit*, a spirit is defined as "an immaterial substance intrinsically endued with life and the faculty of motion." Out of this definition it appears to More to follow that spirit alone has true *unity*, by which he means that it cannot be dissected, cut up into parts which are externally related to one another; it is a unity which is not formed by addition. We shall see this sort of unity emphasized repeatedly among idealistic philosophers and some others, like Bergson, whose views are similar to those of the idealists. Along with unity goes *goodness*, by which More suggests that spirit is oriented toward an end or purpose and that its nature cannot be understood in a nonteleological fashion. If one prefers, it could be said that spirit alone can determine values. In the third place spirit is *true*, by which More means simply that it retains its selfidentity through time. Besides these traits, spirit also exists in time and place and is extended, three characteristics which were traditionally reserved for matter but which More emphasizes because he wishes to oppose the Cartesian idea of the soul as inextended substance. Its substantial nature is accentuated by More since he wishes to prevent anyone's believing that it may be a property of anything else, such as the body, thus eliminating such views as those which Hobbes was propounding. And in spite of its extension, "yet it is utterly *Indivisible* and *Indiscerptible* into real Physical parts. It can *penetrate* the *Matter*, and penetrate things of its own kind; It is understood to have *Life* intrinsically in it self, and the faculty of moving; which in some sense is true in all Spirits whatsoever, forasmuch as *Life* is either *Vegetative*, *Sensitive*, or *Intellectual*. Every Spirit either moves it self by it self, or the Matter, or both".

Whereas most of these traits were commonly accepted by men who believed in the reality of souls or spirits, there is one which was commonly denied, extension. We have already seen the trouble which Descartes faced in making the soul inextended and yet placing it in the pineal gland where it could immediately act upon the animal spirits. More clearly saw that difficulty and avoided it by his theory of extended spirits. They do not occupy much space, to be sure, for their extension may be simply position, but that they occupy space and are, as he says, *somewhere*, does not entail materiality. Spirits can expand and contract apparently at will and all that is required to grant them extension is an *Ubi*. That extension does not entail materiality is demonstrated ingeniously by More when he points out that even if all the matter were removed from the universe, space would remain and such space could be neither divided into parts nor be imagined as objects material and sensible are imagined. That our idea of space can be analyzed logically, he is far from denying, but he is violently opposed to the notion that corresponding to these logical parts or dimensions there are physical parts. Our trouble comes from our imagination, which is so infected with the dregs of the material world that it always tends to think of things in materialistic terms. An example of this weakness, which he does not cite, it goes without saying, would be the use of mechanical models in subatomic physics. Another example would be metaphors drawn from the behaviour of fluids which we use to describe energy systems. If we could only think of extension as dimension without matter, then we would have no difficulty in accepting the idea of extended spirits.

To deny to matter the exclusive right to extension was to diminish the difference between matter and spirit, for it gave all reality at least one common property. Most of the properties of spirit are the polar antitheses of those of matter but this one is that *sine qua non* in More's mind of real existence. It permits him to locate things in the mind and not to think of them as simply presented to the mind. And it also permits him in a curious way to insist that the mind is not a *tabula rasa* until the material world through sensation makes certain impressions upon it. The mind at birth has what he calls "an active sagacity" or "quick recollection" which operates on the occasions of its various experiences and formulates its knowledge. The mind is "jogged and awakened by the impulses of outward Objects" to a fuller understanding of what is before it. This, as is clear, is what Lord Herbert referred to when he spoke of the action of the common notions in perception. That there is actual knowledge in the soul prior to experience is shown by our mathematical ideas. When we are shown a circle drawn on paper, that circle itself is clearly not a perfect mathematical circle, but nevertheless it can represent one to the mind and, when the mind sees it, it can recall all the geometrical properties of circularity. The mathematical circle, he argues, could not come into the mind from the material circle which is drawn on paper for the very reason that it is not out there in it. On the contrary the material circle can be only a hint, a reminder, of what the mind already knows and what it pronounces on the occasion of seeing it. "The Soul sings out the whole Song upon the first hint, as knowing it very well before". This, as readers of Plato will recognize, is derived from the *Meno* in which the slave solves geometrical theorems though he has studied no geometry. Besides certain mathematical ideas the soul also possesses innately relative notions. These notions are those of cause and effect, whole and part, like and unlike. More's technique here is to try to show that there can be no material counterpart to relatives, and that consequently their source must be psychic. There can be no material counterpart to such notions since they are not sensory qualities, like colours and sounds. They cannot be sensory qualities since they may change when the terms by which they are related are not changed. Two similar things can become dissimilar merely by changing one of them, and the dissimilarity is no more in the changed one than in the unchanged. If the former innate idea is based on the argument in Plato Meno, this comes from the *Theaetetus*. But the argument for the subjectivity of ideas of relations is furthered by More's pointing out that some relations may be changed with no change whatsoever in the terms. For a given physical object may sustain contradictory relations to two different other objects, being, for instance, half of one and twice the other. The relation therefore, he concludes, cannot be inherent in the material properties themselves. There are also some complex ideas which he believes to be innate:

axioms of arithmetic and geometry, which are known immediately to be true. An example would be: Things equal to the same thing are equal to each other, or the Law of Contradiction. Such truths arise in all minds that reason at all and arise with no object in the external world corresponding to them. They are "natural emanations of the mind" itself.

It will be observed that up to this point the only disagreement between such men as Locke and a man like More was the terminology that they used. Locke himself knew that the axioms of arithmetic were intuited as true but would not for that reason beleive them to be innate. He did not believe that the rules by which the mind organized its experiences were themselves perceived in experience, in spite of certain sentences in the early books of the *Essay* which would give the reader that impression. If the two men could have agreed on a terminology, they might have agreed on a common epistemology. But behind the epistemology lay a metaphysics which would have been abhorrent to Locke, the peculiar kind of Neo-Platonism which More and his friends found so consoling to their religious feelings. For instance, Locke, though it is perhaps unnecessary to point this out, believed firmly in the existence of the God of revelation, but he believed in His existence on rational grounds; His existence could be demonstrated like all other truths. More, on the contrary, maintained that His existence was another of the innate ideas. The discovery in one's mind of an idea of which one could not rid oneself would have been evidence to Locke of no more than a kind of intellectual stubbornness, a disease of which the cure lay in looking about for people who either did not have the idea or who had actually rid themselves of it. He knew that atheists, whom he detested, did exist and that their existence was evidence that every man did not possess the idea in question. Hume would have looked for an impression which might have been the original of the idea and if he did not find one—and it goes without saying that he could not have found an impression which was the original of the idea of God he would have rejected the idea, though not necessarily that for which it stood. But More, finding the idea of God in his own mind and having eliminated idiots, madmen, and by implication savages from serious consideration, could maintain that since such an idea could not arise from sensation, it must be innate. The idea of God, an eternal substance, infinite in essence and goodness, omnipotent, omniscient, and necessarily existent "of itself," is the same idea which Descartes discovered himself to have. But Descartes by the application of the causal postulate maintained that no finite being could cause such an idea to arise in the mind and that hence only an infinite cause, with the other traits indicated, could have produced it. But the only such being is God Himself and therefore He must exist. More, on the other hand, is satisfied with the inner light and finds the idea of God, like the ideas of the arithmetical axioms, self-substantiated.

Nevertheless, in refuting his opponents he goes beyond the simple acceptance of what the inner light reveals. He points out that his opponents do not see that the idea of God is that of a being whose essence implies existence. The existence of God is necessarily implied in the idea of God, as the sum of the angles of a triangle is implied in the idea of a triangle. To put the matter in other words, More believed that a spiritual being has the same nature as an idea. Whatever is implied in an idea may legitimately be asserted of it which is almost a truism. Thus there may be geometrical figures which have never been exemplified on paper or otherwise. Yet a geometer could frame ideas of them the chiliagon is the stock example and could presumably draw out of the idea a set of theorems which would be true of them. So with the idea of God. If there is no self-contradiction in statements which define Him, then we have a logically consistent idea of Him. If we find that one of the implications of those statements is His existence, then we have a right to believe in His existence. Unfortunately, though the idea as presented by More may not be "arbitrarious and fictitious," he does not show that God's existence follows from his essence but leaves the matter as a string of adjectives which he discovers when he contemplates the ideas. He would have done better to follow the course of Pascal. As it was, his proof of God's existence is a confused statement of St. Anselm's ontological proof.

Behind much of More's metaphysical reasoning lies an assumption which was common in earlier periods, to the effect that matter cannot move itself but is utterly inert. What might be called autokinesis was the exclusive property of spirits or immaterial substances. It is therefore easy for More to argue that a human being could not be simply a mass of matter for he moves himself about voluntarily, moves other bodies, and performs all the mental operations of thinking, feeling, imagining, and the like, which are the very opposite of bodily motions. Therefore the soul cannot be the effect of the body, whether the body be thought of as the brain or the animal spirits, but must be an immaterial substance distinct from the body "which uses the *Animal Spirits* and the *Brains* for instruments in such and such operations". The human soul in this way becomes a "little meddal of God," and as it is to the body, so God is to the universe as a whole. But such an argument would identify God with the Neo-Platonic Soul of the World, the *anima mundi*, and not with that necessarily existent being of which we are said to have an innate idea. One might well ask whether the idea of a triangle could produce a triangle or the idea of the first law of motion could move anything. To this More would reply that it is precisely our ideas which would move our bodies and our concepts which generate our percepts. This becomes plausible only when we remember that for More the Neo-Platonic theory of emanation is taken literally.

In the first book of his work on *The Immortality of the Soul* he argues as follows. An emanative cause produces an effect "merely by being"; it does not move, it does not do anything; it simply is and out of it flow its effects. That there must be some such cause follows from the necessity of avoiding an infinite regress: if we go from effect to cause we must either stop at a First Cause or go on forever. But the First Cause must be selfcaused. The human soul is not self-caused, but nevertheless as a spiritual substance it can generate its effects by emanation, as well as it can act upon matter. For unless it is absolutely impotent, there is no other way in which it could produce anything. For when matter acts upon matter, it does it by the literal contact of its parts. But a spiritual substance has no parts and cannot be said to touch anything except figuratively. Yet it can penetrate matter and indeed More repeats frequently arguments seeking to demonstrate that power. He needs it in order to explain how the soul organizes matter, for he cannot believe that order comes about spontaneously, without direction from some "plastic force." The human soul, like all others, permeates the body. On its lowest levels, it generates the action of the heart and lungs. Next comes perception when a material object is presented to us, though the material object is but the occasion of the perception. The higher faculties, imagination, will, and reason, are similarly her own possessions and cannot be explained as due to any changes in any one part or group of parts of the body. The details of this exposition are of little importance, for they are fanciful in the extreme. What is important is More's attempt to explain such an experience as that of the sensory qualities as psychic emanations, not as effects produced here or there within the body. By spreading the soul throughout the body, while retaining its immaterial nature, he thinks that he is able to give an orderly account of sensation while abandoning nothing to the materialist.

Though there is much in Henry More which is repugnant to rational men, such as his belief in witches, yet it would be foolish to treat him lightly. It must be remembered that he accepted certain presuppositions of most men of his time, such as the inability of matter to initiate movement and therefore to cause anything by itself, and the inconceivability of order which is not given to things by a mind. Once these presuppositions are accepted, one must either land in a blind alley or assume the existence of some nonmaterial being which will cause changes, and a mental being which will bring order into the universe and into our part of the universe. If the human body, for instance, moves, it is either propelled by something outside of it or by something intimately united with it. It would seem reasonable that when we move through space, we are not propelled like leaves in the wind or billiard balls which are hit by cues. If that is so, then it would follow that the motive power is within us. And if the only motive power we know is that which is traditionally called psychic, then we will call it the soul. Furthermore, if our lives manifest order (and if they did not, the life-cycle to start at the point most easily grasped would not be as it is) then there must be some nonmaterial explanation of that order. And since order is always an "expression" of a mental being, we will explain it as the expression of the mind. Whether we use the word "expression" or "emanation" is of small moment; we shall need some term that will not suggest that a nonmental cause effectuates the order. The fundamental difficulty in all this arises from the presuppositions themselves, not from the inferences drawn from them. The whole concept of causality needed further investigation; the notion that processes required agents to perform them was more than dubious, though no one doubted it in the seventeenth century. Little was gained by invoking an ultimate cause when one's reasoning was frustrated except possibly a reputation for frankness. In spite of the repulsive rhetoric of Henry More, he could have been rewritten in a simple and clear style, for the logic, which was often shrouded by the rhetoric, was not hard to grasp. He was not a mere synthesizer of ancient dogmas, though he derived much of his inspiration from them. He was to be sure a Christian apologist, as he understood Christianity; but he tried to base his apologetics on reason. For us he stands as a man who confronted the empiricists with outspoken demands for intelligibility. He asked how it was possible for unthinking matter to produce thought, for inert matter to produce movement, for order to come about by chance rather than plan, for separate and ununited percepts to form judgments. One answer might have been that facts were not questions and that if these things were so, then they were so and that was the end of it. But not even Hume was willing to take that stand.

It is customary, and not faithless to fact, to consider Ralph Cudworth (1617-88) as the alter ego of Henry More, who turned the Platonistic argument of his friend toward ethics. His main work is undoubtedly *The True Intellectual System of the Universe*, first published in 1678, though written much earlier. Cudworth points out in his preface that his purpose is to refute what he calls fatalism, of which he distinguishes three types:

(1) the determinism of a pure materialism in which physical law, i.e., the laws of dynamics, controls all changes in the cosmos;

(2) atheistic fatalism according to which God determines all change without regard to standards of goodness or justice;

(3) atheistic fatalism according to which God does respect moral values but nevertheless predetermines all human behaviour. Cudworth's objection to all three types of fatalism is based on their denial of human freedom. For himself, he believes that (1) "there is a God, an omnipotent understanding Being, presiding over all"; (2) "God, being essentially good and just, there is . . . something in its own nature immutably just and unjust"; (3) "we are so far forth principals or masters of our own actions, as to be accountable to justice for them, or to make us guilty and blameworthy for what we do amiss, and to deserve punishment accordingly". Since he puts the burden of proof upon the atheists, he considers it necessary to analyze their arguments and disprove them one by one.

One of his most pressing anxieties is to establish teleology, which he takes for granted. He can find no atheistic doctrine which permits one to believe in it. To justify it, he assumes the existence of what he calls a plastic nature, below God in rank, but permeating the whole world of matter, both living and inorganic. This plastic nature acts purposively; and, if its existence be denied, he says one is either forced to conclude that all apparent purpose is attained fortuitously, or that God intervenes in the creation and, presumably, behaviour of "every gnat and fly, insect and mite." Both of these hypotheses seem nonsensical to Cudworth. It is to him inconceivable that the infinite regularity of things should come about by chance. Moreover there are many occurrences in nature, such as respiration, "as do plainly transcend the powers of mechanism." There are finally certain phenomena his example is that of the "distant poles of the equator and ecliptic" which are flatly contradictory of mechanism. He cites Aristotle's refutation of mechanism from the example of artistry, wherein it is asserted that no work of artistry could be explained on purely mechanical principles. The second alternative, that God intervenes in creation every time something purposive is achieved, is to "render Divine Providence operose, solicitous, and distractious". It would reduce nature to something so distinct from her creator as to signify nothing. Finally, the slow process of generation would be absurd if it were determined by an omnipotent being. In such processes we often see bungling and error, and surely no one could imagine that God could be guilty of such. Hence Cudworth has recourse to his plastic nature, "an inferior and subordinate instrument," which carries out God's rules and ordinances, but cannot act "electively and with discretion."

The source of the idea of a plastic nature Cudworth attributes to both Aristotle and Plato, though he suggests that Aristotle himself attributed it to Empedocles with his notions of Love and Strife as the two ruling forces in the universe. A plastic nature can harmonize opposites; it introduces discord, to be sure, but it reconciles the discord in a universal harmony. It operates for the achievement of ends and these ends are the good and the beautiful. These values are resident in the orderliness and "artificiality" of the cosmos. Orderliness and beauty, then, become explanatory principles in themselves. That is, we can properly explain why certain things happen by giving their ends. This is clearly a reaction against the mechanistic theories which were contemporary with him, and not merely a set of arguments against Democritus and the Epicureans. It is an attempt to restore the general teleology of Aristotle and to rephrase it in Christian terms. The plastic nature, as he keeps repeating, is a kind of artist; both artisans and nature itself operate as if they were seeking goals. But, again in Aristotelian language, the artist exists outside his materials and impresses a form upon them; nature, as artist, is within the materials themselves. "Whereas human art cannot act upon the matter otherwise than from without and at a distance, nor communicate itself to it, but with a great deal of tumult and hurlyburly, noise and clatter, it using hands and axes, saws and hammers, and after this manner, with much ado, by knockings and thrustings, slowly introducing its form or idea into the materials; nature, in the meantime, is another kind of art, which, insinuating itself immediately into things themselves, and there acting more commandingly upon the matter as an inward principle, does its work easily, cleverly, and silently". Nature, thus, is like the soul, an incorporate law guiding matter according to fixed rules. Nature requires no consultation or deliberation to reach her ends, whereas men do, for nature is the impress of the Divine understanding.

But an impress of the Divine understanding is not the divinity itself. The understanding of God is separate and far removed from all Creation. It is modelled upon the Divine understanding; it follows the rules laid down by it; but it is the builder in relation to God who is the architect. The plastic nature is not conscious of what it does; it imitates the wisdom and art of God. Lest this seem strange to his readers, Cudworth produces the example of such habits as those of singing or playing on musical instruments. "Which habits direct every motion of the hand, voice, and body, and prompt them readily, without any deliberation or studied consideration, what the next following note or motion should be". The main difference between habits and nature is that the former have to be learned, whereas the latter is unlearned and untaught. Yet the plastic nature has to be further differentiated from matter, for an opponent could maintain that Cudworth is simply giving a name to the regularity of natural events. Consequently he is anxious to point out, as Leibniz was also to do, the Cartesian identification of the soul with thinking or consciousness. He insists that wherever there is life some kind of soul must exist; and yet embryos and men in deep sleep and lethargy are not deprived of souls because they have no consciousness. The vegetables and beasts, human beings performing habitual acts, indeed the soul itself as distinct from its effects are not conscious. We have no way of knowing how the body affects the soul. When we think, we are aware only of the objects of our thought, not of the machinery by which these thoughts are produced. There is a long list of psychic operations of which we are unconscious and yet which cannot be termed material. Hence, if the plastic nature is not conscious, it must act "fatally, magically, and sympathetically". By these terms, which Cudworth takes over from Plotinus, he wishes to name a cause which is immaterial, psychic, and yet unconscious, like love, hate, and the other attractions and repulsions which we feel but which in themselves are not rational. We may, after experiencing love or attraction, bring it to consciousness and discuss it intellectually, but it is not itself guided by the intellect nor does it operate in accordance with reason. We ourselves do reason and do control our lives; or can, at any rate, use a faculty which is much higher than the plastic nature that is found in things. It is a lower form of life which emanates from the higher. Yet it is a form of life, however low in the cosmic scale, and hence incorporeal.

Cudworth, like most of his contemporaries, could not believe that matter could be more than a passive something incapable of doing anything. It is, in Cudworth's words, a "resisting bulk, nothing but mere outside, *aliud extra aliud,* together with passive capability," without "internal energy, self-activity, or life belonging to it". Hence when one came upon activity which seemed to be without life or mind, one was bound to interpret it as attributable to the action of something mental or immaterial-either within it or outside it. Since the only mentality outside of the physical universe was that of God, it was necessary to show how God's mind could act upon the purely material world. One could turn to some form of pantheism which would make God's being permeate the world, but that would contradict the belief in a transcendent God, creator and judge of the world. Therefore, God must have His surrogate acting in accordance with His will and intimately united with nature. Its main task would be the harmony and order of the diverse things and kinds of things which are found in the cosmos and the production of unity in that diversity. "It must be one and the same thing, which formeth the whole, or else it could never have fallen into such an uniform order and harmony. Now that which is onc and the same, acting upon several distant parts of matter, cannot be corporeal". In Aristotle no separate being was required to explain these observable features of the world; he could talk of Nature's doing nothing in vain, and yet not identify Nature as anything separate from natural occurrences. Just as in the case of human beings, he was able to speak of our souls as the final cause and purpose of our bodies, being related to them as cutting is to the axe; so he was also able to deny that they have ever existed apart from our bodies. But to Cudworth, as to other Neo-Platonists, this is an absurdity. To them the so-called active principle must be existentially distinct from that which it acted upon. Hence such phrases, as we have seen in Henry More, to the effect that the soul uses the body as its instrument. Unfortunately for Cudworth, he uses the Pseudo-Aristotelian *De mundo* as a genuine work and could therefore find in it the real meaning of Aristotle, which is that there is spirit, living and generative, which accounts for the order and form of the universe.

Having made his universe a manifestation of goodness and beauty and hence governed by a plastic nature a nature operating under God's rule—Cudworth has drawn a portrait of the macrocosm. The laws which correspond to our ideas may then be found exemplified in the cosmos without the cosmos having to go through a course of study to learn them. It needs no experience to teach it. It follows its nature. What then of the microcosm? Our minds possess among other ideas certain general, universal, and abstract theorems of science, which are self-verifiable. They exist only in the mind and have nothing in the material world corresponding to them. They are, of course, the Common Notions of Lord Herbert. When they are understood, or clearly perceived, they are seen to be true. The point here, as in Herbert and More and for that matter in Descartes and Spinoza and even Locke is that to understand such ideas is to see their truth. "No rational understanding being," says Cudworth, "that knows what a part is, and what a whole, what a cause and what an effect, could possibly be so made, as clearly to conceive the part to be greater than the whole, or the effect to be before the cause, or the like." (Yet in teleological explanations, the effect does exist before the cause.) Such knowledge, as distinguished from sensory perception, is absolutely true and will be so granted by all men. It was normal for a man of Cudworth's inclination to move immediately to a proof of the existence of God.

With astonishing ingenuity he proceeds to show all the weakness of the ontological argument of Descartes, which he correctly points out was anticipated by others. The argument which he himself finds more telling is that from the Great Chain of Being applied to a scale of perfections:

> *It being on the one hand undeniably evident, that lesser perfections may naturally descend from greater, or at least from that which is absolutely perfect, and which virtually containeth all: but, on the other hand, utterly impossible, that greater perfections, and higher degrees of being, should rise and ascend out of lesser and lower, so as that, which is the most absolutely imperfect of all things, should be the first fountain and original of all: since no effect can possibly transcend the power of its cause; wherefore it is certain, that in the universe things did not thus ascend and mount, or climb up from lower perfection to higher; but on the contrary, descend and slide down from higher to lower: so that the first original of all things was not the most imperfect, but the most perfect being.*

This most perfect being is God. It is interesting to observe that Cudworth here overtly uses the principle *ex nihilo nihil,* which he says the materialists misunderstand. The intelligence could not, on this principle, come from brute matter which is not intelligent, nor could ideas come from the impact of matter on our sense organs. Knowledge is conferred by the mind on the things with which it comes in contact and it is conferred by the application of intelligible principles which are universal to particular experiences. Otherwise there would be nothing in our minds but several different impacts which moving material particles make upon us. The universal principles by which we know, e.g., the axioms of geometry, by their very nature could not come from experience but are part of our intellectual equipment. And this is a direct reflection of the mind of God. Corresponding to the universal ideas, there must be universal objects, or Platonic essences, and these essences must exist in the mind of God, their sensible existence being merely a vestment in which God has clothed them.

The *Intellectual System*, which is a long and exhaustive set of arguments against atheism, serves as an introduction to Cudworth *Treatise Concerning Eternal and Immutable Morality*. This work, which was published posthumously in 1731, was not transcribed entirely by its author and hence may contain certain errors. But no one, to the best of my knowledge, has ever maintained that it did not accurately represent Cudworth's thought. In the third book of the *Treatise* he elaborates his epistemology, showing first that sensation is not knowledge but a passion, a "dull confused and stupid perception obtruded upon the soul from without". It apprehends objects but does not know what they are. The reason why it cannot know what they are is simple enough; the nature of things is always expressed in the form of a universal, and sensory objects are always particulars, localized and dated. One may see a cat but not know its nature, which is expressed in the term *felinity*. That sensation can only apprehend particulars was traditional, and it was not until recently in American philosophy, when Strong and Santayana insisted that we perceived essences, that it was seriously questioned. To know, then, is to assign a nature to a particular, to classify it under a general term, to grasp its essence as distinguished from its particularity. If the essence cannot rise out of sensory materials, then it must be contributed to knowledge by the mind itself. But if that is so the seat of ideas, the soul, must also be entirely distinct from matter, and its spiritual substantiality is thus justified. Sensation, Cudworth concludes, has merely pragmatic value, a hint of the existence of the external world whose inner nature is unknown to it. The familiar doctrine that experience is but the occasion for knowledge, not its cause, reappears. Sense, he says in the picturesque language of his time and school, is the feeling of "a jog, knock or thrust made upon the body which the soul is united to".

As Hume was to say in his *Treatise*, though motivated by different interests, there is no essential difference between sensations and images. What we see in a dream or in fantasy is really one and the same. The latter are but weak sensations. They may be aroused by our own volition or not;

qualitatively there is no distinguishing between them and what we perceive in waking life. Thus, apprehending a sensory quality is no evidence of anything whatsoever; judgment is required to pronounce it real or imaginary; and judgment is made by us, not forced upon us. Since there are only two possible sources of mental contents, the external world and the internal, matter and the soul, if one is cancelled, the other must remain on the books. Hence he is driven to the conclusion that knowledge is our own activity directed toward the things of the external world. We conquer and master them, as he likes to say, by knowing them. And knowing consists, let us repeat, in applying ideas to the particulars which are before us. "The primary and immediate objects of intellection and knowledge are not things existing without the mind, but the ideas of the mind itself actively exerted, that is, the intelligible rations, reasons of things". Ideas in this sense of the word are assertions, sentences, judgments, not qualities. This is the sense which Spinoza, it will be recalled, also gave to this highly ambiguous term.

To explain how our judgments or ideas are true, Cudworth returns to the vocabulary of Lord Herbert and assumes a conformity between the soul and the world itself. The soul is "all things intellectually", a mirror of the universe. All we have to do is to reflect upon what is contained in, or implied by, our most abstract ideas. Thus knowledge that is abstract and remote from particular facts is the more demonstrable and the truer. The result would seem to be that what is called purely formal science today is always and demonstrably true, whereas imagination and sensation may be, and usually are, deceitful. Cudworth thus has only to list those ideas which we possess without any contact with experience. The outcome is that the faculties of the soul themselves thinking as contrasted with what is thought about, sensing as contrasted with sensory objects cannot be received from without but are expressions of our own psychic powers. Then come the moral notions. Finally relative notions. We are back again at the principle that the sensible objects are simply the occasion of our pronouncing some judgment about them. They are no part of knowledge nor the cause of knowledge.

Though Cudworth is well worth close study, as are his colleagues in the idealistic tradition, for they have all been seriously neglected in favor of those of the same persuasion who came later, we must be content here with what has been already said. The next generation was more sensitive to the criticisms of their doctrine emanating from Locke and his followers and, in turn, developed certain arguments which might well have been considered by that group. That generation was less florid in its rhetorical devices. We shall begin with a man who is scarcely ever mentioned in the histories of philosophy, Richard Burthogge.

BURTHOGGE

As the seventeenth century drew to a close, the members of the idealistic or Platonistic group, under the influence of Locke, undertook more detailed analyses of the problems of knowledge, and the labels which are applied to their views become more and more misleading. This is especially true of Richard Burthogge who, while retaining many of the Platonistic tenets, grants more to sensation than his colleagues do. He believed in the plastic nature which animates the cosmos, in the discovery of some truths by intuition, in the non-empirical form of understanding, but he also believed that the contributions of sensation to the understanding are real, though not identical with the "inner natures" of things. Much of this could as well be found in Locke as in Herbert or More or Cudworth, and we know that Burthogge knew the work of Locke. But his emphasis upon the religious significance of his theories is quite un-Lockean and there is some reason to believe that one of his aims was a reconciliation of the Lockean and the Platonistic theories of knowledge.

One of his fundamental principles is that the world is known to us only through our ideas of it. Things are not known as they are but "as they are in the Sense, Imagination, or Minde". Things thus are transformed into ideas by our mental faculties; they appear as qualities and these qualities are purely subjective. Similarly the values and such relations as that of cause and effect, whole and part, are also subjective.

So much is straight Platonism. Burthogge also assumes that things themselves, though their real nature is unknown and unknowable, do stimulate ideas, though what the stimulation consists in is not clear. Burthogge resorts to metaphors here and speaks of the "notions of the mind" as *"bottomed* on *Sentiments* of Sense." The real things are "grounds to Sentiments"; "the impressions of things without upon the Sensories, produce or occasion in them the Cogitations which we call Sentiments, as Colours, Sounds, Sapours, etc." It can be confidently asserted, then, that he believed in the reality of something external to the mind, and that, whatever that external something is, without it we should have no sensations. Moreover, having made a distinction between first and second notions, the former of which we might call ideas of sensation, and the latter both Locke's ideas of reflection and all the apparatus of thinking, he maintains that knowledge by first notions is clearer and more evident that knowledge by second notions. In fact, "what is against Sense, is against Knowledge". It is therefore impossible for a man rightly to believe in something that is contradicted by sensation, not even if it be something said to be revealed. It is on this around that he rejects the dogma of transubstantiation.

The duality of first and second notions has a parallel in two sorts of truth: (1) that which he calls metaphysical, and which is found in the conformity between our ideas and those in the mind of God; (2) that which he calls logical and which is the conformity between our ideas and the things of which they are the ideas. The former cannot be grasped by us, for we cannot apprehend God's ideas though presumably we can know that they must exist. The latter, however, is our greatest concern. At this point, Burthogge accentuates the difference between apprehending a sensory quality and making a judgment about it. He points out that apprehension in itself is no more true or false than a thing is. Only judgments can be true. Hence the clarity and distinction of a perception cannot be the reason for its truth, though true ideas will be clear and distinct. Calling Lord Herbert to witness, he argues that truth lies in the conformity of things to our faculties. When this conformity exists, then we freely and spontaneously assent. Burthogge, like most idealists, is forced into some such situation as this since he admits that we cannot set idea and its original side by side and compare them. The congruity to which Herbert invited his readers' attention was in this case the logical harmony between two judgments. This was not of course his language but mine. We are enclosed in a world of ideas, and in the long run it is admitted that truth must be a relation between those ideas. There can be both logical consistency and inconsistency, and the judging mind can see for itself when and how its inferences hang together.

Yet Burthogge will not admit that the mind possesses at birth, or, if one prefer, by nature, "a system of notions and first principles" by means of which we might discover all truth and dispense with experience. Were that the case, we should be able by introspection alone to find the truth. The soul is too closely joined to the body to permit us to believe in such theories. "Ratiocination itself is an Animal act," he says, "not an abstract Action of the Soul ; it is the Man reasons". This does not mean that all ideas come to us from sensation, but that there must be a consistency between all our judgments, including those made about the sensory experiences. It follows that the harmony, coherence, congruity, or consistency which is truth must apply to the whole mass of our judgments, and that such a position is attainable he asserts beyond question. That there might be gaps between the various sciences is to his way of thinking nonsensical. All ideas form one system which parallels the system of things. This is analogous to Spinoza's two attributes of God: in each system there is an item corresponding to an item in every other system. That the world of things is a harmony, the parts of which are so ordered that they cannot be torn out of the whole without ruining the whole, is an old Stoic principle which he seems to think is self-evident. But the harmony of the cosmos, though obviously a very influential and indeed inspiring idea, was nothing more than an obscure figure of speech. At most it was based upon a few teleological relations, relations of means to end, such as rainfall and vegetable growth. No one seemed to feel the need of really producing evidence for a completely harmonious world in which there would be no conflict of any sort. In any event, obscure or not, the cosmic order was pictured as an exemplification of God's ideas, which stood in the same relation to His handiwork as the idea which an architect might have would stand in relation to the house which he built. On this foundation there could be erected a theory that an adequate description of the harmonious cosmos could be made in a single system of propositions, and it would follow that separate systems—that is, the various sciences—would be false to the extent that they were separate.

This is a clear anticipation of the doctrine that the: "truth is the whole," as well as of that of internal relations. There seems to be no evidence that Burthogge made anything of it; he simply stated it. It is curious that such men, whose paradigm of formal reasoning was Euclidean geometry, should not have wondered why all the axioms, definitions, and postulates were not reduced to one. It was, to be sure, a commonplace that the natural order is the simplest, and that in some sense of a highly ambiguous word the universe is unified. But the closest approach any of them made to unity was in their fundamental metaphors, by means of which they could advance the view that the universe existed to fulfill one purpose, or was composed of one substance, or was like a great organism. This seems to have satisfied them, though whether it really did or not, we have no way of knowing. In reading speculative philosophy, where there is no test of satisfactoriness but logical consistency, and where even consistency is dubious because of the vagueness and even ambiguity of the terms involved, one usually has to rest content with the simple statement of a man's beliefs. The English idealists of the seventeenth century were all theologians and used theological language as a matter of course. Whatever their pretensions to literal statement, they seldom saw the difficulty of using terms like "God," "the soul," "freedom," "action," and "passion," as if they were beyond the need of definition. Their opponents were usually in the more favourable position of setting all theological questions aside, either by fiat or by laying down the rule that they were beyond the scrutiny of reason.

The influence of traditions other than theological was also accepted without much question. It would seem that if we are confined to the circle of our ideas, there would be no need of looking for a world beyond our ideas, for such a search would be doomed to failure at the outset. But the encirclement of ideas could itself be interpreted in a variety of ways. We could emphasize, as some of the critics of idealism did, the egocentric predicament and point out that all our ideas were personal property, and that by implication one could never emerge from one's own mind at the moment of thinking a position which has been called the solipsism of the present moment. But one could also maintain that ideas, by their very nature, were interpersonal and that they were the one bridge which existed from individual to individual, a bridge whose solidity was proved by communication. A set of ideas was always universal in its meaning, even if particular in its existence. Not even Berkeley or Hume both stout believers in nominalism—when they were talking about the origin of ideas, denied that two people could understand each other when they were discussing a given subject. The signs they used, the common nouns and adjectives, were in origin the children of dated and localized impressions; but in meaning they transcended both the moment and the place of their birth. They represented or stood for "meanings" which several minds could grasp, and the human minds could circulate in this world of meanings as geometers could circulate in a world of perfect triangles and squares and even chiliagons, and know what one another were talking about. But sooner or later the influence of what can only be called common sense made itself felt, and an attempt would be made to discover what ground there could be given for believing in a world of things which were not ideas. When they yielded to this impulsion, they carefully distinguished between ideas in the sense of images and hallucinations, and ideas in the sense of direct observations or sensory data. But even then they wished to show that the latter corresponded to use the most colorless word at my disposal to beings which were not ideas.

Burthogge was thus not peculiar in attempting to discover

grounds for belief in an external world, even though he maintained that substance was "a thing conceived under a certain notion". We do not conceive of substances as they really are but through their accidents, that is, through what Descartes called their attributes. These attributes may be simply their sensory qualities, their colors, sounds, and the like. We believe that attributes must be possessed by something and that thing is called a substance. "But what that something else is, to which [the attribute] belongs, I am willing to learn; and will ever honour as my great Master, that Person who will effectually teach me". So far Burthogge is simply basing his reasoning to our ignorance of substances and yet to their real existence upon language. Our English sentences demand that predicates belong to subjects. And if we seriously and consciously argue in this way, then we are clearly projecting into nature our human customs of thinking. But Burthogge proceeds beyond this state of affairs to arguing that we observe things beginning to be and ceasing to be and that *therefore* there must be some cause of their coming into being and ceasing to be. The regularity of their appearance and disappearance will not suffice. And since he will not permit the existence of an infinity of causes, he comes to the conclusion that there are first causes. These fall into two classes, the first causes of activity and the first causes of passivity, which he identifies with mind and matter respectively. Idealist though he be, he does not deny the real existence of matter: it is the universal patient, that which is always acted upon, which suffers effects but produces none. He cannot conceive of causality in any other way than that of cause, effect, and patient. The patient's behaviour can always be described in terms of motion and it was, as we have repeated *ad nauseam* I should imagine by now, only minds which could produce motion. One might have thought that the first law of motion would have suggested that motion was an inherent characteristic of matter and that rest was simply zero motion. That something is at rest is relative always to something else, and the relativity of position and motion was not unknown at this time. But the habits of thinking in terms of agent and patient, of inert patients and effective agents, of matter and mind, were apparently too strong to be overcome at this date, at least by philosophers, whatever physicists might say. Beyond the point of maintaining what he cannot doubt, regardless of the reasons why he cannot doubt it, Burthogge refuses to advance. He will not adventure into discussing the nature of either matter or mind, of raising Spinoza's question of whether there is but one substance of which mind and matter are two attributes, of the "gradations of life" which correspond to the various levels of substantial reality, or of any of the other hypotheses which might illuminate the dark areas which lie beyond our ideas. He is steadfast in asserting his fidelity to evidence, by which he means "the certain testimony of our faculties". And all that this testimony tells us is that two substances exist, mind and matter. In describing them, he follows the lead of Descartes, trying to discover by the analysis of our ideas and notions just what traits are sufficient and necessary for defining each. He is admirable in his fidelity to the principles which he has laid down to guide him; but he is vulnerable in his too willing acceptance of these principles. Yet here, too, he can scarcely be blamed for doing what philosophers continued to do up to the time of Fichte, and in some cases beyond that time. Fichte was willing to declare that the unknowable must be eliminated from all philosophy. If something is unknowable, one can say nothing whatsoever about it, not even that it exists. This should not entail the belief that the imperceptible, for instance, is non-existent, unless we also have reason to believe that there are no conditions under which any knowledge could be had of it. No one would be so obstinate nowadays as to deny the existence of molecules, atoms, and the inhabitants of the subatomic world, though it is true that Auguste Comte in deprecating the use of microscopes almost approached that state of stubbornness.

JOHN NORRIS

The philosophy of John Norris (1657-1711), insofar as it concerns us, is contained in his *Essay Towards the Theory of the Ideal or Intelligible World*, first published in 1701-4. Norris, who had studied More and Cudworth, and sympathized with many of their views, nevertheless believed that no one had satisfactorily solved the problem of the relation between ideas and the world of particulars. He had great admiration for Descartes and Locke, accepted Malebranche's theory of our vision in God, and used as his most constant source of inspiration the various works of St. Augustine. Like More and Cudworth, he was a clergyman and naturally accepts not only the truths of Revelation, as he understands them, but also the necessity of harmonizing the results of philosophy or science with those of Scripture. Nevertheless one can understand his epistemological theory without having recourse to religion, for the problem which he sets forth in his subtitle, the relation of the intelligible world to human understanding, is much more a problem of science than it is a religious problem. For if one believes that general ideas do exist, and indeed everyone admitted that we make use of them in reasoning, then their relation to sensory experience arises as a question, whether one is an empiricist or an idealist. If one followed the idealistic lead, then one had to recognize that sooner or later one will be confronted with things, localized and dated, and these things are antithetical in their nature to ideas. If, on the contrary, one follows the Lockean direction and begins with the apprehension of these particular sensory qualities, then one sooner or later comes face to face with the question of how we know general laws and rules.

The idea of an intelligible world distinct from the sensible world and characterized by traits the very opposite of the latter's traits goes back at least to Philo Judaeus, but its most influential statement was that of Plotinus. Here the world of ideas was timeless and spaceless, immutable, logically related in a hierarchy of ascending generality, culminating in the One from which all ideas flowed; the world of things was, on the contrary, multiple and mutable, essentially spatial and temporal. The former was known to the intellect, the latter grasped by sensation. The former was the archetypal original of which the latter was the imperfect—because materialized image. In the work of the early English Platonists, the former was known intuitively and its inhabitants were innate ideas in the sense that, at whatever date the mind began to think, it would think only through the medium of them. As we have seen, these inhabitants were mathematical axioms, logical principles, and moral notions. In ancient Neo-Platonism the intelligible world was an emanation from the cosmic Intelligence which in turn emanated from the One. The Plotinian Trinity was the three highest hypostases, or persons, the One, the Intelligence (the *Nous*), the Soul of the World. In medieval Christian thought, the One was identified with God, and hence it was easy enough to maintain that the Intelligible world was composed of the ideas in His mind. The identification was made by St. Augustine, who had gone through a Platonistic period as a young man, and expressions of it and its consequences are found frequently in his works. It will be recalled also that Malebranche had maintained that the human mind sees whatever it sees in God. And since knowledge was impossible if it were to be reduced to the apprehension of particulars—for particulars say nothing Norris, like his colleagues in the idealistic tradition, saw knowledge as an interpretation of the sensible world made through the directing force of the ideas.

The first volume of his major work describes and justifies the existence of such a world as being the ideas in the mind of God. The second applies the conclusion to epistemology. It is argued by Norris, and admitted by most men, that only in formal reasoning could there be absolute-truth. Regardless of whether the theorems of geometry are exemplified or not in our experience, they are true. They necessarily follow from the premises of the system, and the premises were believed to be indubitable. Empirical knowledge, however, is contingent and one can at best maintain that only if the world of things correctly exemplifies what logic demands of it, will statements made about it have unquestioned truth. Moreover, one can proceed logically from the more general truths to the less general and continue the process as far as one wishes: one will never by logical means alone reach existence. In modern language, existence is a surd; it is found, but it is never simply deduced. Yet we do have knowledge of it and reliable knowledge. How are we to explain this apparent paradox?

Norris begins this part of his theory by distinguishing between the act of thinking and the object of thought, both of which, he says, are called by the same name, "thought." The objects of thought may be both ideas and that of which they are the ideas. But in treatises of epistemology we are to limit ourselves to the former. The act of thinking and the ideas about which we think are the whole range of theories of knowledge. Since Norris was a close reader and admirer of Descartes, he included among the acts of thinking all so-called mental processes: willing, desiring, loving, "and all the passions, nay, even *Sensation* itself". Yet after pointing to specific acts of thought, he confesses that he does not know what thinking is, for clearly he could not have an idea of what, by its nature, is not an idea. This is the problem which confronted Berkeley, too, when he came to the nature of perceiving as distinct from that which is perceived. The instrument of perception, it was believed, could not itself be the object of perception, and the analogy of the eye which sees but does not see itself was sometimes invoked to intimate what the problem was. In Berkeley we were said to have only a "notion" of our perceptive acts, and that word was a favourite among the English Platonists. The trouble here again was the vexatious distinction which was believed to be necessary between what a thing is and what it does, between its nature and its behaviour. In our own time the distinction has been rejected and the nature of a thing has been identified with its behaviour: a thing is what it does. In psychology this was the basis of behaviourism, though when the behaviourist came to identifying behaviour, quarrels arose within the group. In Norris our ignorance of the nature of thinking, as an act, did not prevent our knowing somehow a good deal about it. "As unknown as I am to myself, methinks I have a confuse Interview of this involv'd Secret, like the glimmering Light, that trims the edges of a dark Cloud". He could tell when he was thinking and when not (if such times be); he could distinguish between the various acts of thinking; he could observe the difference between thinking about an act, such as moving his hand, and the act itself. Moreover, and he emphasizes this, the act of thinking is always of a uniform nature; it is the objects of our thinking which introduce difference. Whether one think of a triangle or of a horse, the thinking itself is the same; the triangle and the horse are different. In the language of the time, the modes of thinking are the same in nature; the ideas are different. Unfortunately this is obscured by our custom of paying little if any attention to the act and all to its objects.

When we reflect upon our thinking we observe a primary distinction between perception and volition. All understanding belongs to the former, assent to the latter. Knowledge, then, is the simple apprehension of a clear idea; no judgment is needed in order to know. The truth is presented to us and we see it. So long as we restrict our judgment to what we clearly perceive, we shall never err, though we may remain in ignorance of some things, that is, of the things which we do not perceive. Volition is within our own power, so that the mind may be said to be purely passive in sensation. When, however, we attend to certain ideas and here Norris is referring to abstract ideas—the mind is partly active, partly passive, active in studying and attending to these ideas, passive in that it does not fabricate them. For abstract ideas do not exist side by side in complete distinction from one another. On the contrary, they are merely different aspects of a single whole and when we dwell upon abstract ideas, we enlarge our mental powers in the sense that we attend to more and more inclusive objects. Here Norris is invoking the Plotinian theory of a hierarchy of ideas which in his first volume he had called the intelligible world.

By attending to such ideas we see—we do not reason to this conclusion that all are both of a *real* and an *ideal* nature. In essence an idea is whatever it is; but an idea may and usually does represent something beyond itself; namely, its object, that of which it is an idea. All ideas are essentially divine; that is, they are in themselves ideas in the mind of God. But they represent not God but His creatures. Since the distinction between matter and spirit is clear, following

Descartes, and since ideas are always spiritual in essence, they may be discovered to represent either material or spiritual beings. But since ideas, even when representative of material objects, cannot be caused by effluvia from such objects or impressions made upon the brain by them, we are left with representation as a fundamental principle in the system. In vision, for instance, there is to be distinguished the material effect of certain rays upon the eye; but those rays are not the visual idea. Vision differs from the other senses in that it comprises both a sensation (color), and an "ideal perception," which is the representation of the material object that I am said to see. The sensory qualities, whether visual or not, are what we would today call subjective. But whereas the sensory qualities of audition, olfaction, and so on, possess only an "inward feeling," vision also possesses an "outward perception". Regardless of this, it is the mind, not the eye, which sees; and the only reason why Norris spends time on vision is that it appears to put us into more intimate contact with the external world. Yet as far as our ideas are concerned, visual ideas are as mental as any other kind.

Norris cannot deny the connection between certain bodily states and certain mental states. He is not unaware of the neural apparatus and the role it plays in perception. But, because of the causal postulate that only similars can sustain causal relations, he, like so many others, has to resort to some sort of evasion when speaking of the relations between the mind and the body. Representation comes about "by virtue of that Law of Union which is between the Soul and Body". But the Law of Union is no more than a phrase avoiding in its connotations the consequences of psychophysical interaction. The same Law accounts for the two aspects of vision, the sensation of colour and the awareness of an object. The idea itself is occasioned by these experiences, though not caused by them. It stands midway between the spiritual being that it represents and the sensation that arises from the physical object. The idea is intelligible, the sensation unintelligible. We can actively turn our attention to the contemplation of ideas; we passively receive our sensations.

But, again, since bodies can act only upon other bodies, there must be a spiritual being which produces these spiritual effects upon our minds. Norris obviously picks up the clue of Malebranche. The physical impressions are but the occasions on which God produces our sensations within us. But similarly, as the body cannot move the soul, the soul cannot move the body.

From this point on Norris follows his French master very closely. The ideas which we contemplate are really ideas in the mind of God and, when we contemplate them, we have a vision in God. Yet we also experience particular objects and we can be led astray by them. Of these there is no genuine science, for science deals only with necessary truths, not contingent. This is all very well, but even the sensations are produced by God and must have some purpose other than that of misleading us. Norris, like so many other epistemologists, gives us an excellent account of how we reach truth, and of what to do to avoid error, but unfortunately for him he gives no reason why anyone should ever err. We intuit the intelligibles directly, immediately; and among them is God Himself. But we also have ideas of material objects and they, along with many spiritual objects, are known only through the mediation of representative ideas. It is through them that we can have natural science, for science is "only of Necessaries and Immutables" and material things in themselves are mutable and contingent. But again our contact with these objects is established by God, and our mistaking sensations connected with them for knowledge is also presumably caused by God, for there is no other cause left in Norris' universe. Is our erring to be attributed to God? On the contrary, Norris' God, like Descartes', is incapable of deceiving us.

Our ideas, then, are God's ideas. Through them we construct systematic science, eternally true and necessarily so. It comes therefore as no surprise to read that the world of things is not only unintelligible but quite superfluous. That there should be any such world the question which we posed above is left a mystery. It is a desperately imperfect fulfilment of God's plans, for its general features are the very opposite of the plans. Norris does not hesitate to paint the world of material things in the darkest colors. It is never directly known; it is temporal and mutable; it leads us astray from the truth; in itself it is unintelligible. He is, of course, justified in maintaining that insofar as knowledge must always deal with universals, the simple apprehension of particulars could not be knowledge. But what is it? The world of things is not the collection of instances from which we can abstract generalities. It cannot serve as evidence of general ideas, since no particular can prove a universal, though it might disprove one. It simply exists, confronts us, as the twentieth century was to say. Curiously enough, some thirty years before the publication of the *Essay Towards the Theory of the Ideal or Intelligible World*, men like John Graunt and Sir William Petty were laying the foundations of an intellectual technique in which probability would take the place of eternal and immutable truth and in which universals would be replaced by statistical groups. But their influence on epistemology was nil.

BERKELEY'S SIRIS

Though Berkeley is best known nowadays for his theory of knowledge and as a continuator of Locke's so-called empiricism, he became in his later years a representative spokesman for English Platonism. In 1744 appeared his *Philosophical Reflexions and Inquiries Concerning the Virtues of Tar-Water*, re-entitled in the second edition *Siris, the Greek for "chain." It is the second title that points to the ideas which interest us in this study, for though Berkeley's own contemporaries were more concerned with the virtues of the panacea which he explained in his reflections and inquiries, they form now only an incident in the history of medicine, though the arguments for a panacea were, like most such arguments,* based upon a metaphysical assumption. That assumption was, briefly, that all things in the universe possessed a common nature and that, since similars could stand in a causal relation to one another, if one could find a substance which summed up in itself all the properties of the elements, that substance could produce effects which no other substance could produce. Since the human psychophysical organism was believed to be a microcosm, the substance in question would stand in a special relation to it, as a sort of second microcosm. The intimacy of this relation was such that, on the principle of *similia similibus curantur*, all our ills ought to be curable by it. Whether this was because illnesses were held to be an insufficiency of one of the elements—or of one of the humours which corresponded to the elements—or not, I do not know. But in diseases caused by such insufficiencies the panacea could supply what was lacking. In any event, tar-water was an acid mixture derived from the distillation of pine, balsam, and similar woods. In accordance with the chemical ideas of some of the leading scientists of the time-Newton, Homberg, and Boerhaave—whatever characteristics are found in plants come to them from the air. Thus the air is a grand mixture of whatever elementary "principles" a specific scientist found necessary for vegetable life. The details of this part of Berkeley's argument need not concern us, curious though they are. What is of more interest is the use which he makes of his earlier theory of ideas in building up a Neo-platonistic metaphysics. For it is this part of his thought which reappears in later philosophies of nature.

The vegetable soul is then breathed out of the plant into the air and the air is breathed by us. But it is also the "seminary of minerals and metals", which on the principle *ex nihilo nihil* must come from somewhere. Air is thus envisioned as no element but a mixture midway between whatever composes earth and the finer and more volatile spirit that is fire. The latter was itself found in a still purer form known as *aether* or "pure invisible fire." It is this which is the ultimate material substance. Berkeley traces this back to Heraclitus; and, in fact, that even the soul was a sort of fiery particle appears in the common speech of many centuries. But it is only the material substance, not the real motive force in the world, for Berkeley had already demonstrated in the *Principles*, and in this he was in agreement with all his fellow Platonists, that nothing material could ever move anything by its own powers alone. Only something mental or spiritual could move things. The fire which seems to move things is but a sign of the real active principle which, in the long run, is God.

Here Berkeley introduces a paragraph which is essential to an understanding not only of his special views but in part of the views of his school. I quote it almost *in toto.*

The mind of man acts by an instrument *necessarily.* The mind presiding in the world, acts by an instrument *freely.* Without instrumental and second causes, there could be no regular course of nature. And without a regular course, nature could never be understood; mankind must always be at a loss, not knowing what to expect, or how to govern themselves, or direct their actions for the obtaining of any end. Therefore in the government of the world physical agents, improperly so called, or mechanical, or second causes, or natural causes, or instruments, are necessary to assist, not the governor, but the governed.

The distinction between the mind of God operating freely and the minds of men is retained here as in the *Principles.* But whereas in the Principles the mind of God acts as a stable and uniform world, that world which permits invariant scientific readings, here it is the one absolutely free agent. The minds of men need a constant world of order so that they may fulfil their purposes, relying for that on a predictable future. The physical world turns into a set of signs of this orderliness which individual minds may interpret. This set of signs is still God's ideas and still generates ideas in men's minds. But its primary function is to assist human beings in planning their lives. If this is taken literally, then each physical object is not only to be understood as so much sensory quality: colour, sound, and the like; but also as an instrument for human use. If it could be believed that Nature did nothing in vain, it was even easier to believe that God made nothing in vain, and to surround men with the conglomerate mass of sensible objects and to endow them with no human utility would certainly have been vain, unless they were to be considered as obstacles to human desires and thus morally useful. The world of things interpreted as signs of God's purposes and in that way guides for men can also be understood as permeated with a spiritual nature, the Plastic Spirit of Berkeley's predecessors. In Berkeley, however, the Plastic Spirit is replaced by the pure invisible fire, or *aether.*

It is this which explains the presence of life, both vegetable and animal; and again we must point out that, if living beings were entirely material, they would have no power of self-movement, autokinesis. It is this assumption about matter that lies behind all the speculations of the English Platonists. It unifies all creation by giving it a common nature—and a common nature which avoids the errors of pantheism. Since it can be found in several forms, depending on its degree of visibility, it can be made parallel to the different degrees of "reality" from the grossly material to the divine. To use Berkeley's own examples, at the risk of making him appear less intelligent than he was, we find the cosmic pure fire in light, animal spirits, muscular motion, fermentation, vegetation, and "other natural operations". All such changes involve motion, but none appear to be caused through the imposition of outside forces. It must always be recalled that in 1744 chemistry was barely in its infancy, and the theory of the four elements still stood. If fire exists in so many forms, and if these forms exist on so many levels of being, then fire must itself be heterogeneous, a conclusion which Berkeley accepts. It contains in itself the natural causes or "seeds" of all sublunary things, which seeds were the seminal reasons of the Stoics. Parallel to the seeds were ideas, and the ideas of God were parallel to those of men. None of this apparatus would have been necessary if Berkeley had been able to be satisfied with a simple descriptive statement of the laws of nature. He is willing to accept such laws as demonstrated by scientists like Newton, but he believes that descriptions are not enough. They are "rules or methods observed in the productions of natural effects, the efficient and final causes whereof are not of mechanical consideration". Since he believes that explanation must always give efficient and final causes, "it would seem the mechanical philosophers never explained any thing". Mechanical laws are good things to have and Berkeley never makes light of them. They are good because they direct us how to act and teach us what to expect. But we want a more complete account of things and that can be furnished only by the discovery of what purpose is achieved and whose purpose. Thus, one is impelled to proceed from science to philosophy and from philosophy to theology. Only by seeing natural law as the decree of God, and God as the God of the Bible, can we obtain a fuller understanding of the world around us. For by accepting that God as the mind which actuates the aetherial spirit which, in turn, permeates all nature, we immediately see the relevance of moral values to nature.

"Intellect enlightens, Love connects, and the Sovereign Good attracts all things". In that one sentence we have a compendious statement of Berkeley's philosophy as it appears in Siris. For it asserts not only the intelligibility of nature, but also the inextricable intertwining of values and facts in which he so fervently believes. To his way of thinking, the Democritean philosophy, as his school called purely physical science, leaves the universe shorn of goodness and beauty and, at best, relegates them to the human sphere. That might well be enough, but to a man of Berkeley's temperament values could not be substantiated unless they were firmly rooted in the nature of things. Human values must, he believed, be at least an image of cosmic values. The biblical justification of this was, of course, God's seeing that His creation was good, just as the biblical justification of the world's intelligibility was the opening of the Gospel according to Saint John. In Plato the supposed basis was in the *Phaedo*, where Socrates criticizes the physicists for overlooking the link between the good and the necessary. If changes did not occur for an end, which is the good of the change, then God and Nature would be doing things in vain and the whole cosmological scheme would dissolve into "meaningless" operations. They might be regularly repeated but would be no more than that. But if a general plan is discoverable and that plan is the purpose of the Creator, then all incidents in fulfilling it have their significance. If some are in themselves that is, separated out of the totality of things bad or ugly, that is because of the separation. Fitted into their place they are good and beautiful. But we must rise above sensory experience to see this, and consequently Berkeley here departs from his earlier emphases upon sensory experience to accentuate his belief that ideal existences must have all the qualities of the ideal. In other words, he draws out of his epistemology a metaphysics which he thinks is logically entailed in it. One could, to be sure, draw out of it many other metaphysical systems if one were not already convinced of the truths of the Christian religion. But just as even in the *New Theory of Vision* Berkeley's purpose was to confute atheists, so here he was to establish Christianity on a rational basis. The establishment reduced to seeing what reasons he could give for his faith. But, as we have pointed out so frequently in this study, one cannot simply reason without orientation. One has to have, at a minimum, a conjecture that one wishes to prove.

There is but one more item of this phase of Berkeley's philosophy to be noted: his apparent new interest in what he had called *notions* in the *Principles*. Notions differed from ideas in that the latter came from sensation and were what common sense would have called images of sensory qualities, either single or combined. Notions were those intimations which we have of our own existence, of beings that were not in the external world and could not be apprehended by sensation. The notions, which were not closely examined in *Siris*, were much like the innate ideas of the earlier English Platonists; that is, they were latent in the human consciousness and were regulatory principles of knowledge. An active mind, he said in the seventh dialogue of his *Alciphron*, cannot be an idea or like an idea. For ideas were always effects produced in the human mind by the ideas in the mind of God, and they corresponded to objects, which were assumed to be inert. In the third edition of the dialogues, he added the significant words: "Certainly it must be allowed that we have some *notion*, and that we understand or know what is meant by, the terms *myself*, will, memory, love, hate, and so forth; although to speak exactly, these words do not suggest so many distinct ideas." It was precisely this which Hume had denied in the *Treatise*, and it must be admitted that, if the mind can know only its own ideas, then it cannot also have knowledge through notions. But some means had to be provided for knowing what could never be apprehended by ideas, unless one was to fall into the scepticism of Hume or give up rational philosophy as a whole. By suggesting a means for catching activities on the wing, Berkeley, uneasy though he was about it, allowed one to have knowledge of the self and conscious processes without turning them into reflections of sensory qualities. It demands no great philosophic skill to see that once the way is open for notions to be accepted as knowledge, the way to verification is closed. For the notions are by their very nature private and incommunicable. Hume himself was willing to admit that some people might intuit their selves; but that as for him, he could not. This admission is always necessary when one falls back on introspection as evidence. For, in the long run, communication depends upon our possession of a language which refers to common experience, and the only way in which a person can communicate a private experience is by finding some commonly accepted terms that will describe it. The *je ne sais quoi* usually has to be resorted to on such occasions, the simile, the *as if*. But these devices are never satisfactory for the simple reason that they are but approximations to what a man feels. On the other hand, no one can reasonably doubt that another may have inner experiences that he cannot express in commonly accepted terms. One may, like the early behaviourists, flatly deny that there is any private experience, though how one can honestly deny the existence of something the description of which one avowedly does not understand, is as difficult to grasp as the assertion itself.

We shall see later that the hints given by Berkeley about notions were duplicated by the Scottish Realists, who also insisted that there was an act of perception different from that which was perceived. Whether they actually took this over from Berkeley or not, I do not pretend to know, though Reid, the so-called founder of the school, was an early admirer and student of Berkeley. If we could know only our own ideas and if there were some terms which did not name ideas, then they were meaningless or misused. But Berkeley for obvious reasons could accept neither of these consequences. For not only did he need a subject for knowledge, someone who could, at a minimum, judge, assent, and possibly be mistaken; but he also needed something which could escape from the flux of appearances. That permanent being was the perceiving and thinking person, a monad, as he called him, "the indivisible centre of the soul or mind." This monad occupies in the individual's life the same position as God, or The One for Berkeley gladly takes over Plotinus's term—occupies in the cosmos.

15

Revolution in History of Philosophies

Introduction

One of the effects of the French Revolution on Philosophy was to turn men's thoughts again to history. We have suggested how this new interest developed in Hegel; we have now to investigate its appearance in France itself. In doing so we shall first discuss two of the main philosophical trends: that of the so-called Traditionalists and Positivism.

Bonald and Maistre

Traditionalists, Count Joseph de Maistre and the Vicomte de Bonald, who were as closely united as Marx and Engels, were apologists for Catholicism and indeed in their political philosophy maintained that the Pope had supremacy over all the rulers of the earth. For Bonald, men are not simply social atoms living in conglomerate masses, nor do they form societies because of a social contract; they are social by a law of nature. Individuals are whatever they are because of the character of the society in which they live. Just as Hegel was able to speak of Oriental, Classical, and Germanic societies as having each a spirit of its own, so Bonald was able to speak of Jewish, Pagan, and Christian societies as "expressions" of pure theocracy, pure humanism, and the proper balance between the two. But whereas the third stage of social evolution in Hegel was an improvement on its preceding stages, in Bonald this is far from being the case. The Jews and Pagans strayed from the ideal which had been revealed by God to their primordial ancestors and, consequently, a Christian society is one which has regained the original and eternal pattern of right living. Thus history represents the divergencies and approaches of societies from God's will and to it. Change is real enough but it is always bad. The only good society is the eternal society, and if we have moved away from it, that must be because of our inherent wickedness.

Just as the personality of an individual is determined by the society in which he lives, so our ideas are realized only in that social thought which is language. We have seen something like this before in Reid and Jouffroy. But in Bonald the social nature of ideas carries the implication that the individual who resists the common opinion of the group is a pig-headed rebel who deserves punishment. For the tradition which is language, i.e., thought, is by its very nature true, and the rebel is a rebel not merely against a government but against truth. Just as religious tradition is a from the first Revelation to Adam, passed on to subsequent generations through Abraham, Aaron, and the high priests of Israel to the Apostles and from them to the Popes, so language is a steady growth of ideas originating in a source which was implanted in Adam's mind by God. Since language and thought are identical, and since all history is a growth from a seed to maturity, and since everything which is in the plant was potentially in the seed, all truth was given to Adam, and tradition is simply the unfolding of that primitive truth. Traditionalism could perhaps be called a theory according to which history is exfoliation.

The main difference between Bonald and Maistre lies in

what the one or the other omitted from his writings, not in what they included. They both took up their pens primarily to justify their hatred of revolution, for they both thought that the cause of man's downfall was itself revolution. The disobedience of our primordial parents was the first rebellious act of human history, and each succeeding rebellion has brought about disastrous consequences. Both men agree also that change is inevitably a movement from better to worse, for whatever order is established, it is order. In that it resembles the original condition of man before the Fall and, presumably, stability is the greatest social value. Stability is described as an image of eternity, as correct an image as can be found on earth. Prophets and saints have the power of emerging from the temporal sequence into timelessness, and the realm of timelessness is the realm of absolute values and authority. Oddly enough, both men confuse the idea of the eternal with that of the everlasting or long-enduring, so that any institution which lasts for unusually long periods is considered by them to be superhuman. The Church, which had lasted for eighteen centuries, must for that reason alone be considered divine. The Capetian dynasty again has lasted longer than any other known to man; it too must be under divine auspices.

Just as Maistre hates change, so he hates diversity. The temporal and the many, the timeless and the one go hand in hand. All tendencies toward plurality are inherently evil; all the contraries inherently good. But the kind of unity which he longed for was the unity of a hierarchy, the sort of thing which had as one of its earliest expressions the various books of Pseudo-Dionysius. The Middle Ages, on the whole, had accepted the hierarchies of Plotinus as pervasive of the universe, and that mirror of the cosmic hierarchy which was the theoretical feudal system, running from Emperor down to serf, retained in the eyes of even the more sophisticated philosophers the prestige of the celestial hierarchy. Thus, rank was not merely one's place in a larger whole, as it might have been for the Stoics, but conferred on a person a certain degree of value. A baron was supposed to be nobler than a yeoman, not in that he had command over more people, but because his place in the system was nobler. So positions in the universe had varying degrees of value, the periphery being inherently better than the center, a notion reflected in Dante's circles of Hell. It was the social and political hierarchy that Maistre was anxious to preserve. In the Old Regime all power was theoretically in one pair of hands; in the Church it is in the hands of Christ's Vicar, the Pope. The unity of power in the Church is contrasted by Maistre with the diversity of power in Protestant sects according to which, he believes, every individual has authority equal to that of every other individual. Maistre passion for unity is so strong that in his book *Du Pape*, he goes to the extreme of insisting that all secular rulers are subordinate to the head of the ecclesiastical organization. The Pope is called "the natural chief, the most powerful promoter, the great Demiurge of universal civilisation". No Guelph was ever more strident in his claims of sacerdotal supremacy.

The philosophy of history of which these two men were the chief proponents gained few followers in the early nineteenth century, and it was not until after the Vatican Council (1870) and the formation of *l'Action Française* that their influence began to spread widely. The development of their principal ideas is to be found in men like Ballanche and LaMennais where it led, unfortunately, to error if not heresy. But we cannot describe its evolution here. Suffice it to say that in LaMennais traditionalism turned into philosophic anarchism. But this was about as inevitable as anything in the history of ideas can very well be. For if reality is behind the historical scene, then what takes place on the stage must be purely phenomenal and, as Kant and his followers had shown, one of the things that take place is rational thought. If, then, we are to obey commands given by a supernatural source, we must not ask for reasons why; obedience is enough and is all that is asked of us. But a system of government in which there is no rational code of law is hardly a system. Caprice however disguised becomes law and submission the highest virtue. The inner conflict in the set of ideas known as traditionalism lies in the presupposition that truth is one and yet develops in tradition.

How this can happen has never been satisfactorily explained nor is it likely to be, since development by its very nature entails change.

A philosophy of history such as this, moreover, does not explain why men should sin and thus stray from the ideal set before them by their Maker. Sin becomes as mysterious as righteousness, so that both the eternal and the temporal are veiled in obscurity. There is, to be sure, no reason why a philosophy of history should deal with historical causation and thus be able to predict the future. It may maintain that what men do as social animals is utterly undetermined and that the course of history is chaotic. But whether that be true or not, Traditionalism itself is unable to make any predictions, though Joseph de Maistre himself was not reluctant to make them. It may conclude that human beings, in the words of St. Augustine, are incapable of not sinning and that consequently the future will be as disheartening as the past. Yet one might venture the suggestion that if one is to have a philosophy of history, one should first assume that the historical process is real and should not be explained away.

AUGUSTE COMTE

A less anti-intellectual philosophy of history was developed by Auguste Comte and his followers. As early as 1750 Turgot had maintained, in a speech printed in 1808, that men first think in terms of divine wills effectuating all change in the cosmos. The gods were simply human beings blown up to superhuman size, and presumably primitive man thought of all change on the model of changes produced through human effort. Later, says Turgot, philosophers recognized the absurdity of the aetiological myths and "thought to explain the causes of phenomena by abstract expressions, such as *essences* and *faculties*," expressions which had no explanatory value whatsoever but were in reality names for our ignorance. After this period, "while observing the mechanical action which bodies have one upon the other," new hypotheses were elaborated which "mathematics could develop and experiment verify." The essential points in this passage from Turgot's speech are:

(1) that it outlines the course of intellectual history, the way in which men think;

(2) it recognizes three stages: the theological, the philosophical, and the scientific;

(3) it identifies the first with explanation in terms of volitional action, the second with explanation in terms of verbal abstractions, the third with explanation in terms of empirical observation capable of mathematical formulation. The only hint of an explanation of why modes of thinking should change is in the passage from mythology to philosophical abstractions, where Turgot says that the philosophers recognized the absurdity of the myths. But why people brought up on myths and mythological explanations as correct and standard should ever see them as absurd is left in the dark.

That empirical observational science is the only kind of knowledge which is reliable is emphasized by d'Alembert in the Preliminary Discourse of the *Encyclopédie*. Moreover, it is pointed out that the arts and sciences have a reciprocal influence upon each other; that the useful arts, agriculture and medicine, developed first and that the first science to develop was physics, because of its utility. That an art may develop before the principles which its practice illustrates was a relatively novel idea, and one of the reasons why Diderot and d'Alembert included so many articles on the crafts was that they believed technology to be of equal value with science. Science may thus be considered to evolve out of practice. One gradually learns how to do or make something; one finally becomes conscious of the rules which one has been unconsciously following.

A third idea which was to reappear in Comte was that the intellectual history of the individual recapitulates that of the race. This notion is clearly expressed in Condorcet *Esquisse* and, in Comte's own words, man is a theologian in his childhood, metaphysician in his youth, and positivist in his manhood. The inevitability of thought passing through these three stages was formulated as a law by Comte and he considered it to be the fundamental principle of his philosophy. Since he had no special admiration for children, it framed not merely the course of intellectual evolution but also the passage from bad to better thinking. Thinking in the third stage was the goal of all thinking. Such thinking was called positivistic by Comte. It was the logical organization of observations, and all observations were supposed to be neutral as far as the observer's interests or other preoccupations were concerned. In short, they were identical with Hume's perceptions, except that in Hume there was a lingering feeling that the perceptions masked inner natures which were not observable. Comte maintained flatly that there were no inner natures. What is observed alone exists. It is too bad that he did not raise the question of what conditions the observations, for it should be obvious that they are never made in vacuo. The contribution of the problem, of the method, of the instruments used, of the laboratory conditions, and the like, is surely not to be overlooked in a discussion of observation. But Comte was so convinced that neutral observations could be acquired that he even deprecated the use of microscopes. To him the scientific method was essentially the collecting of what the nineteenth century was likely to call the facts; facts were apparently lying about waiting for people to collect them, like seashells on a beach. It was only later in the century that men like Poincare began to question this idea.

Metaphysics, as we have said, is one type of thinking and a type which became obsolete at the close of the Middle Ages. Included in metaphysics was psychology which in the early years of the nineteenth century was still the "science of the soul." Since souls were not observable to the sense-organs, they had to be ruled out of the possible subjects for scientific inquiry. Yet Comte assumed a metaphysics of his own according to which a distinction was made between active and passive senses; a hierarchy of sensation from touch, the most universal, to hearing, the least; and a sort of methodological behaviourism. He insisted upon the disunity of the Ego and the social origin of self-consciousness. Though he rejected the legitimacy of the idea of causation, he did insist upon that of legality. All such notions are based upon a metaphysics, or could be justified only as assumptions tentatively held in order to see whither they might lead one.

But more important than his metaphysics is his idea that all history is intellectual history. The Law of the Three Stages runs throughout his work. One of its supposed implications is that each subject-matter has a history of its own and reaches the positivistic condition at a date peculiar to itself. Thus all science is approaching the condition of mathematics, but a science like astronomy is closer to that goal than physics or chemistry or biology. One can therefore classify the sciences on the principle of where they stand in relation to the general history of thought. Since a completed positive science would be absolutely general and contain no causal residues, it is clear that mathematics is the most perfect science attainable by man. For there is no subject-matter whatsoever which is not describable in mathematical terms. Thus mathematics becomes both the perfect science and the tool by which sciences are to be perfected. Comte's famous classification of the sciences-mathematics, astronomy, physics, chemistry, biology, sociology—is not only an arrangement of subject-matters from the most inclusive to the least, from the most abstract to the most concrete, but it is also a history of science. The various sciences listed could be said to have arisen in the order given, though the determination of the dates of origin is far from simple. Just when shall we say that physics arose? Was there not some biological information in primitive medicine? Can one not speak of even culinary recipes as rudimentary chemistry? But if one is willing to be lenient, the order is reasonable enough, and it is also plausible that the formulation of scientific theorems is always preceded by a long history of practical devices. Thus we have early Egyptian representations of souls being weighed in balances long before Archimedes, to say nothing of Lavoisier. And though alchemical theory was largely mythology, its practice was often fruitful. In any event there is plenty of evidence to back up Comte's generalization that practice is prior to theory.

Primitive practice always operates, as indeed it must, through human volition. One *produces* one's effects, as if the will were somehow competent to change the order of nature. If, then, one thinks that all change comes about in a uniform fashion, one must find a method of influencing the wills that are nonhuman and which may be either beneficent or maleficent. But the only way to influence a will is through threats, promises, and the like. But this is essentially magic and the man who knows the magical recipes will have the most important knowledge of his people. Such a man is the *shaman* or priest. He has the monopoly of the methods by means of which he can control the natural world. His tendency is, of course, to retain that monopoly for himself and his group. But similarly, since all change is produced by wills, government itself must be conducted by a will and that will belongs to the most powerful man in the community, a king. Thus monarchy, the priesthood, magic, belong together on the theological stage of human history and determine a kind of society which is characteristic of the childhood of the race. But Comte is willing to admit that remnants of the childish manner of thinking survive in individuals who live in later stages.

The metaphysical stage also determines the general character of a society. Where everything is expressed in terms of essences or abstractions, only those individuals who can handle them can exercise power. Such men are logicians and jurists, for the essences are always incorporated into legal formulas. Sovereignty itself is abstracted from the person of the king and erected into an essence of its own, popular sovereignty. The theory of popular sovereignty is metaphysical in the sense that the people are in reality a collection of individuals whose wills are often in a state of conflict. To determine the popular will is always to use a fiction, majority rule, or something of that sort. This may be a useful device but cannot be thought of as a real expression of an overindividual will. Certain individuals will obtain power, as they did in the theological period, by understanding the rule in accordance with which the people are governed. In Comte's day, as Daumier saw so clearly, these individuals were the lawyers who were supplanting the military class as the dominant power in society. But he was living at the end of the metaphysical period, he thought, and saw signs of the approaching third stage, the positive. The positive mind would of course stop at perceptual appearances and attempt to order them in constant laws. But these laws would be laws, not of hidden metaphysical essences, but of empirical observations. Scientists alone could possess the necessary knowledge to understand that kind of world, and the scientist and technological expert would take the place of priests and jurists. Utilizing their knowledge, as kings utilized that of the priests, would be the industrialists who would become the real rulers of society through their experts' advice. Comte foresaw a time when the map of Europe would be redrawn so that the location of raw materials, rather than mountain ranges and rivers, would determine frontiers. His dream was a world at peace through economic interdependence. If all the iron on a continent were in one place and belonged to one nation, and if all the coal belonged to another, then the inhabitants of Ironland would have to live at peace with those of Coal-land. The experts would presumably inform the industrialists, who would in turn influence the statutory rulers, that it would be better, in some sense of that term, to agree to interchange the materials essential to prosperity than to make war and to seize them. But one may ask whether the older sentiments of national pride would not arise again in the hearts of the Ironlanders and induce them to feel humiliated if they had to bargain and negotiate for that which their ancestors had acquired by military valor.

This picture of the future was a rationalized account of what history would be if history followed the Law of the Three Stages. Out of the progress of the sciences was to arise the new science of sociology. Sociology, as Comte saw it, considered the individual simply as a constituent part of a society, and he never paid much attention to the strains and conflicts within all social groups, not to speak of the individuals themselves. To him humanity was logically prior to human beings. The latter he saw simply as specimens of the former. Though he was willing to admit a certain degree of heterogeneity in his admission of survivals of older methods of thinking into later periods, he failed to see the psychological effect of those survivals on the total human being. If one thinks theologically about the stellar universe, metaphysically about, let us say, poetry, and positivistically about chemistry, one will sooner or later attempt to iron out these inconsistencies or try to justify them. It is of course possible that one will do nothing whatsoever and live according to different sets of rules. But to Comte's way of thinking that was inconceivable. To him there was always a tendency toward a unification of intellectual processes. If in the theological age there are priests and kings, that is because theological thinking demands them. Comte was dominated by the idea of "unity," an idea which he never analyzed very thoroughly but which he used continually. Thus his admiration for the Middle Ages was based entirely on the unity of culture which it manifested, "the political masterpiece of human wisdom." Concretely, this unity was the supposed pervasiveness of Catholicism in all spheres of human interest. As is customary with admirers of this period, Comte paid no attention to the constant quarrels between various religious groups, the rise of heresies and the manner of exterminating them, the disputes between philosophic schools, to say nothing of the wars between feudal chieftains. The most that one can say of medieval unity is that it should have been the dream of the Church.

The basic question which one must ask in reading Comte's philosophy of history is whether the technique of thinking is the clue to historical change. The discovery of the fact that this technique itself has a history, though Comte's account of it may be incorrect, is of the greatest importance. For if it is a fact, then the results of thinking must always be appraised relative to the technique by which they were found. The notion of absolute and enduring truth would have to be disregarded unless one had reason to believe that a given type of thinking was final and not merely the latest. Both Comte and Hegel did think that they had such reason and that therefore their philosophies were final. In both these men the later stages arise out of the earlier through reflection; that is, the mind itself sees that it must proceed beyond the point at which it has arrived. The obligation is, however, differently grounded in each of them. If, on the other hand, the anti-intellectualists were right and thinking itself is a reflection of something nonintellectual, then that something, the will-to-live, the will-to-power, social utility, the interests of the dominant economic class, personal happiness, will have to be examined to see why it changes as the years go by. Either there is no explanation of any historical change or there are a variety of basically different causes of such change or there is one general cause. Each of these positions has certain definite implications for a philosophy of history. In Comte's case there was one cause of change, methods of thinking. But those methods themselves have a history. It is curious that Comte did not see the possibility of his third stage becoming superseded as its predecessors were.

COURNOT

A philosophy of history similar to Comte's in certain details is that of A. A. Cournot (1801-77). Though his great work, *Considerations on, the Progress of Ideas and Events in Modern Times (1872)*, never had the popular success that Comte's work enjoyed and though even today he is very little known, there are certain germinal ideas in the *Considerations* which have played an important role in recent years.

I refer especially to the doctrine that chance has its part to play in history as well as determinism, accompanied by the doctrine that the history of human societies is intimately linked with the history of all natural processes. It is the latter doctrine which led him to call his point of view "historical naturalism." It is naturalistic in that it accepts the results and methods of science as ultimately true and not simply as descriptions of the phenomenal world. It is historical in that the sciences, arts and industry, which obviously have a history, are an integral part of the natural order. Cournot himself stated the difference between his own philosophy of history and that of others as follows. Whether there are historical laws or not, there are historical facts; and he proposes to examine the interrelations of these facts, which are here independent of one another, there interdependent. In that it studies the facts and their interrelations, it will probably never reach the status of a science which for Cournot must demonstrate laws. Laws are supposed to be always true and to follow from the very nature of that of which they are the laws. But facts are events determined by other events and determining still others. One can discover why an individual behaves as he does; but one cannot have a scientific study of an individual. It is clear that for Cournot, who was a mathematician, deductive science was the model of all science. Deductive science therefore is not causal, and Cournot makes a sharp contrast between implications and causal determinism. History is a causal study, not a series of deductions.

It is interesting to observe that Cournot opens his *Considerations* with a definition of "chance." He points out that chance is not a name for our ignorance, nor a covering of the imperfect state of our knowledge, but a fact of nature, established by reasoning or by observation like any other natural fact. It consists in the mutual independence of several series of causes and effects which collaborate accidentally in producing a certain phenomenon, happening, or event, called for this reason fortuitous. But none of this means that all the links in the chains of events are not suspended from a primordial ring, the will of God. Thus if one puts several dice in a shaker, the sum of the figures which turn up is a fortuitous event; it is not determined by the original position of the dice in the shaker, nor by the shaking which is given to the shaker, nor by the hand which held the shaker. What turns up could not have turned up unless the dice had been in the shaker and shaken. In other words, that preliminary situation is a necessary but not a sufficient cause of the final result. So one can say that a man cannot die without having had parents; but his parents are hardly the cause of his death. In the aetiology of any individual event one must have recourse to chance, since such events by their very individuality extend beyond the boundaries of any class in which they may be located. Cournot does not deny that historical events can be classified; but he insists that each has characteristics which are not those of every other member of the various classes in which someone classifies them. Every war is like all wars, but the explanation of the War of 1812 does not have to be identical with that of the Spanish-American War. When an historian writes about the latter, he does not do so in terms of the former. Briefly, though Cournot does not use these words, one can call an individual, dated, and localized event either self-determined or accidental. The two terms mean the same thing.

At the same time, statistics show us that there is regularity in the universe and even large groups of accidental events will manifest a regular character. This is well known to every Freshman. But what does not seem to be so well known is that there is nothing inconsistent between the existence of chance and that of law, nor of chance and that of causality. The number of events that had to meet when Abraham Lincoln was shot by Wilkes Booth surpasses the imagination. It was pure accident that the murder came off, as we know. And yet the cause of Lincoln's death is far from being unknown. Scientifically all we can say is that Lincoln died because his heart stopped beating. Historically we say that he died because he was shot by Booth. History, then, is the aetiology of events and for that reason must include chance in its considerations. It will of course indicate general tendencies when the historian perceives them, but it will never overlook the effects of chance occurrences. History then must rely on the interplay between chance and law. If everyone were like everyone else, if everything were like everything else, then there might be change, but there would be no explaining it. For causal explanation is relevant only to the appearance of differences. In fields like the history of science, where human caprice counts for so much less than in the history of political institutions, the factor of chance is less important. And, Cournot thinks, the time may well come when human beings will be so standardized that history will become obsolete. At that time, one imagines, rational sociology will have taken its place.

The reality of chance makes "historical Molinism" absurd.

The existence of scientific law does not eliminate either the individual's freedom nor his responsibility. Law is true only of large numbers of facts, never of the individual fact, and the contribution of the individual thing to the events in which it participates the language is mine, not Cournot's does not disappear when a law is established. The behavior of the individual is whatever it is regardless of general statements descriptive of large masses of individuals more or less like him. This important bit of wisdom on Cournot's part has been overlooked by his successors as well as by most of his contemporaries, who find a conflict between the idea that a man may be responsible for his acts even though large groups of men, as groups, act in a regular and fairly predictable manner. As long as one makes a distinction between causality and law, and the distinction seems necessary, there will be an intelligible sense to the words freedom and responsibility. But when one asks Cournot whether there is a general law upon which we may base hopes for a better future or despair, he cautiously points out that we simply do not have enough evidence for either. He is equally cautious when it comes to accepting such grand ideas of history as those of Hegel and his school. The facts show, he insists, a constant interplay between chance and regularity, and the greater part of his two-volume work is given up to pointing this out.

We are too limited in space to do more than hint at what follows in Cournot's book, but a hint at least is necessary. He is only too willing to admit that there are in human history, as in geological, certain events which take time and which we call epochs or ages. These have marked beginnings and develop in a detectable manner. In what we call the modern period, beginning with the fifteenth century, we cannot help noticing a growth of science and industry which was more rapid than one finds in the earlier period, the Middle Ages. It is the predominant interests of a period which give it distinction and a name; these interests may be completely satisfied or not, may therefore come to an end. Their satisfaction will demand certain things, as industries of a given type demand special raw materials, energy to manufacture them, and so on. Should all the iron in the world be exhausted, industry based on steel would have to be abandoned and a substitute for steel would have to be found. It is in that sense of the word that a civilization can be said to decay, though this must not be taken as evidence that Cournot presupposes an entirely material basis for all civilizations. He is arguing against a notion of a period as a sort of living being which is born, matures, and dies. He is willing to use that figure of speech but points out that it is only a figure of speech.

SPENGLER

Though the metaphor of the life-cycle was but a metaphor in the eyes of Cournot, it continued to be used and in two of our most popular philosophers of history, Spengler and Toynbee, it became central. Oswald Spengler (1880-1936) in his Decline of the West was one of the most celebrated prophets of doom in the period between the two wars. To his way of thinking history was the spectacle of ever-recurring cycles analogous to the lives of individuals. One of his essential distinctions was that between cultures and civilizations. A culture "springs with primitive strength from the soil of a mother-region." It clings to that soil throughout its life. Each culture has "its own idea, its own passions, its own life, will, and feeling, its own death". Cultures may be of two kinds, Faustian and Apollinian. The former resembles Nietzsche's Dionysiac will, the latter his Apollinian. But the examples given by Spengler in his typically suggestive rather than explicit manner are as follows. The nude statue, mechanical statics, the sensuous cult of the Olympian gods, the individualistic citystates of Greece, "the doom of Oedipus and the phallus cult," are all Apollinian and all presumably differentiae of a culture. The art of the fugue, Galilean dynamics, Christian dogmatics, the Baroque dynasties, "the destiny of Lear and the Madonna-ideal from Dante's Beatrice to the last line of Faust II," are all Faustian. Apollinian painting defines the body by contours; Faustian forms space by light and dark. [5] The Apollinian culture conceives of history as determined outwardly, Faustian inwardly. The soul of classical culture was

Apollinian, of post-classical western culture, Faustian. We might not be doing an injustice to Spengler to say that the Faustian is passionate, dynamic, expressive; the Apollinian rational, stable, and reflective. But one never knows in dealing with this type of philosophy whether one is just to it or not.

As cultures mature they pass into civilizations. A civilization is the last stage of a cultural cycle. It is the stage of completion in which a pattern is fixed. As a man growing old repeats the acts of his maturity, neither seeks nor acquires new ideas, substitutes ritual for invention, and lives by the inertia of custom, so a senile culture continues meaninglessly to repeat the things which originally were creative and expressive. One cannot deny that communities do reach that stage when they are faced with no new problems witness the old New England villages become summer resorts and indeed it is hard to see how a group of people clinging to its mother-region could do more than maintain the design of the past in the present. When faced with a challenge, people can either meet it or submit to it and die. But to maintain that inevitably a people will die has little if any evidence to support it.

The weakness of Spengler's philosophy of history is common to all men who insist on seeking a uniform spirit of a people or an age or a culture. The delimitations of historical events must be made laterally as well as longitudinally. The frontiers of a nation may be defined in geographical terms clearly enough, though they too have changed significantly, but when one is speaking, for instance, of the French, does one include the people of the northern provinces whose dialects pass by almost imperceptible steps into Flemish on the West and German on the East; does one include the Gascons whose ancestors came from what is now Spain and whose dialect is close to Spanish; does one include the Provençaux and the Dauphinois? If one is considering the plastic arts, would one ever know that the Rhineland was not deeply gallicized? And when one comes to religion, how is one to distinguish its Catholicism from that of any other country? Is the French literature of Canada French or Canadian? And what does one do about modern architecture between, let us say, 1850 and 1930, when architects in both the old and new worlds studied at the Beaux-Arts and followed the principles of Guadet? Each of these and other fields has to be considered separately and the lateral boundaries are never the same for any two except by accident.

Spengler reads into the arts and sciences of the past the feelings they arouse in him, as if their makers had had him in mind. But we have no way of knowing whether a nude statue seemed to a Greek as Apollinian as it did to Spengler, even when it was a statue of Apollo. Could Archimedes have felt about the science of statics as the sculptor of the Apollo Belvedere did? We have no evidence whatsoever for opinions on what the Greeks felt about their most celebrated works of art with the exception of adjectives of praise, like "wonderful," "lifelike," and so on. In order to set tip his cultures as homogeneous, he has to neglect all conflicting trends and, though he would be willing to admit that no culture after a few generations is pure, he does not see the contribution of conflict to the general picture. Ironically enough, his interpretations of the past have actually changed our view of the past. The Baroque, as in Lewis Mumford, has now become Spengler's Baroque and, whether we know it or not, we are likely to see it through his eyes. This has its benefits for it induces us to make new appraisals of periods and works of art which we had learned to appraise through the views of our teachers. But it would be absurd to say that it has led us closer to the truth.

Spengler's popularity has waned since the second World War largely, one suspects, because Mr. Toynbee Study of History, Mr. Northrop Meeting of East and West, and Mr. Sorokin's various studies have taken the place of the Decline of the West. All such books follow the pattern of simplifying civilizations and cultures, peoples and ages and movements, and giving them some name taken from individual psychology. No one has yet arrived to say firmly that a people is a collection of individuals in interaction with one another, loyal to various groups at the same time even when the groups have opposing programs, torn between selfish and altruistic motives, without over-all programs and purposes, now rebellious, now resigned, now led, now leading. What would seem to be needed is a return to analysis and the abandonment for the time being of major syntheses.

In philosophy, the Renaissance refers to the period of the break-up of feudalism (15th to early 17th century), when trade grew up around the merchants and craftspeople of Northern Italy particularly, and a bourgeois society began to flourish and gave rise to a humanist culture in opposition to the official scholasticism.

The revival of the philosophical legacy of the Ancient Greeks (particularly the individualism and scientific interests of the Stoics) and a number of important natural scientific and technical discoveries, and challenges to the authority of the Church promoted the development of Rationalism. The principal figures were the Stoicist Petrarch, the Epicurean Laurentius Valla, and the astronomers and natural scientists Bruno Giordano (who was burnt at the stake for his materialist views), Nicholas of Cusa, Paracelsus, and later Copernicus, Galileo, the founder of political science Niccolo Machiavelli, the German Utopian Thomas Munzer, the English Empiricist Francis Bacon, the French philosopher and mathematician Rene Descartes, the pantheistic philosopher Baruch Spinoza who wrote from the relatively liberal Dutch Republic.

British philosophy had its beginnings in the relatively open social conditions of pre-Revolutionary England with the British Empiricists Francis Bacon, Thomas Hobbes and during the period of the Restoration, John Locke.

The growth of natural science was a major influence on the development of bourgeois thinking prior to the nineteenth century with Isaac Newton (1642-1727) among the most prominent of British natural scientists of the period prior to the Industrial Revolution. It is generally accepted that as the first to make a bourgeois revolution and the first to make an industrial revolution, the British felt the need to accumulate material for theory to work upon, rather than trying to make their way with theory. Even more than this, in order to make their revolution, the English had to launch an attack on the authority of existing (feudal) wisdom, and given conditions of relative political and economic freedom, the most effective way of contesting doing this was science, exploration and technology and industry and making money.

After leading the way in the seventeenth century, the British bourgeoisie has remained strongly wedded to its characteristic Empiricist philosophy which in fact distrusts all theory, preferring to rely on experience and the accumulation of observation. Consequently, the English have not subsequently figured highly among the great figures of the history of philosophy. Apart from early Empiricists, the very many natural scientists contributing to every branch of science and those already listed under the heading of British Political Economy, the notables of British philosophy are the mathematicians Bertrand Russell and Alan Turing and British feminists from Sylvia and Adela Pankhurst to Sheila Rowbotham and Juliet Mitchell.

Bibliography

Aquinas, De Regimine Principum, in Aquinas, Selected Political Writings, ed. A. P. D'Entreves, Oxford, Blackwell, 1965.

Augustine, City of God, ed. V. J. Bourke, New York, Image Books, 1958.

Bauer, F. L. (ed.) Intellectual Movements in Modern European History, London, Macmillan, 1969.

Bentham, J. An Introduction to the Principles of Morals and Legislation, Oxford, Blackwell, 1967.

Bentley, M. (ed.) Companion to Historiography, London, Routledge, 1997.

Bertens, H. The Idea of the Postmodern - a History, London and New York, Routledge, 1995.

Bodin, J. Six Books of the Commonwealth, ed. M. J. Tooley, Oxford, Blackwell, 1967.

Bronowski, J. and Mazlish, B. The Western Intellectual Tradition, London, Hutchinson, 1960.

Bultmann, D. R. History and Eschatology, Edinburgh, 1975.

Burke, E. Reflections on the Revolution in France, ed. C. C. O'Brien, Harmondsworth, Penguin Books, 1969.

Burke, P. Vico, Oxford, Oxford University Press, 1985.

Burns, T. (ed.) After History? Francis Fukuyama and His Critics, Maryland, Towman & Littlefield , 1994.

Cassirer, E. Essay on Man, New Haven, Yale University Press, 1945.

Cohen, B. 'The Eighteenth-century Origins of the Concept of Scientific Revolution', Journal of the History of Ideas, Vol.37, No.2, 1976.

Cohn, N. The Pursuit of the Millennium, London, Mercury Books, 1962.

De Grazia, S. Machiavelli in Hell, London, Picador, 1992.

Deane, H. A. The Political and Social Ideas of St. Augustine, Columbia University Press, 1963.

D'Entrèves, A. P. (ed.) Aquinas - Selected Political Writings, Oxford, Blackwell, 1965.

Earl, D. The Moral and Political Tradition of Rome, London, Thames & Hudson, 1967.

Engels, F. Schelling and Revelation, in Vol. 2, Karl Marx/ Frederick Engels, Collected Works, London, Lawrence & Wishart, 1975.

Evans, E. 'The Theory Man', History Today, Vol. 47, June 1997.

Feuerbach, L. Principles of the Philosophy of the Future, New York, Bobbs-Merrill, 1966.

Fortin, E. L. 'Augustine's City of God and the Modern Historical Consciousness', The Review of Politics, Vol. 41, No. 3, July, 1979.

Frankfort H., et al., Before Philosophy, Harmondsworth, Penguin, 1968.

Franklyn, J. H. Jean Bodin and the Sixteenth-Century Revolution in the Methodology of Law and History, New York & London, Columbia University Press, 1966.

Fukuyama, F. Our Posthuman Future: Consequences of the Bio-technology Revolution, Profile Books, 2002.

Fukuyama, F. The End of History and the Last Man, London, Penguin Books, 1992.

Fukuyama, F. The Great Disruption: Human Nature and the Reconstitution of Social Order, Profile Books, 1999.

Gardiner, P. The Philosophy of History, Oxford, Oxford University Press, 1982.

Hay, D. (ed.) The Renaissance Debate, New York, Holt, Rinehart, & Winston, 1965.

Hegel, G. W. F. Phenomenology of Mind, trans. J. B. Baillie, London, Allen & Unwin, 1966.

Hegel, G. W. F. Philosophy of Mind, trans. W. Wallace and A. Miller, Oxford, Clarendon Press, 1971.

Hegel, G. W. F. Philosophy of Right, trans. T. M. Knox, Oxford, Clarendon Press, 1962.

Hegel, G. W. F. Science of Logic, trans. A. V. Miller, London, George Allen & Unwin, 1969.

Hegel. G. W. F. The Philosophy of History, trans. J. Sibree, New York, Dover Publications, 1956.

Hirschman, A. The Passions and the Interests, New Jersey, Princeton University Press, 1997.

Hobbes, T. Leviathan, ed. J. Plamenatz, London, Fontana, 1962.

Hobbes, T. Thomas White's 'De Mundo' Examined, trans. H. W. Jones, London, Bradford University Press, 1976.

Jaki, S. L. Science and Creation - From Eternal Cycles to an Oscillating Universe, Edinburgh, Scottish Academic Press, 1974.

Jenkins, K. On 'What is History?', London and New York, Routledge, 1995.

Kennedy, P. The Rise and Fall of the Great Powers, London, Fontana Press, 1989.

Kristeller, P. Eight Philosophers of the Italian Renaissance, California, Stanford University Press, 1964.

Kropotkin, P. in The Essential Kropotkin, (eds E. Capouya and K. Thompkins), London, Macmillan, 1976.

Lechte, J. Fifty Key Contemporary Thinkers - From Structuralism to Postmodernity, London and New York, Routledge, 1994.

Lemon, M. C. The Discipline of History and the History of Thought, London, Routledge, 1995.

Levine, J. M. 'Quarrel between the Ancients and the Moderns', Journal of the History of Ideas, Vol. LII, No. 1, 1991.

Lichtheim, G. Marxism - An Historical and Critical Study, London, Routledge & Kegan Paul, 1964.

Machiavelli, N. The Discourses, in The Prince and the Discourses, New York, The Modern Library, 1950.

Machiavelli, N. The Prince, Harmondsworth, Penguin Books, 1961.

Manuel, F. The Prophets of Paris, New York, Harper & Row, 1965.

Marx K. and Engels, F. 'German Ideology', in Vol. 5, Karl Marx/Frederick Engels, Collected Works; London, Lawrence & Wishart, 1976.

Marx, K. A Contribution to the Critique of Political Economy, in Vol, 29, Karl Marx/Frederick Engels; Collected Works, London, Lawrence & Wishart, 1976.

Marx, K. and Engels, F. 'Deutsche Ideologie', in Vol. 3, Karl Marx/Friedrich Engels: Werke, Berlin, Dietz Verlag, 1969.

Marx, K. and Engels, F. Manifesto of the Communist Party, in Vol. 6, Karl Marx: Frederick Engels; Collected Works, London, Lawrence & Wishart, 1976.

Marx, K. Contribution to the Critique of Hegel's Philosophy of Law - Introduction, in Vol. 3, Karl Marx/Frederick Engels; Collected Works, London, Lawrence & Wishart, 1976.

Marx, K. Contribution to the Critique of Hegel's Philosophy of Law, in Vol. 3, Karl Marx/Frederick Engels; Collected Works, London, Lawrence & Wishart, 1976.

Marx, K. Economic and Philosophic Manuscripts of 1844, in Vol. 3, Karl Marx/Frederick Engels; Collected Works, London, Lawrence & Wishart, 1976.

Marx, K. On the Jewish Question, in Vol. 3, Karl Marx/Frederick Engels; Collected Works, London, Lawrence & Wishart, 1976.

Marx, K. Theses on Feuerbach, in Vol, 5, Karl Marx/Frederick Engels; Collected Works, London, Lawrence & Wishart, 1976.

Mazlish, B. The Riddle of History, New York and London, Harper & Row, 1966.

Morrison, J. C. 'Vico's Principle of Verum is Factum and the Problem of Historicism', Journal of the History of Ideas, Vol. 39, Issue 2, 1978.

Munslow, A. Deconstructing History, London and New York, Routledge, 1997.

Nauert, C. Humanism and the Culture of Renaissance Europe, Cambridge University Press, 1995.

Nisbet, R. A. History of the Idea of Progress, London, Heinemann, 1980.

Nisbet, R. A. Social Change and History, Oxford, Oxford University Press, 1970.

Oakeshott, M. Rationalism in Politics, London, Methuen, 1962.

Orynski, W. Hegel - Highlights: an annotated selection, New York, Philosophical Library, 1960.

Raphael, D. (ed.) Political Theory and the Rights of Man, London, Macmillan, 1967.

Reill, P. H. The German Enlightenment and the Rise of Historicism, Berkeley, University of California Press, 1975.

Rice, E. and Grafton, A. The Foundations of Early Modern Europe, 1460-1559, New York, W. W. Norton, 1994.

Rosenstone, R. 'Experiments in Narrative', Rethinking History, Vol. 5, No. 3, 2001.

Rousseau, J-J. Discourse on the Origins of Inequality, trans. G. D. H. Cole, London, Everyman, 1966.

Rousseau, J-J. The Social Contract, trans. G. D. H. Cole, London, Everyman edition of The Social Contract and Discourses, 1966.

Sabine, G. A History of Political Theory, 3rd Edition, London, Harrap & Co., 1963.

Southern, R. Medieval Humanism and Other Studies, Oxford, Blackwell, 1970.

Spinoza, B. On the Improvement of the Understanding, Vol. 2, The Chief Works of Benedict de Spinoza, trans. R. H. M. Elwes, New York, Dover Publications, 1955.

Spinoza, B. Tractatus Theologico-Politicus, Vol. 1, The Chief Works of Benedict de Spinoza, trans. R. H. M. Elwes, New York, Dover Publications, 1955.

Spinoza, B., The Ethics, Vol. 2, The Chief Works of Benedict de Spinoza, trans. R. H. M. Elwes, New York, Dover Publications, 1955.

Strauss, L. Persecution and the Art of Writing, University of Chicago Press, 1988.

Strauss, L. Thoughts on Machiavelli, Seattle, University of Washington Press, 1969.

Trompf, G. W. The Idea of Historical Recurrence in Western Thought - From Antiquity to the Reformation, Berkeley, Los Angeles, London, University of California Press, 1979.

Tuck, R. Philosophy and Government, 1572-1651, Cambridge, Cambridge University Press, 1993.

Vico, G. On the Heroic Mind, trans. E. Sewell and A. Sirignano, in Social Research, no. 43, 1976.

Vico, G. The New Science of Giambattista Vico, revised translation of the third edition (1744) by T. G. Bergin and M. H. Fisch, New York, Cornell University Press, 1968.

Vico, G. Universal Right, trans. and ed. G. Pinton and M. Diehl, Amsterdam - Atlanta, Rodopi, 2000.

Index

A

A Treatise on the Immortality of the Soul, 179
Absolute Possibility, 152
Aeschylus in the History of Philosophy, 53
Ageold Distributions of Power, 60
Alciphron, 375
All Men Are Mortal, 250
Things Intellectually, 355
An Active Sagacity, 341
Elegant Treatise on Nature, 68
Inferior and Subordinate Instrument, 349
Innate Automatism, 228
Analogy of Attribution, 95, 100
of Proper Proportionality, 105
Anti-Cartesianism of Philosophy, 249
Antidote against Atheism, 339
Appellat Suam Rationem, 77
Application of the Analogy Rules to Language about God, 118
Arbitrarious and Fictitious, 344
Articles of Cardinal Curty, 165
Auguste Comte, 381
Augustinian Argument for Philosophical Dialogues, 123

B

Baron D'holbach, 306
Berkeley's Siris, 369
Bernardino Telesio, 184
Black-Letter Law, 57
Bonald and Maistre, 377
Bouquet of Wine, 260
Bruno, 195
Burthogge, 356

C

Cambridge Platonists, 339

Campanella, 188
Cartesian Dream, 208
Catholic Church, 232
Christian Theology, 216
City of God, 209
  of Man, 209
  of the Sun, 190
Civic-Minded, 23
Condorcet, 233
Contra Academicos, 136
Count Joseph De Maistre, 377
Cournot, 388
Creatura Producibilis, 149
Creatural Deas, 143
Crede Ut Intelligas, 125
Critique of Practical Reason, 267

D

D'holbach, 306
De Libero Arbitrio, 125
  Rerum Natura, 184, 257
Deductive Reasoning, 261
Definitions, 89
Deity of the Sun, 86
Demonstratio Propter Quid, 167
  Quia, 167
Detective Story, 77
Dictionnaire Historique Et Critique, 285
  Philosophique, 327
Dilatation, 339
Discourse on Method, 262
  on Universal History, 293
  on Livy, 177
Discursive Thought, 333
Distant Poles of the Equator and Ecliptic, 348
Docta Ignorantia, 197
Doom of Oedipus and the Phallus Cult, 392

E

Encyclopédie of Diderot, 284
Entia Rationis, 148
Entitatis Prae-Eminentiam, 194
Esprit De Finesse, 261, 264
  De Géométrie, 261
Esse Intelligibile, 144
  Objectivum, 144
Examination of This Axiom: Whatever is, is Right, 324
Exhibition Analyses, 87
External Apprehension, 333

F

Femmes Savantes, 260
Fictum Theory, 145
Franc Arbitre, 327
French Revolution, 247, 377

G

Galileo, 203
Geometrical Manner, 205
God Supreme, 190
  Book, 191
Gorgias in Philosophy, 63
Grand Dictionnaire Historique, 285
Grounds to Sentiments, 357

H

Henry More and Cudworth, 339

Herder, 222
High Quality Work, 99
Historical Naturalism, 388
History of Philosophy, 1, 180
How Charming is Divine
  Philosophy, 283
Huet, 269

I

Ideal Perception, 367
Idealist Tradition in England
  for Philosophy, 329
Idealistic or Platonistic
  Group, 356
Ideen Zur Philosophie Der
  Geschichte Der
  Menschheit, 226
Indivisible Centre of the Soul
  or Mind, 376
Instantia Naturae, 146
Intellectual System, 354
Intentional Identity, 85
Internal Apprehension, 333
Intrinsic Possibility, 152
Inward Feeling, 367

J

John Norris, 363

L

La Bonté Naturelle, 290
  Fleur De La Matiere, 260
  Mettrie, 301
Law of Contradiction, 343
  of Nature and of Nature's
  God, 43
Le Christianisme Devoile,
  307
Les Lumières, 283
  Philosophes in
  Philosophy, 281
Lettres Persanes, 292
Little Meddal of God, 345
Lives of the Sophists, 64
Logique De Port-Royal, 261
Lord Herbert of Cherbury, 330
Lumen Naturale, 263

M

Machiavelli, 171
Material Form, 199
Modern Reader, 2
Modus Significandi, 109
Montesquieu, 291
Moreri and Bayle, 284

N

Natural Emanations of the
  Mind, 343
  Instinct, 333
  Theology, 216
New Theory of Vision, 374
Nicholas of Autrecourt, 161

O

Ockham and Intrinsic
  Possibility, 155
  of the Textbooks, 151
  Conception of the Divine
  Ideas, 146
  Solution to the Question,
  150
Oedipus Tyrannus, 19
On the Nature of the Gods,
  31
  the Nonexistent, 68

Only of Necessaries and Immutables, 368
Operations of Reason, 32
Ordinary Language, 88
Other Natural Operations, 372
Outline of Epicureanism, 256
Outward Perception, 367

P

Parity of Reasoning, 83
Pascal, 261
Peloponnesian War, 4
Perplexing and Baffling, 32, 47
Philosophiae Epicuri Syntagma, 256
Philosophic Liberty, 297
Philosophical Treatise of the Weakness of the Human Mind, 274
Philosophy Demonstrated By the Senses, 191
Pindar, 1
Pitilessly Slaughtered Sister, 58
Plastic Force, 346
  Spirit, 339
Plato in the History of Philosophy, 29
Platonistic, 330
Plotinian Theory of a Hierarchy of Ideas, 367
Poem on the Disaster of Lisbon, 324
Political Liberty, 298
  Masterpiece of Human Wisdom, 387
Pomponazzi, 179
Praenotio, 257
Praeparatio Evangelica, 180
Preliminary Discourse of the Encyclopédie, 382
Principles of a New Science, 213
Profession of Faith of the Savoyard Vicar, 267
Proportional Similarity, 116
Pseudo-Dionysius, 379
Pure Invisible Fire, 371

Q

Quasi-Passivus, 144
Quick Recollection, 341

R

Ratio Cognoscendi Creaturas, 159
Ratiocination It Self is An Animal Act, 358
Rationes Cognoscendi Creaturas, 148
Realms of Truth, 191
Recentiores Quidam Cartesianae Doctrinae Patroni, 272
Rejection of Authority in Philosophy, 171
Reverse Copernicus, 45
  Darwinism, 45
Revolution in History of Philosophies, 377
Richard Burthogge, 356
Rule of Meaning for Religious Language, 86

S

Science and the Modern
World, 40
of the Soul, 383
Scienza Nuova, 217
Secundum Se Et Primo, 141
Seipsum, 155
Self-Contraction, 339
Motion, 339
Penetration, 339
Seminary of Minerals and Metals, 371
Senno Supremo, 191
Sensible Signs, 219
Sensory Perception, 333
Shares the Marvelous Munificence of Deity, 8
Similarity of Relations, 122
Similia Similibus Curantur, 370
Socrates is A Man, 250
Socrates is Mortal, 250
Solution of Duns Scotus, 143
of Henry of Ghent, 139
Sophocles in Philosophy, 19
Spengler, 392
Spirit of the Laws, 293
Spiritual Expression, 223
Strange Piece of Fortune, 38
Susceptible of Scientific Corroboration, 310
Sympathetic Insight, 2
System of Notions and First Principles, 358
Système De La Nature, 307

T

Telesio, 184
The Actual Realisation of Perception, 336
Christian Religion, 308
City of God, 39
Cloud of Words, 338
Criterion is Destroyed, 70
Divine Gift of Speech, 227
Fixation of Belief, 207
General Cosmic Motions, 41
Greatest of Centuries, 243
Immortality of the Soul, 345
Mind's Road to God, 189
Nation, 178
Persians' Zeus, 66
Prince, 178
Principle of Plenitude, 201
True Intellectual System of the Universe, 347
True Philosopher Makes Light of Philosophy, 263
Tommaso Campanella, 188
Tone of Dignity, 61
Tragic Effect, 62
Treatise Concerning Eternal and Immutable Morality, 354
Trial is the True Test of Mortal Men, 4

True Notion of a Spirit, 340
True Saying, 4

U

Universal Physical Efficient Cause, 196

V

Vico, 213
Vicomte De Bonald, 377
Voltaire, 321